PROVINCE WITH A HEART

Celebrating 100 years in Saskatchewan

Celebrating Saskatchewan's Century

100
LEADER-POST
The StarPhoenix

CANWEST BOOKS

Published by CanWest Books Inc.
A subsidiary of CanWest Global Communications
1450 Don Mills Road
Toronto, ON
Canada, M3B 2X7

Library and Archives Canada Cataloguing in Publication

Boswell, Randy, 1966-
        Province with a heart : celebrating 100 years in Saskatchewan / Randy
Boswell ; edited by Lynn McAuley.

ISBN 0-9736719-0-4

        1. Saskatchewan--History. 2. Saskatchewan--History--Pictorial works.
I. McAuley, Lynn, 1956- II. Title.

FC3511.B68 2005   971.24   C2005-902723-1

Jacket and text design by Tania Craan
Prepress Emerson Group
Front Cover photograph: Saskatchewan Archive Board R-A 15198 (Hadley Selville)
Back Cover photograph: Regina Leader-Post Files (Legislative Building)
Inside Front Flap photograph: Regina Leader-Post Files, D'Arce McMillian (canola crop)
Inside Back Flap photograph: Regina Leader-Post Files (combine tractor)

Printed and bound in Canada by Friesens

First Edition

10 9 8 7 6 5 4 3 2 1

Contents

INTRODUCTION

The story of Saskatchewan will be told in more than a million ways this Centennial year.

Every person in the province — every family, every community, every school and every organization — is part of that story. Most will be sharing their own personal version in their own special way. Whether it's of the magnitude of a book, television special or community homecoming, or something more intimate like a family reunion or simply a conversation over coffee, the story will be told and retold.

But of all the accounts, none will be quite like the version you hold in your hands.

It's been gleaned from the pages of the province's two major daily newspapers, which have had a perspective like no other, having served as Saskatchewan's unofficial historians for the past hundred years.

The *StarPhoenix* and *Leader-Post* were there from the beginning, sharing ringside seats for Saskatchewan's birth as a province in 1905 and for every other significant event since.

Generations of *Leader-Post* and *StarPhoenix* journalists have come and gone but their daily chronicles of the people and events of the past live on in a century of weathered pages in the newspapers' archives.

From those pages, and through the creative genius of CanWest journalist Randy Boswell, the *Leader-Post* and *StarPhoenix*, in co-operation with CanWest Books, are proud to present their own special version of Saskatchewan's Centennial story.

For those of us fortunate enough to play a role in chronicling our province's history, we salute those who came before us and laid the track for us to follow in recording the hopes, dreams, successes, failures, tragedies and triumphs of the amazing people of Saskatchewan, the Province With A Heart.

Janice Dockham   Steven Gibb
Editor-in-Chief   Editor-in-Chief
Regina Leader-Post   *Saskatoon StarPhoenix*

We forever remain attached to the place we call home and to its symbols and icons. There is no comparable canvas to a prairie sky at sunset, nothing as vividly mystical as Northern Lights nor as hauntingly beautiful as hoarfrost freeze-framing a moment in time.

For me, it's also prairie grain elevators, Saskatoon pie, fall suppers in church basements and Legion halls — and family.

Saskatchewan is, as the cliché goes, a state of mind. So several times a year, I make a ritual but much-needed pilgrimage to my home in Saskatchewan for a refresher course in community, family and the prairie version of common sense.

You see, everything I've learned about people and place, I learned first in Saskatchewan. Despite the fact that I love living in the very heart of New York City, one of the world's largest, nosiest and most intense environments, the experience has only served to enhance my respect for where I come from. This backward view is not through some gauze-filtered lens of nostalgia, but rather the focus is clear and real because every single day I use the life lessons learned at home.

From family I learned to set — and keep attuned to — my own moral compass, which simply means knowing right from wrong and having a sense of responsibility. So for me, home is more than just a geography; it's a moral place. My attitudes were shaped and my value system crafted by witnessing my parents' beliefs in action. It's the place where I learned that character always trumps genius — in other words, that being kind is always more important than being smart.

But at the core of life, as part of any community, are our relationships. In the midst of the city's relentless thrust, our obligations to the stranger are a test of our character because there is no fear of reprisal or consequence for bad behaviour.

But the skill of manoeuvring through the waters of familiarity is what truly tests our humanity. It teaches tolerance. When you must deal with the same folks day in and day out, civility becomes a crucial part of the unspoken social contract. These are the circumstances that call up out of all of us our strengths or weakness, fears or confidence we didn't know was there.

We call that character. We call individual values shared, practised and collected, a community. We call it Saskatchewan.

Pamela Wallin
Canada's Consul General in New York City
Journalist
Birthplace: Wadena

My great grandfather, Chief Gabriel Cote, was the main spokesperson for the Saulteaux tribes at the signing of Treaty 4 at Fort Qu'Appelle on September 15, 1874.

That is a proud part of my people's history; what followed were years of suffering, beginning with the establishment of First Nations reserves. Like so many of my generation, I do not have many good memories of my early years, especially once I started school.

Right from six-and-a-half years old, I was taken into the dreaded residential school. To try to forget that experience isn't possible. It was terrible.

It wasn't until I was allowed to go to the Cote day school for Grades 7 and 8 that I started to learn more than fear and embarrassment at school. That's where I met a very wonderful teacher — Miss Russell. She had an interest in her students and in helping us learn. She made us work hard, but she did it with kindness. That was a turning point in my life.

Mostly, my perspective of Saskatchewan is shaped by the years of residential school experience, control of our lives by the Indian agent and a lack of willingness by government to help with individual initiatives. It wasn't until 1960 that First Nations people were even recognized as citizens and allowed to vote in federal and provincial elections.

When I ran away from home at seventeen to join the army, it was to escape the shame of those years of physical, mental and sexual abuse. But when I came back, I realized that I couldn't keep feeling sorry for myself. If things were going to change for my people, we had to push hard on our own. So I got myself interested in community development.

For the past fifty years, I put most of my energy into working with our young people. As chief of the Cote First Nation, as treasurer and then sports and recreation director with the Federation of Saskatchewan Indians in the 1970s and more recently at the First Nation University of Canada, there have been many opportunities to make things happen.

Cote First Nation built the first arena on an Indian reserve in the early 1970s. As a result, other bands started doing the same thing. In 1974, Cote hosted the first Indian Summer Games. Then in 1980, we held the first Indian Winter Games.

My community became a model for others. Now, around my community near Kamsack, people still say, "You're the guy that started things moving around here." I'm proud of that.

I have less anger, less bitterness. But it has been a lifelong struggle to overcome so many injustices.

My "home" is my community on the Cote First Nation, where I will retire someday soon with pride in what we have accomplished for ourselves.

Tony Cote, First Nation Elder
Former chief of Cote First Nation
Korean War Veteran
Birthplace: Cote First Nation

It happens every time I think of Saskatchewan. I start to feel a bit lonely. I think of home and family. Of happy times and sad. Of Paula, Madeline and Richard. Hot summers, cold winters. Open spaces, decent people. It's not easy to describe. The only way I can explain it is as a kind of vague, empty feeling, like a piece of me that's missing.

After nine years of being away, I realize that I never really left Saskatchewan. That a part of me is so deeply connected to the province where I was born, raised, got married, learned about what matters in life and had a family, that I can never completely leave.

There will be those who say there is nothing particularly unique in having such attachments to your roots. That everyone's sense of self is entwined with where they come from. But, in the case of Saskatchewan, somehow it is a much deeper, more meaningful relationship. In some ways it is spiritual, a kind of emotional bond between ourselves as individuals and the community we call Saskatchewan. Our identity is rooted in something much bigger and more important than ourselves.

So, the issue is not so much to recognize the meaning and importance of Saskatchewan to ourselves. We all feel the same connection to the province. The challenge is to understand why we feel so strongly about Saskatchewan.

Being away from the province, I believe, has given me some perspective on my feelings about it. Missing something forces you to consider the reasons for your emotional attachment to it.

For me, the meaning of Saskatchewan is expressed in two core beliefs: hope and faith. A century ago, Saskatchewan was a place of tremendous hope. People from around the world flocked to the province in pursuit of building better lives for themselves. Saskatchewan was a place where hope abounded.

Throughout the past century, there were times when hope faded, but never died. It merely became expressed in a faith that, together, Saskatchewan people could overcome adversity and build a special community and a better future. Hope and faith became one. There is always hope because we have faith in each other, which is what Saskatchewan means to me.

Dale Eisler
Assistant Secretary to Federal Cabinet
Former political columnist for the Leader-Post *and the* StarPhoenix
Birthplace: Regina

I grew up in the Dust Bowl in the Thirties, when things were so hard for most of the people in Saskatchewan, both farmers and city folk.

But my own early life was a very happy one. I was allowed, at a very young age, to go about the town on my own. I used to visit the police chief and the fire department, the Chinese restaurant where they would often give me a jawbreaker and women I knew at their homes.

People were very kind to me. If they were busy, they would just say, "I'm busy today, Shirley." Or they would say, "Oh, how lovely to see you, Shirley. Come in, I'm baking pies. You can help me."

I was supposed to go home immediately when I heard the whistle that would blow at twelve o'clock. Sometimes the people I was visiting would phone my mother and ask if I could stay for lunch. My early socializing — my love of a visit — started in Weyburn.

We would go to Ottawa in the winter after my father became a Member of Parliament. I never could get the same system of visiting going there!

It was only after I had left Saskatchewan in 1952 to go to London, England to study at the Royal Academy of Dramatic Art that my great appreciation for Saskatchewan took hold.

I had watched my mother and father, and thousands like them, help to build a movement — a united front to fight the injustices and extreme hardships that people were facing during the Great Depression — organizing the unemployed, bringing food and clothing from British Columbia and Ontario, pooling their money for those that needed health care.

But out of these hardships, where people were fighting for their very survival, groups of people started to meet to try to find a solution. They knew they could only survive by working together — building an organization bigger than themselves. Their only hope was co-operation. The CCF (the Co-operative Commonwealth Federation) was born in 1933.

I loved the CCF's "Humanity First." I saw brave, fearless people, trying daily to bring change. And they did. These were Saskatchewan's visionaries. This gave me a belief and a confidence for the rest of my life that there was nothing you could not change if you were willing to try and organize.

In this Centennial year, we need to take time to reflect on our rich heritage of "Humanity First" and continue to build on those foundations.

Thank you to those long ago people of Saskatchewan for everything they taught me.

I have gratitude for the past. It gave me courage for the future.

Shirley Douglas, O.C.
Daughter of late Saskatchewan premier Tommy Douglas
Actress, activist, health-care advocate
Birthplace: Weyburn

1905

CHAPTER ONE

It rises suddenly out of the prairie like a monument of earth, a great grass-and-soil-and-sandstone shrine celebrating the birth of the land and the beginning of history.

The Cypress Hills, upland in the southwest corner of Saskatchewan, are an exquisite accident of geology. Formed by a deep layering of primordial debris washed away from an eroded ancestor of the Rocky Mountains, they withstood the ravages of Ice Age glaciers and today mark a majestic continental divide.

The plateau offers more than a sublime view of the vast plains, which gave life first to a prehistoric people, then to a hardy pioneer culture, and finally — a century ago — to a new province of Canada. It provides more than Saskatchewan's highest point of land, more than its only remnant of rock untouched by the ice sheets that scraped and sculpted every other square inch of this country's sprawling Midwest.

A penultimate perch in every sense, a true touchstone of history and geography, this place is something more to Ross Bierbach: a home, a livelihood and a legacy.

His great-grandfather, cattle rancher William Faulkner, laid claim to a piece of the Cypress Hills at the dawn of the 20th century — on the eve, in fact, of Saskatchewan's inauguration as a province in 1905.

"He came from Pincher Creek in Alberta," says Bierbach. "This was good range land, and there was a very good water source — a spring that runs out of

ABOVE: Bachelor settlers, near Saskatoon, date unknown

LEFT PAGE: "Buffalo Rift" by A. Miller

Cree Chief Piapot, one of the last great Plains chiefs, circa 1880

the hill and starts a little creek that flows into a meadow. So, he settled in Saskatchewan. And we've been here ever since."

The land passed from William Faulkner to his son, Ray, who left it to his daughter, Fay, who married John Bierbach and gave birth, in 1955, to a son.

Ross Bierbach turns fifty as his province turns 100. He has a son of his own, William, who helps run their 600-cattle operation and will eventually take over the ranch that his namesake ancestor started in 1904.

There's a part of the property that Bierbach calls "the bench," a height of land just a stone's throw from the Alberta border and near the edge of Cypress Hills Interprovincial Park, a protected area rich in wildlife and Canadian lore that straddles the boundary between the two provinces.

Bierbach's "bench" is the very summit of Saskatchewan — at 1,392 metres, give or take a mound of grass or two, it's the highest elevation in the province. No point of land between the Rockies and Labrador rises higher than the Cypress Hills plateau. It's the perfect place from which to peer across the Saskatchewan expanse, to ponder the epic sweep of time and space. But mainly, says a rancher not so prone to flights of fancy, it's a good spot for his livestock to graze.

"It's a point of pride," Bierbach says of the highest-land designation.

"And we're also kind of proud that these hills are still the way they always were, native pasture. If my great-grandfather walked out there today, he wouldn't know the difference."

Bierbach has walked those acres many times himself. He sometimes sees deer or elk wandering from the shelter of the park's pine forest to nibble, just like his cattle, on the grassy bench. And sometimes, on his own wanderings, he has found the sun-bleached bones of a buffalo or the discarded stone tool of a long-ago hunter-warrior — relics of the world which gave way, inexorably and too often tragically, to a place that would become a province.

Saskatchewan's first people were hunters who followed bison herds and other big game into present-day Western Canada at the end of the last Ice Age, about 10,000 years ago.

Seven nations from three language groups eventually came to inhabit parts of what would become Saskatchewan. The Athapaskan-speaking Chipewyan, Beaver and Slavey nations occupied lands north of the Churchill River; the Algonquian-speaking Cree and Blackfoot had territories in the central part of the province; and — roaming the southern plains that extend into modern-day Montana and North Dakota — two Siouan nations, the Assiniboine and Gros Ventre.

Territories often overlapped, and clashes — most notably between Chipewyan and Cree warriors — were common over the centuries. Yet stable, productive societies and rich cultural traditions developed in all of these nations, a fact demonstrated by archeology, oral history and, above all, by the strong sense of historical identity among aboriginal communities throughout the province today.

Into this setting, in August 1691, trekked an intrepid twenty-three-year-old explorer and fur trader from England named Henry Kelsey. An apprentice with the Hudson's Bay Company at Fort York, he had been sent west in 1690 — along with several Indian guides — to make contact with native groups and secure fresh supplies of fur. Travelling by canoe up the Churchill and Saskatchewan rivers, and then overland farther south and west, Kelsey is believed to have been the first white man ever to have glimpsed the Canadian Prairies, to have sighted a buffalo and a grizzly bear and to have set foot in the future province.

At a time when explorers' journals often brimmed with detailed accounts of their travels, Kelsey's is frustratingly vague. He composed his thoughts in rhymed doggerel, making him the first and probably still the worst of all prairie poets.

But even so, his witnessing of a once-classic Saskatchewan scene — recorded on August 21, 1691, in a strikingly legible script — is now the foundation document of Saskatchewan history:

Louis Riel, Métis leader

> *So far I have spoken concerning of the spoil*
> *And now will give account of that same Country soile*
> *Which hither part is very thick of wood*
> *Affords small nutts with little cherryes very good*
> *Thus it continues till you leave ye woods behind*
> *And then you have beast of severall kind*
> *The one is a black a Buffillo great*
> *Another is an outgrown Bear which is good meat*
> *His skin to gett I have used all ye means I can*
> *He is mans food and he makes food of man*
> *His hide they would not me it preserve*
> *But said it was a god and they should starve*
> *This plain affords nothing but beast and grass*
> *And over it in three days time we past*
> *Getting unto ye woods on the other side*
> *It being about forty sixe miles wide*

Kelsey's foray into the region was brief — he is thought to have reached the Touchwood Hills northeast of Regina — and his dealings with the Assiniboine people there were fleeting. But the later arrival of other European explorers, fur traders and, eventually, hundreds of thousands of settlers profoundly altered the aboriginal way of life that had reigned for millennia.

The contact period was not without peaceful interaction — the building of trade relationships, the sharing of knowledge and resources, even the emergence of a new race of people born with mixed European and native ancestry: the Métis. However, the introduction of disease and liquor, the decimation of bison populations and other overwhelming effects of European immigration — including the systematic displacement of native groups from their traditional territories — had a devastating impact.

In 1870, not too many lifetimes after Kelsey had travelled to the Touchwood Hills, military officer William Francis Butler passed through the same country.

"This region bears the name of the Touchwood Hills," he wrote. "Around it,

far into endless space, stretch immense plains of bare and scanty vegetation, plains scarred with the tracks of countless buffalo which, until a few years ago, were wont to roam in vast herds between the Assiniboine and the Saskatchewan. Upon whatever side the eye turns when crossing these great expanses, the same wrecks of the monarch of the prairie lie thickly strewn over the surface. Hundreds of thousands of skeletons dot the short scant grass; and when fire has laid barer still the level surface, the bleached ribs and skulls of long-killed bison whiten far and near the dark burnt prairie. There is something unspeakably melancholy in the aspect of this portion of the North West."

Non-native settlement of Saskatchewan did not happen quickly. After the Hudson's Bay Company established a trading post in 1774 at Cumberland House — the first permanent European outpost in what was then called Rupert's Land — the flow of white settlers into the territory remained a relative trickle for generations.

At first, it wasn't clear that the dry, flat grasslands of south-central Saskatchewan held much potential for agricultural production. An 1857 expedition led by British Captain John Palliser identified a "fertile belt" that cut a wide, diagonal swath through the region. He believed it could support farming, though a semi-arid area to the southwest — later to become known as "Palliser's Triangle" — was declared "unsuitable" for agriculture.

It would prove to be a famous geographical misjudgment. Subsequent studies by geologist Henry Youle Hind and field naturalist John Macoun made clear that the Triangle lands, too, had vast potential for both grain growing and cattle grazing, despite the risk of periodic drought.

The transfer of Hudson's Bay Company land to the new Canadian confederation in 1870 set the stage for a series of key initiatives in what was then known as the North West Territories: the federal promotion of homesteading; the construction of a transcontinental railroad; the forceful push to have native groups sign treaties and move onto reserves; and (on Butler's recommendation), the establishment of a new law enforcement agency — the future RCMP — to bring order to Canada's version of the Wild West.

Between 1874 and 1906, the First Nations of Saskatchewan formally surrendered to the new Dominion of Canada all but a few pockets of the vast territory that had been commanded by their ancestors for hundreds or thousands of years.

Known as the numbered treaties — 4, 5, 6, 8 and 10 — the five agreements were typically negotiated between senior government officials eager to assert Canadian sovereignty and secure unencumbered land for settlers and native chiefs desperate to preserve the pride — or secure the survival — of their peoples. Hunger, sickness and economic hardship among the First Nations — which faced dwindling numbers of buffalo and increasing competition for resources from settlers, traders and miners — were the backdrop to bargaining.

"We heard our lands were sold and we did not like it; we don't want to sell our lands; it is our property, and no one has a right to sell them," Plains Cree Chief Weekaskookeensayyin (Sweet Grass) wrote to a government negotiator before the 1876 talks that resulted in Treaty 6.

But he added that "our country is getting ruined of fur-bearing animals, hitherto our sole support, and now we are poor and want help … We want cattle, tools, agricultural implements and assistance in everything when we come to settle — our country is no longer able to support us. Make provision for us against years of starvation. We have had great starvation the past winter, and the small pox took away many of our people, the old, young and children. We want you to stop the Americans from coming to trade on our lands, and giving firewater, ammunition and arms to our enemies the Blackfeet.…"

The Indian chiefs typically understood they would be "sharing" land with newcomers and that they were not, in the words of one present-day native leader, "giving up anything more than the depth of a plough." But the written text of treaties routinely stipulated that the First Nations "do hereby cede, release, surrender and yield up to the Government of the Dominion of Canada for Her Majesty the Queen and her successors forever, all their rights, titles and privileges whatsoever to the lands …"

In exchange, Queen Victoria's designates offered Her Majesty's "bounty and benevolence" — assurances of emergency medical care and supplies of food, manufactured goods and clothing, as required. Along with these items and the land set aside for native communities, there were provisions made for education, agricultural training, hunting, fishing and other concessions shaped by local circumstances.

What precisely was agreed to, and whether those promises were, in fact, kept by the government, has been fodder for much modern controversy.

It was a tragic clash between a Saskatchewan band of Assiniboine and an unruly group of mostly American wolf hunters that hastened Ottawa's creation of the North West Mounted Police in 1873. The "wolfers" were notorious for killing the animals by poisoning bison carcasses — a practice that natives detested because it frequently killed their dogs and sometimes people, too. When a group of wolfers accused some Assiniboine men of stealing their horses, a confrontation in the Cypress Hills — just a few kilometres from Ross Bierbach's

Buffalo bones, railway siding, Saskatoon, August 9, 1890

ranch — turned tragic. Between twenty and thirty natives and one wolf hunter were killed, and news of the Cypress Hills Massacre prompted outrage across Canada and swift action by the government.

A bill to create the NWMP was sped through Parliament. And in the summer of 1874, 275 Mounties rode out from Manitoba to the Saskatchewan country, extending the long arm of the law to Fort Walsh and initiating Regina's role as headquarters of the national police force.

The Mounties went west "not as Americans have done for the purpose of … controlling the Indian tribes, but with the view of avenging injuries inflicted on the red man by the white," Canada's governor general, Lord Dufferin, said at the time.

"If the North West Mounted Police fell short of Dufferin's grand design," observes historian John Herd Thompson in *Forging the Prairie West*, "for the rest of the century they nonetheless maintained a remarkable peace between Euro-Canadian settlers and native people — remarkable, that is, when contrasted with the violent conflict between the U.S. Cavalry and the plains tribes on the other side of the forty-ninth parallel."

One notable exception, Thompson acknowledges, is the North West Rebellion of 1885 — Métis leader Louis Riel's final, failed revolt against what he viewed as Canada's illegal westward expansionism and unjust suppression of aboriginal self-government.

Widely seen as a pivotal moment in Canadian history, the rebellion is rich with reasons for ambivalence. The familiar traitor-or-hero controversy about Riel, who was hanged at Regina that November, is just as easily applied to his military chief Gabriel Dumont, who escaped to the U.S. Indian leaders Poundmaker and Big Bear — each of whom intervened at times to prevent the killing of Canadian settlers or soldiers, but whose followers also initiated deadly attacks. Both Riel and Dumont can be viewed as feckless troublemakers, thwarted peacemakers or tragic heroes witnessing a sorrowful end to their nation's former glory.

The rebellion had been put down. The railway had been completed. The police were in place. And the land had been declared fertile and free for the taking.

Business district, Regina, circa 1890s

All that Saskatchewan awaited was an invigorating influx of settlers ready to embrace pioneer life on the prairie.

An 1881 census showed that fewer than 20,000 people lived in the entire district, which consisted of a few fledgling settlements and a scattering of farmsteads. But the push was on to fill it. And by the start of the early 1890s, the two major cities of the future province, Regina and Saskatoon — each with a crucial railway stop — were in the midst of modest but promising growth spurts.

An official federal government campaign to attract immigrants was already having some success by the turn of the century, as shown by a March 1903 Saskatoon newspaper report on the Barr colony — the founding settlers of Lloydminster — headlined "WESTWARD HO! Midnight Departure of Fifteen Hundred London Pilgrims for Western Canada."

Reporting from a London train station, a correspondent described "a crowd of men, women and children who were putting England behind them and setting out to seek their fortunes in the heart of Canada — Our Lady of the Snows."

More and more land was being put to the plough. And more and more settlers, like William Faulkner in the Cypress Hills, were hitching their wagons to Saskatchewan, enthusiastically peopling what Butler had described as "the great, lone land."

Barely thirty years later, the great, lone land was poised to become a province.

THE BENEVOLENCE AND THE BOUNTY

The advent of the white man changed life dramatically for the people of Saskatchewan's First Nations. Thousands died in epidemics of small pox and tuberculosis while thousands more like Chief Big Bear and his band were faced with starvation for refusing to sign treaties with the Dominion. Big Bear finally capitulated in 1882 and signed Treaty Number 6. In addition to becoming eligible for government rations, each band member was given a $12 annuity; each chief was given $25, a Queen's silver medal, farm implements and a flag. The government called this "the benevolence and the bounty."

Mistahimaskwa, Chief Big Bear, Cree leader

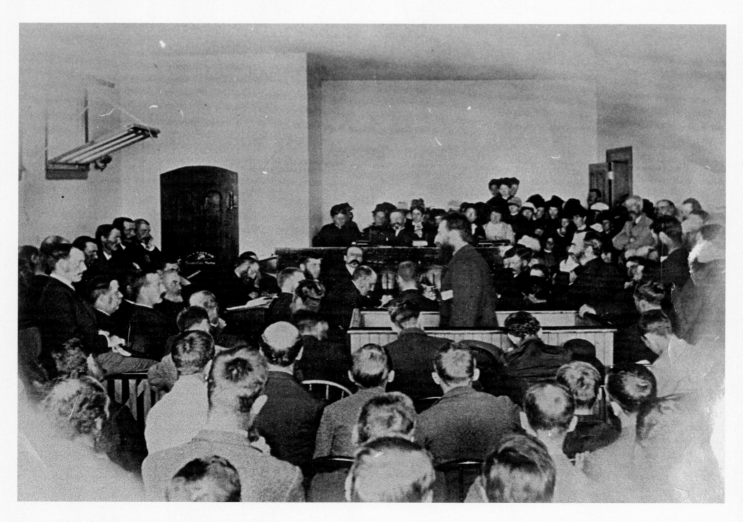

Louis Riel in the prisoner's dock, Regina, November 1885

Pitikwahanapiwiyin, Chief Poundmaker, "This is our land ...
it is ours and we will take what we want." August, 1876

Cree woman, Broadview Reserve, circa 1880s

Cree family, circa 1900

THE DEAD RIEL.

story of His Disfigurement a Wanton Lie.

(From the Supplement of the 19th inst.)

THE LEADER.

We have had to publish a second edition of the LEADER so great was the demand for it.

JUSTICE.

We wrote with indignation over alleged indignities to Riel, which we find to have been never committed. We probed the matter to the bottom. Father Andre told us of them. Another gentleman who spoke at the time as an eye witnees, but who now informs us his evidence was "hearsay," told us. The LEADER has always ranged itself on the side of the weak, and nothing can be weaker than a dead man. We are glad no men disgraced themselues and that nothing but what was respectful took place. Louis Riel's body has been given to his church. He has had the same service a French king would have had read over him. The first men and women in Regina—some of whom had no sympathy whatever with his projects—attended the service and reverently and respectfully bent over his remains. His motivas were undouhtedly mixed, but this is no time to probe every weak spot in his chequered life, every flaw in the composition of his character. We have put it on record that his doom was just. Let us, sinful creatures that we are, try to rise to the grandeur of judging as He judges who is without sin.

We publish the following with great pleasure:—

"We have visited the body of Louis David Riel and certify that there is no word of truth in the statement that the body was disfigured. Nof a hair was improperly removed. In the presence of Sheriff Chapleau attending officially, and a number of Riel's friends, we saw the corpse and repeat there is not a word of truth in, not a title of foundation for the statement that it was in the least ill-treated.

NICHOLAS FLOOD DAVIN,
Justice of the Peace.
FATHER A. ANDRE,
O. M. I.

Regina, November 19th, 1885.

Obsequies of Riel.

Last night the body of Riel, in the plain black coffin, was taken to Father Andre's house at about 12 o'clock. In the presence of the Rev'd Pére André Sheriff Chapleau, N. F. Davin, J. P.; A. L. Lunan, Pascal Bonneau and several others, including the LEADER reporter, the coffin was opened. The body was found to lie as decently there as his mother, wife or child would wish. Not a hair sacriligiously touched. Father André turned round to Mr. Davin and said:—"Its a lie —nothing has been done." He examined him closely and again said:—"No, no —it was quite untrue."

Mr. Davin—The whole story was evidently founded on Father McWilliams and one or two of Riel's friends taking a small piece of Riel's hair as a memento.

Sheriff Chapleau—His shoes are gone.

Father André—Ah, that is nothing. That would be done as a memorial.

Pascal Bonneau—Only friends would care for them. There has been nothing.

A. L. Lunan—Evidently nothing whatever.

Father André—Does he not look beautiful?

The face wore a look of smiling calm.

This morning—after the body had been washed—it was seen again and Riel's face looked positively beautiful. It enabled one to realize the full force of the exquisite lines.

He who hath bent him o'er the dead
Ere the first day of Death is fled,
The first dark day of nothingness,
The last of danger and distress,
Before Decay's effacing fingers
Have swept the lines where beauty lingers,
And marked the mild angelic air—
The rapture of repose that's there—
The fixed yet tender traits that streak,
The languor of the placid cheek,
And—but for that sad shrowded eye,
That fires not, wins not, weeps not now—
And but for that chill changeless brow,
Where cold obstructions apathy
Appals the gazing mourner's heart,
As if to him it could impart
The doom he dreads, yet dwells upon—
Yes, but for these and these alone,
Some moments, ay, one treacherous hour,
He still might doubt the tyrants power,
So fair, so calm, so softly seal'd,
The first last look by death reveal'd!

The service in the church was attended by protestants as well as Catholics. The coffin lay outside the railing that separates the altar from where the laity are. It was covered with black, a white cross of linen was sewn on to the black covering. The altar was in part covered with black with white crosses. Father Andre said the Mass for the dead and the members of the congregation sang the responses. Eight wax candles burned on the altar, two white, two pink, two green, two red. Two burned at the head and two at the foot of the coffin. After mass there was a collection and then the

FUNERAL SERVICE

took place. Father Andre took off the chasibule and manipule and said in Latin: "Enter not into judgment with thy servant." Then he chanted "Libera me Domine." During the service the priest sprinkled holy water on the coffin and and the clerk put coals into a silver vessel held by a chain, and then the priest put incense into this and the clerk swung it, and the church was filled with a thin cloud of incense, having a pungent odour. "*Requiescat in pace*" sang the clergyman, "Amen" came from the clerk and the members of the congregation.

"*Anima ejus, et animae omnium fiddium defunctorum per misericordiam Dei requiscat in pace*".

"Amen".

The priest took off his vestments. The cover of the coffin was moved aside so as to show the face which wore an expression of glorification.

"*Il n'est pas chang*", whispered the clerk. But he *was* changed. The *ruse* look the face wore at times in his days of earthly life, was gone and he looked beautiful and at peace.

The Rev. Mr, Pooley, (Methodist minister)—"How quiet and even beautiful he looks."

"Yes" said someone—"he looks as if he acquiesced in his fate. He is at rest."

Father André—I never saw anything more beautiful.

"If", whispered another, "the spirit can affect its late tenament then Riel is happy."

Father André—Oh indeed he is.

The coffin was lowered into the grave, seven feet deep, on the right of the altar; all was over and the writer left the church and passed out into the bracing air and springlike sunshine which made one fancy he would hear the lark sing up in the blue concave fretted with golden fire. If men's spirits are indeed immortal and Riel had made his peace with Heaven what a change from the cell of the Regina prison to glory.

One moment here, so mean, so low,
The next——*beyond the stars!*

RIEL EXECUTED.

He Des without a Speech.

A Sane and Beautiful Death.

REGINA, Nov. 16.—As fair a morning as ever dawned shone on the closing act—the last event—in the not uneventful life of Louis Riel. The sun glittered out in pitiless beauty, and the prairie, slightly silvered with hoar frost, shone like a vast plain sown with diamonds. We drove Mr. Sherwood, Chief of Dominion Police, who had arrived on Sunday evening with the warrant. As we neared Government House, two armed mounted police drew up their horses across our path and demanded our pass which read as follows:

To Mr. Gibson—"Admit representatives of the LEADER."

(Signed)

SHERIFF CHAPLEAU.

When we neared the bridge there was a force commanned by an inspector. Two traps were at a standstill. One of the troopers shook hands with Mr. Percy Sherwood, an old friend. We had a pleasant word with Mr. F. J. Hunter and Mr. W. C. Hamilton. Our pass was again vised and on we drove. Arrived at the prison we met outside the representatives of the press, Dr. Dopd, Mr. Pugsley, Mr. Marsh, Messrs. Gillespie, Dawson, Bole and several citizens. The beauty of the morning was the chief theme of conversation. Towards eight o'clock we crushed our way thro' troopers, Col. Irvine kindly doing all in his power for us: ascended the stair case; walked the length of the prison and there, at the door of the gastly place of execution knelt Riel, his profile showing clearly against the light, Father André, a surplice over his soutane kneeling, his back to us, Father McWilliams, with a stole thrown over his traveling coat, kneeling, his face to us, and holding a lighted wax candle. In Riel's hand was an ivory crucifix silver mounted which he frequently kissed. Father McWilliams and Pere Andrè ever and again sprinkled holy water on the condemned man. Riel was pale—deadly pale—and his face looked most intellectual.

Father André, in French—Do you pardon all your enemies from the bottom of your heart?

Riel: I do *mon pere*—I pardon all my enemies for the love of the good God.

Father André: Have you any sentiment of malice, any feeling of malice against any one?

Riel: No, my father, I forgive all.

Father André: Do you offer your life as a sacrifice to God?

Riel: I do *mon pere*.

Father André: My child, the flesh is weak and the spirit strong, do you repent you of all your sins of thought word, and deed?

Riel: I do my father, I have committed many sins and I ask my God's pardon for them, all in the name of Jesus, Marie and Joseph.

Father André: You do not wish to speak in public? You make that a sacrifice to God?

Riel: *Oui mon pere.* I make to my God as a sacrifice the speaking to the public in this my last hour.

Father André: God has been good to you my son to give you an opportunity of repenting; are you thankful for this?

Riel: I thank the good God that in his Providence he has enabled me to make my peace with him and all mankind before I go away.

The two clergymen then placed their hands on his head and pronounced the absolution.

Riel then in an affecting and childlike way prayed God to bless his mother, his wife, his brothers, his friends and his enemies. "My father bless me" he said looking up to heaven "according to the views of your Providence which are ample and without measure." Then addressing Pere André:—"Will you bless me Father?"

Father André blessed him, as did Father McWilliams. He then rose from his knees and was pinioned, he meanwhile praying and the clergy praying. When he was ready to pass out to the scaffold Pere André said to him in French "There go to Heaven." *(Bon! Allez au Ciel.)* He then kissed Pere André on the lips, and Father McWilliams embraced him giving him the side of each cheek. Riel then said ere he turned to pass thro' the door which went into that room built of coarse lumber and which, if Pere André is right, and Riel was really repentent, and Christianity is true, was for him the poor dingy portals of eternal day and unending peace and blessedness:—

"I give my life a sacrifice to God. *Remerciez Madam Forget et Monsieur Forget.* "O my God" he cried still speaking in French as he went down the stairs, "you are my support". *Mon Soutein C'est Dieu.*

He now stood on the drop. The cord is put on his neck. He said "*Courage mon Père.*"

Pére André in subdued tones:—"Courage! Courage!"

They shook hands with him as did Dr. Jukes, and Riel preserving to the last that politeness which was so characteristic of him and which was remarked during the trial said:

"Thank you Doctor."

Then he prayed in French: "Jesus, Mary and Joseph have mercy on me. *J'espére encore.* I believe still. I believe in God to the last moment."

Father McWilliams: "Pray to the sacred Heart of Jesus."

Riel: Have mercy on me Sacred Heart of my Jesus! Have mercy on me. *Jesu Marie et Joseph assistez moi dans mes derniers moments, Assistez moi Jesus, Marie et Joseph!*

Father McWilliams held the cross to him which he kissed.

Mr. Deputy Sheriff Gibson: Louis Riel have you anything to say why sentence of death should not be carried out on you?

Riel, glancing where Pere André stood about to ascend the staircase anxious evidently to leave the painful scene, said in French, "Shall I say something?"

Père André: "No."

Riel: (in French) Then I should like to pray a little more.

Père André: He asks to pray a little more.

Deputy Sheriff Gibson: (looking at his watch): "Two minutes."

Father McWilliams: say "Our Father" and addressing Mr. Gibson, "when he comes to, deliver us from evil" tell him then—

Mr. Gibson gave the directions to the hangman who now put on Riel's head the white cap.

Riel and Father McWilliams: "Our Father which art in Heaven, hallowed be thy name, Thy Kingdom come, Thy will be done on earth as it tis in Heaven, give us this day our daily bread, and deliver us"———

The hangman pulled the crank and Riel fell a drop of nine feet.

Dr's Dodd and Cotton were below. The knot in the fall had slipped round from under the poll. The body quivered and swayed slightly to and fro. Dr. Dodd felt the pulse.

LEADER Reporter—How is his pulse Doctor?

Dr. Dodd—It beats yet—slightly.

LEADER Reporter, addressing Dr. Cotton—I hope he is without pain.

Dr. Cotton—O quite. All sensation is gone.

The body ceased to sway. It hung without a quiver. Dr. Dodd looking at his watch and feeling the pulse of what was Riel:—"He is dead. Dead in two minutes". Dr. Cotton put his ear to where that restless heart beat: "Dead". While inside that solemn and mournful tragedy was being enacted, outside the prison were many of the public and the reporter of the LEADER, whose duty it was to watch what took place outside, gives the following description.

The barrack square was suggestive of something unusual though all was so calm. At the door of Col. Irvine's house stood Lord Boyle, Col. Irvine and Col. MacLeod. Before the prison talked the citizens, most of them members of the jury. There were many who were disappointed at not being allowed in to the execution. Jokes were made. The troopers stood in groups on the verandah of the prison and their conversation was not edifying. Sometimes a pause—but no sound came from within. No sign that the tragedy was finished. At last a thud was heard and one of the police said—"The G—d d——n s—n of a b——h is gone at last".

"Yes" said another as if saying 'amen' to this noble prayer—"Yes, the s—n of a b——h is gone for certain now". And then followed some civilized laughter.

As the reporter drove away from the barracks he saw the mounted patrols all on the *qui vive* and everything looked as everything has looked for days as if some attempt at rescue had been expected.

Near Government House a friend was met who asked the writer how Riel died and the answer was:

"He died like a Christian".

"How about his sanity?"

"Any man who saw him die could not doubt his sanity. A more rational, self-controlled, sequent mind could not be conceived than he displayed."

"Did he die game?, Was he pale?"

"He was pale. A man would naturally be pale. He showed the highest reason on the eve of going into eternity to crush down his natural love of display and occupy himself solely with that world to which he henceforth belonged. He died with calm courage, like a man and a Christian, and seemed to me a triumph of rationality as compared with the brutes who could blurt out ribaldry over his death or the atheists who thought it a sign of insanity that in the position in which he had been placed he should have given himself to prayer."

Nothing in his life so became him as the leaving of it.

BY ANOTHER REPORTER.

Some ten minutes after the drop had fallen the door at the base of the enclosure that immediately surrounded the scaffold. opened revealing a ghastly spectacle the lifeless remains of Louis Reil with the hangman's rope around his neck, and the doctor feeling the pulse which had ceased forever four minutes after the drop was sprung. The body appeared in full view dressed in dark homespun, the white cap drawn down over the face which was turned northward towards the wall of the barracks from which the gallows projected, the large massive head was very much bent forward, with the bearded chin resting on his broad full chest showing the back of the strong neck, bare to the skin, and that the once long shaggy locks of Louis Riel had been shorn off. The large hangman's knot showed up very conspicuously and pressed itself against the back of the head just above the base of the brain square in line with the spinal chord. After hanging thus for some thirty minutes, the white cap was turned up showing the face which indicated a painless death. Within three quarters of an hour the body was cut down and placed on a rough table or bench in the walled enclosure that surrounds the gallows; here the rough clothes and pinions were taken off, and then, in full view, surrounded by the doctor, jurymen, civilians and soldiers, lay the body dressed in a black suit with white shirt and collar, the once firey piercing eyes closed forever as if in sleep, the strongly marked features, and massive high brow looking peaceful.

"THE RAPTURE OF REPOSE WAS THERE."

Some present wore a careless thoughtless smile as they removed locks of hair from the dead man's brow; others seemed to realize the terrible character of the situation. Soldiers who had shared the fortunes of war in the late rebellion and whose labours had been greatly increased on account of strict guard over the prisoner while living, expressed themselves as glad that his troubled spirit was at rest, but all seemed to think kindly of the dead who had always acted corteously towards his guards. We turned away from this aweful and never to be forgotten scene, shortly after the body was laid in the plain coffin in which it was about to be buried, in a grave beneath the scaffold.

INTERVIEW WITH RIEL.

His Parting Messages to Mankind.

The reporter of the LEADER having received the orders of its proprietor to see Riel before his death and have an interview with him, waited on Captain Deane who was suffering from a severe accident, and who said he would be most happy to oblige the LEADER, but he doubted if he could do so were he in charge, but his superior officer was here and he had no authority to act without his orders.

"Who is he?" asked the reporter.

"Col. Irvine."

Reporter: "I fear Col. Irvine is not friendly to the LEADER; which, in the public interest has felt bound to criticize him. However I must not enlarge on that head with you. My marching orders were to 'See Riel,' who it was understood desired to see the Reporter of the LEADER with whom during his trial he frequently communicated." Believing it to be useless to wait on the gallant Col. I repaired to the Queen City of the plains and went to my lodgings where I had the 'Materials' with which I had long been armed in preparation for this crisis. When first the officer in command of the LEADER said: An interview must be had with Riel if you have to outwit the whole police force of the North-West.' I revolved various schemes. I reflected what great things had been done by means of the fair sex, and I thought, suppose I enlist on my side the fair 'Saphronica' and get her to put the 'Com hether' on Irvine's susceptible fancy, and let her represent the LEADER. Saphronica was willing. A young lady of undoubted charms and resolute will, she essayed the officer in command, and strange to say, his sense of duty or his fears of the Government, were stronger than his gallantry and Saphronica utterly failed. To corrupt the guard? But on this the Editor in chief frowned. At last I hit on a plan of my own. Accordingly on the evening of my refusal by Deane, I repaired to my lodgings, put on a *soutane*, armed my chin with a beard, put on a broad brimmed wide awake, and stood Mr. Bienveillée the *ancien* confesseur of the doomed Riel. I hung at my bosom an enormous silver crucifix and now, speaking French, presented myself at the Barracks. The guard made no difficulty, and I believe they took me for Pere André. Entered his cell, I looked round and saw that the policeman had moved away from the grill. I bent down, told Riel I was a LEADER reporter in the guise of a prêtre, and had come to give his last message to the world. He held out his left hand and touching it with his right said: "Tick! Tick! Tick! I hear the telegraph, ah *ca finira*," "quick, I said, have you anything to say? I have brought pencil and paper—Speak."

Riel: "When I first saw you on the trial I loved you.

MESSAGES.

I wish to send messages to all. To Lemieux, Fitzpatrick, Greenshields. I do not forget them. They are entitled to my *reconnaissance.* Ah!" he cried, apostrophizing them, "You were right to plead insanity, for assuredly all those days in which I have badly observed the Commandments of God were passed in insanity *(passe dans la folie).* Every day in which I have neglected to prepare myself to die, was a day of mental alienation. I who believe in the power of the Catholic priests to forgive sins, I have much need to confess myself according as Jesus Christ has said, 'Whose sins you remit they are remitted.'"

DEATH.

Here he stopped and looked in his peculiar way and said:

"Death comes right to meet one. He does not conceal himself. I have only to look straight before me in order to see him clearly. I march to the end of my days. Formerly I saw him afar. (Or rather "her" for he spoke in French). It seems to me, however, that he walks no more slowly. He runs. He regards me. Alas! he precipitates himself upon me. My God!" he cried, "will he arrive before I am ready to present myself before you. O my God! Arrest it! By the grace, the influence, the power, the mercy divine of Jesus Christ. Conduct him in another direction in virtue of the prayers eneffable of Marie Immaculate. Separate me from death by the force the intercession of St. Joseph has the privilege to exercise upon your heart, O my God! Exempt me lovingly by Jesus, Marie and Joseph, from the violent and ignomineous death of the gallows, to which I am condemned.

"Honorables Langevins, Caron, Chapleau, I want to send them a message, let them not be offended if a man condemned to death dares to address them. Whatever affairs hang on you don't forget, 'What shall it profit a man to gain the whole world and to lose his soul?'

Honorable Messrs. Blake and Mackenzie, I want to send them a message. For fifteen years you have often named me, and you have made resound the echoes of your glorious province, in striking on my name as one strikes on a tocsin. I thank you for having contributed to give me some celebrity. Nobly take from me an advice nobody else will dare to give you. Prepare yourself each day to appear before your God.

The Vice-Regal throne is surrounded with magnificence. He who occupies it is brilliant, and my eyes cannot fix on him without being blinded. Illustrious personages the qualities with which you are endowed are excellent. For that reason men say 'Your Excellency.' If the voice of a man condemned to death will not appear impertiment to you; it vibrates at the bottom of the cells of Regina to say to you: Excellencies! you also, do not fail to hold yourself in readiness for death, to make a good death, prepare yourself for death!

Sir John Macdonald! I send you a message. I have not the honour to know you personally. Permit me nevertheless to address you a useful word. Having to prepare myself for death I give myself to meditation and prayer. Excuse me Sir John. Do not leave yourself be completely carried away by the glories of power. In the midst of your great and noble occupations take every day a few moments at least, for devotion and prayer and prepare yourself for death.

"Honorable and noble friends! Laurier, Laflamme, Lachlaelle, Desgardins, Taillon Beaubien, Trudel, Prud'homme, I bid you adieu. I demand of God to send you the visit of Death only when you shall have long time desired it, and that you may join those who have transformed death into joy, into deliverance and triumph.

"Honourable Joseph Dubuc, Alphonse, C. Lariviere, Marc. A. Girard, Joseph Royal, Hon. John Norquay, Gov. Edgar Dewdney, Col Irvine, Captain Deane, I would invite them to think how they would feel if they had only a week to live. Life here below is only the preparation for another. You are good Christians, think of eternity. Do not omit to prepare yourself for death.

"O my God! how is it death has become my sweetheart with the horror I feel towards her? And how can she seek me with an attention proportioned to the repugnance she inspires. O Death the Son of God has triumphed over your terrors! O Death I would make of the a good death!

"Elezear de la Grinodière! Roger Goulet, and you whom I regard as a relative Irené Kérouak, prepare yourself for death. I pray God to prolong your days. Louis Schmidt, I ask of the good God to enable you to come to a happy old age. Meanwhile prepare yourself for death. Listen to the disinterested advice of one condemned. We have been placed in this world of pain only for the purpose of probation.

"And you whom I admire and respect, glorious Major General Middleton you were kind to me, you treated me nobly. Pray see in my words the desire to be as little disagreeable as possible. Life has been smiling and fortunate for you, but alas! it will also finish for you. General if there is one thing I have appreciated more than being your prisoner of war it is that you chose as my guard Captain Young, one of the most brave and polite officers of your army. Captain Young! Be not surprised that I send you a message through the LEADER newspaper which I understand with *reconnaissance* has not called out against me, prepare yourself all your days. Death also disquiets himself about you. Do not sleep on watch. Be ever well on your guard.

MESSAGES TO FATHER CHINUIQUY.

"And you whom death spares and does not dare to approach and you whom I cannot forget, Ancien Preacher of Temperance, Chinuiquy, your hairs are white. God who has made them white slowly, wishes to make your heart white right away *(tout d'un coup).* O be not angry at the disinterested voice of a man who has never spoken to you, to whom you have never given pain, unless it be in having abandoned regretably the amiable religion of your fathers. The grace of Marie waits for you. Please come."

The prisoner paused, and in the pause one heard the skirr of the spurred heel of the Mounted Policeman and the neighing of one of the horses in the stables hard by, and I said:—"Is this all? Have you no more to say?"

"No more," replied Riel, "Father André has been here. He has told me there is no hope, that he has had a letter from my good friend Bishop Grandin. I have made my confession. I have taken the Sacraments. I am prepared. But yet the Spirit tells me, told me last night I should yet rule a vast country, the North-West, with power derived direct from heaven, look!" and he pointed to the vein in his left arm, "there the spirit speaks, 'Riel will not die until he has accomplished his mission' and—"

He was about to make a speech and I left him with some sympathy and no little sadness. I felt that I had been in the presence of a man of genius *manqué*, of a man who, had he been gifted with judgment might have accomplished much; of one who, had he been destitute of cruelty might even command esteem, and as I rode over the bridge and looked down on the frosty creek, and cast my eye towards the Government House where happy people were perhaps at dinner at that hour, I said to myself, "Why did he murder Scott? Why did he seek to wake the bloody and nameless horrors of an Indian massacre? Why did he seek the blood of McKay and his fellow peacemakers? Unhappy man there is nothing for it. You must die on Monday."

Here as I passed near the trail going north-west the well known voice of a home returning farmer saying "Good night!" woke me from my reverie. In twenty minutes I was seated at dinner. I joined in the laugh and the joke, so passingare our most solemn impressions so light the effect of actual tragedy. Our emotions are the penumbras of rapid transitions of circumstances and vanishing associations and like clouds we take the hue of the moment, and are shaped by the breeze that bloweth where it listeth.

Testimony to Leader's Enterprise and Accuracy.

We yesterday received respecting the report of the Riel execution in our daily the following letter from Pere Andre:

Monsieur le redacteur du LEADER: I have been reading your morning report of the execution of Riel and in comparing it with with the reports published in the *Free Press* and *Manitoban* which I have seen this morning I can say your report IS THE MOST EXACT AND TRUTHFUL. *You alone have correctly reported the words I addressed to Riel and his responses in front of the scaffold.* You may make this letter public if you wish and I hope you will believe me,

Yours etc.
PERÉ ANDRÉ.

MAPLE CREEK.

A Thriving Town,

The Mounted Police.

MAPLE CREEK, Nov. 15.—To a stranger entering the town the most imposing structures are Messrs. T. C. Power & Bros. store and the Commercial Hotel. T. C. Power & Bros. are one of the oldest and wealthiert firms in the North-West, having some 28 stores besides several stage, freight and steam boat lines in Montana ann several business places in the N.W. T. The store here is operated by Mr. Horace A. Greeley, a cousin of the great journalist, and a thorough and pleasing gentleman. Messrs. Dixon Bros. and J. Clanstie are the other merchants. They are both substantial firms and their stores have a very business like appearance. The Commercial Hotel, which is the largest in the N. W. T., is owned and run by Mr. T. M. Rasin, and old employee of the firm of T. C. Power & Bros., and a pleasant gentleman to deal with. The International Hotel, which was the first one built in the town, was built by Mr. J. J. English, is now being operated by Hr. J. D. Pearson, an eastern gentleman who seems thoroughly acquainted with his business and is making friends. Mr. V. Levesque has a modal Blacksmith shop with the modern appliances for his trade, also does tinsmithing and carriage blacksmithing. W. A. Laurence, cabinet maker, turns out some splendid work from his shop. Mr. P. Bradley, builder, has had a hand in the construction os the entire town, and is one of the oldest settlers in the N. W. T. E. Hartley has a blacksmith shop located a little out of town. Mr. Flack, a most affable gentleman, is the C. P. R. agent. Mr. Thos. Jones has a well stocked livery stable which is o model of neatness. Mr. H. Holtorf's point shop, J. Quesnelle's dairy, J. Hasty's Bakery, J. J. English, Agricultural Implements; and Mrs. W. D. Hay's laundry complete the business portion of the town. Beside the school house; Methodist church and parsonage there are a number of comfortable looking dwellings which speak well for the enterprise and thrift of the future city. There are about two hundred quarter sections under cultivation within 16 miles of the town. The grain crops, considering the dry season, were good, and root crops were splendid as they always are.

One of the oldest and weaithiest settlers, Moj. A. Shurthff, late of the N. W. M. P., died in Colorado a few days since. He was largely interested in cattle here and his wife, it is believed, will return to their beautiful home located scarce three miles out of town. The ranch has been carried on by the mayor's brother-in-law, Mr. Geo. W. Wood, a gentleman thoroughly posted in the cattle business. They moved here some four year's ago from McLeod to gain the benefit of the superior winter range in this district. The census taker, I am told, gathered together the names of 500 souls, within a radius of 16 miles of the town. There are several large herds of cattle, horses and sheep in the district, and am told a great many more are expected in next spring. Quite an interesting case was going on while at the creek. The school house which is being erected by Mr. Laurance, is of logs, and of course there are a great many chips which make good fuel, scattered about the grounds. Mrs. Hay who runs the laundry, asked permission of two of the committee to take some of the chips, and they thinking them worthless, granted it. When she sent her children to gather the chips, the builder told them they were the property of the school house and therefore could not be used by any one else. Mrs. H. then came herself and carried off a washboiler full, while Mr. Laurance went off for another member of the committee, Mr. Jno. Dixon, who came up at once to intercept the lady but she would not intercept. Mr. D. then snatched the boiler from her and emptied the chips and Mrs. H. claims, tore her dress. Forthwith she whaled away at him with the boiler and a battle ensued, of which we are told the lady was winner. Both parties put in a charge of assault and battery and were each fined $8 and costs. Mr. D. brought witnesses to prove against the lady's character without avail and has nearly laid himself liable to suit for defamation of character.

RIEL'S LAST WILL AND TESTAMENT.

Silver or Gold Had He None.

A Remarkable Document.

The following will, written in French, was handed by Riel to Father André:

"Prison de Regina, Nvo. 6, 1885.

"Testament of Louis David Riel."

I make my will according to the advice given me by the Rev. Father Alexis Andre, my kind confessor and most devoted director of my conscience.

In the name of the Father and of the Son and of the Holy Ghost, I declare this to be my last will and testament; that I have made it freely and in the full use of my faculties.

Men having fixed the 16th November next as that of my death and as it is possible the sentence will be executed, I declare beforehand that my submission to the orders of Providence is sincere. My will is ranged with entire liberty of action under the influence of the Devine Grace and our Lord Jesus Christ, on the side of the Roman Catholic and Apostolic church. I was born in it and it is by it that I have been led into the way of grace. It is by her also that I have been regenerated. I retracted what I have said and professed contrary to her teaching; and I retactr i again. I ask pardon for the scandal I have caused. I do not wish there should be a difference between me and the priest hood of Jesus Christ, as great as the point of a needle. If I should die on the 10th of the month—that is to say——in four days—I wish to do all in my power, with the Divine Succors of my Saviour, to die in perfect harmony with my creator, my redecmer, my sanctifier, and with the Holy Catholic Church. And if my God wishe well, not to accord me the gift inestimable of life, I wish on my side, to mount the scaffold, and to resign myself to the will and end of Providence, by holding myself apart, as I am to-day from all earthly things. For I understand the most certain means of doing well and of having durable fruits, it is to practice and perform all enterprises in a manner entirely disinterested, without passion, without excitement, entirely in sight of God, while loving your neighbor, your friend, and your enemy as yourself for the love of God. I thank my good and tender mother for having loved me, and for having loved me with a love so Christian. I demand of her pardon for all the faults of which I have been guilty, against t helove, the respect and obedience that I owe her. I beg of her to pardon also the faults that I have committed against my duty towards my well-loved and regretted father, and towards his venerable memory. I thank my brothers and sisters for the great love and kindness to me. I also ask their pardon for my faults of all kinds, and for all the errors for which I have been culpable in their eyes. I thank my relatives and the relatives of my wife, for having always been so good and gentle to me, in particular my affectionate and well loved father-in-law, my mother-in-law, my brothers-in-law and my sisters-in-law. I beg of them also to pardon whatever has not been right in me, all that has been evil in my conduct. I give the hand of true friendship to my friends of all ages, of all ranks, of all conditons, of all positions. I thank them for the services they have rendered me. Particulary am I grateful towards my friends who have deigned to busy themselves with my affairs in public, both on this and the other side of the line. To the Oblates of Marie Immaculate, to the Society of St. Sulpice, to the Grey Nuns for all the good and kindness I have recieved from my infancy, I return them my thanks.

I have benefactors on the other side of the line, friends whose goodness to me has been beyond measure. I beg of them to accept my thanks and to charitably excuse my defects. And if my conduct has in any way been offensive to them, whether in small or great matters, I beg of them to pardon me while taking into account the excuses that may be in my favor. And as to the real sum of my faults, *(mes culpabilites)*, I hope they will have the goodhess to forgive them all before God and man.

I pardon with all my heart, with all my mind, with all my force, with all my soul, those who have caused me chagrin; who have given me pain; who have done me harm; who have persecuted me; who have, without any reason, made war on me for five years; who have given me the semblence of a trial; who have condemned me to death. And if they really mean to give me to death, I pardon them this entirely, as I ask God to pardon me all my offences entirely, in the name of Jesus Christ.

I thank my wife for having been so good and charitable to me, for the part she has so frequently taken in my painful works and difficult enterprises. I pray her to pardon me the sadness I have voluntarily and involuntarily caused her. I recommend to her the care of her little children; to bring them up in a christain manner, with particular attention to all that relates to good thoughts, good words, good actions and good companions.

I desire that my children may be brought up with great care in all that belongs to obedience to the church, their masters and superiors. I urge them to show the the greatest respect, the greatest submission and the most complete affection towards their good mother.

I do not leave to my children gold or silver but I beg God of his infinite pity *(je supplie les entrailles de la misericorde de Dieu)*, to fill my heart and my mind with the truly paternal blessing which I desire to give them.

Jean mon fils; Marie—Angélique, ma fille, I bless you in the name of the father and of Son and of the Holy Ghost, so that you may be attentive to know the will of God and faithful to accomplish it in all piety and in all sincerity; that you may practice virtue solidly but simply, without parade or ostentation; that you do the most good possible, while holding to your self without being wanting to others within the limits of just obedience to the bishops and priests, especially to your bishop and your confessor. I bless you; that your death may be sweet, edifying, good and holy in the eye of the church and in that of Jesus Christ Our Lord. I bless you in fine that you may seek and find the kingdom of God and that you may have moreover rest in Jesus, in Marie and in Joseph, Amen.

Pray for me. I leave my testament to Rev. Pere Alexis André, my confessor, I pray my friends everywhere to hold the name of Pere Andre side by side with my own. I love Father Andre.

LOUIS "DAVID" RIEL,
Son of Louis Riel and of Julie de la Gimodire.

THE LAST, BEST WEST

With the election of the Liberal party in 1896, the federal government made settlement of the Prairies — the final frontier of North America's West — a priority. The promise of land and freedom lured cowboys and colonists, shopkeepers and schoolteachers, farmers and dreamers to the territory. A steady stream of immigrants from Great Britain, Eastern Europe and the United States foreshadowed the flood that would follow in the next decade. This was a land of opportunity for 2,300 Barr colonists who arrived in 1903 and a haven from persecution for the 7,400 Doukhobors who were granted land near Yorkton in 1899. The Doukhobors, persecuted in their native Russia, were championed by Count Leo Tolstoy and the Quakers. Their history in the province would prove tumultuous and controversial.

Lawrence's haying crew, Cypress Hills, circa 1902

Barr colonists encampment, Saskatoon, 1903

Barr colonist homestead

Relaxing in the "Ram's Pasture," a bachelor wing, Didsbury House, Cannington Manor, 1894

Doukhobor woman and children, Veregin, circa 1905

PILE O' BONES

As its Cree name *Oskana-Ka-asateki* — "the bones that are piled together" — suggests, the site of the future provincial capital was known by native hunters as a spot where buffalo grazed and as shelter from winter blizzards and summer grass fires. It became a settlement — Pile of Bones — in 1882, the year the Canadian Pacific Railway decided to lay tracks there. New homesteaders, taking advantage of the newly enacted Dominion Lands Act, could claim 160 acres of land for $10. It was renamed Regina in 1882 in honour of Queen Victoria and named the provincial capital in 1883 after Lieutenant-Governor Edgar Dewedney decided that Battleford, the capital until then, was too far from the railway line.

Nicholas Flood Davin, who founded the *Regina Leader* in March 1883, circa 1873

The original *Regina Leader* building, Regina, 1885

SASKATOON

John Lake, leader of the Temperance Colonization Society, surveyed the site at a bend in the Saskatchewan River in 1882, seeking to found a town true to the philosophy and ideals of the Temperance League. The first settlers arrived in August 1883 and by 1899, Saskatoon consisted of a few houses on the east side of the river: a railway station house, the North West Mounted Police barracks and a hotel. It was incorporated as a village in 1901, with a population of 113.

Saskatoon businessmen and land agents, circa 1889

Victoria School, Saskatoon's "little stone school," where classes were first held in January, 1888

SHOOTING ACCIDENTS

SASKATOON'S M. L. A. SHOT AND KILLED.

Mr. W. B. Sinclair, a Newly-Elected Member, Meets With a Deplorable End While Goose Shooting---Received the Full Charge in His Breast.

A dispatch from Saskatoon, N. W. T., of Sept. 28, says: Mr. W. H. Sinclair, the newly-elected member of the Territorial assembly for the district of Saskatoon, was accidentally shot this afternoon about three miles east of the town. He was replacing his gun in the wagon after having fired a shot at a flock of geese, and received the full charge from the remaining barrel in the left breast. He lived only a short time, breathing his last before medical aid could reach him. He was a comparatively young man, a widower, with a small family in the east, and was extensively engaged in ranching. He has been a man of great business energy and will be much missed in Saskatoon. Two brothers-in-law from Toronto were with Mr. Sinclair at the time of the shooting.

Medicine Hat Victim.

A sad accident happened south of Medicine Hat on Friday. Wm. Rutherford was one of a party of duck shooters out for a day's sport. He and a companion were together and while the latter had put a shell in his gun and was closing it, the shell exploded, the contents going into Rutherford's right foot. He was taken to Medicine Hat to the home of his brother-in-law, Wm. Rutherford, and Dr. Calder summoned. The doctor endeavored to save the foot for the young man, but on Tuesday it was found necessary to amputate it. Blood poisoning set in however, and death came to his relief in the evening.

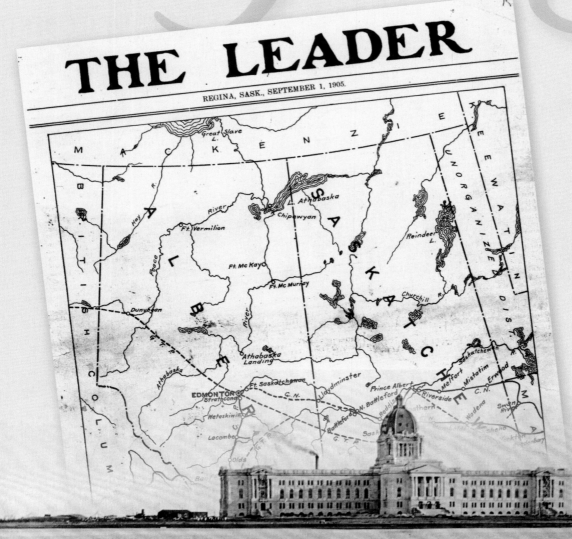

THE LEADER

REGINA, SASK., SEPTEMBER 1, 1905.

1914

CHAPTER TWO

The weather, one grateful scribe noted, "was magnificent." Clear skies, tolerable heat, a mercifully light wind. All in all, a true bargain of a day for the thousands who gathered at Regina on September 4, 1905, to celebrate Saskatchewan's birth as a province.

She was, in fact, already a few days old. But the dignitaries — Canada's prime minister and governor general among them — had decided to mark a simultaneous, September 1st entry of Alberta and Saskatchewan into the federation. Beginning at Edmonton, the entire entourage then hopped an eastbound train to repeat the performance in Regina. If the second billing to a sister province prompted any resentment among the newly minted residents of Saskatchewan, the hard feelings were well-hidden or forgotten by the time the special rail car arrived carrying Sir Wilfrid Laurier, Governor General Earl Grey and the rest of the sharp-dressed notables.

"Monday morning broke clear and fine," observed the *Regina Leader*, "with fresh breeze fluttering out the innumerable flags that flew in every direction above the city. From early dawn, the special excursion trains from the north, south, east and west began to pour in their human loads and by nine o'clock the greatest crowd ever met within Regina was thronging the sidewalks and roadways."

The good weather was no trivial matter. This day, this august moment of metamorphosis in the life of the old North West, had come in defiance of

Wilfrid Laurier, Mrs. Laurier, Inauguration Day, Regina, September 4, 1905

decades of conventional wisdom that said there was really nothing to be had here in the Prairies but the desert misery of summer followed by the unspeakable horrors of a polar winter.

What the agents of progress recognized was that while Saskatchewan's weather had its truly wicked moments, that its wild isolation had some indisputably frightening aspects, there was another way of seeing the starkness: as a landscape with untapped and unlimited potential, as an unsettled expanse ready to welcome a world of newcomers weary of cramped quarters and crimped prospects in their native countries.

It was Clifford Sifton, Laurier's interior minister for nearly the entire decade preceding Saskatchewan's 1905 inauguration, who had championed the West as a sellable commodity in the global market of human opportunity. Sifton looked not only to eastern Canada but also to the United States and especially to Europe for customers keen to have a piece of "the last, best West." And, by all accounts, he was a salesman *extraordinaire*.

When a group of 1,500 Londoners, bound for western Saskatchewan in 1903, were described by a British newspaperman as being destined for "the heart of Canada — our Lady of the Snows," the challenge facing Sifton and the other would-be proponents of western settlement was made clear. But in coming to Canada, those Londoners were a testament to the success of a federal promotional campaign that played down the wintry imagery, played up the golden sheaf of wheat and billed the unpopulated Prairies as a potential home to millions in posters and advertisements sent around the globe.

The pitch was more than elaborate spin doctoring. The scholarly studies of naturalists, soil scientists and climatologists had all been marshalled in a bid to contradict, in the words of historian John Herd Thompson, "the perception, crafted by the fur traders, of the western interior as a wilderness wasteland."

Laurier biographer H. Blair Neatby also noted that "exhibitions of Canadian farm products at American state fairs, combined with free railway excursions to the Canadian West for American newspaper editors, helped to destroy the myth of a 'frozen north.'"

Common folk, too, were enlisted in the campaign to attract homesteaders to Saskatchewan and other parts of the West. An essay contest, sponsored by the territorial government in the late 1890s, offered a prize and widespread publication in newspapers to the author of the best argument for becoming a prairie pioneer.

"To a man in any temperate quarter of the globe, who wishes to carve out a successful career, there is no place which offers such grand opportunities leading to the desirable position, expressed by the words 'a self-made man,' than the North West Territories of Canada," the winner, a certain E. Hagell, expounded. "To a man of energy and pluck, whether with little or considerable capital, the vast extent and illimitable resources of the great North West offer a field of exploitation such as can nowhere be found in conjunction with the healthfulness of which the robust farms and vigorous movements of those raised in the country bear witness."

The campaign, made easier by federal control over Saskatchewan's natural resources, allowed Ottawa to offer free of charge a 160-acre plot of land to any qualified homesteader from inside or outside of Canada.

Concerns muttered by some that members of "undesirable" ethnic or social classes were being let in just to fill the prairie void were brushed off by Sifton and Laurier as nonsense — though there was unanimous and almost unconscious agreement at that time in Canada that any worthy immigrant would be white.

Yet, as much by necessity as any deliberate adoption of egalitarian values, the foundation of the multicultural mosaic for which Canada has become famous was being assembled in those years village by village, farm by farm, on the Saskatchewan plains.

"I think that a stalwart peasant in a sheep-skin coat, born on the soil, whose forefathers have been farmers for generations, with a stout wife and a half-dozen children, is good quality," Sifton once memorably argued in response to his critics.

Saskatchewan, a Cree word for "swiftly flowing river," was finally living up to its name, with a relative torrent of newcomers — British, German, Ukrainian,

Charles Saunders, inventor
of Marquis wheat

Scandinavian — arriving in the early years of the 20th century compared with the trickle that had come to the region in the 1870s, Eighties and Nineties. The meagre population of 19,114 recorded in the 1881 census of the North West Territories would blossom to 492,432 by 1911 in the opening era of Saskatchewan proper.

And so it was to a genuinely thriving Regina, on as fine a Monday morning as one might find in any temperate quarter of the globe, that the official party arrived in the late summer of 1905 to proclaim Saskatchewan a province.

"The air was full of music, played by the various bands in the different portions of the town," the *Leader* observed. "School children numbering seven or eight hundred started the day with a parade, marching four abreast towards Victoria Park to sing for the prime minister and governor general, the girls in white and the boys in blue caps and sashes, each waving a Canadian flag, followed by a general parade that even had elephants …"

Earl Grey, his imperialist fervour checking any multicultural sympathies he might have harboured, rose to express his desire that Saskatchewan "become the happy and prosperous home of millions of Britons" loyal to the King — then Edward VII — and his vast overseas empire.

"The sight which I was privileged to witness at the children's parade," Grey went on, "where the healthfulness of your province was proclaimed by the fresh and bright loveliness of the most beautiful flowers Canada can produce, coupled with the fact that Regina is, as you say, the centre of the vast wheat belt, leads me to share your conviction that your expectations will be abundantly fulfilled."

Among those on parade, according to one newspaper account, was "a band of Indians in full regalia" — men, women and children marching in feathered headdresses to the delight of Grey and other esteemed onlookers.

That colourful spectacle was in sharp contrast to the dark cloud that, at that moment, loomed over the First Nations of the new province. Despite the fine rhetoric of the occasion and the genuine benefits that provincehood would bring to thousands of residents of Saskatchewan, the land's native inhabitants still faced a long and desperate struggle to preserve slim portions of their ancestral territory, to assert elusive treaty rights and to maintain some semblance of control over their indigenous heritage.

The rise during these years of a residential school system aimed at "civilizing" and Christianizing native children — some, no doubt, on parade that day in Regina — would eventually be understood to have deprived them of their families, languages and cultures, all the while subjecting many to unspeakable forms of abuse. But such bitter realizations and a nation's belated regrets were still generations away on September 4, 1905, a day dedicated to inauguration hoopla.

Laurier, architect of the expanded Confederation, echoed the governor general's joyful sentiment and, like Grey, made clear that the fortunes of Saskatchewan's people depended on their capacity to produce wheat — and that the success of that project could reap great benefits for all Canadians.

"I would vision," the prime minister said, "those vast prairies inhabited by a strong, independent patriotic people building towns, cities and villages and making the stubborn prairie soil yield its wealth in order to provide happy and prosperous homes for multitudes, and helping to furnish sustenance for dwellers in less favoured regions, living in harmony and peace, and fulfilling their destiny as patriotic Canadians."

Yet to come that day in Regina, the newspaper records, were "a fancy inaugural ball" and "the biggest and most magnificent display of fireworks ever in the Dominion." And if the revelers or dignitaries made their way along South Railway Street following the formal ceremony, they would have passed under "four great arches of golden grain" meant to symbolize Saskatchewan's number one hope for prosperity.

But in reality — despite all of Sifton's upbeat advertising for immigrants, despite all of the stirring speeches and the ubiquitous wheat-sheaf totems of hope — Saskatchewan's economic dependence on grain was still a great gamble. Scientific studies and alluring immigration posters notwithstanding, farmers in the early 1900s remained largely at the mercy of nature's whims, and wheat-killing early frosts routinely wiped out a whole season's crop in some parts of the fledgling province.

It was fortuitous, then, when a gaunt and bespectacled flutist-turned-cereal scientist from Ontario got his hands on a transplanted batch of Saskatchewan wheat and — within a few years of the inauguration — helped turn the new province into the breadbasket of the world.

Charles Saunders worked at the federal government's central experimental farm in Ottawa, hub of a national network of test fields where hybrid strains of key Canadian crops were developed to improve agricultural output. Along with his father, William, the Dominion cerealist, and his brother Percy, Saunders was attempting to create grains better suited to Canada's northern climate.

Ladies' group, Moose Jaw, pre-1910

Red Fife was the most popular variety of wheat in western Canada during the early 1900s. But the fact that it matured late in the summer meant it was vulnerable to early frost — those sub-zero August nights that were never played up in "the last, best west" promotions.

The susceptibility to frost restricted Red Fife's growing range to the southern part of the Prairies, and even there entire crops could be lost if a farmer's luck ran out and the mercury plunged before harvest time.

In 1892, Percy Saunders had taken samples of Red Fife grown in Saskatchewan — at the Indian Head test farm — and crossed them with an early-ripening variety of wheat from India called Hard Red Calcutta.

Planted at the Ottawa farm, the hybrid's best kernels were selected year after year for re-seeding until a distinctive strain of wheat, Markham, was developed.

In 1903, after Charles Saunders had nurtured the Markham crop through several more generations, he selected four samples for a series of tests that finally yielded early-ripening wheat — now named Marquis — that still possessed the bread-making qualities of Red Fife. By 1907, Saunders had enough seeds for field tests to be conducted in the West, and the results at Indian Head confirmed that Marquis was a major breakthrough. In some cases, it matured a week or more before Red Fife and yielded twice as many bushels per acre.

The news — and the magic seeds — spread quickly. Marquis was soon being planted widely across North America, and the amount of land suitable for growing wheat in Saskatchewan and throughout the Prairies was doubled in a matter of years. The 2.5 million acres of wheat sown in 1901 had shot up to 10 million in just over a decade, and total yields soared from 63 million bushels to 209 million in 1913.

Civic reception, Duke of Connaught's visit at City Hall, Regina, 1912

Significantly, that year Canada exported more than half of its total wheat crop, signalling the country's arrival as a major supplier in the world market. And with most of Canada's prime wheat-growing land lying within its borders, Saskatchewan stood poised to fulfill even the most optimistic expectations that had been expressed just a few years earlier, on the day it became a province.

But farmers throughout the West began to question whether they and their communities were getting the benefits they deserved from the boom.

Resentment was building over the federal government's control of provincial resources, and many grain growers in Saskatchewan began pushing to reap greater rewards from their international wheat bonanza.

The province, however, was about to go global in a much different way. And thousands of young men — some of them schoolboys in 1905 who had heard Laurier thunder about patriotic Canadians "fulfilling their destiny" — were about to leave the sunny wheat fields of Saskatchewan for the muddy trenches of Belgium and France.

THE LEADER.

VOL. 22.—NO. 29. REGINA, N.W.T., WEDNESDAY, SEPTEMBER 6, 1905. PRICE FIVE CENTS.

HAIL PROVINCE OF SASKATCHEWAN!

HIS HONOR GEORGE HEDLEY VICARS BULYEA
Sworn in September 1st as First Lieutenant-Governor of Alberta

New Province Enters Confederation Under Happy Auspices---Brilliant and Spectacular Scenes---Imposing Military Review---Lieutenant Governor Sworn in---Civic Addresses Presented to the Governor-General and Lieutenant-Governor---Luncheons and State Dinner---Grand Display of Fireworks--Dazzling Illuminations--State Ball

Officially Created September 1, 1905

THEIR EXCELLENCIES THE GOVERNOR-GENERAL AND LADY GREY
Who Honored the Inauguration Ceremonies With Their Presence Last Monday

Formally Inaugurated at Regina September 4, 1905

HIS HONOR AMEDEE EMMANUEL FORGET
Last Lieut.-Gov. of North-West Territories, Sworn in Sept. 4, as First Lieutenant-Governor of Saskatchewan

The great, the long-expected and much-prepared-for day has come and gone, and amidst much pomp and ceremonial and boundless popular enthusiasm Saskatchewan has taken her place in the confederation of Provinces that constitute the Dominion of Canada.

All day Saturday, bands of workmen, re-inforced by a small army of volunteers, were busy far into the night putting the finishing touches to the fitting preparation of Regina for the ceremony of September the fourth. Sunday dawned with the city in gala array and its hotels already thronged with those who had come to view the ceremonies. The decorations had been prepared upon the most elaborate scale, both those of a public nature and those due to private enterprise. Between Broad Street and Scarth Street on South Railway Street, four great arches had been prepared, artistically built up of golden grain, both wheat and oats, and evergreens that the generosity of the city of Prince Albert had supplied for the occasion. Starting at Broad Street and working westward, the arches bore the following inscriptions: "World's Granary," "North-West Forever," "Saskatchewan"j and "God Save the King." The places of business along the route of the procession were, almost without exception, profusely and artistically decorated with flags of all sizes, bunting, heraldic and other devices. One of the most elaborately prepared buildings was the Michaelis Block, the home of the Regina Trading Co., and containing the offices of the late Territorial Government. Tiny vertical masts had been erected upon the parapet of the building, from which streamers flowed and to which festoons of tri-colored bunting were attached. The decorations of this building were not, however, confined to the exterior, an elaborate and amusing tableau having been prepared in one of the windows, showing the infant "Saskatchewan" in a baby carriage with a bottle of "Scott's Emulsion" by its side, and the portraits of the late Sir John A. Macdonald, Sir Wilfrid Laurier, Hon. F. W. G. Haultain and Walter Scott, M.P., placed around it and directions to "Watch the Baby Grow." From Broad Street to Scarth Street South Railway Street was a mass of gaily colored bunting, every building being decorated with more or less elaboration. In other parts of the city also, both in the business and residential sections, decorations had been carried out, though, while most of the humblest dwellings of the city hung out their tribute of respect for the occasion, some of the houses of people from whom a great deal might have been reasonably expected were absolutely devoid of everything in the shape of special preparations. The schools and public buildings were all gaily bedecked with flags and bunting and upon the brickwork of the High School the words "Peace and Progress" had been inscribed. "Peace," indeed, seemed everywhere a prominent word, coupled generally with the words "progress and prosperity," seeming to indicate the direction towards which the eyes of the people of the new province were turned.

About 11.30 a. m. the special train with the 90th Regiment from Winnipeg steamed into the station amid the cheers of the big crowd waiting to receive them. With practically no delay the Regiment detrained and were marched to the camp that had been prepared for them at the Exhibition Grounds.

Church Parade

In the afternoon the Regiment attended a church parade in Victoria Park, at which it was estimated that over three thousand people were present. The service, which was conducted by the Presbyterian, Baptist, Methodist and Church of England ministers, will long be remembered by all those who were present at it. The ministers occupied the bandstand, in front of which the 90th were drawn up. The service started with the singing of "Old Hundredth" the regimental and the Regina Citizens' Bands providing the music. A reading from the Old Testament by Rev. J. J. Paterson came next, followed by the singing of the hymn "O Praise One God Today." Rev. H. G. Mellick then read a selection from the New Testament, after which came the hymn "Oft in Danger, Oft in Woe." Prayer was then offered by Rev. C. W. Brown, followed by the singing af "O God, Our Help in Ages Past." The brief address was delivered by Rev. G. C. Hill, who chose as the source of his inspiration the words found in verse 1, Psalm 127—"Except the Lord build the House, they labour in vain that build it; except the Lord keep the city, the watchman waketh but in vain." In simple language the preacher applied the words of his text to present circumstances. During the next few weeks, he said, our ears would be filled with accounts of what men had done in the building up of the great North-West. But all the labour and ability of men came to nought unless divine co-operation was sought for. Nothing could prosper without God's blessing. There were what was known as "tricks of the trade," smart things done to help a man forward in his business, against which he warned his hearers, urging them to adopt principles of righteousness in their place. Addressing himself to the farmers, many of whom he believed were in the congregation before him, the preacher said the words of his text were in an especial sense applicable to them. They might use good seed, the latest implements that the skill of man had been able to devise, they might build great barns and elevators, but unless God gave good harvest weather everything else would avail nothing. How many, he asked, took God into partnership? God wished for some of the profit, for an active interest in their business concerns. He prayed God that virtue and uprightness should be upheld in the new province, only so could it be lastingly built up. Fearing and trusting God, the people of Saskatchewan could confidently face the future.

At the end of the address, the National Anthem was sung, after which Rev. G. C. Hill pronounced the benediction, invoking the Almighty to bless the country with peace and prosperity. The service concluded, the 90th marched back to camp, while the Citizens' Band entered the bandstand and gave a selection of sacred music.

In the evening the principal streets of the city were thronged with sight-seers, viewing the decorations and illuminations. All the churches of the city were crowded to the doors and special sermons suited to the occasion were preached. In Victoria Park the Band of the 90th Regiment and the Brandon Band played sacred selections to an immense gathering.

September 4th

Monday morning broke clear and fine, with a fresh breeze fluttering out the innumerable flags that flew in every direction above the city. From early dawn the special excursion trains from the north, south, east and west began to pour their human loads and by nine o'clock the greatest crowd ever met within Regina was thronging the sidewalks and roadways. The air was full of music, played by the various bands in different portions of the town. Among the bands present were the following:—90th Regiment, Neepawa, Brandon City Band, Wolseley Silver Band, Rosthern, Indian Industrial School, Regina Citizens' Band and Cox's Drum and Fife Band, all of which gave their services gratuitously for the occasion.

Children's Parade

At nine o'clock, in accordance with the official programme prepared for the occasion the children of the various city schools, numbering some seven or eight hundred, assembled at their appointed places, and those from the Grattan and High Schools joininb those of the Public School, all started on their march towards Victoria Park. Walking four abreast, the girls in white and the boys with blue caps and blue sashes, each waving a Canadian flag, they presented what was without doubt the prettiest and at the same time the most imposing spectacle of the whole day. At the head of the procession, led by Mr. Jameson, chairman of the School Board and Mr. McMurchy, the principal of the High School, marched the Regina Citizens' Band, playing patriotic airs. After almost circling the city, the procession swept into Victoria Park, marching in admirably orderly array to the bandstand in front of which they were drawn up with almost military precision. Shortly afterwards, accompanied by an escort of the R.N.W.M.P. under Inspector Church, the vice-regal party arrived from Government House. Accompanying the Governor-General were Lady Grey and Lady Evelyn Grey, with Col. Hanbury Williams (private secretary), Captain Newton, aide-de-camp and Major Saunders of the R. N. W. M. P. In another carriage were Sir Wilfrid Laurier and Sir Gilbert Parker. On reaching the bandstand, the distinguished party was received by the Mayor, H. W. Laird, Judge Newlands, Speaker Gillis, Rev. G. C. Hill and Mr. A. F. Angus of the Reception Committee and Mr. Wm. Trant, secretary of the Celebration Committee.

The members of the Governor-General's party having taken up positions on the band stand the children proceeded to sing "Canada, The Land of The Maple" and "The Maple Leaf Forever," waving their hundreds of flags in the air as they sang. The effect was beautiful in the extreme and elicited the applause of those upon the stand and of the thousands of spectators massed around the children. So pleased was Lady Evelyn Grey with the picture presented by the children, that she requested that the singing of "The Maple Leaf Forever" should be repeated in order that she might bring her camera to bear upon it and obtain a picture of the occasion.

Earl Grey's Speech

Silence having been obtained Earl Grey advancing with Lady Grey was received with a great outburst of cheering. His Excellency said:

Children of Regina, I wish that the salutation that you have given me as the representative of His Majesty, King Edward, had been seen and heard by the King himself, instead of only by the eyes and ears of his deputy. You, the children of Regina, do a special honor for your city in which you are fortunate enough to live, as it is called after our great and good Queen Victoria, the mother of our Gracious King. I wish to say to you that if you are worthy of being called children of the Queen, for that is what it means by being children of Regina, you must each of you try your utmost to live as the prince and princess of whom you have read. Among the virtues of that distinguished true prince and princess is the love of fair play (Cheers) and a fearless determination to do nothing that is mean or dishonorable. I would, therefore, say to you children of Regina, children of the Queen, just to you boys, that you are under a special obligation to keep high the standard of fair play in your schools and over this city and never allow it to be lowered except over your prostrate bodies. (Loud cheers.) The honor of Regina demands this championship, it is of more importance than the championship of baseball or lacrosse. Strain every nerve to win the prize but rather die than win the victory by foul or dishonorable means. And to you young maidens of Regina I may also say that the honor of Regina is in your keeping. Do not give your sunny smiles or the approving clasp of your hands to anyone who is unfair in sport or business.

I speak to you in the name of the King, who looks to you to uphold the honor of your province in this great Dominion that is so fair a portion of the Empire. Your lives will show you are worthy of the proud title of children of Regina, that is children of the Queen, and now consequently children of the King, ready to die, if ever the occasion should arise that you are called upon for your services. (Loud applause and waving of flags.)

Sir Wilfrid Laurier's Speech

At the conclusion of the Earl's address, Sir Wilfrid spoke as follows: My dear children, you have just heard His Excellency who has spoken as the representative of the King. It so happens that at this moment I am the prime minister, the first servant of the crown in this country. I have nothing to add to the words given you, but if I were able to forget and not occupy the official position I occupy at this moment, and which I am proud to occupy, it would be to change positions with you. It would give me more pleasure to sing "God Save the King" as you have sung it than to serve the King in the position in which I am proud to serve him. The time will come when there will be another prime minister among you, therefore, live up to the advice already given you and grow up as good as has been recommended to you by His Excellency (Applause) Cheers were then given for the King, for His Excellency, and Sir Wilfrid Laurier, and after singing the National Anthem the proceedings terminated.

The vice-regal party then returned to their carriages and made their way to the viewing stand that had been erected on South Railway St., facing Scarth Street, to watch the monster general parade. The great crowd that had filled the park quickly melted away, following in the wake of the Government House procession.

General Parade

Hardly had the Governor-General and the other distinguished guests taken up their positions upon the stand prepared for them, than strains of music from the direction of Albert Street heralded the approach of the big procession under the directorship of Messrs Geo. Whitmore and Mr. N. S. Edgar.

To the music of half a dozen bands the procession filed eastward, past the viewing stand in the following order:

90th Regiment, under Col. Chambre, headed by the regimental band.
Mounted Indians.
Cox's Fife and Drum Band.
"Westward Ho!" being a "prairie schooner" representing early settlers entering the country.
Procession of Old Timers.
Regina Citizens' Band.
"Our Fair Dominion," being an elaborate float in the shape of a vessel bearing Canada, represented by Miss Laubach and the various provinces of the Dominion, including Albertg and Saskatchoincluding Alberta and Saskatchewan, represented by Miss Bessie Williams, British Columbia; Miss Julia McIntyre, Quebec; Miss Fern Dowswell, New Brunswick; Miss Peverett, Prince Edward Island; Miss Lila Ross, Ontario; Miss Barner, Nova Scotia; Miss B. Friel, Manitoba; Miss Sault, Alberta and Miss Dorothy Scott as Saskatchewan.
Brandon City Band.
Regina Fire Brigade (present time.)
Regina Fire Brigade (20 years ago.)
Rosthern Band.
Ex-M.L.A.'s, M. P.'s and other public men in carriages.
City Aldermen and officials in carriages.
Labour Day Floats.
Neepawa Band.
Procession of Germans and other nationalities.
Wolseley Silver Band.
Floto Shows.

As the various contingents passed along the crowd heartily cheered them, the mounted Indians and Old Timers receiving especially enthusiastic ovations. The old-time fire brigade provided great amusement, being in the nature of a burlesque, while the "prairie schooner" with its occupants cooking slap-jacks, was also provocative of much mirth. The rear end of the procession had hardly passed by the viewing stand, when the head of it marched down Scarth Street, facing the stand, on its way to the Exhibition Grounds for the military review and swearing-in ceremony.

To the Exhibition Grounds

No sooner had the procession passed than the crowds began to make their way towards the scene of the great central event of the day. Large numbers followed the vice-regal cavalcade by road, both on foot and in rigs of every description, whilst thousands took advantage of the 15 minutes service of trains run by the C. P. R. between the grounds and the city. Within an incredibly short space of time, the vast throng that had filled the streets of the city were transferred almost by magic it seemed. The great grand-stand, that had been much enlarged for the occasion, was filled to the limit of its capacity, presenting a veritable sea of faces towards the arena in which the military review was to take place, while for a considerable distance on either side immense crowds gathered to get a glimpse of the imposing spectacle. The review was watched by the Governor General's party from their carriages, while among the large number of distinguished guests who witnessed first the military manoeuvres and later the swearing-in ceremony were Countess Grey, Lady Evelyn Grey, His Honor, the Lt.-Gov., and Madame Forget, Sir Wilfrid and Lady Laurier, Sir Gilbert Parker, Hon. Wm. Patterson, ex-Lt. Governor Hon. David Laird, ex-Lt. Governor Hon. C. H. Mackintosh, Senator and Mrs. Watson, (Portage la Prairie), Senator T. O. Davis, (Prince Albert), Walter Scott, M.P. and Mrs. Scott, D. W. Bole, M.P., Winnipeg; A. J. Adamson, M.P., (Rosthern), J. H. Lamont, M.P., (Prince Albert), J. E. Cyr, M.P., (Provencher), and Mrs. Cyr, A. E. Dyment, M.P., W. F. Maclean, M.P., and Mrs. Maclean, H. J. Logan, M.P., Thos. Burrows, M.P., Dr. E. L. Cash, M.P., R. S. Lake, M.P., Hon. F. W. G. Haultain, Dr. Elliott, late commissioner of agriculture, Mrs. Bulyea, wife of Lt.-Gov. of Alberta, Speaker Gillis and Messrs. McNutt, Prince, Finlay, McDiarmid, McIntyre, Greeley, McDonald, Hawkes, Brown and Smith, (members of the last legislative assembly), ex-speaker Eakin and Mrs. Eakin, Chief Justice Sifton, ex-Chief Justice MacGuire, Mr. Justice Newlands, Dr. Douglas, ex-M.P., S. McLeod, ex-M.L.A., B. Richardson, ex-M. L. A., Wm. Mackenzie, president C. N. R., Miss Mount, Montreal, neice of Madame Forget, and the Mayors of a large number of the North-West cities and towns.

Military Review

The Royal North-West Mounted Police mustered to the number of over 200, under the command of Commissioner Perry and Asst. Commissioner McIllree, while the 90th Regiment of Winnipeg paraded 328 strong under the command of Col. Chambre. The review started with a march past by the Police, followed by the infantry, both bodies of men presenting an unusually distinguished appearance and winning the warm applause of the spectators as they marched past. Various movements were then gone through by both the mounted men and the infantry, the men throughout showing to advantage the splendid discipline and training that they had received. Upon the termination of the review their Excellencies the Governor General and Lady Grey and the other members of the vice-regal party took their seats upon the specially prepared dais ready for the formal inauguration ceremonies.

Civic Address to Governor-General

Upon the Governor General's party taking its place on the specially prepared pavilion in preparation for the swearing-in ceremony, the following address from the Mayor and Aldermen of the City of Regina was read to His Excellency by the City Clerk, Mr. J. Kelso Hunter:

To His Excellency, the Right Honorable Sir Albert Henry George Earl Grey, Viscount Howick, Baron Grey of Howick, in the County of Northumberland, in the Peerage of the United Kingdom, and a Baronet, Knight Grand Cross of the Most Distinguished Order of St. Michael and St. George, etc., etc., Governor General of Canada:

May it please Your Excellency:

We, the Mayor and Aldermen of the City of Regina, on our own behalf and on behalf of our fellow-citizens, desire to express our high appreciation of the great honor conferred upon us by a visit from Your Excellencies, and being accorded an opportunity of assuring you of our sincere respect and bidding you welcome to Regina.

We take this opportunity of renewing, through Your Excellency, our assurance of unswerving loyalty to the Crown and person of our most gracious King, and of expressing the hope that he may be long spared to reign over the Empire; and that our dearly beloved Queen may also be long spared as his Consort.

In 1877 Battleford became the first capital of the North-West Territories and from thence the capital was moved to Regina in 1883, where it remained until the other day, when the districts of Alberta, Saskatchewan and Assiniboia ceased to form part of the North-West Territories and Regina became the provisional capital of the new Province of Saskatchewan.

It is in honor of the birth of our new Province of Saskatchewan and to take part in the celebration ceremonies connected therewith that Your Excellencies have been so graciously pleased to visit out city.

Regina is the centre of a vast wheat belt, and the process of filling up this great area, has, until recent years, been very slow, but now we have the prospect of a greater tide of Immigration being directed towards our province—intensified by the abundant harvest which it has pleased Providence to give our farmers.

The growth of our city depends largely upon the growth of the country. During the past three years the population of Regina has increased by leaps and bounds. From a small prairie town it has developed into a city of no mean importance and everything is being done to keep it abreast of the times. It is well provided with Churches, Schools and Hospital; it possesses an abundant supply of beautiful, clear, spring water; and ample provision has been made for making it one of the healthiest cities in the Dominion. Its trade is increasing enormously, and, financially, it stands unique amongst the cities in Canada, as our civic surplus surpasses any of the smaller cities of the Dominion.

In both city and country you will find a happy, contented and prosperous people, who have successfully grappled with the problems and difficulties which usually arise in a new land; and we trust that you will find much to interest you in connection with our public and private institutions, and in the fact that our Province can provide happy and prosperous homes for millions of subjects loyal to the Sovereign and Crown of the British Empire.

The pleasure we feel in welcoming

(Continued on page 3.)

METEOROLOGICAL REPORT

Date.	Maximum Temperature.	Minimum Temperature.	Velocity of Wind. (Miles per hour.)	Direction of Wind.	Snowfall. (inches.)	Rainfall. (Inches.)	Remarks.
Wed. Aug. 30	71	41	Light	E.	—	—	Fine.
Thurs. Aug. 31	63	46	10	E.	—	—	Heavy rain at 7.45 a. m.
Fri. Sept. 1	54	43	Light	W.	—	.96	Light showers.
Sat. Sept. 2	60	38	10	N. W.	—	.01	Fine.
Sun. Sept. 3	69	37	8	E.	—	—	Fine.
Mon. Sept. 4	60	39	10	E.	—	—	Fine.
Tues. Sept. 5	70	46	14	E.	—	—	Fine.

WAR ON LIBERALS BY CANADIAN PACIFIC

Open Fight on the Grand Trunk Pacific Also---Notice Given That the Railway Will Also Attack Liberals in New Provinces

The Toronto Star of August 28th published under the above heading, the following special despatch from Montreal:

(Special to The Star.)

Montreal, Aug. 28.—It would be difficult to over-estimate the extent to which the directors of the Canadian Pacific Railway have been aroused by the Grand Trunk Pacific being allowed to invade its territory for a distance of 275 miles.

An interest close to the company stated to The Toronto Star that it would certainly mean the beginning of open war by the C. P. R. both against the Grand Trunk Pacific and the Liberal Government.

A prominent director, in conversation with your representative, when asked what was the opinion of the directors, said: "It would not be going too far to say that we regard it as an outrage. From one standpoint it would be difficult to exaggerate the harm that might be done the country by showing foreign investors that it is impossible to get a permanent good investment in the country because there is no telling when your rights may be set aside. The C. P. R., with its system of hotels, its steamship connections on the lakes and two oceans, is just in a position to take up the present fight, but we had thought it would be so arranged that the C. P. R. and G. T. P. would have been brought together and an agreement reached as to what territory each line would cover."

A gentleman who is in close touch with the C. P. R. in the West says that in the approaching elections in the Territories the big railway will lend every possible assistance to Haultain and his followers.

City clerk J. Kelso Hunter speaks at inauguration ceremonies, Regina, 1905

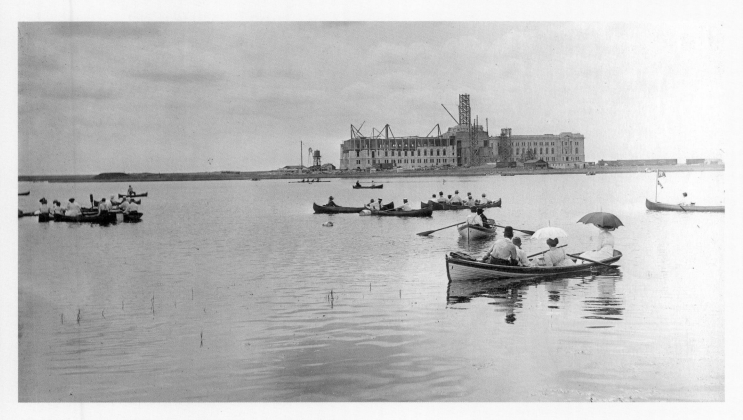

Legislature under construction, Wascana Lake, Regina, circa 1910

IMMIGRATION

The arrival of the Canadian Pacific Railway brought lumber, goods and farm equipment to grateful prairie homesteaders, but it also carried with it the first wave of agricultural immigrants who had begun to arrive in Canada from overseas. The Canadian government hoped to encourage the immigration of European farmers as a means of populating the Prairies and developing increasing amounts of arable land. In the 1880s, fewer than 1,000 non-aboriginal people were reported to live in what would become Saskatchewan. Over the next twenty years, a surge of Ukrainian, Russian, Scandinavian and British immigrants settled in the province, becoming important members of Saskatchewan's growing agricultural base.

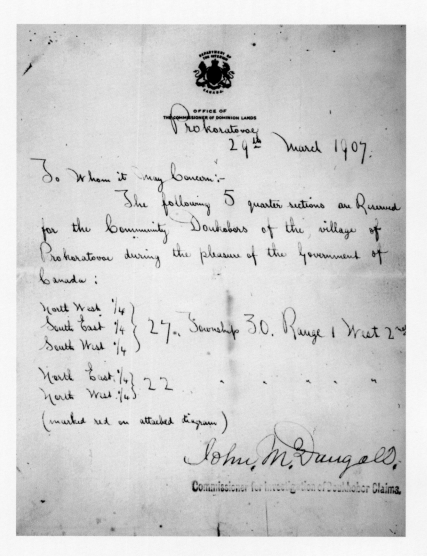

Letter addressing Doukhobor lands, Prokoratavos, 1907

European immigrants, Yorkton

Ignite coal miners, Estevan, 1902

Ukrainian children in front of sod house, circa 1903-1907

Russian family, Kerrobert, circa 1907

Homesteading and Farming

Setting up camps near Wascana Lake in 1882, homesteaders relied on well-water, horses and, later that year, the Canadian Pacific Railway to help carve out new lives for themselves in the Saskatchewan Prairies. Under the Dominion Lands Act, each new homesteader could pay $10 for 160 acres of land — on which they often built tents or shacks, gave birth to young, pioneering families, and solidified their prairie dreams. At the beginning of the 20th century, prairie farmers still used horse-drawn plows to turn the soil surrounding their new homesteads and scattered seeds over their new-found promised land by hand.

Homesteaders, circa 1905

Threshing at Seager Wheeler's Maple Grove farm, Rosthern, circa 1905

Regina Comes of Age

After Regina was officially named a city in 1903 and Saskatchewan a province in 1905, the next step for Saskatchewanians was to find a home for their growing political aspirations. When Regina became the provincial capital in 1906, a 168-acre site was chosen on the south side of Wascana and two brothers from Montreal — Edward Maxwell and W.S. Maxwell — were hired to design a new provincial legislative building. According to the City of Regina, 300 men worked day and night for a year-and-a-half to prepare the stone front of the building and the entire construction took four years to complete. When Governor General Earl Grey laid the building's cornerstone on October 4, 1909, he deposited a time capsule, a possible foreshadowing of Regina's rich history to come — a city always mindful of its strong pioneering roots. By the time the building officially opened in 1912, it had cost $1.7 million.

Rose Theatre Orchestra, musical accompaniment for silent films, Regina, 1914

Regina Leader Building, Hamilton Street and 11th Avenue, 1910

CYCLONE

The city of Regina, eight years after incorporation and on its way toward a sunny future as the province's new capital, was struck by a storm June 30, 1912, that destroyed its downtown and left many residential areas in ruin. Winds travelling at 500 miles per hour — then believed to be a cyclone, but later described as two tornadoes — began south of Regina and tore through the city just before 5 p.m. that afternoon. Twenty-eight people were killed and 2,500 people were left homeless. Property damage was estimated at more than $1.2 million.

1800 Block, Scarth Street, Regina, 1912

Lorne Street and 13th Avenue, Regina, 1912

THE MORNING LEADER

VOL. IX., NO. 157 TO-DAY'S PAPER—16 Pages REGINA, SASK., TUESDAY, JULY 2, 1912 PROBS—Cool; Showers PRICE FIVE CENTS

STORM DEATH LIST STANDS AT 27

CITIES OF WEST OFFER AID IN TIME OF NEED

TELEGRAMS PRESSING HELP ON REGINA POUR IN TO MAYOR McARA

CHICAGO SENT MESSAGE

SAYS OPTIMISTIC AND COURAGEOUS PEOPLE HERE WILL WIN OUT

FINANCIAL AID IS NEEDED

Mayor Tells all Offer is Appreciated Deeply and Very Acceptable

Rivals as they may be in prosperity, the cities of the West are one in adversity and they feel that the loss of one is the loss of all. Until a late hour last night messages of condolence continued to pour in from the civic authorities of every city in the west and some from as far east as Chicago and Fort William. All are willing to help and ask only to know in what form assistance would be most acceptable.

The sister provinces are taking their places beside the province of Saskatchewan in the calamity to its capital. The railway companies have been among the first to tender sympathy and the C.P.R. has already donated five thousand to the relief fund. The C.N.R. has offered to send any special trains.

The gifts to the relief of the sufferers so far are as follows:

Govt. of Saskatchewan	$25,000.00
C. P. R.	$5,000.00
His Worship, Mayor McAra	$1,000.00
H. Anderson, check	$5.00
Collected on north side by Ad. Halleron	$43.65

The messages from other cities with the replies made by His Worship are as follows:—

The following wires were received:

MAYOR MAYBERRY Moose Jaw—"Much distressed at fragmentary news of your calamity. We have no particulars, but are sending some nurses on the 22 k train. Can we do anything else?"

MAYOR WAUGH, Winnipeg—"Winnipeg shocked at dissater which has befallen your city and sympathizes with bereaved and sufferers. Can we do anything to assist you?"

MAYOR MITCHELL, Calgary—"Appalled at great loss and disaster your city has experienced. City of Calgary anxious to relieve. Wire quick what is most needed; our sympathy to all sufferers."

W. E. BURKE, Board of Trade, Moose Jaw—"We have 50 or 60 tents which we would be glad to ship to you by first train. If you need them wire immediately."

R. P. ROBLIN, Premier Manitoba—"On behalf of government and people of this province I desire to extend deepest sympathy in the great misfortune which your city has sustained. If there is any service or financial aid which we can render to alleviate distress I shall be glad to have your command."

G. S. ARMSTRONG Mayor of Edmonton—"On behalf of the citizens of Edmonton, I extend the deepest sympathy to those who have suffered by the terrible storm that swept through your city. Kindly advise if monetary aid is acceptable."

R. ROGERS, Minister of Interior—"Just returned from Kenora and learn of the terrible disaster that overtaken Regina. Will arrange to send Bruce Walker or someone else by tonight's train with full authority to act for the department in rendering assistance."

Mayor McAra will answer all wires and accept in the name of the city all aid offered.

Mayor McAra met the military committee at the close of this meeting.

EUGENE V. KIMBARK, President Chicago Association of Commerce:—

The Association notes with deepest sympathy your city's severe loss in life and property by cyclone. Chicago nkows the influence of disaster upon people of spirit and purpose like yourselves. We mourn with you over your dead and foresee with you the immediate restoration of the stricken sections of your wonderful city. Our delegation which visits you July 12th will confirm Chicago's message of consolation and confidence.

COLONEL GASKIN, Winnipeg:—

Be assured of Salvation Army's deepest sympathy in great disaster.

M. H. McLEOD, Winnipeg, Man.:—

Deeply regret sad catastrophe to your city this afternoon, only meagre details at hand. Please advise if Canadian Northern can assist in any special train service.

M. ISBISTER, Pres. Sskatoon Board of Trade:—

On behalf of the Saskatoon Board of Trade I extend to the citizens of Regina our heartfelt sympathy and sincere condolence in their hour of disaster. Inform me by return if we can render any assistance.

MAYOR CONNOR, of Arcola:—

The residents of Arcola extend to the citizens of Regina their deepest sympathy in this their sad hour of affliction.

MAYOR STEADMAN, of McLeod, Alta.:—

The people of McLeod are shocked and sorry for the terrible disaster to your town. Can we be of any assistance?

GEORGE A. GRAHAM, Mayor Fort William:—

We wish to express deep sympathy with Regina in its great calamity. Our reports so far are very meagre. Can we do anything to assist you?

SIR T. SHAUGHNESSY, Montreal:

The directors of the company join with me in extending to you and the people of Regina, more particularly those who had relatives killed or se-

(Continued on page 5.)

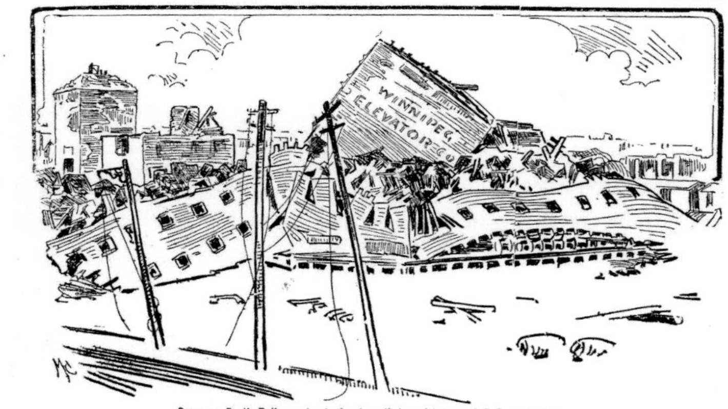

Scene on South Railway street, showing piled up debris on C.P.R. main line.

CONNECT UP LINE TO MOOSE JAW

Phone Communication With Winnipeg Completed Early This Morning

SWITCHBOARD FROM EAST

Will be Four or Five Weeks Before Service Comes on, Experts Say

The management of the Saskatchewan Government Telephones System have accomplished a great deal during the past twenty-four hours and out of the chaos of tangled wreckage of overhead wires a temporary service on long distance lines to the Moose Jaw and points west has been effected.

During the afternoon the service to Moose Jaw which was cut off was resumed and tonight a number of wires were working. But for the untimely rain of this afternoon the service to Winnipeg and points east would have been resumed. It is hoped, however that this will be completed some time tomorrow.

An exceptionally fortunate circumstance occurred when a switchboard was located in Montreal which it is thought will take care of at least four-fifths of the customers in the city.

Month Without Phones.

Citizens, however, will be forced to forego the luxury of making the "Hello girls" work for at least four or five weeks after the arrival in the city of the switchboard, as it will take this ength of time to install it. However, it is understood that an effort will be made to establish a temporary service, from fog stations at different points in the city, before this length of time.

The work of picking up connections in the underground conduits will be commenced at once. Several linemen have been brought from Moose Jaw to aid in the work of restoring the service.

VISITOR FORGOT POLITICS WHEN HE SAW WRECKAGE

Chicagoan Thought it Funny Town Before He Knew—Then Offered Help

Yesterday afternoon a gentleman visited the editorial offices of The Leader and enquired of a reporter. "What's the latest from Baltimore about the nomination."

The reporter informed him that no telegraphic news of any description was being received, the whole efforts of the editorial department being centred on other things.

"This is a funny sort of town," said the visitor. "I've just got in from Chicago on the train and came straight to the newspaper office to hear the latest news from the convention.

"Take a look around the next two or three blocks south," suggested the reporter, "and then perhaps you'll understand."

Within the hour, the same man returned and said: "Where does a fellow go to offer assistance. I didn't know when I was in before what had happened. I've seen everything and, my God, it's awful. Tell me where to go and I'll do anything I can. I want to help."

He was directed to the city hall, where men were being asked for.

DUCHESS MAY COME WEST.

OTTAWA, July 1.—The following announcement was given out this afternoon at government house: "Although the health of the Duchess of Connaught has improved so much that her Royal Highness hopes to be able to accompany his Royal Highness, the governor-general, to the Maritime provinces and on the western tour it is not expected that her Royal Highness will attend any official functions."

(Signed) H. C. Lowther, Lieut. Colonel, Military Secretary.

REPORT TO BLACK BLOCK

It is urgent that all injured who are being tended in private houses be reported at Room 4, Black Block in order that friends may know that they are safe and also where to communicate with them.

It will also be of assistance in checking up the lists of injured, missing and dead.

All requests for nurses or doctors should be made at Room Four of the Black Block.

PLAN MEMORIAL TO STORM VICTIMS

Funeral Arrangements as Yet Incomplete—May Not be For Few Days

ALL BODIES ARE EMBALMED

Expect Some Bodies Will Be Taken to Old Homes in East For Burial

Funeral arrangements have not yet been completed, but it is comparatively certain that a public memorial service will be held in the course of the next few days.

Messrs. Guggisberg and Dickson have charge of this part of the work and when seen last evening Mr. Guggisberg stated that all the bodies recovered had been embalmed and that it would be possible to keep them for several days or until practically all had been recovered from the ruins. Fifteen graves have already been provided and working in conjunction with the undertakers who will endeavor to learn the wishes of the friends in the matter, other graves will be dug today.

Many bodies will doubtless be taken to oid homes in Eastern Canada for interment but no arrangement has been made for shipping them yet.

While some of the bodies, and it may be the greater number, may be buried privately, it is almost certain that a public memorial service will be held in which a Regina without creed or distinction will unite in mournng for her dead and in thanksgiving for the miraculous escapes and also for the spirit of her citizens who in the hour of disaster thought only of the rescue of those in danger and the care of those who were destitute.

PART OF CANOE BREAKS IN 4TH STOREY WINDOW

Man in Film Exchange, Kerr Block, Almost Struck by Flying Splinterrs

Another marvellous canoe incident has come to light. Mr. Soskin was barricaded behind a door in the Film Exchange on the fourth floor of the Kerr Block when a large section of a canoe crashed through the window and smashed to atoms against the opposite wall. The craft had been snatched up by the cyclone from the side of the lake.

MR. WEEKS WILL RECOVER

Dr. Morrison Says His Injuries Not Likely Fatal

The report in the second extra edition of The Leader yesterday that a man named Weeks was dying now happily proves to be false. His injuries are of a most serious nature, but Dr. Morrison, who is attending him, stated last evening in response to a question as how his patient was progressing that Mr. Weeks will pull through.

Mr. Weeks received his injuries when his house fell in. He is suffering from severe scalp wounds but yesterday he took a turn for the better and Dr. Morrison entertains every hope of a rapid recovery.

NEBRASKANS HERE CALL IT WORST EVER

Family Which Has Seen Other Cyclones Tell of What Happened Then

WOULD TAKE TO CELLAR

Elements in Fury Play Queer Pranks in South—Trees Cause Havoc

A family who have recently come from Nebraska, where they have witnessed cyclones, declared to a representative of The Leader they had never seen anything to equal the Regina holocaust.

On Sunday afternoon they had been on their verandah with friends watching the approach of the storm. As the whirling, funnel shaped cloud was noticed, "I would say that was a cyclone coming if I were in Nebraska," said one of the daughters, adding, "but you don't have cyclones in Canada."

She had been reassured by a Canadian who had spent a number of years in the west.

As the Nebraska family are living on a street outside the cyclone zone, their house escaped with a broken chimney and cracked plaster. What has most impressed them has been the calm of the people following the terrible catastrophe, the splendid courage shown by those who have lost their property and the fine order and lack of excitement that prevailed.

Admire Officials and Police.

Their admiration for the administration of the city officials and the trusty mounted police has been unbounded.

"Had we been in Nebraska," continued this young lady, "we should have taken to the 'cyclone' cellar. One knows by watching the clouds when to expect it.

"I saw a cyclone hit another town 10 miles from where we were. It came whirling along and one could see trees and parts of buildings high in the air.

"Once I saw a large tree in which a strip of hardwood had been driven as if it were sharpened steel. Trees always make it seem worse.

"Stories, outsiders would not believe, could be told about these Nebraska cyclones," she said.

"Another time a cyclone hit a train. It turned it completely over, down a short embankment. Nearly everybody was injured but no one was killed outright.

"Another time I saw a hole in the ground that was made when the funnel of a cyclone hit the earth. There were no houses nearby It was a huge well, with the ground torn and earth scattered in all directions.

"After three days of such intense heat as we have had in Regina one would be on the watch for a cyclone in Nebraska," she said in conclusion.

SUBSCRIPTION LIST IS BEGUN AT CITY HALL

Those Whose Property Escaped Injury Asked By City To Chip in for Needy

A subscription list has been opened at the City Hall to supply the most pressing needs of the sufferers and all contributions will be thankfully received.

At present many have been housed temporarily in the homes of the nighbors but in a few days it will be necessary to take steps to set them upon their feet again and while the immediate need is not a most pressing one, within the next few days many will suffer serious hardships unless generous contributions are forthcoming to tide them over. It is not charity in the ordinary sense, for much of the material purchased will remain the property of the city and will be held to meet such unforeseen situations as might arise through a general conflagration. For the rest it will be impossible for many men to earn enohgh from day to day to keep their houses going and at the same time furnish it with the barest necessities.

Generous contributions have been made by the Government, the railways and his worship and the citizens who escaped the cyclone uninjured and whose property did not suffer destruction are asked to do their share towards helping the others to again gain a footing in the tide which has swept away their all.

CASUALTIES

THE DEAD

J. J. BRYAN, 2155 Albert St. Born Thorndale, Ont.; age 51; Church of England; manager of Tudhope-Anderson.

SCOUT MASTER APPLEBY.

GEO. E. CRAVEN, age 35; born New Zealand; Church of England; dairy instructor.

JAMES PATRICK COFFEE, Lisbon Island.

FRANK BLENKHORN, and his wife Bertha; born in England.

ARTHUR DONALDSON, contractor.

MISS ELLA GUTHRIE, seamstress, Barries, Ltd.; lived 2134 Lorne St.

MRS. F. W. HARRIS, 2134 Lorne St., wife of F. W. Harris, accountant Reeves & Co.

LAURANCE R. HODSMAN, son of James R. Hodsman, 1947 Smith St.

MR. McDOUGALL, of North Side.

ROBERT FENWICK, killed in Mulligan's barn.

FRED HINDSON, medical student, son of James Hindson, merchant, 2220 Lorne St.

Child of Mr. and Mrs. H. N. LOGIE.

MRS. W. T. McDONALD.

MRS. ISABELLA McKAY, resided at Hodsman house, 1947 Smith St.; widow.

CHARLES D. McKAY, age 3, son of Mrs. Isabella McKay.

MRS. PAUL McELMOYLE, wife of Paul McElmoyle, grocer, corner of Lorne and 14th.

JAMES SCOTT.

MRS. MARY SHAW, wife of Samuel D. Shaw, 2320 12th Ave., age 50; born at Elgin, Ont.; Presbyterian.

PHILIP ARTHUR RICHARD STEELE, 1915 Rae St.; age 11; father a carpenter.

JOHN RICHARD STEELE, Church of England.

VINCENT H. SMITH, real estate Agent, Balgonie.

YE WING.

ANDREW BOYD, retired farmer, formerly of Sherwood; died this morning.

TWO UNIDENTIFIED CHINAMEN.

THE MISSING

WM. BRADSHAW, C. P. R. checker; last seen near shops.

MRS. BULLOCK, four children, 2110 Lorne St.

MISS DAVIDSON, Prince Albert, 2775 Cameron St.

MISS N. GRIER, nurse, Creelman, Sask.; last heard of on Lorne St.

S. P. JONES, 1057 Rotallack St.

ROBERT BLACK, wife and child, 1254 Hamilton St.

SAUNDERS, child.

MISS ALICE HATHERLEY.

MR. BULLOCK.

(Continued on Page 4.)

WORK OF RESCUE PROMPT; INJURED ALL DOING WELL; REBUILDING IS PLANNED

Regina Will Remember Dominion Day for Reason All Her Own — Flags Yesterday had Deeper Significance to Many as They Flew at Half-mast—Volunteers Were Numerous; There was Much Work to Be Done, and Much Was Done.

EVERY TRAIN BRINGS SIGHT-SEERS HERE

Amazing Amount of Work Done in Clearing Away Debris; Patching up Houses, Erecting Tents, Serving Out Supplies, Caring for Wounded and Planning New Work

DOMINION Day has come and gone, and with it has passed a day into Regina's history that will be remembered as long as the Dominion of Canada remembers the birth of Confederation.

Strangers to the city years hence will look around them on the first day of July in wonder, and inquire with smiles the reason of the glorious, gruesome splendor of flags.

"This is Dominion Day," they will be told.

"But why at half-mast?" they will persist.

"Because Regina could fly them no other way on the First of July."

It was a glorious, gruesome sight that met the eye yesterday in the city.

Flags there were indeed. Not in the abundance usual on fete days or days of mourning.

But there were flags—where flag staffs stood to support them—and there were many places where neither flag staffs nor any other thing stood high enough to flaunt aloft the bunting—

—Even at half-mast.

This was the day for which great preparations had been made for entertainment at home and excursions abroad.

The day of celebration for the Confederation of the greatest of Britain's Dominions beyond the seas.

Instead of a day of rejoicing was a day rife with sadness—yet not with mourning.

There was no time for mourning.

There was work to be done and the citizens of Regina showed that they were capable of forgetting for the time what cause they had to mourn while help was wanted, needed, demanded, on every hand.

Volunteers were called for, and volunteers were at hand. Nurses were divided into "shifts" and took their turns caring for their patients and snatching a few hours' sleep.

The hours of care were greater than those of sleep.

Doctors, wearied with their all night and all day vigil, still labored self neglectingly over the injured and dying, and started bravely upon the second night of the most enervating work the human system can undergo.

Crowds Near City Hall.

On Hamilton street and Eleventh avenue around the city hall where the crowds gathered the thickest not a hint of this fierce fight against death could be found.

Early in the morning—long before six o'clock—the crowds commenced to gather. They swarmed around bulletin boards, crowded the cafes, and poured in a steady stream in and out of the telegraph offices—a stream that has hardly abated since the first crash, and may not abate for days—relative calling to relative, friend to friend, afar off, perhaps, the glad or sad tidings that all are waiting to hear.

The air was tense with excitement. All wanted to do something—all were looking for someone to tell them what to do.

The call for volunteers was not in vain.

A civic telephone service was installed on short notice.

You smile.

Ask the boy scout who waited patiently at the city hall, waiting patiently to speed on his errand to any part of the city.

There were many of him, and none in all the city did better service for the general weal.

Carpenters, masons, teamsters, laborers, electricians—all offered gratuitous service, and the service of all was welcome.

Sightseers on Every Train.

But in addition to those engaged in work of various natures were the sightseers who came in their crowds from every train that drew up at the station.

Many were looking here and there for friends and relatives.

Many were present out of mere morbid curiosity.

All were shocked—dumfounded—at the calamity which had fallen upon the city.

It was the one from outside who really grasped the full horror of disaster. To those who saw it, the tale was old before it was fully told.

All that was left for them was work.

City Officials on the Job.

Of all the hosts of workers the city fathers were first on the job. Theirs was the authority—theirs also was the responsibility.

Not an instant were the reins allowed to slacken. From the first a firm hold was kept, and all was orderly as a lifeboat drill. Carpenters hurried out to their work close upon the heels of the daylight. Teamsters in scores were busy from dawn to set of sun, carting away the debris as though it were their life custom to clear away the wanton ruins of the storm fiend.

Clear them away!

That is the cry already.

It is not the custom of the west to weep over spilt filk, and the truth of this was pounded home yesterday more convincingly than ever before.

Regina does not look upon that trampled footpath of the wind as ruins.

Already in the minds of the far-seeing conceptions are formed of a Regina that has grown up and spread once more over the vacant land in more luxurious growth than ever.

Regina Retains Her Nerve.

For the present let the work of rescue and succor continue, but even as it does, Regina is cleaning out the ugly gash with no timid knife, that the wound may heal all the quicker.

It was more than a pleasure yesterday to watch the tired face of His Worship, Mayor McAra, as message after message of sympathy came in throughout the day from brother Chief Magistrates of cities all over Western Canada, and from men big in other walks of Canadian life.

Many offered to do what they could if they were only told wherein they could be of assistance.

To all His Worship replied accepting offers of help as freely as they were given, and offering sincere thanks for kinidly offered sympathy from afar.

Moose Jaw Prompt to Aid.

Two special trains ran from Moose Jaw during the afternoon.

The first bore members of the Board of Trade, the City Council and Mayor Mayberry, together with several nurses.

With them they brought one hundred tents for the homeless of the city, and a small army of men to pitch them.

More help, if it was needed, was offered without reservation.

Moose Jaw proved herself a true friend in need.

A remarkable feature of the preparations made for the homeless was that scarcely any of the food provided free by the committee in charge of relief work was needed.

Poverty and hunger have not yet shown their face in the desolate camp.

It was a good sign.

Another matter of congratulation was the splendid discipline kept throughout the city.

With only a handful of city police

QU'APPELLE HIT BY STORM.

QU'APPELLE, Sask., July 1.—This town was visited by worst hail and wind storm it has ever experienced this afternoon about 4 p.m. While of only short duration most of the windows on the west and south sides are demolished, Caswell's hardware store, the Anglican church and the school being the worst off in this respect. A portion of the large barn being erected by Stewart and Acres was demolished. Hail stones fell of great size and were found after the storm.

SASKATOON

In 1906, three settlements along the South Saskatchewan River — Saskatoon, Riversdale, and Nutana — incorporated as a city with a population of about 4,500. Immigrants started flooding to the community and Saskatoon became the fastest growing city in Canada — a prairie boomtown. By 1911, the population had more than doubled and, thanks largely to the railway, Saskatoon had become a major hub city for the surrounding agricultural region. The board of trade published pamphlets promoting Saskatoon as a "wonder city" — a place to settle and invest. By 1912, the population was estimated at 28,000 and was predicted by many to grow to 50,000 within three years and to 100,000 by 1920, according to the City of Saskatoon archives. But Saskatoon would not reach a population of 100,000 until the 1960s. Boomtown saw grand hotels, small businesses, cabarets and vaudeville theatres lining the streets of Saskatoon. The boomtown era, which lasted until 1914, also saw the construction of a railway station, hospitals, bridges, municipal public transit and the first University of Saskatchewan buildings. A life-size tourist attraction now looks back at this exciting time in Saskatoon's history — the Western Development Museum's Boomtown 1910.

Canadian Northern Freight yard, Saskatoon, 1914

Saskatoon skyline, 1915

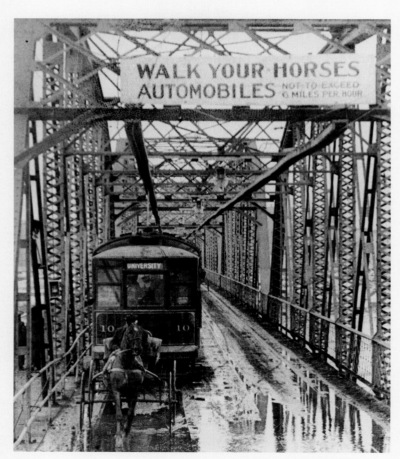

Victoria Bridge, circa 1912

WOMEN

Early in the 20th century, women began to organize. In Saskatchewan, groups like the Homemakers' Club helped prairie women form bonds and build community ties. Members of the Homemakers' Club met to discuss matters of home and community and to socialize. A key leader in the early women's movement in Saskatchewan was Violet McNaughton, who had been involved in radical movements in her native Kent, United Kingdom. When McNaughton came to Saskatchewan as a homesteader, she was convinced women should be part of the burgeoning agricultural movement in Canada. At meetings of the Grain Growers Association, she proposed a women's section be created. Soon, the Women Grain Growers was born. McNaughton became the group's first president and she worked with farm women from all over Canada. McNaughton was also involved in the suffrage movement. In March of 1916, Saskatchewan became the second province to give women the right to vote. Many of the people involved in women's rights were also part of the temperance movement, whose followers pushed to stop the consumption of alcohol. Temperance colonists played a key role in the establishment of settlements that would become Saskatoon.

The Grain Grower's Guide, February 26, 1913

Pioneer women of the Grain Growers' Association, Violet McNaughton, S.V. Haight and Mrs. Arthur Thompson, 1914

Putting Out Fires

As houses and shacks were being built and communities established in settlements near both Regina and Saskatoon, a new community awareness was evolving — leading toward the pioneering of essential city services, even if only on a very basic level. In 1884, Regina firefighters began the city's first "bucket brigade." A rope attached to the Catholic Church bell acted as the first alarm until the fire department finally purchased its own bell — weighing 2,500 pounds — in 1890. By the late 1880s, a horse-powered fire engine was used to pump water from underground cisterns, replaced in the mid-1890s by a horse-drawn steam fire engine and later with a horse-drawn hose wagon and ladder truck in 1905. Three years later, Regina's first street fire alarm system — consisting of twenty-five fire alarm boxes — was installed.

Édouard Beaupré, the Willow Bunch Giant, with Octave Gaudry and Mr. Lauzière, circa 1902

Jack Spindel at Purim Dance, Rossie, Regina, circa 1913

William Wallace Gibson with his first aeroplane engine, Regina, 1907

Grand Challenge Winners, Regina Bonspiel, 1909

Baseball team, Moose Jaw, 1913

Rugby Club, Regina, 1910

1915

The Saskatoon Phœnix

Exhibition Story And Awards On Pages 10-11

Local Weather
For 24 hours ending 7 p.m.
Maximum 73
Minimum 55
Prob.: Fair and cooler.

FIVE CENTS A COPY

SASKATOON CANADA WEDNESDAY AUGUST 5 1914—FOURTEEN PAGES

VOL XXIV NO 28

"CAPTURE OR DESTROY ENEMY'S SHIPS"

GREAT BRITIAN DECLARES WAR AGAINST GERMANY AND NAVY IS ORDERED TO STRIKE AT ONCE

TO MAKE POLICE
PART OF MILITIA
Order Anticipated to Make R.N.W.M.P.
Part of Canadian Militia.

CANADIAN PARLIAMENT WILL MEET ON AUGUST 18--READY TO EQUIP 60,000 SOLDIERS

All Cable and Wireless Stations Guarded By Military And Strict Censorship Established Over All Messages for Abroad or for Domestic Publication.

Germany Summarily Rejects British Ultimatum Requiring Germany To Respect Neutrality of Belgium and War Follows Expiry of Date Set-- All Europe Now in Arms, Austria-Hungary and Germany Being Actively Engaged by Great Britain, France, Russia, Belgium Servia and Montenegro While Italy, Spain, Portugal, Holland, Norway, Sweden, Denmark, Switzerland and Turkey Have Mobilised their Armies and Are Waiting Events.

WILLIAM II.
Emperor of Germany and King of Prussia, First Cousin to King George

WAR BRIEFS

RAYMOND POINCARE

President of the French Republic.

MOBILISATION ORDERS WILL BE ISSUED TODAY TO MOBILISE CORPS D'ARMEE

DOMINION NOTES ARE LEGAL TENDER

PREMIER SAYS WAR UNJUSTLY PROVOKED

France Did Not Seek War But Will Defend Herself

TRIED TO AVOID IT

Belgium Has 250,000 Men Prepared to Defend Native Land

HUGE GOLD RESERVE

Cabinet In Session

Canadian Censorship Strict

Parliament to Meet

CHAPTER THREE

It is tempting to imagine a scene unfolding in Moosomin, circa 1907, with Saskatchewan's birth as a province fresh in everyone's memory and its potential still seeming as boundless as the wheat fields stretching out around the town.

Bob Combe, twenty-seven years old, is clad in his apron, behind the counter at the drug store where he has been working as a pharmacist since arriving in Canada from England the year before. Harry Mullin, an Oregon-born teenager who has lived in Moosomin since he was two, is across the counter with a prescription, perhaps for an ailing brother. And waiting in line behind him is one of the town's most distinguished young men: Andy McNaughton, nineteen, born in Moosomin and son of its leading merchant. A distinctively gifted student, he'll soon be bound for college — and presumed great things — in the East.

All three, in fact, are destined for greatness, and their stories — momentarily mingled in one small, southeast Saskatchewan town nearly a century ago — tell much about how life in the province would be shaped and shaken by the First World War.

Britain's declaration of war against Germany in August 1914 automatically enmeshed Canada in the coming European conflict and arrived at a time when Saskatchewan was in the midst of its own futile battle against a heat wave that was ruining that year's wheat crop. But neither the immediate disappointment of a lost harvest, nor the grim prospect of a protracted, bloody fight in Europe dampened the province's jubilant reaction to the advent of war.

J. Thomas Clinkskill, the mayor's son, was the first man in Saskatoon to enlist. He was killed in the Battle of the Somme, September 1916

"There was, on that warm night of August 4, 1914, spontaneous patriotic response in the streets of Regina, Moose Jaw and other Saskatchewan centres," noted Jim Wright in his book *Saskatchewan: The History of a Province*. "Citizens joined in impromptu and sometimes tumultuous parades. There was cheering from flag-draped automobiles and horse-drawn vehicles decorated with red, white and blue bunting."

In Saskatoon, the *Phoenix* reported, young men rushed to enlist in defence of freedom and, unwittingly, in defiance of enormous odds that they would not return from overseas unscathed.

"The local militia paraded and enlisted several hundred men all anxious to serve the empire should they be required. After the parade, the military band marched through the city with a standard bearer carrying a huge Union Jack in front. Following the band was half the male population of the city who joined in singing such patriotic airs as *Rule Britannia*, *The British Grenadiers* and the national anthem."

Meanwhile, Regina residents crowded the offices of *The Leader* for news bulletins — "item by item they were breathlessly followed, and between the announcements, flags were raised, patriotic songs sung and cheer followed cheer, the greatest being for the confirmation of the declaration of war."

In less than three weeks, 1,500 Saskatchewan men had boarded trains for a military boot camp in Quebec. Barely three months after that they had sailed to Britain. And by April 1915, they were somewhere in France, marching inexorably toward enemy guns.

More than 20,000 soldiers from the province were in action by the end of 1915 and among them were the three young men whose paths had crossed in Moosomin nearly ten years earlier, perhaps even at the town drugstore.

Robert Grierson Combe, the English immigrant who identified himself as a "chemist" in his enlistment papers, is known to have opened a pharmacy in Melville before joining the 53rd Battalion at Prince Albert. Initially appointed a major and made an instructor, he requested a demotion to lieutenant and a battlefield assignment.

On May 3, 1917, now fighting in France with the 27th Battalion at Acheville, near Vimy, Combe helped direct a 3 a.m. assault on a German stronghold. The battalion's own diary records how, with "his few men" and the "remnants" of another decimated platoon, Combe led "a gallant and successful effort to drive

KEEPING UP WITH THE JONESES.   —By Pop.

Pupils prepare to work in school garden, Lang, 1917

the Hun from the trenches," used captured German bombs to sustain his attack after "he had used up his own supply," and "succeeded in taking over 250 yards of this line." His actions and wonderful spirit made his men carry out the impossible. Just as the reinforcements were arriving, he was killed.

It was a sacrifice more than worthy of a Victoria Cross, which would be awarded posthumously to Combe's widow in 1919 during a visit to Saskatchewan by the Prince of Wales, the future King Edward VIII. The official citation recounted how Combe "steadied his company under intense fire and led them through the enemy barrage" and had shown "great coolness and courage" in the successful pursuit of his goal before finally falling to a sniper's bullet.

"His conduct inspired all ranks, and it was entirely due to his magnificent courage that the position was carried, secured and held."

Some 4,400 other Saskatchewan soldiers, like Combe, would be buried in European soil before the war had ended, robbing the province of a good portion of an entire generation of factory workers, teachers, farmers and merchants — and druggists.

War meant sacrifice on the home front, too, and not just for the widows and families forced to nurse thousands of wounded men who returned from the war, often as shadows of themselves. Farmers continued to battle a host of wheat-killing plagues — rust, hail, frost and drought. And on May 1, 1917, the Saskatchewan government was forced to declare war on gophers. More than 500,000 of the pests, blamed for destroying hundreds of thousands of acres of farmland, would be killed by schoolchildren enlisted for the fight.

All the while, dedication to the overseas war effort was unstinting. Women knit clothes, rolled bandages and prepared supply kits to send to the front and made up for the shortage of male farmhands by pouring into the fields by the thousands.

"I have given all I have," Mrs. C.T. Spooner of Saskatoon said about the enlistment of her husband and three sons. "But I am not the only one to suffer, and if I had more I don't doubt that I should give them as it is the least we can do for our country."

Prairie farmers during the 1918 influenza epidemic

More than 1,500 Saskatchewan horses were shipped to Britain and the Patriotic Acre Fund — organized by the Saskatchewan Grain Growers' Association — encouraged every farm to donate an acre's worth of grain as a gift to the people of Britain. In 1915, a port-bound train of forty rail cars, each filled with forty tonnes of flour, was a perfect manifestation of the "Patriotism and Production" motto Saskatchewan had adopted at the outset of the war.

Just weeks before Combe's fatal act of heroism, another Moosomin soldier distinguished himself at Vimy Ridge on April 9, 1917. George Harry Mullin, twenty-five, earned a battlefield promotion from corporal to sergeant during the famous assault in which Canada itself is said to have advanced a rank among nations of the world.

Mullin, remarkably, had already sustained wounds to his head and groin in a 1916 battle in France. The farmer recovered and returned to fight with distinction at Vimy. Yet his most glorious hour was still to come.

At Passchendaele, on October 30, 1917, Mullin was with the Princess Patricia's Canadian Light Infantry when his unit encountered heavy machine-gun fire in defence of a German pill-box that held stores of weapons and other supplies.

At stake in this war's bloody game of inches was a critical summit called Meetcheele Ridge and it was another Canadian — Lieutenant Hugh McKenzie — who first rushed to capture the enemy garrison that blocked the Allies' advance. McKenzie made it, miraculously, to the pill-box entrance before being cut down by a sniper, never knowing that his act of valour would be recognized — like Combe's — with a posthumous Victoria Cross.

Then Mullin tried his luck. Slogging through mud and in the face of relentless gunfire, he approached the pill-box from a different direction. "He rushed a sniper post in front," reads the official account of his heroics, "and crawling on top of the pill-box, shot the two machine gunners with his revolver. He then rushed another entrance and compelled the garrison of ten to surrender."

Mullin's uniform was said to have been "shredded" by bullets that somehow never found his flesh. Later, when King George V awarded Mullin his VC for the daring operation, the citation noted how he had "actually performed the incredible feat of taking the pill-box single-handed. His gallantry and fearlessness were witnessed by many, and although rapid fire was directed in his purpose, he not only helped to save the situation but also indirectly saved many lives."

Mullin would survive and return to work the wheat fields of the family farm outside of Moosomin. He later served as Sergeant-at-Arms of the Saskatchewan legislature and, like Combe, was honoured in the re-naming of a lake in the northern part of the province. Mullin received the Victoria Cross in 1918. He died in Regina on April 5, 1963.

In all, seven other soldiers with Saskatchewan connections — Michael O'Leary, Arthur Knight and George Pearkes of Regina, Edmund DeWind of Yorkton, Gordon Flowerdew of Duck Lake, Raphael Zengel of Humboldt, and Hugh Cairns of Saskatoon — would earn Victoria Crosses during the First World War.

And what of Andy McNaughton? The other young man from Moosomin didn't win a VC. But he did receive a Distinguished Service Order, serious wounds at Ypres and Soissons, and a string of remarkable promotions. He ended the First World War as a brigadier-general in charge of the Canadian Corps Heavy Artillery. And three decades later, when Canadians again went to war in Europe, General Andrew G. L. McNaughton would command the entire Canadian army.

Saskatchewan, in fact, had produced tens of thousands of heroes during the Great War, some from among the unheralded home front volunteers who raised funds and food for the prolonged struggle, and others in the front-line forces where men were often maimed or buried before their bravery had even been tested.

"It was a glorious experience worth paying any price for," Lieutenant Charles McCool, former city editor of the *Saskatoon Phoenix*, reported in a letter from a battlefield hospital during the final days of the war in November 1918. He had lost his right arm, had taken a bullet through his left lung and had received shrapnel wounds in too many places to mention.

But, he wrote, with an oddly irrepressible cheeriness, "I am having a first-rate time and getting the very best of attention and treatment. From everything except the loss of the arm, I hope to recover fully and I am still looking forward to making Saskatoon my home when I get back to Canada."

Sarah Ramsland, first woman member of the Legislative Assembly, elected 1919

Saskatchewan Stationers, Regina

The world to which the soldiers were returning was changed — for better and for worse — and still changing. Ukrainian Canadians, thousands of whom had helped open the West by homesteading in Saskatchewan, were nursing a justified bitterness over the internment of many of their people during the war as "enemy aliens." Urban unemployed were agitating for better working conditions and wages throughout the West. But women, citizens only in theory before the war began, had finally achieved the vote by the time the Armistice was signed and they would see the election of the first female provincial legislator — Sarah Ramsland — in 1919.

The growing influence of women in Saskatchewan politics had already been felt in the success — short-lived though it was — of the prohibition movement. The ban on booze, imposed in 1917 and lifted in 1923, had transformed parts of the province into a bootleggers' paradise and left as a colourful legacy the famous rum-running tunnels of Moose Jaw along with a legend (or perhaps a truth) about Chicago gangster Al Capone laying low for awhile in Saskatchewan.

But the global war spawned a global plague as returning soldiers helped spread the Spanish influenza that eventually killed twenty million worldwide and some 5,000 residents of the province — more, in fact, than had perished in the combined carnage of all the battles of the war.

A poignant report in the November 12, 1918, *Leader Post* described the death of car salesman Elmer Brownlee, "one of the best known and deservedly popu-

Hedley Saville, 1928

lar men in Saskatchewan," after a bout of pneumonia caused by the influenza epidemic.

"A very sad part of Mr. Brownlee's death is the fact that he fell into unconsciousness a bare few minutes before news of the end of the war reached Regina."

The Armistice re-focused the attention of Saskatchewan farmers on many long-standing complaints — dutifully suppressed, for the most part, during the war — about the marketing of prairie wheat and the perceived exploitation of western farmers by eastern economic interests.

"The war that had begun as a great English-Canadian national quest ended by intensifying the Prairie West's emerging sense of regional grievance," notes historian John Herd Thompson, "and advancing the gradual process by which the people who had come west as the colonizers came to see themselves as the colonized."

The stage was set for a Saskatchewan-led movement that would ultimately re-balance the country's political scales and help make the West a voice — and a force — to be reckoned with.

95th Saskatchewan Rifles, Regina, circa 1914-1918

Members of the 68th Regina Regiment from File Hills Indian Colony, their relatives and the inspector of Indian agencies, W.M. Graham, Regina, circa 1918

Lieutenant John G. Diefenbaker,
Canada's Officers Overseas Draft, 1916

The people of Saskatchewan embraced the war effort with an enthusiasm usually reserved for dances, weddings and hockey games. More than 20,000 men from across the province had enlisted by the end of 1915, many of them heading east to join the British forces in the days after war had been declared. Included among these young men were members of the province's First Nations, like the File Hills Reserve recruits, even though the Indian Act exempted them from service. One hundred and seven volunteered, many earning acclaim as battlefield runners, sharpshooters and scouts. For the first time, they were free of the restrictions of the Indian Act and that experience radicalized them politically. First Nations veterans were denied standard veteran benefits and were expected to accept once again the conditions of the Indian Act. They were unwilling to submit. By 1919, the Indian League of Canada had been established in Ontario; two years later, the league's Annual Congress was held at the Thunderchild First Nation in Saskatchewan. By the end of the decade, the League of Indians of Western Canada had formed a delegation to protest the Soldier Settlement Act that expropriated land from the province's Indian Reserves to give to veterans. As a result, reserve lands were being eroded.

27th Light Horse ready to leave for England, Moose Jaw, circa 1916

Make Your Victory Bonds Measure Up With the Victory

1st Extra THE MORNING LEADER

"OVER THE TOP" SASKATCHEWAN; DON'T BE A SLACKER

VOL. XV, NO. 270. PROBS—FAIR AND MILDER REGINA, SASK., MONDAY, NOVEMBER 11, 1918. TODAY'S PAPER: 24 PAGES By Mail, $5 a Yr. City Daily, 15c a Wk. Saturday Edition, $1.50 a Year.

ALLIES' TERMS OF ARMISTICE

Berlin and Other Large Cities Given Over to the New Republic

PARADE STARTS AT 7 O'CLOCK THIS EVENING FROM THE CITY HALL

All citizens with automobiles will turn out and join in the triumphal procession. The order of the parade will be:

Salvation Army Band.
Returned Soldiers' League.
Rotary Club autos.
Canadian Club autos.
American Club autos.
Citizens with decorated cars.

Lieut.-Col. Hodson will give a display of German flares, captured at the Somme, at Wascana Park at 8 p.m.

COMPLETE Peace Terms of Great War

WASHINGTON. (1 p.m.)—The terms of the armistice with Germany were read to congress by President Wilson at one o'clock this afternoon. The President spoke as follows: Gentlemen of the Congress: "In these times of rapid and stupendous changes it will in some degree lighten my sense of responsibility to perform in person the duty of communicating to you some of the larger circumstances of the situation with which it is necessary to deal.

The German authorities who have, at the invitation of the supreme war council, been in communication with Marshal Foch have accepted and signed the terms of armistice, which he was authorized and instructed to communicate to them.

"The strictly military terms of the armistice are embraced in eleven speifications which include the evacuation of all invaded territories, the withdrawal of the German troops from the left bank of the Rhine and the surrender of all supplies of war.

"The terms also provide for the abandonment by Germany of the treaties of Bucharest and Brest-Litovsk.

Military Clauses on Western Front

1. Cessation of operations by land and in the air, six hours after the signing of the armistice.

2. Immediate evacuation of invaded countries: Belgium, France, Alsace-Lorraine, Luxembug, so ordered as to be completed within fourteen days from the signature of the armistice.

In Germany, troops which have not left the above mentioned territories within the period fixed, will become prisoners of war. Occupation by the Allied and U. S. forces jointly will keep pace with evacuation in these areas.

All movement of evacuation and occupation will be regulated in accordance with a note annexed to the stated terms.

II.—Repatriation

3. Repatriation beginning at once and to be completed within fourteen days of all the inhabitants of the countries above mentioned, including hostages and persons under trial or convicted.

4. Surrender in good condition by the German armies of the following equipment: Five thousand guns, (two htousand five hundred heavy, two thousand five hundred field) thirty thousand machine guns. Three thousand minenwerfer. Two thousand airplanes (fighters, bombers, firstly D-73's and night bombing machines) the above to be delivered in situ to the Allies and the United States troops in accordance with the detailed conditions laid down in the annexed note.

5. Evaucuation by the German armies of the countries on the left bank of the Rhine. These countries on the left bank of the Rhine shall be adminstered by the local authorities under the control of the Allies and United States armies of occupation. The occupation of these territories will be determined by Allied and United States garrisons holding the principal crossings of the Rhine, Mayence, Cologne, together with bridgeheads at these points in thirty kilometre radius on the rightbank and by garrisons similarly holding the strategic points of the regions.

A neutral zone shall be reserved on the right of the Rhine between the stream and a line drawn parallel to it forty kilometers to the east from the frontier of Holland to the parallel of Gernsheim and as far as practicable, a distance of thirty kilometres from the east of stream from this parallel upon Swiss frontier.

Evacuation by the enemy of the Rhinelands shall be so ordered as to be completed within a further period of eleven days, in all nineteen days after the signature of the armistice.

All movements of evacuation and occupation will be regulated according to the note annexed.

6. In all territory evacuated by the enemy there shall be no evacuation of inhabitants; no damage or harm shall be done to the persons or property of the inhabitants. No destruction of any kind to be committed.

Military establishments of all kinds shall be delivered intact as well as military stores of food, munitions, equipment not removed during the periods of evacuation.

For evacuation—Stores of food of all kinds for the civil population, cattle, etc., shall be left in situ, industrial establishments shall not be impared in any way and their personnel shall not be moved. Road and means of communication of every kind, railroad, waterways, main roads, bridges, telegraphs, telephones, shall be in no manner impaired.

The naval terms provide for the surrender of 160 submarines, fifty destroyers, six battle cruisers, ten battleships, eight light cruisers and other miscellaneous ships.

The immediate repatriation of all allied and American prisoners without reciprocal action by the allies also included.

7. All civil and military personnel at present employed on them shall remain. Five thousand locomotives, fifty thousand wagons and ten thousand motor lorries in good working order with all necessary spare parts and fittings shall be delivered to the associated powers within the period fixed for the evacuation of Belgium and Luxemburg.

The railways of Alsace-Lorraine shall be handed over within the same period, together with all pre-war personnel and material. Further material necessary for the working of railways in the country on the left bank of the Rhine shall be left in situ. All stores of coal and material for the upkeep of permanent ways, signals and repair shops left entire in situ, and kept in an efficient state by Germany during the whole period of armistice.

All barges taken from the Allies shall be restored to them. A note appended regulates the details of these measures.

8. The German command shall be responsible for revealing all mines or delay action, fuse disposed on territory evacuated by the German troops and shall assist in their discovery and destruction. The German command shall also reveal destructive measures that may have been taken (such as poisoning or polluting springs, wells, etc.)

9. The right of requisition shall be exercised by the Allies and the United States armies in all occupied territory. The upkeep of the troops of occupation in the Rhineland (excluding Alsace-Lorraine) shall be charged to the German government.

10. Immediate repatriation without reciprocity, according to detailed conditions which shall be fixed, of all Allied and United States prisoners of war. The allied powers and the United States shall be able to dispose of these prisoners as they wish.

11. Sick and wounded, who cannot be removed fro mevacuated territory will be cared for by German personnel who will be left on the spot with the medical material required.

Disposition relative to the eastern frontiers of Germany.

12. All German troops at present in any territory which before the war belonged to Russia, Roumania, or Turkey shall withdraw within the frontiers of Germany as they existed on August 1, 1914.

13. Evacuation by German troops to begin at once and all German instructors, prisoners and civilian as well as military agents, now on the territory of Russia (as defined before 1914) to be recalled.

14. German troops to cease at once all requisitions and seizures and any other undertaking with a view to obtaining supplies intended for Germany in Rumania and Russia (as defined on August 1, 1914.)

15. Abandonment of the treaties of Bucharest and Brest-Litovsk and of the supplementary treaties.

16. Allies shall have free access to the territories evacuated by the Germans on their eastern frontier either through Danzig or by the Vistula in order to convey supplies to the populations of those territories or for any other purspose.

III.—Concerning East Africa

17. Unconditional capitulation of all German forces operating in East Africa, within one month.

IV.—General Clause.

18. Repatriation, without reciprocity, within a maximum period of one month, in accordance with detailed conditions hereafter to be fixed, of all civilians interned or deported who may be citizens of other allied or associated states than those mentioned in clause 3, paragraph 19, with the reservation that any future claims and demands of the allies and the United States of America remain unaffected.

19. The following financial conditions are required: Reparation for damage done. While such armistice lasts no public securities shall be removed by the enemy which can serve as a pledge to the allies for the recovery or reparation for war losses.

Immediate restitution of the cash deposit, in the National Bank of Belgium, and in general immediate return of all documents, specie, stocks, shares, paper money, together with plant for the issue thereof, touching public or private interests in the invaded countries.

Restitution of the Russian and Roumanian gold yielded to Germany or taken by that power. This gold to be delivered in trust to the Allies until the signature of peace.

V.—Naval Conditions

20. Immediate cessation of all hostilities at sea and definite information to be given as to the location and movements of all German ships. Notification to be given to neutrals that freedom of navigation in all territorial waters is given to the naval and mercantile marines of the allied and associated powers, all questions of neutrality being waived.

21. All naval and mercantile marine prisoners of war of the Allied and associated powers in German hands to be returned without reciprocity.

22. Surrender to the Allies of 160 German submarines (including all submarine cruisers and mine laying ssubmarines (with their complete armament and equipment in ports which will be specified by the Allies. All other submarines to be paid off and completely disarmed and placed under the supervision of the allied powers.

23. The following German surface warships which shall be designated by the Allies shall forthwith be disarmed and thereafter interned—in neutral ports, or for the want of them in allied ports to be designated by the Allies and placed under the surveillance of the Allies, only caretakers being left on board, namely: Six battle cruisers, ten battleships, eight light cruisers, including two mine layers, fifty destroyers of most modern type.

All other surface craft (including river craft) are to be concentrated in German naval bases to be designated by the Allies and are to be paid off and completely disarmed and placed under the supervision of the Allies.

All vessels of the auxiliary fleet, trawlers, motor vessels, etc., are to be disarmed.

24. The Allies shall have the right to sweep up all mine fields and obstructions laid by Germany outside German territorial waters and the positions of these are to be indicated.

25. Freedom of access to and from the Baltic to be given to the naval and mercantile marines of the Allied powers; to secure this Allies shall be empowered to occupy all German forts fortifications, batteries and defence work of all kinds in all the entrances from the Battegat into the Baltic, and to sweep all mines and obstructions within and without German territorial waters without any question of neutrality being raised, and and the positions of all such mines and obstructions are to be indicated.

26. The existing blockade set up by the Allies and associated powers are to remain unchanged and all German merchant ships at sea are to remain liable to capture.

27. All naval aircraft are to be concentrated and demobolized in Geramn bases to be specified by the Allies.

28. In evacuating the Belgian coasts and ports, Germany shall abandon all merchant ships, tugs, lighters, cranes, and all other harbor materials, all materials for inland navigation, all aircraft, and all materials and stores, all arms and armaments, and all stores and apparatus of all kinds.

29. All Black Sea ports are to be evacuated by Germany; all Russian war vessels of all descriptions, seized by Germany in the Black Sea, are to be handed over to the Allies and the U.S.A. All neutral merchant vessels seized are to be released; all warlike and other materials o fall kinds seized in those ports are to be returned and German material as specified in clause 28 are to be abandoned.

30. All merchant vessels in German hands belonging to the Allies are to be restored in ports to be specified by the Allies, without reciprocity.

31. No destruction of ships or, of materials to be permitted before evacuation, surrender or restoration.

32. The German government will notify the neutral governments of the world, and particularly the governments of Norway, Sweden, Denmark, and Holland, that all restrictions placed on the trading of their vessels with the allied and associated countries, whether by the German government or by private German interests, and whether in return for specific concessions such as the export of shipbuilding, materials or not, are immediately cancelled.

33. No transfers of German merchant shipping of any description to any neutral flag are to take place after signature of armistice.

The duration of the armistice is to be thirty days, with option to extend during this period, on failure of execution of any of the above clauses, the armistice, may be denounced by one of the contracting parties on 48 hours previous notice.

—BUY VICTORY BONDS—

VICTORY HAS CROWNED HIS LEADERSHIP IN FIELD

FIELD MARSHAL SIR DOUGLAS HAIG, BRITISH COMMANDER-IN-CHIEF

IRON CROSS BAN ON IN GERMANY

COPENHAGEN, Nov. 9—The Danish frontier is being strictly guarded by the German soldiers' council. This is being done, it is stated, in order to prevent the escape of rich people, generals and other high officers

TWO MILLIONS FOR NEW HOSPITAL

WINNIPEG, Nov. 10.—(Special)—The Dominion government will erect $2,000,000 worth of new buildigns at Tuxedo military hospital. The contracts are let for the first $1,000,000 work of work, to commence immediately and to be pushed through the winter to an early completion. The contractor is Sam Browne, of Winnipeg.

The new buildings will be one "long active reatment" building, one "neurological" hospital building, two "short active treatment" buildings, and three large convalescent hosuital buildings.

—BUY VICTORY BONDS—

An inventor has given a shirt an adjustable collar band.

A water cooled motorcycle engine has been invented in England.

THE MAN WHO HAS CARRIED OUR EMPIRE TO FINAL VICTORY

MARSHAL FERDINAND FOCH

Germany Seethes In Revolution In Its Cities

KAISER BEING DEPOSED, "PEOPLE'S GOVERNMENTS" ARE FORMED IN GERMAN CAPITAL AND IN MANY OF BIG CITIES OF EMPIRE—NEWS DIFFICULT TO GET, BUT IT IS ALLEGED THERE WAS NO BLOODSHED.

(By the Associated Press.)

William Hohenzollern, the former German kaiser and king of Prussia, and his eldest son, Frederick William, who hoped some day to rule the German people, are reported to have fled to Holland.

The revolution which is in progress in Germany, although it seemingly is a peaceful one, probably threw fear into the hearts of the former kaiser and crown prince and caused them to take asylum in a neutral state.

William II, reigning king of the monarchy of Wurtemburg, is declared to have abdicated Friday night, and reports have it that the grandduke of Hesse, ruler of the grand duchy of Hesse, has decreed the formation of a council of state to take over the government there. Every dynasty in Germany is to be suppressed and all the princes exiled, according to Swiss advices.

GREAT CITIES IN MOVEMENT.

People's governments have been established in the greater part of Berlin and in other cities of the kingdom and empire.

(Continued on Page Two)

War Bulletins

LONDON, Nov. 11—(2.35 p.m.)—Field Marshal Von Hindenburg has placed himself and the German army at the disposal of the new people's government at Berlin, says a despatch from the German capital by way of Copenhagen.

PARIS, Nov. 11. (9.50 a.m.)—The Prussian minister of Hamburg has been arrested at his home in that city, according to a Basel despatch sent on Sunday but delayed in transit.

Mons Captured.

LONDON, Nov. 11—Mons, the Belgian town near where British troops engaged in bitter fighting with the Germans at the beginning of the war, was captured early this morning by Canadian troops under General Horne, according to Field Marshal Haig's announucement today.

Germany Hoists Red Flag.

COPENHAGEN, Nov. 11—The revolution in Germany is today to all intents and purposes an accomplished fact.

The news of the revolt spread throughout the whole empire, but fourteen of the twenty-six states including all the four kingdoms and all important states are reported securely in the hand of the revolutionists.

Frontier Garrisons in Revolt.

AMESTERDAM, Nov. 11.—German garrisons along the Dutch frontier are reported in revolt. Officers are being disarmed and are being treated roughly in some instances. Many of the guardsmen threw down their arms and have gone home.

Thousands of Dutch workmen are streaming homeward from Kruppe, at Essen.

Saxon King Dethroned

COPENHAGEN, Nov. 11.—King Friedrich Augustus of Saxony has been dethroned according to an official telegram from Berlin.

Kaiserlet Tries Suicide

PARIS, Nov 11.—Many sensational rumors became current here as a result of the signing of the armistice between the Allies and Germany.

These reports were to the effect that Prince Eitel Fredrick, the second son of William II, was prevented from committing suicide and that the Empress was dying. Three German generals are said to have committed suicide.

Suspicions of Socialists

LONDON, Nov. 11.—In view of the irregular and uncertain position of the new German government anxiety is expressed by some London newspapers lest difficulties arise to prevent acceptance and enforcement of the allied armistice terms.

The pleas of some German papers that the Allies ought not to crowd Germany to the wall so hard that she would be unable to establish herself under a democratic government tend to confirm suspicions in some quarters here that the transfer of power to the Socialists really is a subtle device by which the former emperor and the military, hope to obtain easier terms. It is contended that if such a scheme gained even partial success it might easily lead to reaction in favor of the formr autocrats.

The Times and the Daily Mail, for instance recall that all Germany, including the Socialists, assented to the war, the failure of which alone leads them to abjure it now. They insist that the change in administration is nowise removes the necessity for reparation and restitution.

Allied with this view is doubt voiced by the Daily Express and elsewhere as to whether the armistice arrangement with the present government would provide the guarantees demanded, as Chancellor Ebert's administration is conceived to be so fragile that it may fall at any moment.

Fighting in Berlin.

BASEL, Nov. 11.—Fighting between revolutionary forces and imperial troops was still going on in Berlin Sunday morning. The struggle which began Saturday evening broke out afresh at nine o'clock Sunday morning.

COPENHAGEN, Nov. 11. — The Grand Doke of Oldenbnrg has beenu dethroned and the Grand Duke of Mecklenburg-Schwerin has abdicated according to despatches from Hamburg.

AMSTERDAM, Nov. 11.—Public authority in the Prussian North seaport of Danzic is in the hands of a soldiers' and workmen's council formed by both social parties. There were no disturbances Sunday but a general strike has been declared for today.

THE PILOT KING

The visit by Edward, Prince of Wales, the future Edward VIII, to Saskatchewan in late September, early October, 1919, was marked by large, zealous crowds, anxious to express their patriotism in the wake of victory. His itinerary — which included visits to Regina and Saskatoon and whistle-stops at Maple Creek, Gull Lake and Swift Current — reflected his gratitude for the sacrifices Saskatchewanians had made as he stopped at veteran convalescent homes and awarded the Victoria Cross to the widow of Robert Combe. He would become the first pilot king, which might explain his appreciation for the Canadian Prairies (he would own a ranch in Alberta), home to the country's aviation pioneers. The most accomplished of these pioneers was Lieutenant Roland Groome, who had been a flight instructor during the war. In 1919, he and two war-time pals, Edward Clarke and Bob McCombie, formed the Aerial Service Company in Regina, Canada's first licensed aerodrome. Groome was the first licensed commercial aviator in Canada and flew the first intercity airmail in Saskatchewan between Saskatoon and Regina. He would remain president of the Regina Flying Club (founded in 1927) until he died in a plane crash in 1935.

Edward, Prince of Wales, and Ray Knight, Saskatoon, October 1919

The widow of Robert Combe receives his posthumous Victoria Cross from
Prince Edward, Regina, October 4, 1919

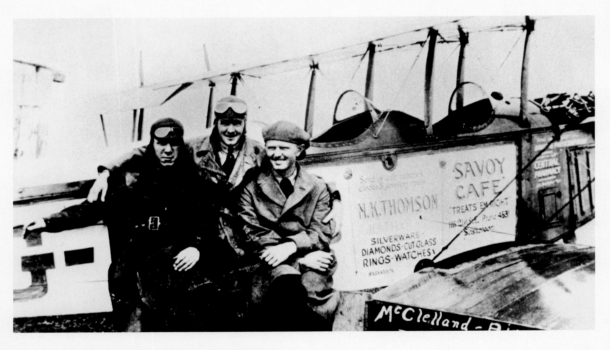

Hyslop McClelland with crew at Campbell Aviation, Saskatoon, 1921

THE MORNING LEADER

VOL. XIV, NO. 178. PROBS: DECIDEDLY WARM. REGINA, SASK., THURSDAY, JULY 26, 1917. TODAY'S PAPER—18 PAGES By Mail, $4 a Year. City Delivery, 10c a Week.

EXHIBITION CROWD COOL IN FIRE DANGER

FIRE IN THE GRAND STAND AT ITS HEIGHT

VIEW OF THE GRAND STAND 5 MINS. EARLIER

Big Stand and Industrial Building Burned But Fair Will Go On Today As Usual

TOTAL FIRE LOSS IS ESTIMATED AT ABOUT $100,000

The total loss at the big exhibition fire yesterday will, it is estimated, run in the neighborhood of $100,000. The grand stand cost about $20,000, on which there is some $14,050 insurance. The main building is valued at about $16,000, on which there is insurance to the extent of about $12,500. It was impossible last evening to secure the total value of the contents of the main building, but it is estimated that it is in the neighborhood of $50,000. The loss to the World-at-Home shows is estimated at about $7,000 and Mr. Brooks, who had the ice cream and cigar concession at the grand stand places his loss on goods at about $1,500. The various concessions burned out are valued at approximately $15,000, while the members of the grand stand attractions company lost about $2,000 worth of apparatus and clothes.

FIRE RACES THROUGH BIG WOODEN GRAND STAND BUT SPECTATORS WHO HAD PACKED STRUCTURE TO LIMIT ALL GOT OUT SAFELY—MAIN BUILDING, WITH ITS FINE EXHIBITS, AND MANY CONCESSIONS ARE LOST—LOSS IS ESTIMATED AT $100,000

FACTS OF THE FIRE

Fire discovered, 4.45.

Grand stand emptied of 5,000 people in seven minutes.

Buildings burned—Grand stand, Main building, judges' and starter's boxes at the race track and about a dozen concessions.

Total loss estimated on incomplete figures, $100,000.

Cause of fire is believed to be a lighted match or cigaret dropped through a crack in the floor of the grand stand and falling on rubbish on the roof of the underneath part of the grand stand.

No fatalities occurred and only three people were injured severely enough to be taken to the hospital for treatment.

The loss to the World at Home Shows includes the sideshow "The Whip," valued at $6,000, the cars of the Ferris wheel and minor damage to other shows.

At a quarter to five yesterday afternoon fire broke out in the grand stand at the exhibition buildings and before it burnt itself out had totally destroyed the stand and the Industrial building in addition to doing damage to other buildings.

While no official cause of the fire has been given out, it is pretty well agreed by those in a position to know that the fire was started through a lighted cigaret, match or cigar being dropped through a crack in the floor of the grand stand falling on rubbish between the floor and the roof of the underneath part of the stand.

Another story of the start of the fire was given to The Leader late last evening. It was stated by a citizen that the fire started in the babies' rest room through a coal oil stove on which milk was being heated. He added that he personally pulled a baby carriage away out of the room that was scorched and that he also assisted in taking the babies out before the alarm had been given in the stand.

(Continued on Page Two)

Batteries In Use Only On French Front

PARIS, July 25—The official communication issued by the war office tonight reads:

"The activity of the two artilleries was very spirited, particularly on the Casemates and California plateaux, in Champagne, in the region of Moronvilliers, and on the left bank of the Meuse. Everywhere our batteries very vigorously took to task the enemy artillery. There was no infantry action.

Still Shelling Reims.

"Shells to the number of 567 were fired into Reims.

"Belgian communication: The enemy artillery was active during the night against our communications in the region of Woesten and near Saint Jacquescapelle. There was grenade fighting before Dixmude and artillery fighting in the region of Ramscapelle and Rippedgaele.

"Army of the East, July 24: There was moderate artillery activity in the region of the Vardar. Enemy patrols were dispersed by the Serbians near Staravina. Lively artillery actions occurred northwest of Monastir during the night of July 23-24. Calm was re-established in the day."

MORE VICTIMS OF SUBMARINES IN WEEKLY LIST

LONDON, July 25.—Twenty-one British vessels of more than 1,600 tons each and three of less than 1,600 tons each were sunk last week by mines or submarines, according to the weekly admiralty report on shipping losses. One fishing vessel was also lost.

The announcement of the British admiralty given above shows an increase of seven vessels of more than 1,600 tons sent to the bottom as compared with the report of the previous week, when 14 were sunk. In the smaller category the losses are the same as those given in the report of the previous week—three, while there was a falling off by seven in the number of fishing vessels sunk.

FORCE GERMANS TO RETREAT IN EAST AFRICA

LONDON, July 25.—British troops in German East Africa have won new victories over the remaining German forces there and the main body of the enemy is now in retreat toward the south after having suffered heavy losses, says an official statement issued today. The text reads:

"An engagement on July 19 at Naroncombe resulted in the enemy being driven from all his positions. The main body is retreating southward. The enemy's losses were heavy.

"A small German column is at large on the north shore of Lake Manyara.

"We are in touch at Libuka with the enemy retreating toward Mahenge (in the southeasterly section of the colony).

"In Portuguese East Africa we are pursuing the enemy from Mwimbe toward the Rovuma river."

IGNOMINIOUS RETREAT CONTINUED IN GALICIA TOWNS FALL TO TEUTONS

In Galicia the precipitate retreat of the Russians continues almost everywhere from the Carpathian foothills to the region around Tarnopol, the government apparently not yet having had time to put in force its strong repressive measures which M. Kerensky, the head of the government, has promised to apply in order to stay the debacle.

Nadvorna, in the fringe of the foothills, Stanislau and Tarnopol, and numerous smaller towns have been taken by the Teutons, who are now approaching the important railroad junction of Buczacz, which lies thirty miles east of Halicz. The German emperor was an observer of the battle on the Sereth front and saw his men put down the only effort of moment that was made to hold them back—an attack by the Russians between Tarnopol and Trembowla.

Since the penetration of the German lines near Krevo, in which the women took a notable part, despite which large numbers of the Russians ignominously retreated to their old positions without even the vestige of harassment by the enemy, the Russians have not stirred from their trenches again to face the foe.

PETROGRAD, July 25—The Russian Guards Corps defending Tarnopol retreated, unpressed by the Germans, says the official statement issued by general headquarters tonight, but the Probrajensky and Semoszky regiments remained faithful to their duty and are fighting southeast of Tarnopol.

In the streets of Stanislau, there were stubborn bayonet engagements. The populace threw grenades on the retiring Russian troops. The text of the statement reads:

"In the direction of Vilna, in the region north of Krevo, our detachments occupying a portion of the enemy trenches east of Mihalcze retired to their former trenches owing to the enemy's powerful artillery fire.

"The guards corps, with the exception of the Petrovsky brigade, defending Tarnopol, voluntarily and without pressure from the enemy left its positions and retired eastward, the Petrovckie brigade, comprising the Probrajensky and Semoszky (Semenovcky) regiments, remain faithful to duty and are fighting southeast of Tarnopol.

Some Opposition.

"The enemy crossed to the left bank of the Sereth in the region of Beresovica, Czertory and Mikulice, driving back our troops to the Smykovce River-Gniezna-Trembowla line. East of Mysczkovice great opposition was offered to the Germans by the Smolensky and Kolyvansky regiments, which developed counter-attacks.

"Between the Sereth and Stripa rivers the Germans continued their offensive, concentrating their chief efforts along the western bank of the Sereth. Three infantry divisions in the region northwest of Romanovki left their positions and moved to the rear. On Tuesday towards evening our detachments halted on the Romanovki-Paaskovce-Getidovce line. West of the Stripa the Germans penetrated our positions in the region of Oesha, and towards Tuesday evening our troops retired to the Prjevlok-Egirjany-Baryl front.

One Brave Regiment.

"Particularly noteworthy was the gallant work of two cyclist battalions, which fought furiously against superior enemy forces. According to the testimony of a German officer, the one hundred and forty-third German regiment was almost completely destroyed by the 5th Cyclist battalion.

"South of the Dniester, as far as the Carpathians, our troops continued to retire eastward. On the Bystritza at Solotvina, in the Stanislau region, our rearguard engaged in action with enemy advanced patrols. Great support was given to our infantry by Polish Uhlans, who delivered six mounted attacks against the German infantry.

"In the streets of Stanislau stubborn engagements with the bayonet were fought with enemy forces which had broken into the town. The inhabitants of the city threw grenades from the balconies and windows on our departing troops.

REFUSE TO WORK WITH ENEMY ALIENS

CALGARY, Alta., July 25.—Freight handlers in the local C.P.R., yards three times today threatened strikes as a protest against the introduction of alien enemy labor by the C.P.R. As a result each time the aliens were removed.

The officials declare that enemy labor is necessary to sustain traffic but at a meeting tonight freight handlers announced their decision to decline to work with enemies. The aliens sent to work today admitted they were Austrians. The men insist that Italians and Russians can be found if sufficient wages are offered.

Monthly Bank Statement

OTTAWA, July 25.—A falling off in both the total assets and liabilities of the banks of Canada, is noted in the bank statement for June, issued by the finance department. The total assets for June were $2,033,622,960, as compared with $2,066,702,590, in May. The total liabilities were $1,790,343,357, as compared with $1,822,959,711 the previous month.

Wesley Allison's Counsel Is to Probe O'Connor Report At Flavelle's Request

OTTAWA, July 25.—In the house of commons miscellaneous estimates were taken up. Before the item covering the expense of the high commissioner's office in London and his staff, Sir Wilfrid Laurier remarked that "there ought to be an increase in this for I hear we are going to have a new high commissioner."

Hon. George P. Graham asked if the government had yet decided in filling that vacancy. Sir Thomas White replied that the matter of the high commissioner was not under consideration.

Mr. Macdonald brought up the question of the board appointed to investigate the O'Connor report on cold storage. He presumed that the board was not intended as a reflection upon Mr. O'Connor.

The prime minister replied that Mr. O'Connor in his report had recommended further enquiry.

F. B. Carvell was inclined to criticize the government for its appointment of G. F. Henderson, K. C., as chairman of the new commission. He was afraid that the chairman would be more inclined to prevent the truth coming out than to get at it for the benefit of the public. He was of this opinion because of experiences he had had with Mr. Henderson in connection with another enquiry (the shell enquiry in connection with which Mr. Henderson was counsel for Col. J. Wesley Allison). Mr. Carvell thought that in view of the appointment of Mr. Henderson, counsel should be named to represent the people. If this were not done, he was afraid that a truthful report would not be forthcoming.

Sir Robert said that Mr. Henderson was a capable lawyer of judicial temperament. He had no doubt but that he would discharge his duty with impartiality and ability.

George Kyte, of Richmond, said that the government had established a new record for investigating investigators. The report made by Mr. O'Connor was not satisfactory to the government and its friends, who had complained. It had been decided therefore to appoint a court of appeal which would make a satisfactory report for the parties interested at public expense.

Sir Robert Borden explained that provision is made in the order-in-council regarding control of the cost of living for appointment of examiners in a case of this kind. The new commission had also been given additional powers under the Enquiries Act.

Russians and Rumanians Broke Powerful Enemy Line and Captured Villages

From the Baltic to the Black Sea only at one point along the long line—in the southern Carpathians—have the Russians risen to the occasion and shown some of their old fighting spirit. Here, fighting shoulder-to-shoulder with their Rumanian allies, they have attacked and captured several villages from the Germans and broken the heavily fortified line on a wide front.

PETROGRAD, July 25.—A report of the general staff of the Rumanian army received here today says:

"In the south Carpathians troops under General Rofoza Averesco assumed the offensive and occupied the villages of Meresci and Volochany and captured several hundred prisoners and 19 guns, including some heavy ones. We owe this success to the skilful manoeuvring and close co-operation of the Rumanian and Russian forces and also to the vigorous activity of our allied artillery.

"The powerfully organized enemy line has been broken on an extensive front. The bravery and devotion of our troops was incomparable. Among other incidents one battery lost its entire personnel except seven men, who continued firing without cessation and finally succeeded in silencing the enemy's fire. Lieut.-General St. Cherbatcheff (commander of the Russian forces in Rumania) decorated all these men with the St. George's Cross."

KAISER HANDS OUT MORE HARDWARE

COPENHAGEN, July 25.—The arrival of Emperor William at the Galician front yesterday morning is reported in a Berlin despatch. After hearing the report of the commander-in-chief the emperor visited the troops on the Sereth.

The emperor awarded the Order Pour Le Merite with oak leaves and chain to Prince Leopold of Bavaria, Gen Hoffman, Prince Leopold's chief of staff and Major Franz, chief of staff of all army corps.

Seeds of Discontent

The war changed everything for Saskatchewan wheat farmers. Poor crop yields began in 1914 and dropped dramatically during a drought after 1917, the same year the federal government began marketing grain as part of the domestic war effort. Farmers lost control of the market and prices fell dramatically. Thousands abandoned their farms, homesteads that the federal government had frantically tried to settle only a decade before. After the war, the mistrust of the federal pricing policy intensified and, when wheat prices took another dramatic plunge in 1920, organizers for a co-operative wheat pool found their campaign would fall on fertile ground.

Farmer sowing seeds, Prince Albert, circa 1920

Horse-drawn adjustable harrows, Lloydminster, circa 1920

Racing cars, Regina, circa 1921-1922

Radio station CKCK, Regina, 1922

The Roaring Twenties

Like most of North America, the Twenties in Saskatchewan were a time of bustle, innovation, good times and fast times. Within a year of the Armistice, the celebration seemed cemented in the social life of the times. In Saskatchewan, sports took root and grew. Bowling boomed; golf club memberships soared; traditional sports — baseball, football and hockey — were the entertainments of the day. On the fifth floor of the *Leader* building, radio station CKCK made its debut on July 29, 1922. In February 1923, the station became the first in the British Empire to broadcast a church service and in March that same year, the station again made history airing the Regina Pats vs. Edmonton Eskimos game, the first hockey game to be broadcast in Canada.

Pre-Prohibition bar of Fielding Hotel, Fielding, late 1916

Swimming at York Lake, Yorkton, circa 1920

CHAPTER FOUR

There is a letter, penned on April 3, 1926, which tidily encapsulates a new coming-of-age spirit — call it the Great Awakening — that swept Saskatchewan in the years between the Great War and the Great Depression.

The writer, Alexander James McPhail, was a leading organizer of the province's grain growers, spearhead of a new co-operative movement aimed at pooling the prairie wheat harvest to build farmers' bargaining power and stabilize incomes as they shipped their crops to markets in the East and around the world.

The letter's recipient, Violet McNaughton, had already led the women of Saskatchewan in their successful battle for the right to vote. Now, she was a key player with McPhail in the push for a pool against speculators, corporate grain handlers and other middlemen — in Winnipeg, Toronto and Chicago — who were seen to be getting rich off western wheat at the expense of its growers.

"The people today are different to what they were eight, or ten, or twenty-five years ago," McPhail wrote to McNaughton in those fledgling days of the Saskatchewan Wheat Pool. "They are more widely awake. They are doing more thinking for themselves than ever before. Perhaps some wrong thinking but that does not matter so much. They are not any longer going to allow any man or men to think they know better what is good for them. They may make mistakes but they will be their own mistakes."

LEFT PAGE: Saskatchewan
Wheat Pool Drive.
A.J. McPhail is on the
far right

ABOVE: *Saskatoon Phoenix*
carrier boy, circa 1928

Cree and Métis pilgrimage to Duck Lake, where, in 1884, Louis Riel gave a seminal speech calling for responsible government and the creation of provinces in the North West and where, on March 26, 1885, the North West Rebellion began, July 1928

This fresh confidence was on display, too, during official celebrations to mark the sixtieth anniversary of Confederation in 1927. Saskatchewan had only been a full-fledged member of the Canadian family for twenty-two years by then, but its relatively recent entry into the Dominion didn't prevent towns and cities throughout the province from mounting colourful Jubilee pageants on July 1. And those parades, parties and pronouncements, argues University of Regina historian James Pitsula, marked the emergence of a distinct "Saskatchewan consciousness" alongside the Union Jack nationalism commonly exhibited across Canada.

"Saskatchewan in the Twenties considered itself the 'granary of the world,' a self-definition that reflected the pre-eminent place of agriculture in the provincial economy," Pitsula wrote in a 2002 essay published by *Saskatchewan History*.

Citing Saskatchewan's booming population (more than 820,000, third largest in Canada by 1927), its soaring gross domestic product (also third in Canada at the time) and relatively high personal incomes (third again), he notes that "the people of the province had reason for pride in the rapid growth of their economy. The prevailing mood can be summed up in the phrase 'muscular Saskatchewan.'"

Newspapers of the era, such as the *Saskatoon Star-Phoenix* and *Regina Leader*, helped burnish the province's self-image with upbeat stories and illustrations extolling Saskatchewan's virtues — including one cartoon that showed a prairie wheat sheaf and an oat stalk anthropomorphized as two triumphant strongmen standing beside best-in-show trophies won at a U.S. farm exhibition.

Pitsula points, too, to the text of a full-page advertisement — headlined "Saskatchewan: Its Place In, and Contribution to, the Canadian Confederation" — published in the *Regina Leader's* Jubilee edition: "FIRST Province in Canada in

Ethel Catherwood with Saskatoon Mayor George Wesley Norman and other dignitaries, Saskatoon, September 13, 1927

per capita wealth; FIRST in production of wheat; FIRST in production of oats; FIRST in production of rye; FIRST in production of flax; FIRST in the breeding of horses."

There were, indeed, signs of tremendous progress everywhere. Saskatchewan's 1905 population of a quarter-million residents at the time of provincial inauguration had more than tripled by the 1926 census. The rapid mechanization of farming was evident in the number of combine harvesters in operation, which shot up from 148 in 1926 to more than 2,300 by the end of the decade. The number of automobile licences doubled from 60,000 in 1920 to more than 128,000 in 1929. And the number of movie theatres tripled that decade from 110 to 343.

"FIRST in quantity of commercial clays; FIRST in production of sodium sulphate; FIRST in number of rural telephones per capita."

And first at the Olympics. The 1928 gold medal won at the Amsterdam Games by Saskatchewan high-jumper Ethel Catherwood — a prairie sweetheart nicknamed the "The Saskatoon Lily" — only stoked the optimism of a province already bursting with pride.

Saskatchewan's surging sense of self-assurance followed years of hardship and frustration. Farmers who had pluckily endured war, influenza, pestilence and drought found themselves in the early 1920s facing another plague: rock-bottom prices for the grain they had managed to grow. Their disgruntlement had sparked the formation of powerful farm unions and a break-away political party — the Progressives — that would seriously challenge the status quo of governance throughout the Prairies and at the national level, as well.

And the most significant product of these dizzying changes and the rising tide of Saskatchewan pride was the creation of the wheat pool McPhail and McNaughton were corresponding about in 1926.

The postwar dismantling of a federal agency that had set fixed rates for each

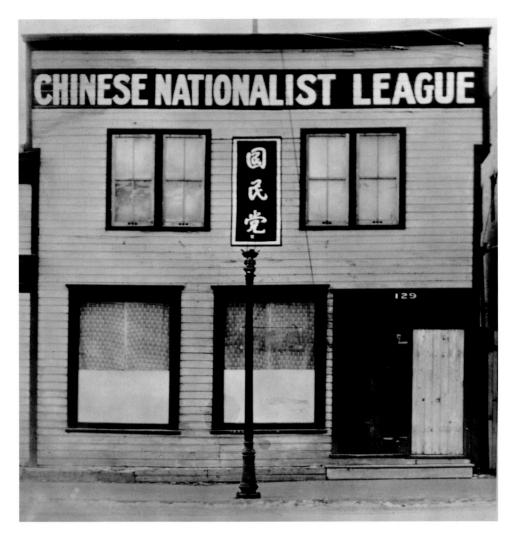

Chinese National League Headquarters, 129-19th Street East, 1917-1931. Former offices of the *Star-Phoenix*, Saskatoon

bushel of wheat left growers at the mercy of vague market forces which, in their minds, seemed to favour big grain companies over individual farmers.

For a province still populated largely by men and women working the land — more than sixty per cent of Saskatchewanians still lived a farm life during the mid-1920s — perennially poor returns on its prime agricultural product added up to a large-scale crisis.

So when the campaign for a farmer-controlled wheat pool was launched in 1923, the provincial government voiced support for the idea. And the arrival in Canada that summer of Aaron Sapiro, a charismatic California co-operative organizer, signalled the start of a township-by-township, field-by-field sign-up drive across Saskatchewan. It was a grassroots movement in every sense, with success hinging on whether fifty per cent of the province's total acreage in wheat would be pledged to the pool. Anything less, organizers believed, represented insufficient support for the concept among farmers and a doomed co-operative.

"The wheat pooling movement of the world cannot be started anywhere else, except in Canada, because you are the key to the surplus exports of the world," Sapiro thundered in one speech. "And the best place — the one place where it ought to be done, more than any other province — is Saskatchewan, where you raise more than one-half of the wheat of all Canada. I tell you, people of Saskatchewan, that it can be done! If you only will to do it, no power can stop you."

But by the end of 1923, the champions of the Wheat Pool had signed up barely half of the farmers needed to put the plan in motion. It took six more months of speeches, pamphleteering and farm-gate conversions before the pool advocates achieved their goal.

Finally, on June 16, 1924, in a diary entry that registers the start of a new era in Saskatchewan history, McPhail scribbled six words: "Wheat pool over the top today."

More than 46,500 farmers representing about fifty-one per cent of all the wheat acreage in Saskatchewan had signed contracts to deliver their crops to the Pool. Within two years, the Pool had purchased 451 grain elevators and four terminals from the Saskatchewan Co-Operative Elevator Company for $11 million. And between 1924 and 1929, the total wheat delivered to the Pool grew from fifty million to 150 million bushels.

Whether they realized it or not, the Pool proponents and the tens of thousands of farmers they recruited during the 1920s were building far more than a grain handling co-op, far more even than the largest provincial corporation that the Saskatchewan Wheat Pool would become. The distinctive Pool elevators that were constructed to hold the harvest would define the prairie landscape just as surely as the economic, social and educational activities of the Pool would reshape Saskatchewan society.

"Firey Cross" Ku Klux Klan postcard, Regina, May 24, 1925

"My father was a 'Wheat Pool man,' as were all the farmers in the neighbourhood where I grew up," recalled Verne Clemence, the former *Star-Pheonix* writer, in his 2004 book *Saskatchewan's Own.* "Among my earliest memories of growing up on a farm near Kindersley in the heart of the Saskatchewan grain belt is one of accompanying my father in his old one-ton International truck when he hauled grain to the grain elevator. To me, as a child, the elevator was a fascinating technological miracle with the huge 'Saskatchewan Wheat Pool' lettering that could be seen for miles."

Though the Wheat Pool would struggle mightily to survive the Depression, and would remake itself regularly in subsequent decades to adjust to new threats and opportunities in the agricultural industry, its dominant and enduring presence in the province would stand as a symbol of Saskatchewan's vitality and values. A strategic amalgam of individual enterprise and pragmatic co-operation, the Pool was a potent expression of how the people of the province had come to see themselves by the 1920s.

"Co-operation is a combination of the practical and the ideal," McPhail explained in one of the scores of speeches he gave during the decade. "It offers ample scope for putting into practice the ideals of the practical man as well as the ideals of the idealist. It is not only the most efficient, economical and practical way of doing business, but, when carried to its ultimate conclusion, it recognizes equality and the interdependence of all human beings. It provides a business medium through which progressive and socially minded men and women with high ideals can find satisfaction and peace of mind in useful work."

The farmer-led movement that had made possible the creation of the Saskatchewan Wheat Pool also reshaped the province's political landscape during the 1920s. The rise of the Progressives forced a realignment of Liberal and Conservative platforms as all parties vied for the support of the increasingly powerful farmer bloc. The Liberal party had dominated Saskatchewan politics from the province's birth, and a string of Grit premiers — Walter Scott, William Martin, Charles Dunning and Jimmy Gardiner — steered the legislature from 1905 through to the late 1920s.

But in 1929, an alliance of Progressives and Conservatives forced Gardiner from office and put James Anderson in the premier's chair. Historians generally believe that Gardiner was hurt by his intense opposition to an anti-immigrant, anti-Catholic movement that had a brief spell of popularity with the arrival of the Ku Klux Klan in Saskatchewan in the late Twenties. A gathering of the Klan had drawn some 8,000 people to Moose Jaw in June 1927 — just days before the July 1 Jubilee celebrations — but the Klan's crusade had largely petered out by the end of the decade.

"It had been a bewildering decade as new politics, new pools, new fashions struggled to find some stability in a postwar world that yearned to be 'normal' again," wrote John Archer in his 1980 history of the province. "It was a time of change, a time to gamble on the exchange, a time to vibrate in harmony with the four cylinders of the Model T, a time to glimpse a world of wider vistas and interests brought on the magic of air waves. It was a time of prejudice and bigotry which, forced into the open and exposed to the public for what it was, had its brief day and night and began to dissipate."

The new Wheat Pool was in place, a new government was in office, a new culture of prosperity and self-possession was in vogue across the province. But with the 1930s and a dust storm gathering on the horizon, Saskatchewan's character was about to be tested in ways no one could have imagined.

THE LEADER-POST

MORNING

VOL. XXIX. NO. 41   PROBS: SNOW FLURRIES; COLDER   * * *   REGINA, SASKATCHEWAN, THURSDAY, FEBRUARY 18, 1932   TODAY'S PAPER: 16 PAGES   Single Copy 5c

"MAD" TRAPPER DIES BATTLING POLICE

Wounds Officer Before Bullets End Wild Chase

Hersey Shot as He Lifted Gun After Seeing Johnson

(By Canadian Press)

AKLAVIK, N.W.T., Feb. 17.—Albert Johnson came to the end of his blizzardy trail Wednesday. The wild man of the Arctic went down fighting, but Canada's red-coated Royal Canadian Mounted Police won out.

Battling cold, hunger, blizzards and overwhelming odds, the eccentric trapper defied the police for eight wild weeks, now running through the bleak hills of the Arctic, now standing at bay and shooting down his pursuers if they came within range of his deadly rifle.

Doubled Back on Trail

When his fate overtook him, Johnson was perpetrating one of the foxy, trail-muddling tricks with which he has managed to keep out of range of the police and trapper pursuers. He was doubling back on his trail. This time, however, his pursuers were too close.

He was seen by Staff Sergeant S. F. Hersey and a trapper named Noel Verville, plugging along in advance of the main posse. Hunter and hunted at once prepared for a gun battle. Hersey and Verville jerked their rifles from their tobog gan.

ALBERT JOHNSON

Slain Trapper Deadly Shot, Says Albertan

(Leader-Post Special Press Bureau)

SASKATOON, Feb. 17.—"From what I know of Albert Johnson after him shooting those policemen up there—I wouldn't go on his trail if the government offered me all of Saskatchewan."

These words were spoken here by P. R. Lehmann, homesteader of the Empress district, on the Saskatchewan-Alberta border, who reported that he had recognized the picture of the man as a former resident of the community, who went into the north country in 1920.

"He was a smart, intelligent fellow," Mr. Lehmann declared, stating that Johnson came of a good family and that the hunted man was a native of Canada, possibly of the Empress district.

TWO BRITISH SAILORS DIE FROM WOUNDS

Shanghai War Rages While New Peace Move Made

By MORRIS J. HARRIS

(Associated Press Staff Writer)
(Copyright, 1932, by the Associated Press)

SHANGHAI, Feb. 18.—(Thursday)—Renewed words of peace were whispered in the councils of diplomacy Thursday as preparations for war went forward along the lines.

Winnipeg Hold-Up Trio Get $18,600

Early Returns Show Result To Be Close In Free State Vote

Both President Cosgrave and De Valera Head Polls in Their Ridings

(Canadian Press Cable)

DUBLIN, Irish Free State, Feb. 18.—(Thursday)—Tabulation of 25 returns out of 145 in Tuesday's general election in the Irish Free State early Wednesday showed President William Cosgrave's government party and Fianna Fail (Republican party), headed by Eamonn De Valera, running close together in their fight for supremacy in the Dail Eireann.

KNOCK PLUCKY MESSENGER TO INSENSIBILITY

Daylight Robbers Make Escape in Stolen Auto

(By Canadian Press)

WINNIPEG, Feb. 17.—Police cars crashed Winnipeg Wednesday night seeking a trio of bandits who ambushed George Ridd, provincial treasury messenger, slugged him into insensibility and escaped with a satchel containing $3,600 in cash and $15,000 in cheques and money orders.

ESTIMATES CUT BY $7,760,972

Expenditures for 1932-33 Are Placed at $21,927,303 as Figures Tabled

GAS INQUIRY IN PROVINCE IS APPROVED

Committee of House to Investigate Situation

A special committee of the Saskatchewan legislature, yet to be named, will investigate the buying, selling, transportation and storage of petroleum products in the Province of Saskatchewan.

KATHLEEN KEELY

who was crowned queen of the colorful orange festival at Winter Haven, Florida.

Blossoms Out

U.F.A. MEMBERS CLASH IN HOUSE

Party Leader, Gardiner, Takes to Task Follower Over Wheat Bonus Stand

(By Canadian Press)

OTTAWA, Feb. 17.—A brisk clash between Robert Gardiner, Alberta United Farmers' leader in the house of commons, and M. N. Campbell (Prog., McKenzie), two of his supporters, featured Wednesday's debate on a resolution urging the payment of a $1 per acre bonus on wheat.

PAIR SEEKING BAYCHIMO FUR SHIP MISSING

WHITEHORSE, Yukon, Feb. 17.—No word has been received here Wednesday of William Graham and Mrs. Edna Christofferson, who were missing since Monday while on a flight from Hazelton, B.C., to Atlin, B.C.

CUT OUT FOUR LEGAL AREAS IN PROVINCE

Four judicial districts of the province will not operate the year so far as no appropriations have been provided for the department for the fiscal year 1932-33.

REGINA WOMAN HEADS TRUSTEES

Mrs. Ashley Walker Re-elected to Presidency of Urban Section

Leader-Post Special Press Bureau

SASKATOON, Feb. 17.—Mrs. Ashley Walker, Regina, was re-elected president of the urban section of the Saskatchewan School Trustees' association at a meeting of the group here Wednesday afternoon.

LABOR CENSURE VOTE DEFEATED

British House Passes Measure to Speed Enactment of New Trade Bill

(Canadian Press Cable)

LONDON, Feb. 17.—The National government Wednesday night defeated a Labor motion of censure, the third it brought forward since December, by a vote of 413 to 39.

BEER STORES IN PROVINCE SHOW LOSSES

B.C. ACCOUNTS SHOW DEFICIT OF $4,819,261

VICTORIA, B.C., Feb. 17.—Hon. J. W. Jones, minister of finance, in the legislature Wednesday filed officials accounts showing a deficit of $4,819,261 on government financing for the last fiscal year ending March 31, 1931.

ATTACK MADE ON BROWNLEE BY F. C. MOYER

(By Canadian Press)

EDMONTON, Alta., Feb. 17.—A blazing attack upon Premier J. E. Brownlee by F. C. Moyer of Drumheller, leader of the Independent group in the Alberta legislature, who charged that the government's record was one of "indecision and inaction" caused verbal clashes in the house Wednesday.

Weather

Tidal Wave Sweeps Ice Mountains Over Arctic; Eskimos Face Starvation

(By Associated Press)

FAIRBANKS, Alaska, Feb. 17.—Great damage resulted from tidal waves which swept over the western Alaska coast from the Kuskokwim river delta northward and spread many miles inland, Clark M. Garber, superintendent of the Indian affairs bureau, said here Wednesday.

Hockey Scores

NATIONAL LEAGUE

	1	2	3	Fls.
Canadiens	2	0	1	3
Chicago	0	0	1	1

INTERMEDIATE

Melville	0	1	0	2
Regina	0	1	3	4

(Melville wins round, 8-4.)

EXHIBITION

Ottawa All-Stars, 4, Winnipeg, 3.

Canadian Military Flyers, Victims of Economy Slash, Offer Services to Chinese

(By Canadian Press)

OTTAWA, Feb. 17.—Ready to face the dangers of aerial battle in far away China, 80 officers of the Royal Canadian Air Force, soon to be released from the service, Wednesday offered their services to Lt. Tchuin, Chinese consul-general for Canada.

Willie Willis
By ROBERT QUILLEN

"I wish our family was rich like the Smiths an' had servants to do the dirty work instead of me."

The Prairie Sentinels

On June 26, 1924, when the Saskatchewan Wheat Pool succeeded in signing up almost 46,000 farmers representing the necessary fifty-plus percentage of the province's acreage, their next task was to acquire grain elevators at stops — towns were spaced a day's wagon ride apart — along the sprawling railway network. Grain elevators had stood on the Prairies since the late 1870s and within sixty years would grow to 6,000. Until the 1920s, styles and sizes varied but, with the emergence of grain elevator builders the now familiar, once ubiquitous, Prairie Sentinels were standardized. The Wheat Pool opened its first elevator at Bulyea on July 1, 1925. By 1930, it would own 1,000. Each elevator could warehouse 25,000 to 35,000 bushels of grain and house an ingenious mechanical lift and gravity mechanism to unload, distribute to storage bins and eventually load on to boxcars.

Grain elevators, Meadow Lake

Saskatchewan Wheat Pool Inuagural General Meeting, Regina, February 26–27, 1925

Aaron Sapiro, California lawyer who won Saskatchewan farmers over to the co-op, Saskatoon Industrial Exhibition, July 19, 1926

Start the Day Right With The Phœnix

THE SASKATOON PHŒNIX

Read a Day's News At Your Breakfast

VOLUME LVI—No. 28 SASKATOON, SASK., MONDAY, AUGUST 6, 1928. PRICE ON TRAINS—5 CENTS

ETHEL CATHERWOOD SETS WORLD RECORD

LILY OF SASKATOON TAKES LADIES' HIGH JUMP HONORS AT OLYMPIAD, AMSTERDAM

Saskatchewan Girl's Running Leap Clears Bar At Five Feet Three Inches, Leading All Entries

Wild Enthusiasm Greets "Our Ethel" As, Carried Shoulder High, Athlete Receives Great Acclaim

By W. H. INGRAM
Canadian Press Staff Correspondent

AMSTERDAM, Aug. 5.—Canadian girls take equal honors with men from the Dominion in the track and field sections of the ninth Olympiad, which portion of the program concluded today after eight days of intense competition.

The girls' 400 metres relay team, composed of four Toronto girls—Fanny Rosenfeld, Ethel Smith, Jane Bell and Captain Myrtle Cook—won the 400 metres relay finals in new world's record time of 48 2-5 seconds, with United States second, Germany third, France fourth, Holland fifth and Italy last.

STATUESQUE BEAUTY

Miss Ethel Catherwood, of Saskatoon, broke the world's record to win the women's running high jump today with a leap of 5 feet 3 inches.

Thus the two victories of Percy Williams, of Vancouver, in the 100 and 200 metre sprints are balanced by the female contingent's achievements.

The day was an outstanding triumph for Canadian girlhood, for the two events captured by the Dominion girls were the only finals of the day for women.

Ethel Catherwood the "most photographed girl at the Olympic games," statuesque beauty, was jubilant after her feat. She was lifted to the shoulders of Canadians, athletes and spectators alike, and smilingly received the plaudits of the huge crowd. She waved her arms to the cheering watchers and smiled again as the Canadian flag soared to the top of the main Olympic pole in token of her victory. It was the second ascension of the day, the flag having been sent to the top by the relay team earlier.

Miss Catherwood's victory was received with possibly more enthusiasm than any other Canadian win except that of Percy Williams in the 100 metres last Monday, for she had placed no less than 17th in the qualifying events in the morning.

Miss Gisolf, of Holland, and Miss

TURN TO PAGE 5—COLUMN 1

PROTECTION ISSUE OUT IN OLD LAND ELECTION

Stanley Baldwin Pledges Party Following Reports of Members' Speeches

Associated Press

LONDON, Aug. 5.—Stanley Baldwin Saturday pledged his party not to introduce protection as an issue in the coming general election. The prime minister made this promise in a letter which he sent to Commander Bolton M. Eyres-Monsell, chief government whip in the House of Commons. The letter explained itself as having been written "because of some confusion of thought among Unionist members arising from condensed reports of certain speeches."

The epistle stated the government's attitude on "safeguarding duties."

It said, "safeguarding has been the law of the land since it was established as a principle of Lloyd George's government in 1921. It was the policy we adopted at the last general election and it will be continued.

"We pledge and shall continue to be pledged not to introduce protection. We pledged and shall continue to be pledged not to impose any taxes on food."

The prime minister wrote that the boldness and originality of the government's tax plan for permanent relief of productive industries has been "no doubt the reason why both opposition parties have been trying to drag in a protectionist red herring in the vain hope of causing dissension in a party whose unity and enthusiasm have aroused their envious admiration."

Prunella Says—

FORECASTS

Manitoba and Saskatchewan—mostly fair and warm, a few scattered showers. Alberta—mostly fair and moderately warm. Lake Superior—moderate winds, fair, not much change in temperature.

"How did the fight come out?"

"It was a double knockout. They both bumped into each other running backwards."

Bright

Dominion Observatory

TORONTO, Aug. 5.—The weather in the west today has been mostly fair and warm.

	Min.	Max.
Prince Rupert	48	—
Victoria	52	63
Vancouver	54	74
Kamloops	60	—
Calgary	44	78
Edmonton	44	—
Swift Current	56	80
Battleford	52	—
Prince Albert	54	76
Moose Jaw	52	87
Medicine Hat	56	84
Regina	45	84
Winnipeg	58	84
Port Arthur	52	65
Parry Sound	62	—
London	68	80
Toronto	68	79
Kingston	66	78
Ottawa	64	70
Montreal	68	—
Quebec	56	82
St. John	54	—
Halifax	—	54

Britishers Win In Flat Events

By Associated Press

OLYMPIC STADIUM, Amsterdam, Aug. 5.—The ninth Olympiad's track and field events closed today featured by sensational advances in the scoring columns of Canada which produced a winner in both sprints.

The British Empire, with two victories won by Canada, two by Great Britain, one by Ireland and one by South Africa, has triumphed six times. All these victories were won "on the flat" and gives the British dominions supremacy in the track events by a margin of two events over the Finns, who with a total of five, scored one of their championships in the field.

NO HARVESTERS' TRIPS UNTIL JOBS ARE OPEN

Arrangements Governing Labor Movement in B.C. Are Announced

Canadian Press

VICTORIA, B.C., Aug. 5—Arrangements governing the movement of harvesters from British Columbia to the prairies this fall were announced by the department of labor today. While the usual low harvesters' fares will go into effect on Canadian railways on August 8, no men will be allowed to proceed to the prairies then unless they have made definite arrangements individually to secure employment.

Some hundreds of jobs already have been arranged and the inauguration of the low fares will see the annual trek to the grain fields under way.

The main movement, however, must wait until actual orders for men are received from the prairies. Harvesters from here will be sent then as they are required so that no men will arrive on the prairies to find that they cannot get work.

The movement to the prairies will not reach its peak until the middle of the month. Latest estimates place the total number of men likely to go from British Columbia at 5,000 or less, as against nearly 8,000 last year.

EDITOR SHOT DEAD

United Press

BELGRADE, Aug. 5.—Vlada Ristovich, editor of the opposition newspaper Jedinstov, was shot and killed this morning in a street in Zarub. The assailants of the editor were identified.

Archbishop S. P. Matheson To Resign In September

Canadian Press

WINNIPEG, Aug. 5.—Archbishop Samuel Pritchard Matheson will retire as primate for all Canada September 22. He will continue in service however, as Bishop of Rupert's Land and chancellor of Manitoba University.

Today the archbishop, who is 78 years of age, made known his intention to resign, expressing the belief that he should hand over the reins of the primate's office to a younger man. His resignation has been submitted and a successor will be chosen at a meeting of the House of Bishops called for September 22.

For 20 years he has been primate of the church in Canada. Three archbishops are mentioned as probable successors. They are the archbishops of Nova Scotia, New Westminster and Huron.

Archbishop Matheson, who is a native Manitoban born in the old Selkirk settlement of East Kildonan, succeeded Archbishop Robert Machray to the primacy.

Vets March Roads Of Old War Days

Asociated Press

LONDON, Aug. 5.—A great pilgrimage was in progress last night with the migration of 11,000 British men and women to the battlefields of northern France. The pilgrimage was begun on the fourteen anniversary of Britain's entry into the colossal struggle.

The veterans will march along the familiar roads of war days and through the fields of blood red poppies, singing the same old songs as of yore.

The Prince of Wales, who served in France with the Royal Guards, will join the pilgrims.

The culminating feature of the visit will be a solemn ceremony at Ypres.

KING WILL OPEN NATIONAL PARK

Premier Speaks En Route To Prince Albert For Ceremony

Canadian Press

WINNIPEG, Aug. 5.—Premier Mackenzie King passed through Winnipeg tonight en route for Prince Albert, where he will open the new national park. The prime minister was here for a little more than an hour. He will address two political meetings on his way to Prince Albert. Tomorrow afternoon he speaks at Brandon, where Hon. Robert Forke, minister of immigration, has arranged a meeting. On Tuesday afternoon Mr. King will address a meeting at Davidson, Sask., in the constituency of Long Lake which is represented in the House of Commons by J. Fred Johnston, deputy speaker. Mr. King will reach Prince Albert on Wednesday morning and remain there for a couple of days before returning to Ottawa.

The prime minister's trip from Ottawa to Winnipeg was uneventful. At Cochrane, a crowd gathered at the station and Mr. King got off his car and chatted with some of those present. Similarly, at Redditt there was a gathering of people, among whom was Hon. Peter Heenan, minister of labor. Again Mr. King conversed with them until the train pulled out.

WIND DAMAGE HEAVY

United Press

HAMBURG, Germany, Aug. 5.—Damage estimated at more than $250,000 resulted from a cyclone accompanied by cloudbursts which struck Bavaria today. Some injuries but no deaths were reported.

NOBILE GIVES OPINIONS OF POLAR EXPLORATION

Says If Going North in Future Will Use Ship Similar To Lost Italia

Canadian Press

ROME, Aug. 5.—Many scientific observations, including the notebook of Dr. Finn Malmgren, Swedish meteorologist who sacrificed himself in order to better the chances of other members of the expedition, were saved from the dirigible Italia disaster off Spitzbergen. This was revealed by General Umberto Nobile in an interview published in the Fascist newspaper Brillante.

General Nobile said in the interview that the valuable notebook was found between slabs of ice.

The leader of the expedition added that if he were to return to the pole he would employ a dirigible of the same type as the Italia. He said his experiences had suggested only a few minor changes as desirable.

He points out that the Italia had spent 134 hours in the air frequently under unfavorable conditions and had covered more than five thousand miles. He said that most of this mileage was gained over regions that were previously unexplored.

War Is Declared By Taxi Owners

United Press

DETROIT, Aug. 5.—Stench bombing, beating of drivers and passengers and smashing of windows with sledge hammers marked the first day of Detroit's taxi cab rate war.

The cutting of rates to five cents for each third of a mile by a large company brought on the war, which, police said tonight, showed no signs of abating.

Forty-five cabs belonging to the company which cut the rate have been damaged. Cabs of other companies which did not cut their rates were stolen and later found wrecked.

Western Gazelle

ETHEL CATHERWOOD

Performing with the same grace and poise that has characterized her sensational work in Canada, Saskatoon's own Ethel jumped her way into the hearts of Amsterdam Olympic spectators and officials Sunday, won the women's high jump with a leap of 5 feet 3 inches and scored another triumph for Canada. Ethel's performance was heralded with enthusiasm second only to the ovation given young Percy Williams of Vancouver for winning the 100 and 200 metres sprints at the Olympic games. The former local collegiate girl is credited with a new world's record at Amsterdam, although she cleared the bar at the same height in the Canadian women's Olympic finals at Halifax some weeks ago.

WARSHIP CHIEF LOSES HIS POST

Commander of Dauntless, Grounded at Halifax, Is Sentenced

Canadian Press Cable

LONDON, Aug. 5.—A naval court martial held at Portsmouth yesterday found the charge proved against Lieut. Commander T. R. Beatty of giving a wrong course for the British cruiser Dauntless, which grounded when entering Halifax harbor on July 2. The court sentenced Beatty to be dismissed from his ship and severely reprimanded.

The prosecution alleged the accused officer had failed to take reasonable care in checking his chart, considering the weather conditions for entering Halifax harbor.

Lieut. Commander Beatty admitted his error in giving his course but contended the mishap was caused by his scrupulous care in trying to identify a buoy, which, he said, was incorrectly charted which caused the ship's grounding.

RAID NIGHT CLUBS

LONDON, Aug 5.—Scotland Yard has raided more than 20 London clubs during the last four months in connection with a general cleanup campaign here, police revealed today.

Deny Examiners Sight Of Books

Canadian Press

ST. LOUIS, Aug. 5.—The International Life Insurance Company with headquarters here is "apparently short approximately $2,500,000 in securities," says a statement issued tonight by Charles R. Detrick, insurance commissioner.

"When six of the examiners were in Chicago July 23 and 24 to check about $3,500,000 of securities alleged to be in possession of R. C. Toombs, president of the International Life Insurance Company, the examiners were denied sight of the securities by Mr. Toombs, or access to books by Mr. Toombs," the statement reads.

Daddy Must Pay Daughter's Keep

United Press

PARIS, Aug. 5.—French courts have decided that a man is his daughter's keeper.

Mlle. Germaine Cahen D'Anvers went to court to oblige her father, Count Hubert Cahen D'Anvers, to support her when she established a separate home in Paris after failing to agree with her parents.

She went to work in a business office at a salary of 400 francs a month but it cost her 1,500 francs a month to live. She sued her father to collect the difference and the court decided in her favor.

FINDS WIFE IS VICTIM OF DEGENERATE KILLER

Los Angeles Clubman Returns Home to Find Battered Body; Man Held

Canadian Press

LOS ANGELES, Aug. 5.—Victim of a degenerate slayer Mrs. Myrtie L. Mellus, 41, wealthy and socially prominent, was found murdered in her home here late this afternoon. A suspect, who gave his name as Pat Kelly, 38, was found hiding in a closet in the house and was captured by the police.

The nude and battered body of Mrs. Mellus was found by her husband, Frank Mellus, clubman and vice-president of a wholesale canvas goods company when he returned from an all-day fishing trip. Officers from three police stations were rushed to the scene and a cordon of men was thrown about the entire neighborhood.

While the premises and house swarmed with police, a slight noise was heard in downstairs closet. In a corner of the closet Kelly was found crouching. He made a futile attempt to escape through a window but was immediately overpowered by two detectives.

How She Does It

Ethel Catherwood, former Bedford Road Collegiate athletic star, is shown here practising at her favorite event, the high jump. The photograph was taken here last summer when Ethel was in training for the Canadian women's championships at Toronto. Incidentally the popular local girl went east and won the high jump with a leap of 5 feet 1-8 inch.

GIVE DETAILS FOR HARVEST AID IN WEST

Arrangements Made to Bring 10,000 Men From Old Land

Only Healthy Workers of Manual Type Will be Sent to Canada

Canadian Press Cable

LONDON, Aug. 5. — Wireless telephone conversations between British and Canadian Immigration authorities in London and Ottawa figured in the successful conclusion to the negotiations whereby 10,000 British unemployed will be sent to Canada to assist in the harvesting operations.

FILL THE JOBS

According to details announced here today, up to 10,000 men are required to fill the jobs and the Dominion government has expressed a preference for men from the mining areas. A special reduced fare of £12 (about $60) each way is announced. Men wishing to undertake the journey must be used to hard, manual work and be between 28 and 40 years

TURN T OPAGE 5—COLUMN 2

DOMINION TRADE FIGURES HIGHER

Increase in Imports is Responsible; Drop In Exports

Canadian Press

OTTAWA, Aug. 5.—The foreign trade of Canada during the fiscal year ended March 31, 1928, reached a greater physical volume than in any previous year.

The increase in imports was responsible for this improvement as there was a slight decline in exports.

The total trade of Canada for the fiscal year ended March 31, 1928, was valued at $2,359,412,000 compared with $2,298,446,000 in 1927 and $2,256,029,000 in 1926. The increase over 1927 amounted to $60,946,000 or 2.2 percent and over 1926 to $103,383,000 or 4.6 percent.

Imports in 1928 show a decided improvement over 1927 and 1926 while exports show a decline. Imports in 1928 amounted to $1,108,956,000 compared with an importation in 1927 valued at $1,030,893,000 and in 1926 at $927,329,000. The increase in the imports over 1927 amounted to $78,063,000 or 7.3 percent and over 1926 to $181,627,000 or 19.6 percent. The statistics show that the export trade (domestic and foreign combined) was valued in 1928 at $1,250,456,000. This was divided between $1,228,207,000 Canadian produce exported and $22,249,000 foreign exports. This total compares with $1,267,573,142 in 1927 or a decrease of 1.1 percent.

LIBERALS WIN

United Press

BALBOA, Aug. 5.—Early returns in the National election here today indicated an overwhelming victory for the Liberal (Government) party ticket headed by Floren-Clo Harmodio Arosmena, only candidate for the presidency.

SOVIET WANTS TO SIGN KELLOGG'S PEACE PACT

Foreign Minister Hinting of Necessity of Permitting Russia to be Party

United Press

MOSCOW, Aug. 5.—George Tchitcherin, foreign minister of the Soviet republic, issued a statement to newspapers today, hinting at the necessity of the Soviet being one of the original participants in secretary of state Kellogg's anti-war treaty.

Tchitcherin said the United States' failure to invite the Soviet to sign the pact indicates "a desire to make the pact an instrument of isolation and struggle against the Soviet."

The statement asserted that the pact was incapable of preventing wars "because it does not provide for obligatory disarmament."

Blame Labor Fight For Bakery Blast

Canadian Press

SPOKANE, Aug. 5.—The plant of the Silver Leaf Baking Company in an outlying business section was dynamited early today. The bakery has been operating for three months on an open shop basis and police ascribe the dynamiting to labor troubles.

Both the large ovens in the plant, valued at $5,000 each were damaged so badly that the owner, L. L. Francis, said they will have to be rebuilt.

ENGINE THROWS TRIO TO DEATH

Speeding Maritime Train Hurls Automobile Off Level Crossing

Canadian Press

MONTREAL, Aug. 5.—Three persons were killed and three others injured, two of them seriously, when an eastbound Canadian National Railway passenger train and a light open touring automobile came together at a railway crossing at St. Basil, 20 miles from St. Hyacinthe, Quebec, today.

THE DEAD

William Burrows, 43; his wife, 40, and a brother, Charles, 35.

The injured are:

Willie Burrows, 18; Alberta Burrows, 14, and Gertrude Burrows, 9.

Willie and Gertrude are in a critical condition. The dead and injured were all residents of Montreal.

There were no eyewitnesses to the accident but the train was travelling at a high rate of speed. The bodies of the dead were picked up 200 feet from the crossing. The automobile was completely demolished. The accident occurred within one thousand feet of the St. Basil station.

The train is known as train No. 2, the Maritime express. It proceeded for the maritimes after arrangements had been made to postpone the inquest until Wednesday.

A statement issued by the railway states that the public crossing at which the accident occurred gives a clear view in both directions and that the warning bell was ringing and that the engine whistle had been blown.

The bodies were taken to Hyacinthe and the injured placed in the hospital. Willie is reported to be so badly cut about the face as to be hardly recognizable. Gertrude suffered a fractured thigh and ankle, her face was badly cut, her skull was gashed and she is thought to have internal injuries.

HUNDREDS OF OFFICERS AFFECTED BY SHAKEUP

Complete Reorganization of Chicago Police Force Is Forecast

United Press

CHICAGO, Aug. 5.—Complete reorganization of the Chicago police department was forecast today as Acting Police Commissioner William F. Russell recently appointed to succeed Michael Hughes, engaged in further conferences with his aides regarding the shake-up.

John Stege, new deputy police commissioner, today ordered the payroll list of the entire department revised. This order followed closely the sweeping edict Saturday of Commissioner Russell, transferring 328 officers, including 19 captains, 13 lieutenants and 26 sergeants.

The Russell order affected officers in the "bloody twentieth" ward where gambling and racketeering, the cause of much violence in Chicago in recent months, had been flourishing.

The underworld was startled by Russell's move and many were said to have closed their doors Saturday night before the new regime, which started work today, had moved into the ward. Bootleggers, gamblers, racketeers and other vice lords were said to be preparing to "hide out" until after the November election.

Aleep At Wheel, Pilot Suspended

Canadian Press

MONTREAL, Aug. 5.—Sentence of twelve months suspension of his license was imposed to Pilot F. X. Rivard, of Groundines, Que., for sleeping at his post aboard the Meaford, of the Canada steamship lines, which grounded off Cape De La Madeleine, July eighth. The court took into consideration his 17 years service and suspended him until July 17, 1929.

Violent Storms Causing Great Damage In Ontario

Canadian Press

OTTAWA, Aug. 5.—A series of brief wind, rain, hail and electric storms which raked this district over the week-end did thousands of dollars damage to vegetable and standing grain crops. It was the second week-end in succession in which silos were blown over, houses unroofed, large trees cracked at their bases and phone and electrical utility services disrupted by posts being flattened.

Violent thunderstorms, coming on the heels of a four-day heat wave, and accompanied by high winds, hail and rain, swept over the eastern states on Saturday night, leaving a trail of death and damaged property.

At Sharon, Mass., Paul Reader, Salvation Army captain, was killed by a bolt of lightning while he was helping to bring several hundred children bathers to safety as the storm broke over Lake Massopaeg.

Two bathers drowned near Boston and considerable property damage

TURN TO PAGE 5—COLUMN 1

VESSEL PICKS TWO FLIERS FROM OCEAN

Polish Aviators Fail To Make Westward Hop to N.Y.

Circle Over Sea; Injured In Crash Off Coast Of Portugal

Canadian Press

LISBON, Portugal, Aug. 5.—The Polish aviators, Majors Idzkowski and Kubala, after being rescued at sea off Portugal yesterday when their attempt to span the Atlantic came to an abrupt end, were landed today at Leixoes, near Oporto, Portugal.

IN HOSPITAL

The German steamer Samos which took them from their smashed plane also brought the Sesqui plane into port.

One of the two aviators injured his arm in a fall aboard the steamer. So serious was it that he was sent to the military hospital at Oporto when the ship docked this morning. It was said later, however, that both airmen, injured in the crash, expected to be able to leave tomorrow for Paris which was their starting point.

HEAD FOR HOME

The aviators had been in the air since 4.46 a.m., Greenwich meantime, Friday, and in 35 hours of flying had made a great circle out over the Atlantic toward the Azores, during which they had been sighted by two steamships. It was radio reports from these vessels which first gave the world intimation that the Poles had abandoned their attempt to span the Atlantic and were headed back towards Europe. They had reached a point only 60 miles off Cape Finistere when trouble with their gasoline feed pipe forced an abrupt descent into the sea. The big plane struck the waves with such force that the wings were smashed. The crew of the Samos with difficulty extricated the aviators and turned their vessel for the nearest port.

PLUCKED BY SHIPS

For the second time in a week trouble with the fuel supply system had forced a plane into the sea while on an attempt to make the westward crossing of the Atlantic which has only once been accomplished in a plane.

For the second time, too, in so brief a space, aviators have been plucked by steamships from the waters in which so many of their daring predecessors had met death.

On Wednesday, Captain Frank T. Courtney, with three companions, had set out in a flying boat from the Azores to fly to Newfoundland. Half way across, a broken gas line had sprayed fuel against the hot motors so that the plane caught fire and forced a rapid descent. The flying boat made a safe landing and floated ten hours until a steamship reached the spot. That plane was abandoned.

MOTOR IS SANDWICHED BETWEEN STREET CARS

Four Have Narrow Escape in Toronto as Automobile Crushed on Track

Canadian Press

TORONTO, Aug. 5.—When the taxi in which they were riding was crushed between two street cars here Saturday, four persons had an almost miraculous escape from death. All four of them were taken to the hospital but only two required attention there, Mr. and Mrs. J. H. Kastener, whose injuries are painful but not serious. Mary, their two-month-old baby, and M. C. Moffatt, the driver, were unscathed. The taxi was struck with terrific impact by one street car and hurled against another coming from the opposite direction and was then sandwiched between the two. The automobile was so badly demolished that the passengers were removed through the roof.

FLAPPER FANNY SAYS:

Pity the poor chiropractor. He never gets anything but back pay.

HIGHER, STRONGER, FASTER

Many of Saskatchewan's athletes put the province on the world map in the 1920s. Earl Thomson, who was born in Birch Hills and moved to California at age eight, won a gold medal for Canada in the 100-meter hurdles and set a world record at the 1920 Olympics in Antwerp. Wrestler James Trifunov of Regina competed in three Olympic Games and won a bronze medal at the Amsterdam Olympics in 1928. Saskatoon's Stan Glover helped Canada win the bronze in the 4x400 relay that same year. But none were as outstanding as Ethel Catherwood, "The Saskatoon Lily." Catherwood was born in Hannah, North Dakota, in 1908, but she grew up in Scott. She won her first high-jump competition at a meet in Wilkie. Her family moved to Saskatoon in 1925, and Catherwood participated in baseball, basketball, and track and field. She set a world high-jump record in Regina, and then headed to the Amsterdam Games. At those 1928 Olympics, the first in which women were allowed to compete, she cleared five feet, two and 9/16 inches in the high jump to win the gold medal. Catherwood was also named the prettiest athlete of the Games by a New York correspondent.

Ladies' driving competition, Wascana Golf Course, Regina, August 23, 1925

Members of Canada's 1928 Olympic team. Ethel Catherwood, "The Saskatoon Lily," is third from the left

The Regina Pats Memorial Cup champions, Regina, 1925

Girls' softball team, Success, 1928

Ukulele players, Saskatoon, 1926

Leader-Post carrier boys, Capitol Theatre, Regina, 1929

CHAPTER FIVE

In July of 1937, Annie had given birth to twin daughters. "Never thought he had it in him," Sean had said at the time, then added almost sadly, "Twill be the only seed to yield a crop around this goddamn place this year."
— From Who Has Seen The Wind, *by W.O. Mitchell*

Hope was a thing already in desperately short supply on July 5, 1937, as residents of southern Saskatchewan woke to another of the hot, dry mornings that had become cruelly commonplace during eight straight summers of drought. But on that day, newspapers across the province were inviting readers to squander what little hope they had left on the rescue mission for a missing American aviator named Amelia Earhart and on peace talks between Great Britain and Germany.

By day's end, the only news that mattered to anyone anywhere on the Prairies was once again the weather. Nearly a decade of living in the Dust Bowl had hardened many of the farmers and townsfolk to the disastrous whims of nature, but on July 5, the souls who lived in the south Saskatchewan plains near the American border would endure the hottest day in Canadian history.

The record books recall that temperatures soared to 45°C (113°F) in both Midale and Yellow Grass, farming villages about eighty kilometres apart in the southeast corner of the province. What the record books don't recall is that it was perhaps even hotter that day in the city of Weyburn — located midway between Midale and Yellow Grass along the Canadian Pacific Railway's famous

LEFT PAGE: Army engineers en route to Dundurn, 1937

ABOVE: Bennett buggy outside Mooney's Hardware Store, Biggar, 1933

Sanitorium van, Regina,
circa 1930s

Soo Line — where a reading of 45.5°C (114°F) was taken on a federal government thermometer.

Wherever the record was precisely set, Canada's all-time high temperature marked a dramatic low point in the history of Saskatchewan, which in 1937 would suffer its greatest crop failure and its greatest economic crisis, and where it seemed the Great Depression might drag on forever.

The newspapers recorded the sense of panic that gripped the province as temperatures reached unprecedented levels.

Under the July 6 headline "Droughtland Disaster," the *Regina Leader-Post* described how federal agriculture minister and former Saskatchewan premier James Gardiner declared "a disaster of the first magnitude" and cancelled meetings scheduled in Edmonton to rush back to Regina. Within days, special relief programs were announced for stricken farmers.

"The searing blasts of heat waved into Weyburn and over the surrounding area from the southwest — appearing to blow straight off the great desert area of the northwestern United States," said that week's *Weyburn Review*. "It was the most devastating type of day ever experienced in the Weyburn area."

The stock market crash of October 1929 had sent the whole Western world reeling and tossed all of Canada's provinces into social and economic turmoil. But in Saskatchewan, the crisis would be compounded by a climatic catastrophe — nine consecutive years of drought, season after season of skeletal harvests and a gathering dread that the scorched-earth summers of the Thirties would become a permanent feature of life in the province.

"With little money available to buy gasoline for tractor, truck and car, farmers turned back to horses in those areas where they could at least grow enough feed for the horses," noted Jim Wright in his 1955 history of Saskatchewan.

Bennett buggies — automobiles stripped of their motors and pulled by

horses — became the Depression's most famous symbol of lost prosperity, immortalizing the country's Conservative prime minister, R.B. Bennett, as a hapless figure in the face of disaster.

Despair turned to political dissent in July 1935 when nearly 2,000 protesters from across Western Canada arrived by rail in Regina as part of a planned On-to-Ottawa trek aimed at pressuring the federal government to create jobs and improve relief programs. On July 1, a peaceful demonstration in the Saskatchewan capital turned ugly after police ill-advisedly moved in to arrest protest leaders. A city police officer was killed in what became known as the Regina Riot, and scores of protesters were hurt — including one, it has only recently been revealed, who probably died of his injuries.

Bennett was ousted in an election that year, just as Saskatchewan's Conservative premier James Anderson had been a year earlier. The Liberal tide that put Gardiner back in power in Regina and Mackenzie King in the prime minister's office in Ottawa brought more financial relief to the West but no end to the misery of drought and unemployment that seemed more and more likely to go on forever.

The crushing weight of that possibility was never greater than on the sizzling Monday afternoon of July 5, 1937, when Isabelle Eaglesham and several of her co-workers at Weyburn city hall retreated to the coolest place in the building for some relief.

"We all went into the vault where they would lock up the important papers and all that," she has recalled. "It was a little better, but not much."

Eaglesham, perhaps better than anyone left alive, remembers Canada's hottest day. It is her mission to remember; she is Weyburn's leading keeper of the past, author of its best-known local history book, one of the founders of the town museum and — at the age of ninety in this centennial year — a revered citizen nearly as old as the province itself.

She says the wheat fields around Weyburn were already beginning to wilt that summer of '37, but the searing heat of early July "finished the crops off. Everything was brown. The grass on July 1 was usually bright green, but not in 1937."

She believes the Souris River, which runs through Weyburn, became so dry that year that "it disappeared" along one stretch near the town. At home "you could hardly get a trickle" from the bathtub faucet, which in those days was always "covered with the dust that would seep through every crack and crevice" of every house.

Weyburn, Midale and Yellow Grass lie along an edge of the area known as Palliser's Triangle, named for the 19th-century explorer who had warned against ever settling the arid lands of southern Saskatchewan and Alberta. The record heat wave of 1937 had folks wondering if their towns would be swallowed forever by blowing topsoil and silt.

"That year of drought, dust, heat and grasshoppers will be remembered as the most complete crop failure ever experienced," writes John Archer in *Saskatchewan: A History*. "An infestation of army worms and an epidemic of encephalomyelitis added to the miseries of the worst year yet."

"I think everybody was kind of depressed at that moment," remembers Eaglesham. "People were saying, 'This place is going to turn into a desert.'"

Bizarre scenes were witnessed across the province on July 5, the excessive heat perhaps stoking some imaginations. Or perhaps not.

"One enterprising citizen (in Weyburn) broke an egg on the city pavement which evaporated and dried up before it had a chance to cook," reported the

Storefront promoting the City of Saskatoon relief effort, circa 1935

Leader-Post. "Even with fans in operation, thermometers in a large city store had a reading of 104 with chocolates and other perishable goods melting in their show cases."

Candles, it was said, "wilted and drooped into half moons," and "gramophone records in a downtown shop window withered into streams of wax." Asphalt roads "became soft and oozy and car tires screamed as motorists turned corners."

And for "fair-skinned people the day was bad," one writer noted. "Many, despite the use of oil and other preparations, found their necks and backs blistering."

Lake Johnston, south of Moose Jaw, once "the Mecca of duck hunters from the United States," dried up and exposed "its eye-burning bed of white alkali." Farmers are also described "picking up buffalo bones" from other evaporated lakes and ponds.

"Strange cyclonic winds," "dust clouds resembling fog" and fires wrought by "the blazing sun on dry timber" were also reported.

"With Weyburn limp and listless under the terrific heat pressure, a wild dust storm suddenly swept over the area around six o'clock Monday night," the *Review* recounted in its description of Canada's hottest day:

"The sky in all directions apparently miles high was quickly transformed into a swirling mass of dust. Huge black and white storm clouds showed at intervals towering to great heights while lower formations were driven northwards by swirling wind currents, which made the whole sky an ominous looking sight.

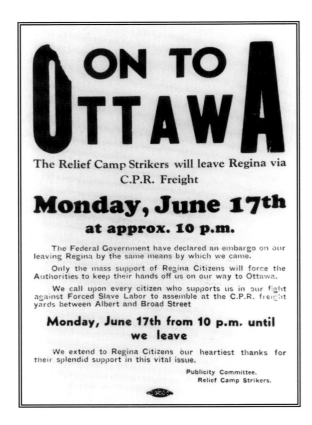

Poster, 1935

Poster, 1939

"But nothing serious developed. A few drops of rain fell in Weyburn. The clouds were driven rapidly northwards and out of sight, dissipating the promise of precipitation to ease the denseness of the hot, dusty atmosphere."

Even the day's breathless news accounts, peppered with strange sights and wild stories of freak weather, reflected the deeper social upheaval being created by the relentless heat:

"No organized exodus was seen of drought land farmers to greener pastures," said the *Leader-Post*, "but a few families were on the highways, moving out with what possessions they could assemble on trucks, touring cars of ancient vintage or in wagons."

Eaglesham describes Weyburn as a city prone to climatic extremes, where "it gets very cold and very hot and you just have to learn to be adaptable." The title of her own local history, *The Night the Cat Froze in the Oven*, suggests a community shaped by its rich experience of bizarre weather — from cat-killing winters to the dog days of summer.

"He wondered why such days were called 'the dog days,'" wrote W.O. Mitchell, Weyburn's most famous native son, inside the mind of the young boy whose experiences of the Depression in south Saskatchewan are captured in the literary classic *Who Has Seen the Wind*.

"Because the dogs lay sprawled in the dust, perhaps, their long, wet tongues spilled from a corner of their mouths; or because the days themselves had the loose laziness of a hot and tired sheep dog …

Cree reserve, 1931

"The air was hot and dry without a hint of rain in it, or in the sky decked with high puffs of cloud. Houses across the street were submarine in the distorting lift and tremble of rising heat."

The rains finally came to south Saskatchewan in mid-July — too late to prevent the worst-ever harvest in the province. The next year's crop was pretty much a wipeout, too, thanks to an infestation of grasshoppers.

Finally, just in time for the alternative anguish of another world war, the drought ended in 1939 and farmers in the Weyburn area began reclaiming their lands through irrigation, improved agricultural methods and massive federal government support.

"There was always something," says Eaglesham, describing how the plucky farmers and townsfolk of south Saskatchewan always kept a reserve of humour during their darkest days.

"People used to say when it was so hot and dry that at least we wouldn't have so many mosquitoes."

The drought years, for all of the crops ruined and hardships weathered, did yield something good and lasting: an unshakable Saskatchewan spirit that's not only central to the province's identity today but also part of the psyche of the nation. In his eloquent assessment of the Depression experience in the province, historian Edward McCourt recounted how the trials of the 1930s — and particularly the nadir of 1937 — had a galvanizing effect on Saskatchewan's character.

"The wheat crop that year averaged two-and-one-half bushels to the acre. But there was little thought of quitting — and none at all of moving to the Ontario bush," McCourt wrote. "The bewilderment and despair of the earlier years had by 1937 given way to a sterner emotion, and the people now took a kind of defiant pride in showing the world their strength to endure, without flinching, the worst that nature could do to them. 'The country is dismal, scorched, smashed,' the mayor of Assiniboia said, 'but the people are magnificent.' He was right. No one could survive nine years of hell without courage. Nor without faith — not in a benevolent god, but in one's own capacity to endure."

Earth, Wind and Fire

The collapse of the stock market in October 1929 alone would have been enough to destroy the optimism enjoyed by Saskatchewan's farm families, but the vagaries of nature is what crushed them. Canada's greatest farm emergency saw the province's population decline dramatically after so many had been battered by poverty and hopelessness. "I tell you, God must have been punishing us for sins of the world in them years," one farmer told Dave Broadfoot in his oral history *Ten Lost Years*. Battered by a steady unforgiving wind, blinded by dust storms and burned by a searing heat, Saskatchewan families subsisted on pig mash (mixed with hot water and molasses), wizened vegetables and the kindness of strangers as their fellow Canadians held tag days and bake sales to raise money for their relief. Drifting soil seeped under doors and windows, dusting everything in a filmy, grey powder. By 1937, two-thirds of Saskatchewan's farm population was destitute — and many abandoned their farms for the cities or left the province entirely.

Sand-blown corn crop, near Rosthern, August 23, 1938

Estevan-Kirby area, 1939

Settler leaving the homestead, Kindersley, 1935

THE REGINA RIOT

For the people of Regina, the 2,000 young men — mostly refugees from the relief camps in British Columbia — who got off the train in late June 1935 could have been their sons, brothers, even their husbands. Many of Regina's unemployed had been enlisted in make-work projects to drain Wascana Lake and build the Albert Street Bridge. Reginians understood: they welcomed the On-to-Ottawa trekkers, housed them in Exhibition Stadium and raised $1,100, which they could ill afford, for their cause. Prime Minister R.B. Bennett was determined that the trekkers not show up en masse at Parliament Hill and ordered the RCMP to stop them at Regina. On July 1, a handful of the trekkers gathered in Market Square to address a rally. The RCMP and local police moved in. And the strikers retaliated. In the end, one city police detective was killed and many bystanders, police and trekkers were injured. One hundred and eighteen trekkers were arrested.

Newly arrived trekkers at Exhibition Stadium where they would stay for the two weeks they remained in Regina, Exhibition Stadium, June, 1935

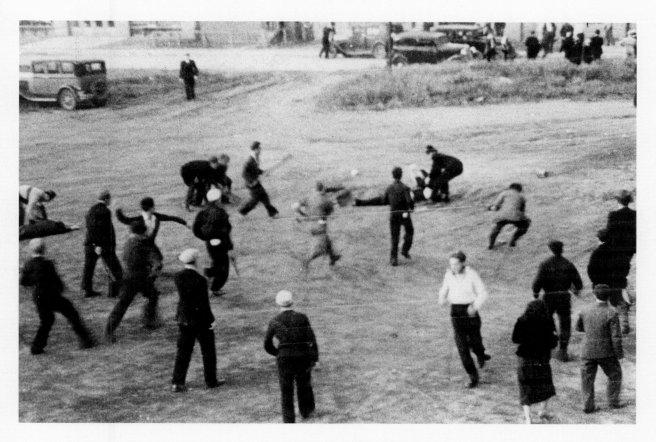

Trekkers move in on an injured police officer, now believed to be Detective Charles Miller who was killed during the riot, Market Square, July 1, 1935

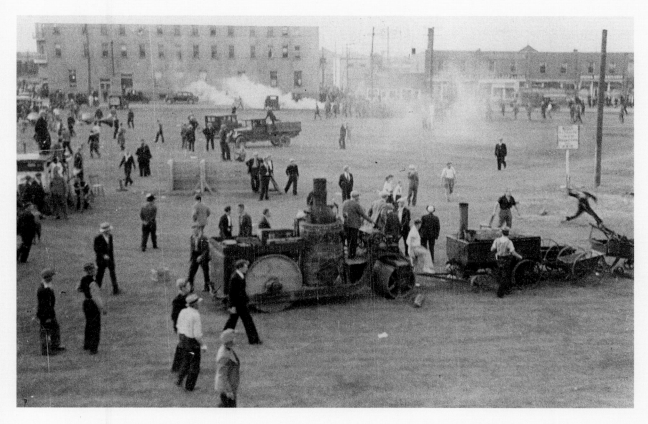

Trekkers attacked police with sticks, stones and parts from the city's tar-making machine, Market Square, July 1, 1935

Last EDITION

The Regina Daily Post

WEATHER FORECAST

FAIR AND COOL

VOL. XIV. NO. 247 TWENTY PAGES REGINA, SASKATCHEWAN, MONDAY, OCTOBER 21, 1929 PRICE FIVE CENTS

WALL STREET MARKET COLLAPSE VIOLENT

STOCK HOLDERS LARGE, SMALL, GLAD TO SELL

MOST VIOLENT COLLAPSE IN RECENT TRADING OCCURS TODAY

Efforts of Banking Interests to Allay Liquidation, Unavailing

BULLETIN

NEW YORK, Oct. 21.—Powerful banking interests fought tooth and nail to save the stock market from complete demoralization today in one of the wildest storms of selling in the history of the New York Stock Exchange. Scores of leading issues were swept down $5 to $45 a share, some $2,500,000,000 in paper values disappearing during the decline, before mid-afternoon, when bull forces were able to present a firm front and lifted several important shares out of the low levels to which they had fallen.

By STANLEY W. PRENOSIL
(Associated Press Financial Editor)

NEW YORK, Oct. 21.—The stock market experienced one of the most violent collapses in recent financial history today, as large and small holders fell over each other to get rid of their stock at any price.

The trading facilities of the stock exchange were taxed to the limit. By early afternoon the ticker was more than an hour behind the trading which went forward at a pace equal to if not exceeding that of March 26 when the record day's turnover of 8,246,740 shares was reached.

Gains More Than Lost

Efforts of powerful banking interests to stay the tide of liquidation were unavailing. A score of important shares were bid up 3 to 13 1-2 points at the opening, but this only attracted new selling and the gains were more than lost in short order. Leading issues such as United States Steel receded from time to time. Scores of issues droped from five to 35 points and scores of new lows for the year were recorded.

Call money renewed at 6 per cent. but soon dropped to 5 and went begging at that figure.

U.S. Steel Drops

U.S. Steel after selling up three points to 212, dropped to 205, a new low for the movement, then rallied a few points. Such shares as General Motors, Montgomery Ward and Packard reached new lows for the year.

Auburn Auto broke 35 points to 340 which is 174 points below its 1929 peak. Simmons, People's Gas, Stone and Webster, General Electric, Radio, Youngstown Sheet, Standard Gas, Anchor Gas, Air Reduction, Columbia Carbon, Atchison, Pere Marquette, American Waterworks and Pacific Lighting were among issues dropping from six to twelve points.

The selling represented an enormous liquidation of weakened margin accounts and unloading by discouraged traders, who have felt keenly the sharp decline of the past six weeks. Selling orders poured into the market from all parts of the country and from abroad.

Auburn Auto went to $340, which contrasts with its high point of the year of $504. Such issues as American Waterworks, American Power and Light, North American Electrical Investors, Pacific Lighting, Standard Gas and Electric, Stone and Webster dropped $6 to $14.

The closing was weak.

High-priced shares continued to hold a prominent place in the demoralized selling.

Commercial Solvents (old) broke to 527, a loss of 138 points; Auburn Auto lost 45; People's Gas, 16; and Second National Investors, 10.

In the final hour the ticker was running 75 minutes behind.

Sales amounted to 7,000,000 shares.

Flapper Fanny Says:

Modernistic furniture is all about—but most people don't know what.

SHYNESS AMONG V.C.'S CAUSES FEW TO DECIDE

By THOMAS T. CHAMPION
(Canadian Press Staff Correspondent)

LONDON, Oct. 21.—The Prince of Wales, who will represent the King at the service before the cenotaph on Armistice Day, will again attend the celebration at Albert Hall in the evening of November 11, which will be under the presidency of Earl Jellicoe, head of the British Legion of Ex-Servicemen.

There is still a certain shyness among Victoria Cross holders in connection with the dinner to be given in the parliament buildings on November 9, when the Prince of Wales will preside. So far 185 V.C.'s have indicated their desire to attend, and this figure represents only a comparatively small proportion of the number of V.C.'s still living.

Gas in Suite Brings Death To 7 in N.Y.

(By Associated Press)

NEW YORK, Oct. 21.—A father and six motherless children were asphyxiated by illuminating gas as they slept in their three-room apartment on West 46th street Sunday.

Police found a pan of water on a kitchen stove which apparently had boiled over, extinguishing the flames and permitting the gas to flow into the rooms.

The bodies were discovered by a neighbor who went to the apartment to tell the father, Walter Cavanagh, a private chauffeur, that his employer had called him on the telephone.

SCULLIN MADE NEW PREMIER OF AUSTRALIA

(Canadian Press Cable, Via Reuters)

CANBERRA, Australia, Oct. 21.—James Henry Scullin is the new prime minister of Australia. The leader of the Labor party, he was commissioned to form a new ministry by Lord Stonehaven, governor-general, today, after Premier Stanley Bruce had tendered his resignation.

Premier Bruce had been in office since 1923. His Nationalist party was defeated and he lost his own seat in the recent general elections.

The new prime minister is 52 years of age and he started life as a farmer's boy near Ballarat. He goes into office pledged to uphold the federal system of arbitration of labor disputes. On arrival at the federal capital today he received a great popular welcome.

Probably Mr. Scullin will choose Hon. Edward G. Theodore, former premier of Queensland, as his treasurer and right-hand man.

Another member of the cabinet is expected to be Hon. J. A. Lyons, former Labor premier of Tasmania. Of the other prospective ministers, none have had any cabinet experience.

FOUR KILLED IN FREIGHT WRECK

SEATTLE, Wash., Oct. 21.—Four men were killed early Sunday when a Seattle-bound Great Northern train broke in two and then crashed together near the eastern entrance to the Cascade tunnel. It was thought that more bodies might be found under an overturned freight car which was to be raised today. The dead:

George Davis, 48, itinerant laborer.
George Ellsworth, 42, member of the Industrial Workers of the World.
Frank Sutton, Morton, Wash.
An unidentified man past middle age.

ACCLAMATIONS TOTAL SEVEN FOR ONTARIO

TWO CANDIDATES DISQUALIFIED, ADDING TO CONSERVATIVE ACCLAMATIONS

In All 237 Candidates in 112 Constituencies for October 30 Vote

(By Canadian Press)

TORONTO, Oct. 21.—The number of acclamations in the forthcoming provincial elections was raised to eight today when the nomination of Rev. A. E. Smith, Communist, in the constituency of Port Arthur, had been disallowed. This decision brings about an acclamation in that constituency for Brig.-General D. M. Hogarth, Conservative nominee.

There will be an election in Welland. After an investigation of the signatures on the nomination paper of Benjamin Hewitt, Liberal, the returning officer this afternoon ruled that there were sufficient bona-fide signatures thereon to render the nomination legal. To validate his nomination, Mr. Hewitt opposes Marshall Vaughan, Conservative member of the last legislature.

Errors Disqualify

The chief electoral officer, Allan M. Dymond, ruled that errors had disqualified Charles Marriott, Communist, in Sudbury and Mrs. Stewart Dies, Prohibitionist, in East Hastings. As a result, Hon. Charles McCrea, minister of mines, will receive an acclamation in Sudbury and James F. Hill, Conservative, will be elected without opposition to represent East Hastings.

Hon. Edward A. Dunlop, North Renfrew; Hon. J. R. Cooke, North Hastings; George W. Ecclestone, Muskoka; Col. T. A. Kidd, Kingston, and Arthur Ellis, South Ottawa, received acclamations.

Two More Protests

Mr. Dymond is expected to rule today on two protests involving candidates at Welland and Port Arthur. At Welland the returning officer was not satisfied that papers filed by Benjamin Hewitt, last night, Liberal nominee, were entirely in order. At Port Arthur, a protest was entered against the nomination of Rev. A. E. Smith, Communist. A number of signatories to his papers are under question on the ground of residence and nationality.

Nomination meetings produced few surprises. Considerable interest attaches to the statement by Anthony Marentette, Liberal candidate in Essex North, that W. E. N. Sinclair had approved his (Marentette's) stand on the liquor question. Mr. Marentette had advocated sale of beer by the glass in the dining rooms of hotels and reputable cafes. Mr. Sinclair refused last night to comment on the statement, but indicated he might have something to say today.

Ferguson Ill

Premier Ferguson, suffering from bronchitis, planned to continue his speaking campaign today with meetings in the constituency of Halton. Mr. Sinclair and J. G. Lethbridge, Progressive leader, also speak today.

At Brantford on Saturday, the Liberal leader called on Premier Ferguson to repudiate Clifford Case, Conservative candidate in North York, for his letter to applicants for old-age pensions. It was not enough, he said, for the premier to point out the result of the election would make no difference to pension payments.

The Canadian Press summary of official nominations shows the party designations and the nominees for each as follows:

Conservatives, 112.
Liberals, 87.
Progressives, 10.
Prohibitionists, 7.
Independent Conservatives, 7.
Communists, 6.
Labor, 3.
Independents, 3.
United Farmers of Ontario, 2

(Continued on Page 13)

Steamship Lines Offer Free Trip for V.C. Men

Three Lines on St. Lawrence Route Issue Joint Statement

(By Canadian Press)

MONTREAL, Oct. 21.—Free transportation from their homes in Canada to England to attend the Prince of Wales' dinner is assured to all Canadian holders of the Victoria Cross. Today, the Canadian Pacific Steamships, the White Star line and the Cunard line issued a joint statement announcing free ocean transportation. On Saturday the Canadian National Railways, through Sir Henry Thornton, announced they would carry any V.C. holder from his home to the seaboard.

Today's statement by the steamship companies says: "It is felt to be a distinct privilege by the steamship lines of the St. Lawrence route to act as hosts to Canadian wearers of the Victoria Cross on the ocean of their passage to England to attend the dinner to be given on November 9 by H.R.H. the Prince of Wales.

"As the latest possible sailings by which England may be reached in time are Ascania, Cunard line, October 25; Duchess of York, Canadian Pacific, October 25; Laurentic, White Star and Minnedosa, Canadian Pacific, October 26. Applications should be made immediately through accredited veterans' organizations."

Huge D.O-X Aeroplane Lifts 169 Passengers

Here's the great flying boat, D.O.-X, which performed the amazing feat today of flying for an hour carrying 159 passengers and a crew of 10 over Lake Constance, Switzerland. The great flying monster weighs 34 tons. Photos were taken on the ship's trial flight last August.

(By Associated Press)

ALTHENRHEIN, Switzerland, Oct. 21. D.O.-X, huge 12-engined flying boat, which was launched here last July, today made an amazing one-hour flight with a human load of 169, the first time in the history of aviation that so many persons have been carried into the air on any conveyance. The machine flew over Lake Constance, her motors working perfectly. The D.O-X carried 159 passengers and a crew of 10.

The flying boat, which may be used for a trans-Atlantic crossing for the purpose of trying out her capacities, was built in the greatest secrecy. She was designed to carry 40 passengers normally, but has accommodation for 100 if necessary. Her 12 engines can develop a total of 6,000 horsepower and each engine can be treated individually without affecting its neighbors.

10 Feet Thick Wings

The D.O-X measures 150 feet from tip to tail. Its wings are 10 feet thick and 150 feet from wing tip to wing tip. Six great turrets poject from each wing and each turret is equipped with two engines of 500 horsepower. The turrets are manned by mechanics who walk along a passage on the inside of the wings from one turret to another.

When the D.O-X was launched, last July, she carried 34 tons of weight and was able to get into the air with the greatest ease after a take-off run of only 500 yards. Other trials were similarly successful.

One of the features of the 'plane is her three decks, while another is that the machine can fly with only eight motors in use.

Dr. Dornier built the 'plane at Althenrhein, on the Swiss side of the German-Swiss frontier, because of the limitations on German aircraft imposed by the treaty of Versailles.

U.F.C. Backs McGeer Over Rates Fight

(Special Despatch)

OTTAWA, Oct. 21.—The Saskatchewan section, United Farmers of Canada, have decided definitely to support the appeal now before the governor-in-council for the removal of the mountain differential and the reduction of grain rates—domestic and export—to the Pacific coast.

G. G. McGeer, whose appeal to the governor-in-council was heard by the cabinet last week, received a telegram this morning from Frank Eliason, secretary of the Saskatchewan section of the U.F. of C. It reads:

"We are in full accord with your demands for equalization of grain and freight rates and for the removal of the mountain differential. Carry on the good work."

In recent hearing the government of Saskatchewan took no positive part in the proceedings. W. H. McEwen, K.C., counsel for the province, stated that the new government was not prepared to take a position on these matters at this time. Mr. McEwen, however, was careful not to commit the province in any way and reserved the right of the province when the appeal of the three far western provinces is heard a few months hence, to go into all the points raised in the McGeer appeal.

SASKATCHEWAN AND MANITOBA CONFERRING

WINNIPEG, Oct. 21.—Representatives of Manitoba and Saskatchewan are now planning to confer with a view to reaching a solution of the freight rate problem on the prairies, stated Jules Prud'homme, K.C. With A. B. Hudson, K.C., Mr. Prud'homme represented the city of Winnipeg in protesting before the Dominion cabinet last week against freight rate changes.

If the Saskatchewan-Manitoba parley is successful, said the solicitor, Alberta will be invited to join the discussion and later British Columbia. An agreement, points out Mr. Prud'homme, would obviate necessity of preceeding with the western government's petition now pending and due to be heard in three months. It would not, however, interfere with the cabinet giving its decision on the appeal just heard from British Columbia farmers.

Mr. Prud'homme considered that there was every indication that the mountain differential would not be removed.

Grain Grown Any Year Is Now Eligible

Federal Department of Agriculture Makes World's Grain Fair Announcement

(Special Despatch)

OTTAWA, Oct. 21.—Grain grown in any year is eligible for competition at the World's Grain Exhibition which is to take place at Regina in 1932, the Department of Agriculture announces.

No restrictions are put upon the year in which the grain is grown and grain which has been entered in other competitions is eligible for participation in the prize list which totals $200,000.

The British Columbia government has offered a challenge trophy to the B.C. exhibitor scoring the highest aggregate number of points in the world's grain show classes at the winter fairs of 1929, 1930 and 1931.

QUICK GLANCE AT MARKETS

Winnipeg Grain—1⅛ to 1⅞ higher.
Chicago Grain—Early average lower.
Toronto Mines—Unsettled.
Toronto Stocks—Unsettled.
Montreal Stocks—Unsettled.
New York Stocks — Violent break.
Calgary Oil—Steady.

The Weather

The weather in the Western Provinces has been mostly fair and mild.

Temperatures

Minimum and maximum temperatures for the 24-hour period ending at 6 o'clock last night follow:

	Max.	Min.	Prec.	
Vancouver	56	51		Fair
Victoria	58	49		Cloudy
Edmonton	54	26		Clear
Calgary	54	40		Fair
Indian Head	55	34		Cloudy
Broadview	55	36		Cloudy
Moosomin	50	35		Cloudy
Brandon	55	29		Cloudy
Winnipeg	54	30		Clear
Toronto	66	59		Cloudy
Montreal	68	52		Fair
Halifax	60	46		Fair
Elbow	60	27		Clear
Moose Jaw	63	38		Fair
Regina	**58**	**38**		**Clear**
Saskatoon	56	36		Clear
Prince Albert	60	38	.04	Clear
The Pas	52	38		Clear
Melfort	57	41	.10	Cloudy
Humboldt	49	28		Fog
Kamsack	62	32	.38	Clear
Yorkton	55	37		Cloudy
Medicine Hat	58	42		Fair
Lloydminster	55	34		Cloudy
Kindersley	55	33		Clear
Vidora	60	32		Clear
Assiniboia	58	40		Clear
Yellow Grass	59	34		Clear
Estevan	56	40		Clear
Shaunavon	54	31		Clear
Swift Current	62	40		Clear
Ottawa	74	46		Cloudy

Forecasts

Manitoba — Fair and somewhat cooler tonight and Tuesday.

Saskatchewan and Alberta—Fair and quite cool tonight and Tuesday.

BIG WELCOME FOR M'DONALD AT MONTREAL

HUGE CROWD GATHERS AT STATION TO HONOR LABOR PREMIER

Pipe Band Enlivens Proceedings; McGill to Confer Degree

By RAY BROWN
(Canadian Press Staff Writer)

MONTREAL, Oct. 21.—Montreal welcomed the Labor premier of Great Britain today. A great crowd, held back by lines of policemen, Bonaventure Station, gay with bunting, a pipe band with its stirring Scottish tunes and a beautiful warm day, furnished appropriate setting for the official welcome of Canada's largest city to the Dominion's distinguished guest.

The welcome was conveyed to Premier Ramsay MacDonald and his daughter by Mayor Camillien Houde, who, with a gold chain about his neck, climbed aboard the prime minister's car at 10 o'clock this morning.

Crowd There First

But long before the Mayor of Montreal arrived at the station, the populace was doing the honors. The special train which bore Mr. MacDonald from Ottawa to Montreal arrived here at 9 o'clock, and the crowd had already begun to gather. It grew and grew until, by the time that the British premier was ready to descend and drive from the station to his rooms at the Ritz-Carlton hotel, it was packed closely about the station and neighborhood. To the ears of Mr. MacDonald on board the car came the music from the Point St. Charles Pipe Band, which marched up and down the station platform, regaling him and the waiting crowd with music.

Sir Henry Thornton, president of the Canadian National Railways, was one of the first callers. He visited the train shortly after 9 o'clock and remained on board until Mr. MacDonald, his daughter and members of their party were ready to descend. Then Sir Henry accompanied them. As the British premier stepped down from his train to the red carpet laid on the station platform, a dozen or so photographers demanded pictures. Mr. MacDonald, his daughter, Mayor Houde and Sir Henry lined up obligingly, with the pipers as a suitable background, and the photographers had an excellent opportunity to do their work.

Police-Lined Lane

Then the party moved through the police-lined lane, between crowded humanity, to the motor cars waiting in front of the station. The cars moved off as people cheered, and proceeded up Windsor street to the hotel, where the British premier had a numbr of engagements before speaking at a luncheon of the Canadian Club.

Among those who greeted Mr.

(Continued on Page 13)

B.C. GOVERNMENT OUT $5,279,000 IN LAND SCHEMES

VICTORIA, B. C., Oct. 21.—Losses suffered by the government of British Columbia on land settlement schemes launched since the war will total $5,279,000, according to an estimate prepared by special auditors who have been making an intensive investigation of the province's finances.

In this estimate the auditors find that the land settlement boards deficits since 1917 have totalled approximately $1,561,000. The loss on the Sumas reclamation scheme is placed at $1,750,000 and on the South Okanagan irrigation project at $1,827,000.

To Drill for Oil in Pasquai Hill District

Area South-west of The Pas in Saskatchewan to Be Investigated

(Special Despatch)

THE PAS, Man., Oct. 21.—The first big effort to probe the oil possibilities of the Pasquai hills, 100 miles southwest of The Pas in Saskatchewan, will be made in the near future, it was announced here Saturday by James Lawrence, representative of three eastern interests who are backing the projects. On the heels of a favorable report by Dr. K. Feige, who conducted a seizmatic survey, comes the decision to drill the properties as soon as machinery can be transported to the region.

The companies besides the venture are the Hamilton Petroleum of Hamilton, a firm of $1,000,000 backed by easterners; the Economic Petroleum, bonds and brokerage, of Hamilton, capitalization $500,000; and the Pasquai Oil Co., of Toronto, capitalization 1,000,000.

The Pasquai hills were prospected for oil several years ago and development work was undertaken, but lack of capital brought suspension of operations.

FORD HONORS EDISON WITH HUGE "PARTY"

DETROIT, Mich., Oct. 21.—Henry Ford's long planned project for a "big party" for his old friend, Thomas Edison, was realized today when 500 noted Americans, headed by President Hoover, joined in personal tribute to Edison while the rest of the world listened to the celebration by radio.

The occasion was the golden jubilee celebration commemorating the creation 50 years ago tonight of the inventor's incandescent light.

The day's program in honor of Edison started at 10 o'clock when President and Mrs. Hoover and Mr. and Mrs. Edison arrived at the Old Smith's Creek, Mich. railroad station in Ford's early American village at Dearborn. Almost 60 years ago the train butcher and newsboy Edison was running along the Grand Trunk at Smith's Creek to board a moving train with his wares. A kindly baggage man reached down and lifted Edison into his car by the ears. His ear drums were broken and he has been deaf since.

The station was moved to Dearborn last summer by Ford for the preservation as a part of the collection of Edisonia.

Four Aeroplanes Will Resume M'Alpine Search In Hinterland, Tuesday

W. Brintnell, Director, Will Hop Off For Bathurst Inlet

(By Canadian Press)

WINNIPEG, Oct. 21.—Four aeroplanes Tuesday are to resume the search for Col. C. D. H. McAlpine and seven companions marooned in the sub-Arctic for more than six weeks.

For two weeks, the "in-between" season has halted all air operations in the barrens, but it is now believed it is possible for ski-equipped 'planes to land on the frozen lakes.

With W. Brintnell directing the air hunt from Winnipeg, the advance squadron plans to hop off Tuesday on the trail of the lost McAlpine party, which disappeared from Baker Lake on September 8. From Baker Lake, the quartet of machines will follow the McAlpine route to Bathurst Inlet, 430 miles away on the Arctic coast of Canada.

The four 'planes will scour the entire route to Bathurst within four or five hours. If the McAlpine party is "down" somewhere between Baker L. and the ice-locked inlet, they should be discovered on the first hop. If, however, they have missed their bearing and flown off their route, they will probably be frozen in somewhere along the Arctic coast.

To Direct 'Planes

Captain G. S. Blanchet will direct the 'planes on their winter dash to the north coast. Aiding him in directing navigation will be Andy Cruickshanks, who came all the way from Prince George, B.C. The other three pilots will be Roy Brown, H. Hollick-Kenyon and William Spence. Pilot J. D. Vance is to remain at Baker Lake for the present, and four other 'planes are awaiting orders at Stoney Rapids and Cormorant Lake in the northern section of the prairie provinces.

In four days of fine flying weather, the entire search area can be covered, in the opinion of Brintnell. He considers that if it is possible for the four Blanchet 'planes to get away tomorrow on schedule, they may have discovered the lost McAlpine group before the end of the week.

Three of the advance quartet of 'planes are super-Fokkers of the Western Canada Airways fleet and the fourth is a Dominion Explorers' Fairchild.

Perfect flying weather seemed to be promised for the renewal of search activities. At Bathurst, where the temperature over the week-end dropped to eight degrees, a cloudless sky shone clear blue before a rising sun today. Reports quoted the temperature as 14 degrees above zero. The wind was negligible and visibility "good."

En route to Winnipeg for repairs, Pilot "Punch" Dickins, at Prince Albert, Sask., Sunday expressed confidence that the McAlpine party would be found safe and sound. He considered that with the winter garb they carried they would be able to dress warmly enough to offset the falling temperatures. Though Dickins, in two daring dashes to the north coast two weeks ago, covered more miles than any search flyer, he is not at present a member of the hunting ensemble and probably will not be summoned unless grave necessity arises at some later time.

Four Charred Bodies Discovered in Hay Stack

THINK FARMER KILLED WIFE, TOOK OWN LIFE

BELIEVE ALLGROVE MAN BURNED BODIES IN HAY STACK

Meagre Police Reports Reveal Tragedy in the Wadena District

The discovery of the remains of four charred bodies in a burned hay stack on a farm in the Allgrove district, north of Wadena, this morning is believed by police to have uncovered a triple murder, followed by a suicide.

Information received by R.C.M.P. headquarters from Prince Albert this morning was to the effect that it is believed that Laurin Berewin, farmer of the Allgrove district had taken the lives of his wife and two daughters during the night of Saturday, Oct. 19, or Sunday, Oct. 20.

He had then apparently placed the three bodies on a large haystack and set fire to it. When the stack was well alight Berewin is alleged to have himself walked into the flaming inferno to his own death. Police are inclined to think that the man carried a fire-arm with him into the flames and instantly killed himself before he was burned seriously.

The light of the burning stack lit up the sky for a large area and neighbors who went to the scene were surprised when they saw no trace of the Berewin family. Human remains were later found in the embers and R.C.M.P. informed. Sergeant Wood and Constable May, Rose Valley detachment, R.C.M.P., are investigating at the present time.

Poincare and Clemenceau On Sick List

"Tiger" of France Suffering From Effects of Cold; Operation on Poincare

(By Associated Press)

PARIS, Oct. 21.—Raymond Poincare, former French president and premier, underwent an operation for a pelvis disorder today, the second he has had in recent months for this trouble.

The physicians early issued the following bulletin:

"The second operation on M. Poincare was performed this morning under good conditions by Dr. Marion with the assistance of Drs. Gossett, Boivin and Pevard."

At the same time Georges Clemenceau, former premier and minister of war, was under the treatment of his physicians, who found him suffering from a slight cold.

They prescribed an application of ventouses or heated glass cups which have the same effect as mustard plasters.

In Private Clinic

M. Poincare resigned his premiership in the summer after he had secured ratification of the Young reparations plan by the French chamber of deputies. He at once submitted to a first operation for his troubles and began to rest and build up his health in preparation for the second ordeal today.

He was removed only last night from his home to a private clinic for the operation.

The former premier was in the best of spirits when he was taken to the operating room. He laughed as he told his doctors he did not want all the bedside details of his illness broadcast.

Briand, Visitor

"I don't want the newspapers discussing the color of my pyjamas or the form of my bed socks," he told them.

The first visitor to inquire as to the result of the operation and inscribe his name in the new visitors' book was Aristide Briand, who followed M. Poincare as head of the French government.

Other members of the government and notables came after him.

The former president was resting tranquilly, it was said at noon at the clinic, and his condition was most satisfactory.

N.Z. DEBATERS WIN

VANCOUVER, Oct. 21.—The debating team from Victoria College, New Zealand, opened its North American tour here Saturday by a victory over University of British Columbia debaters. The visitors upheld the negative of a resolution, "Resolved that the British Empire is in grave danger of disintegration," and received the unanimous decision of the three judges. The program includes debates with several universities in Canada and the United States.

So Let's Sing a Song of Cheer Again

Like all North Americans feeling the burden of the Depression, Saskatchewanians sought refuge in the popular culture of the day: feel-good movies starring Shirley Temple, Busby Berkley musicals, classics such as *Snow White and the Seven Dwarfs*, *Gone with the Wind*, *The Wizard of Oz*; bubbly anthems such as *Happy Days are Here Again*, *We're in the Money*, *Life is Just a Bowl of Cherries* and the daily comics in the newspapers that featured Popeye, Superman and Batman. Even during these desperate years, an appreciation of parties, dances and music remained.

Rex Theatre matinee, Regina, circa 1930s

The Third Page

The Star-Phoenix Goes Home. SASKATOON, SASKATCHEWAN, SATURDAY, OCTOBER 30, 1937. The Star-Phoenix Goes Home.

THOUSANDS FLOCK TO CITY FOR FIRST HOCKEY

Rink Epitomizes Unbounding Faith Of Saskatonians

West's Finest Ice Palace Ready for Today's Events; Building Represents Unswerving Optimism of Northern Saskatchewan

From the highways and byways, from the drouthland south of Regina to the lonely fringes of civilization in the North, from prosperous Manitoba and from Social Credit Alberta, they were converging on Saskatoon last night—coming here for a hockey game which had no significance (except to some players), for a game in which no Stanley Cup, Allan Cup or other bauble was at stake—but coming for a game and to see a rink which epitomized the courage of Saskatchewan.

SUCCESS DESPITE DEPRESSION

For today's game between two New York professional teams is the fulfillment of an old Saskatoon dream, a vision which was undertaken in depression times and carried to a successful conclusion in the darkest days Saskatchewan has known, in the days which will always go down in history as the year of the big crop failure.

Today these professional teams, representing the ultimate in hockey perfection, are playing on an artificial ice rink, which began as a small community enterprise and before its conclusion had aroused such widespread interest it had grown to be almost a north Saskatchewan undertaking.

ALL HELPFUL

It is the finest rink in Western Canada, made possible through the efforts of the $10 subscriber, through school children who donated their nickels to buy one share for their room, and finally through the untiring efforts of a group of local businessmen who demonstrated that old 'Saskatoon spirit' is still a vital force and that, despite depression and drouth, Saskatoon and its citizens will carry on.

This afternoon, the results of long and arduous months of worry, some pessimism and also inexhaustible optimism will be seen as the finest ice palace in the West, its playing area exactly the same as the famed Maple Leaf Gardens in Toronto, were flung open to public gaze.

Farmers who had not been in Saskatoon for several years, rural business folk who have had to watch the pennies in recent times, and hosts of others were among the teeming thousands on the city's streets this morning. The man with a safe job and the man on relief both managed to get tickets somehow. It was the occasion of a lifetime and not to be missed.

SPECIAL TRAINS

By noon Friday the eager spectators from the hinterlands had started to arrive here. Last night hundreds had reached the city and this morning they poured in by automobile, special trains and any conveyance they could grab.

At noon hotel accommodation was rapidly being exhausted and the folks were lined up at restaurants and lunch counters for lunch.

Today is Saskatoon's day! And royally are visitors and citizens preparing to enjoy it. The kids won't be the only persons shouting and yelling as Hallowe'en is observed in this city of pioneer history.

Workmen scurried about the rink last night, putting final touches here, smoothing out obstructions there and in the early hours of this morning the rink was ablaze with lights as the minutest detail was inspected in order to accommodate the expected 11,000 persons who will watch the first hockey games on artificial ice ever played in this Province. The ice surface itself was in perfect shape, the big clock had been placed in position, the radio announcing booth was ready and all those accoutrements which comprise a modern 'gardens' were being carefully scrutinized by Architect David Webster, smiling as the product of months of labor assumed shape.

TWO GAMES

There will be two games today. So great was the demand to see the noted players and to greet the accomplishment of Saskatoon's artificial ice rink, it was necessary to arrange for a second game instead of the one match originally scheduled. The first game, which was certain to attract a sell-out crowd, began at 2 o'clock and the night game, for which all tickets were sold before they were printed, starts at 9 o'clock.

There are other attractions in Saskatoon today but they shrink before this evidence that the West may be down but is never out.

Alright. There's the bell. Let's go.

Won't Permit Any Rowdyism Tonight

Taxpayers Have Been Hard Pressed, Police Chief Reminds Older Boys

Hallowe'en is the night when witches are said to romp across the countryside, and when little boys and girls enjoy parties where they "duck" for apples and generally have a good time.

Chief Donald this morning expressed the hope that the children would have lots of fun. The chief, however, did caution against property damage in the city; and stated that police would be on duty to see that no rowdyism would be tolerated.

He reminded older boys that taxpayers had been hard pressed during the past few years to keep their premises in good order, and that any attempts to damage property would be met by forces entrusted with the duty of upholding the law.

Patterson Visits Famous Parents

Saskatoon's most famous parents had a distinguished visitor on Friday.

Mr. and Mrs. George Cairns, parents of Hugh Cairns, V.C., were delighted when Premier Patterson, taking time from a busy day, visited them at their home and recalled incidents from last year's Vimy Pilgrimage.

The Premier unveiled the tablet in honor of Hugh Cairns at Valenciennes, France, during the Vimy trip and at that time became acquainted with the parents of the Saskatoon hero.

Premier Patterson was in Saskatoon for ceremonies centred on the formal installation of Dr. J. S. Thomson as president of the University of Saskatchewan.

TELEGRAPHY CLASS

Registration are still open for the telegraphy class at the Technical Collegiate.

The Weather

At 1 o'clock this afternoon the Star-Phoenix thermometer registered 49 degrees.

University of Saskatchewan readings at 8 o'clock this morning: Temperature, 26.3; barometer, 30.36; humidity, 85.

Summary of preceding 24 hours: Maximum temperature, 52; minimum temperature, 19; minimum mean temperature, 47; wind, average velocity, 14; maximum velocity, 30; direction northwest; 9.3 hours of sunshine; no precipitation.

Elevator Razed; Loss Is $50,000

Canadian Press

PRINCE ALBERT, Oct. 30. — Loss estimated at more than $50,000 in addition to 2,000 bushels of wheat was caused today, in an early morning blaze of unknown origin which levelled the Searle Grain Company's elevator and annex at Holbein, 22 miles west of here. The proportion of insurance carried is not known. The elevator was built about eight years ago and the annex was added two years later.

When Saskatoon Was Younger

From the Files of the Phoenix and the Star

TWENTY YEARS AGO

October 30, 1917.

The Canadians gained their position on Passchendaels Ridge.—Undine, the former Italian headquarters, was occupied by Austrian forces.—Plans were being considered by labor organizations for the formation of a provincial labor party.—Snow in the city brought an increase of 40 per cent in tram revenues.—The Sinn Fein organization in Ireland announced the draft of a constitution for the "New Irish Republic."

TEN YEARS AGO

October 30, 1927.

Heavy westerly gales in the Old Country took nine lives and wrought heavy property damage.—The City Park Ratepayers Association decided to run candidates in the civic elections.—Dr. Arthur Wilson, city medical officer, urged the improvement of organization for rural health.—Snow fell over much of the Province during the week-end.—The fifth anniversary of the Black Shirts march on Rome was celebrated by Fascists throughout Italy.

Latest Transportation

THIS is one Saskatchewan youth who hasn't let the times get him down. He is pictured here on the highway north of Prince Albert as he was approaching his Winter trapping grounds near the end of a 250-mile trek with his dogs and equipment. He is Joe Snyder and he spent the Summer on a farm near Quinton where he trained his three dogs after a day's work in the fields. On the express wagon he has most of his worldly possessions including his rifle and his blankets. On the trip he has made about 20 miles a day. His dogs get a loaf of bread each at the end of the day's run. He will spend the Winter near Meath Park trapping. The picture was taken by Mrs. J. M. Stevenson of Saskatoon near Red Deer Hill.

Collections $330,000

Ruling Soon if Education Levy Will Apply to Rummage Sales

REGINA, Oct. 29.—With most of the vendors' returns in for the two months' collections, the education tax total stood at $330,000 on Friday.

MAY REACH $360,000

L. S. Sifton, provincial tax commissioner, said he expected that additional collections from individuals, sources from outside the Province and contractors, banks and other institutions which are not licensed vendors, would bring the total up to $360,000.

Next week a ruling will be made by the commission as to whether the tax will be applied to church bazaars, rummage sales and similar functions.

News in Brief

FALLS TO DEATH

REGINA, Oct. 29.—Richard East, 73, suffered fatal injuries in a fall from a second storey ward window at the General Hospital this afternoon. He had been a patient there less than 24 hours. An inquest has been ordered.

BAND CONCERT

Well away to another big season, the Saskatoon Boys Band will give its third concert in the Tivoli Theatre at 9 o'clock Sunday evening. A well balanced program awaits the patrons, who are advised to come early for seats.

TOO MUCH BEER

Charged with purchasing six gallons of beer in one day, Phyllis Seidel, 435 Avenue F, south, pleaded guilty in city police court this morning through her attorney. A fine of $25 and $2.50 costs was imposed. The offense took place on October 23. The law permits purchase of one case of beer in one day. The accused purchased three cases in one day.

TO HEAR OULTON

First supper meeting of South Side Businessmen's Association for 1937-38 season will be held in Westminster Church dining room Monday evening at 6.15. C. A. Oulton will be the guest speaker.

STILL SEEK RADIUM

Search for the missing tube of radium lost in City Hospital on Monday or Tuesday continued at the institution today.

It was expected that a detector borrowed from a Calgary clinic would be put in operation during the afternoon. The Calgary instrument will be used in addition to the apparatus constructed at the University of Saskatchewan in Saskatoon.

Oliver Dealers Hold Session

Fifty-five dealers met in the branch office of Oliver Limited here recently to attend the preview showing of a new model tractor and hear addresses by officials of the company.

Merle Tucker, assistant general sales manager of the Chicago office, addressed the meeting in the afternoon on the policy of the company and new model machines for 1938. D. S. Swinton, Canadian manager, spoke on the aims and sales policies of the Canadian organization. A. R. Fee, Saskatoon branch manager, was in charge, and dealt with advertising and sales helps for the coming year.

A dinner was held in The Bessborough in the evening at which Mr. Tucker gave an address on the progress of the company and plans for the future.

Youth Training Classes Listed

The national and provincial youth training program will start classes at the Technical Collegiate as follows:

Carpentry and construction, Wednesday, November 3 at 4.30; diesel engine instruction, Monday, November 1 at 7.30; electricity (practical), Monday, November 1 at 4.30; motor mechanics, Wednesday, November 3 at 4.30; machine shop, Wednesday, November 3 at 4.30; prospecting and mineralogy, Wednesday, November 3 at 4.30; radio servicing, Wednesday, November 3 at 7.30; oxy-acetylene welding, Thursday, November 4 at 4.30.

Relief Rate To Be Higher

City Authorized to Give Physically Unfit Single Jobless 60 Cents Daily

Mayor Pinder today received authorization from the Bureau of Labor and Public Welfare to increase the relief allowance of the physically unfit single unemployed persons from 52 to 60 cents per day. This will bring these unemployed in line with transients who are receiving direct relief through the Government employment office.

The new rate will go into force November 1, and will apply only to those who are taking cash instead of a voucher for board and room. In the past the board and room vouchers were for 60 cents per day, but the money was not handled by the recipient. It was paid direct to the landlord providing the room and board.

Since the cash rates and voucher rates are now the same, it is anticipated that the majority will take the cash.

LATE RECIPES NEXT WEEK

Owing to a large number of recipes arriving late for the Star-Phoenix cook book, a special kitchen column will be run on the woman's page beginning next week.

Y.M.C.A. Funds Drive Starts Here Wednesday

Final arrangements for the Y.M.C.A. financial campaign have been completed by the Board of Directors and Wednesday morning 75 Saskatoon business men will begin a week's canvass to obtain $6,500, necessary to carry on the work of the association in 1938. Last year the campaign committee was successful in getting $7,300 and officials of the institution hope that the same amount may be realized from this year's effort.

The general chairman of the committee for the current campaign will be J. S. Woodward, who directed the campaign last year. He will be assisted in the management of the campaign by R. H. Potter, who has been long associated with Y.M.C.A. work in Saskatoon.

The Y.M.C.A. has outlined a program for next year which will extend the variety of its service to boys in this city. This Autumn, a membership drive was conducted and classes now meeting at the institution are larger than they have been for several years.

In spite of this expanded activity, the directors feel that the full program can be carried out if the full amount of the objective of the association is reached. However, they believe that they could operate more efficiently if a larger sum was collected during the campaign.

Men who are giving up part of their time for a week's assistance of the Y.M.C.A. are:

George Armstrong; C. E. Arnold; W. C. Arscott; J. C. Baker; George Barclay; A. M. Blue; D. Beckerman; A. S. Boxer; L. P. Bromham; G. W. Brooks; S. E. Bushe; W. I. Byers; D. D. Campbell; H. Carpenter; P. Carpenter; J. Carver; A. D. Cavers; M. J. Champlin; John Collins; A. Cuthbert; N. Gyprus; R. G. Dilke; H. D. Elliot; G. H. Fletcher; A. J. Foster; R. C. Forrest; J. W. Gibson; V. E. Graham; T. H. Hamill; E. A. Hardy; E. L. Harrington; J. W. Hair; Tom Henry; E. C. Hope; H. Hurwitz; A. J. Irving; George Jarvis; S. Kaplan; J. H. LaRoche; M. Lerman; P. H. Maguire; H. C. Manuel; Jack Miller; J. B. Miller; J. Mighton; J. Mitchell; P. M. McCarrell; T. H. Newell; W. P. Noble; W. L. Noyes; R. V. Real; Norman Reid; A. Robinson; A. Ross; W. Ross; G. Sanford; N. W. Shaffer; William Scott; A. H. Silvester; T. Skerratt; S. S. Squarebriggs; W. N. Stewart; Roy Todd; G. C. Weir; R. Wentz; W. J. Weston; W. J. White; J. Whitehouse; W. T. White; W. J. Young.

These men will meet for supper in the Y.M.C.A. building at 6.15 on Wednesday to inaugurate the 1937 campaign.

Consumer Is Paying 4 Per Cent

Cost of Collection Is Charged to Public, Retailers Report

$1,140,000 MORE

EDUCATION TAX UNECONOMIC, ASSOCIATION SAYS IN LETTER TO PRESS

Saskatchewan's education tax will cost the consumers 4 per cent instead of 2 per cent, members of the Regina Branch of the Retail Merchants' Association declared in a letter to the press this week. Increases in the merchant's overhead because of the tax, which must eventually be passed on to the consumer, will impose an additional levy of $1,140,000 on the consumers of the Province, the merchants' organization claimed.

QUOTE RETURNS

"Naturally one must conclude that the education tax is only another name for lack of economy, and this would still be true if the figures for the cost of collection were decreased by half," the statement reads.

The merchants have supported their arguments on the uneconomic nature of the tax by quoting figures from returns given to the Government so far and from the cost of business which they have experienced.

They have pointed out that there are 16,000 merchants in Saskatchewan and on returns made for the first quarter, the average tax collected amounted to $21. The merchant received 4 per cent of this amount for collection. This works out at an average of 1.6 cents a business day for each merchant.

Additional overhead costs placed on the merchant because of the tax would amount to at least 25 cents a day on the average of small and big businesses alike, the organization declared. The total cost, then, is was computed would be $1,200,000 annually for collection alone. Deducting the commission to be paid by the Government, this left a net cost to the merchant of $1,140,000 which must be met out of increased prices to the consumer.

COMBINE FIGURES

The uneconomic nature of the tax was said to be shown by combining these figures. The yield to the Government after all expenses were paid on a total tax of $1,500,000 would be $1,350,000. The total cost to the consumer, including the additional overhead for the merchant, will be, they estimated, $2,640,000.

Comparison of these figures, the merchants pointed out, will mean that only 51 per cent of the cost of the tax to the consumer will reach the Government treasury.

The brief also expresses the opinion that the Government could not foresee this situation. The brief concludes: "We are equally sure that no Government would willingly continue so uneconomical a means of raising revenue."

BANK CLEARINGS

Saskatoon bank clearings totalled $6,651,067.16 in October. For October last year they were $8,639,144.70.

RAIL UNIONS MEET

The Saskatoon Joint Council of Railway Unions will hold a meeting in the I.O.O.F. Hall at 2.30 o'clock Sunday. All railway unions and women's auxiliaries' members will be welcomed.

Young Wife Loses Legs In Tumble Under Train

Special to the Star-Phoenix

HUMBOLDT, Sask., Oct. 30.—The girl wife of S. J. Rollins of Portage la Prairie, Man., lost both her legs under a freight train here at 4.30 o'clock this morning.

Husband and wife were travelling as transients on a through freight from Kamsack. The train stopped on entering the Humboldt yard, and the couple alighted. When the train started they made an attempt to board it again and Mrs. Rollins fell under the wheels. The engineer heard her screams and stopped the train.

A doctor was called and the victim was taken to the hospital here. One leg had been ground off below the knee, the other had to be amputated above the knee.

New Policies

J. G. DIEFENBAKER, K.C.

unanimous choice of Saskatchewan Conservatives as their provincial leader at the Regina convention a year ago, who will make his first official pronouncement of policy at the Conservative rally in the Canadian Legion Hall on Monday evening. Marked changes in the Conservative platform have been forecast following lengthy deliberations of party supporters. Mr. Diefenbaker was in the city today.

Text Ready For Course

Composite Book Prepared at University for Tuition Starting Monday

Information dealing with every farm operation, including guidance on the planting of forage crops, the repair of farm machinery, caring for poultry, cattle, hogs, sheep and horses, tanning hides, churning milk, plowing, soildrifting control, and many other subjects, is contained in a composite text book prepared by the University of Saskatchewan agricultural extension department, under direction of Professor R. D. Ramsay.

The text will be distributed to farm lads taking two-week courses in practical farming under the youth employment training program, which starts in ten Saskatchewan towns and villages, Monday. Instructors for the courses left Saskatoon today, following a short "refresher" course.

Obituary

MRS. J. A. JOHNSON

Alice, aged 49 years, wife of John A. Johnson of North Battleford, died in a Saskatoon hospital early today. Surviving are the widower and four children. They are Stanley, Elsie, Nancy and Martha. A sister, Mrs. Charles Engwall lives at Morland. There are also a brother and sister in Sweden. A service will be held in the chapel of the Saskatoon Funeral Home at 2 o'clock Monday.

LOUIS GENDRON

The death occurred on Thursday at his Makwa home of Louis Gendron. He is survived by his widow, Mrs. H. Few, Mrs. F. Hobbs and Mrs. W. Smith and Arthur, all of Saskatoon, and by Mrs. A. Kirkup, of Loon Lake, and Alford, of Sudbury, Ont. Burial will take place at Makwa this afternoon at 2 o'clock.

CHESTER CARLTON

Funeral service for Chester Howard Carlton, 837 Third Street, was held in McKague's chapel, Friday afternoon, the Rev. Nelson Chappel officiating. Pallbearers were: John Storr, Fred Mulvey, John French, Dr. J. Wilhelm, William Gibson and Tom Maybin. Burial was made in Woodlawn Cemetery.

MRS. FRANK HARBURN

Aged 58, Florence Ethel, wife of Frank Harburn of Donovan, died in a local hospital on Friday. The Harburn family has resided in the Donovan district for 32 years. Survivors are: Three daughters, Mrs. Carl McKenzie, of Fort Saskatchewan, Alta., Flora at Vancouver and Alma, at home. Her mother, five sisters and brothers also survive. The funeral will be held at Donovan Sunday afternoon at 3 o'clock when the Rev. H. G. Reese will officiate. McKague's Funeral Home has charge of arrangements.

Anderson Statement Is Absurd

So Says Estey in Reply To Charge of Politics In Relief Handling

WITHOUT GROUNDS

DECENTRALIZATION SEEN AS BAR TO ANY ADVANTAGE BEING POSSIBLE

Allegation by Dr. J. T. M. Anderson, former Premier of Saskatchewan, of partisanship in Saskatchewan Government relief administration, was seen as a direct attack on the integrity of municipal officials throughout the Province and "absolutely false and unfounded," by the Hon. J. W. Estey, K.C., minister of education, in a press statement today.

CHARGED INTIMIDATION

Pointing out centralized relief administration as established by the Anderson Government lent itself more to political influences than the decentralized system instituted by the present Government, Mr. Estey termed the Anderson statement "absurd."

Doctor Anderson gave a press statement on Friday charging the Government with intimidating rural relief recipients to cash their vouchers with Liberal merchants.

In his comment, Mr. Estey said, "Exception will be taken to the allegation by municipal officials, elected and appointed, throughout the Province. There are 170 rural municipalities in the Federal official drouth area and outside that there are many municipalities in addition to urban centres, where relief is administered by co-operation of the Provincial Government and municipal bodies.

ISSUE IN 1934

"Relief administration was an issue in the 1934 provincial election when the people voted against centralized administration and for the decentralized system.

"Under the centralized system with all the officials in one place and friendly to the Government of the day, it was possible for the Government to use the organization for party purposes.

"Under the decentralized system it is necessary for the Government to co-operate with the elected representatives of the people regardless of political affiliations. It is impossible for political considerations to obtain and it makes Doctor Anderson's charge absurd."

Food Aids 450People

Shipment From Ontario Church Is Received at Grasswood

The generosity of Ontario people, which has been evident on many occasions in the south of the Province, came close to Saskatoon this week with the arrival of a car of food at Grasswood siding. Containing thousands of pounds of produce from the Eastern Province's fertile fields, the car came from the congregation of the United Church at Exeter, Ont., of which the Rev. A. E. Elliott is pastor.

128 FAMILIES

One hundred and twenty-eight families, including close to 450 individuals received the benefit of the gift. The produce was distributed among people of the Grasswood, Victor and Floral districts, all of whom were absolutely destitute. They harvested no crop this year, have no money and 90 per cent of them depend on Government assistance to keep their animals alive.

Some of these families have as many as 13 children, and for the little ones particularly the outlook was bleak. Telling of the joy with which the food was received, Percy Holland, pioneer farmer of the Victor district, said that the car's arrival had turned despair to hope in many hearts.

The produce was distributed by a committee consisting of men who, like Mr. Holland, have been resident in the farming country south and southwest of Saskatoon for many years. They are: Hastings Baker, W. Ennis, George Bailey, Mike Herman (and Mr. Holland). John Manson, Pool elevator agent at Grasswood, gave valuable help in distribution.

The committee found in the car: 480 bags of potatoes, 150 bags of turnips, 28 bags of carrots, 30 bags of cabbage, 28 bags of beets, 25 bags of citrons and pumpkins, 35 bags of apples, three bags of onions, 17 bags of dried beans, 36 packages corn flakes, 100 pounds of flour, 24 pounds of tea and coffee, 37 cartons of canned fruit, pickles, honey, peas and corn.

Child in Court, Shooting Result

A boy under 16 years of age was brought to juvenile court this morning on a charge of shooting a loaded revolver near Nutana Collegiate on Saturday, October 15, and unlawfully wounding a child. An adjournment was made until next Saturday.

+ I SEE— +

Installation of officers will occupy the Cosmopolitans at their dinner Monday.

* * *

A musical program has been arranged by Tom Austen for the meeting of the Wesley Macs at 2.15 Sunday afternoon, in St. Thomas-Wesley Church.

* * *

Dick Mayson of the M. and C. Aviation Company, visiting in the city today, said that a report of several days ago that commercial flying in the north had stopped owing to a freeze-up was incorrect. He said all aviation companies were still on Summer schedule and were having no difficulties.

* * *

Dr. William Allen of the farm management department of the university, will continue the discussion of rural credits at the meeting of the Adult Education Association in room 16, Technical Collegiate, at 8 o'colck Monday evening.

* * *

Ex-service men from the country adjacent to Saskatoon visiting the city this week-end for the Arena rink opening games are cordially invited to visit the clubrooms of the Canadian Legion. Local members of the Legion will be on hand to welcome visitors immediately after the evening game. The Legion building is immediately east of the rink.

* * *

The executive committee of the Saskatoon Figure Skating Club will meet at 5 p.m. Monday at the offices of James Richardson and Sons, Limited.

* * *

The Lions Club of Saskatoon by way of entertainment at their dinner meeting on Monday will see films on Russia released by Entourist Incorporated, official tourist bureau of the Russian Government and brought to Saskatoon specially for this showing.

* * *

The Saskatoon Poultry Association will meet at 8 o'clock Tuesday evening in the office of W. W. Ashley, Second Avenue, south. There will be a debate on the advantages of Government poultry services.

* * *

The 65th Battalion Old Boys Association will meet at 8 o'clock Tuesday evening in the Canadian Legion Hall. The president is asking a large attendance due to important business.

* * *

Jay Fox, official photographer for Toronto Saturday Night, will entertain the Canadian Club at dinner Tuesday with an illustrated talk on "Camera Conversations." The dinner will be held in The Bessborough at 6.15 o'clock.

* * *

Rotary's weekly luncheon meeting on Monday will be featured by discussion of the Saskatoon Arena, with David Webster leading. The club's community service committee of which Reg Munkley is chairman, will have charge.

* * *

At the Kinsmen Club's dinner Monday, Captain D. Jamieson-Bell, gentleman adventurer, will be the speaker. A man who has travelled widely, he will draw on interesting experiences and observations for his address.

* * *

"One Hundred Years in Agriculture in Saskatchewan," will be the subject of Prof. J. W. Grant MacEwan of the animal husbandry department, University of Saskatchewan, when he speaks at the Kiwanis Club's luncheon Tuesday.

Grey Owl

He was born an Englishman, but Grey Owl became the most noted aboriginal of his time, spending the latter part of his life in Saskatchewan as an advocate for nature conservation. Grey Owl was born Archibald Belaney in Hastings, United Kingdom, in 1888. Belaney immigrated to Canada in 1906, eventually moving to Northern Ontario. There, he adopted the name Grey Owl and the story that his father was Scottish and his mother Apache. Grey Owl set to work as a fur trapper, wilderness guide and forest ranger. In 1925, Grey Owl met Anahareo an Iroquois woman who encouraged him to focus on his writings about wilderness life. Those writings attracted the attention of the Dominion Parks Service, which hired Grey Owl to work as a naturalist. Grey Owl, Anahareo, and their pet beavers settled in Prince Albert National Park in the early 1930s. There, they established a beaver sanctuary on Ajawaan Lake. He lived in the park until 1938 when he died of pneumonia.

Grey Owl with pet beaver, circa 1934

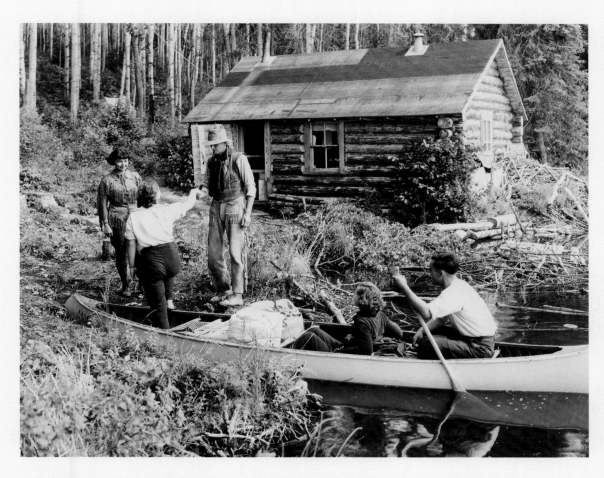

Grey Owl and Anahareo receive visitors at the log cabin, Prince Albert National Park, circa 1934

WEATHER FORECAST
Fair, a little warmer

THE LEADER-POST

REGINA, SASKATCHEWAN, TUESDAY, JUNE 6, 1944

WEATHER YESTERDAY

VOL. XLI No. 132

D-DAY HERE!

ALLIES DRIVE
CANADIANS LAND
INTO FRANCE

SMASH NORTH COAST
'chutists spilled over Normandy

By WES GALLAGHER
Associated Press War Correspondent

SUPREME HEADQUARTERS, ALLIED EXPEDITIONARY FORCE, June 6 (AP).—Allied forces landed in northern France early today in history's greatest overseas operation, designed to destroy the power of Hitler's Germany and wrest enslaved Europe from the Nazis.

Prime Minister Churchill told the house of commons today that an immense Allied armada of 4,000 ships with several thousand smaller craft had carried Allied forces across the channel for the invasion of Europe.

Mr. Churchill also said that massed airborne landings had been successfully effected behind the Germans' lines.

Batteries silenced

"The fire of shore batteries has been largely quelled," said Mr. Churchill. He added that obstacles which were constructed in the sea have not proved so difficult as was apprehended."

The prime minister said the Allied forces are sustained by about 11,000 first-line aircraft, which can be drawn upon as needed.

"So far," he said, "the commanders who are engaged report that everything is proceeding according to plan."

"And what a plan!" he declared.

The German radio said the landings were made from Le Havre to Cherbourg, along the north coast of Normandy and the south side of the bay of the Seine.

Allied headquarters did not specify the locations, but left no doubt whatever that the landings were on a gigantic scale.

Ringing in their ears, the British, American and Canadian forces who made the landings had these words from their supreme commander, Gen. Dwight D. Eisenhower:

"You are about to embark on a great crusade. The eyes of the world are upon you and the hopes and prayers of all liberty-loving people go with you ...

"We will accept nothing less than full vic[tory]

Roughly three hours after the invasion started, Canadian fighter pilots reporting back to their station said "things seemed well organized on the beach," though there was "lots of shooting going on at the beachhead."

One pilot said: "I've never seen so many ships in all my life."

The German radio filled the air with invasion flashes for three hours before the formal Allied announcement came at 7:32 a.m. G.M.T. (2:32 a.m. C.D.T.).

It acknowledged deep penetrations of the Cherbourg peninsula by Allied parachute and glider troops in great strength.

Berlin said the "centre of gravity" of the fierce fighting was at Caen, 20 miles southwest of Le Havre and 65 miles southeast of Cherbourg.

Caen is 10 miles inland from the sea, at the base of the 75-mile-wide Normandy peninsula.

Heavy fighting also was reported between Caen and Trouville.

The assault was supported by gigantic bombardments from Allied warships and planes, which the Germans admitted set the coastal areas ablaze. The fleet included several British and United States battleships.

A senior officer at supreme headquarters said water caused "awful anxiety" for the seaborne troops, but that the landings were made successfully, although some soldiers were troubled by heavy seasick.

The sun broke through a daybreak shower. The wind had blown fairly hard during the night but moderated somewhat with the dawn. The weather outlook remained somewhat unsettled.

Supreme headquarters' first communique was this single sentence:

"Under command of Gen. Eisenhower, Allied naval forces supported by strong air forces began landing Allied armies this morning on the northern coast of France."

Montgomery commands

It was announced moments later that Britain's Gen. Sir Bernard L. Montgomery, hero of the 8th Army victories in North Africa, Sicily and Italy, was in charge of the assault, and the announcement added: "This army

(Concluded on Page No.)

KING WILL BROADCAST

NEW YORK, June 6.—The BBC, in a broadcast recorded ... said that King ... broadcast tonight at 9 p.m.

War II

Chapter Six

The lights went out in Saskatoon one night in September 1941. And in the darkened stillness of that moment, the residents of the city on the banks of the South Saskatchewan River — some 10,000 kilometres from occupied Paris and bombed-out London — made themselves imagine the drone of enemy warplanes, the whine of plummeting bombs, the palpable fear of invasion and defeat that gripped so much of the free world at that time.

"The citizens of Saskatoon, Thursday night, were given some remote idea of what is now the nightly routine experience of millions of people in the cities and towns of battle-torn Europe, Asia and Africa," the *Star-Phoenix* reported in its account of a Second World War black-out drill. "As the whistles of the power house sounded the 'alert' and other whistles and sirens in the city took up the cry, the lights of Saskatoon blacked out street by street, sign by sign and house by house, until in a very few moments blackness prevailed.

"From the roof of the Bessborough Hotel, the outline of river, bridges and streets became dimly discernible as eyes grew accustomed to the darkness. Lights beyond the city limits outlined the boundaries of the university, Sutherland, the airport …"

The mayor is described congratulating residents for making the drill a success, while soberly reminding them in a radio address that "the people of Britain had been forced to go through the real thing many times and might, at the very moment he was speaking, be crouching in shelters while the Huns

LEFT PAGE: South Saskatchewan Regiment, Zwiggelte, Netherlands, April 12, 1945

ABOVE: Victory Bonds rally, Regina, 1941

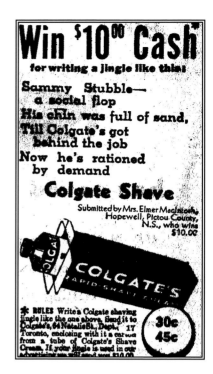

bombs were falling in the streets, killing children and other non-combatants, and destroying property."

Though far from the front lines, the effects of the 1939-45 war were, in fact, keenly felt throughout the province — and not just when the lights were doused to trick Phantom fliers of the Luftwaffe. More than 70,000 residents of Saskatchewan enlisted for service in the great struggle against Germany and her allies, and many times that number — as during the First World War — volunteered their time and effort at home to support the troops overseas.

The wide, open sky of the Prairies provided ideal conditions to train pilots and other members of flight crews for the air war that would be so crucial to victory. As part of the 1939 agreement that launched the British Commonwealth Air Training Plan, air force flight schools were created at fifteen sites in Saskatchewan. These training schools, which produced thousands of pilots, navigators, wireless operators, gunners, bombers and other air force personnel, were set up at Assiniboia, Caron, Dafoe, Davidson, Estevan, Moose Jaw, Mossbank, North Battleford, Prince Albert, Regina, Saskatoon, Swift Current, Weyburn, Wilcox and Yorkton.

"As the war progressed, nationals of France, Poland, Holland, Czechoslovakia, Belgium, Norway and other countries took their training in Saskatchewan, finding some kinship among the province's ethnic strains and adding common understanding through devotion to a common cause," writes provincial historian John Archer.

Even before the war was officially declared, Saskatchewan had begun feeling the impact of Adolf Hitler's rise to power and the European tumult caused by his imperial ambitions. The 1939 invasion of Czechoslovakia and the Nazi takeover of the Sudetenland had sent a wave of refugees to Canada, including about 150 families destined for the St. Walburg, Bright Sand and Loon Lake areas.

"They saw the little wooden dwellings of St. Walburg huddled along the muddy streets," Rita Schilling writes in Sudeten in *Saskatchewan: A Way to Be Free*, one of many classics of Saskatchewan non-fiction excerpted in the 1996 anthology *The Middle of Nowhere*. "The wooden sidewalks were invisible beneath the great patches of mud and snow. They saw the primitive post office, the strange buildings called elevators, and huge barns, far bigger than the houses, on the outskirts of the community."

The refugees, noted Schilling, were stunned by the frontier landscape they encountered and the locals, in turn, were initially cool toward the German-speaking newcomers. But a local newspaper, she observed, captured the determination among Saskatchewanians to oppose Nazism and to give comfort to its victims.

"Not one — not even those political acrobats who denounce immigration in all its shapes and forms — could quarrel with the decision of Ottawa to allow several hundred Sudeten German families to come to Canada this spring to settle on Canadian farms," Schilling quotes the *St. Walburg Enterprise*. "These people are refugees in one sense, but there is nothing shabby about this label for them."

Across the Atlantic, Saskatchewan native Gladys Arnold was among those forced to take flight from the advancing German army. The intrepid newspaper reporter was filing stories from Paris for the Canadian Press and *Regina Leader-Post*, where she had earned her stripes as a scribe in the 1930s — a time when few female journalists were able to overcome the prejudices of colleagues and carve out decent careers in the profession.

"When the German Blitzkrieg rolled into Paris in the spring of 1940, Arnold was the only Canadian reporter still on the scene," writes Verne Clemence in *Saskatchewan's Own: People Who Made a Difference*. "She escaped with a stream of refugees just hours before the occupying forces entered the city. It was an unforgettable experience...."

Clemence quotes Arnold's signature piece of reportage, a richly detailed account of the hurried exodus from the besieged French capital:

"We left Paris in the grey dawn of June 12. The shabby and shuttered buildings seemed to draw back within themselves as we passed.... Within a kilometre we ran into a solid wall of refugees. Though we had passed many bedded down along the avenues, it was impossible to imagine what we were seeing now. An endless river of people on foot, in carts, wagons and cars; animals and bicycles so tightly packed across the road and sidewalks that no one could move more than a step or two at a time."

While Arnold went on to promote the Free French movement, in Canada scientists from Saskatchewan were making major contributions — secretly — to the technological battle against the Germans' formidable military research and development machine.

Andrew McNaughton, a Moosomin native and a brilliant military engineer who had risen rapidly through the ranks of Canada's military during and after

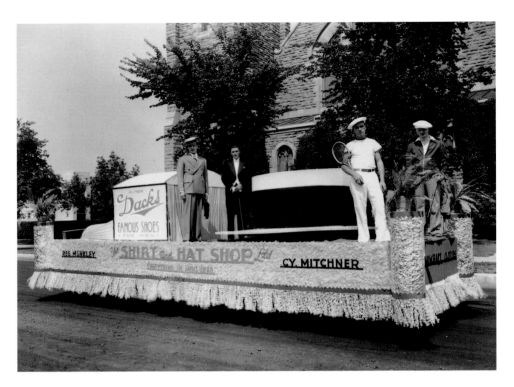

the First World War, was by 1939 serving as the country's top science administrator — president of the National Research Council. Having led a successful effort to devote scientific know-how to Canada's defence capability, McNaughton was called back to the battlefield in 1939 as the country's top general.

So he called upon a trusted friend, University of Saskatchewan's dean of engineering, C.J. Mackenzie, to take over as the NRC's wartime president.

Mackenzie, in turn, tapped other Saskatoon scientists, such as chemist John Spinks (a future University of Saskatchewan president) and Gerhard Herzberg (a U of S physicist and future Nobel Prize winner), to work on a variety of projects aimed at bolstering the Allies' war effort. Their research — on search-and-rescue systems, convoy protection, explosives, anti-submarine technology and even nuclear fission — helped make Canadian science a key part of the Allied arsenal that eventually tilted the technological balance against Germany.

Spinks, in his 1980 autobiography *Two Blades of Grass*, recalled how one of his scientific missions to Britain in the early 1940s revealed the depth and diversity of Saskatchewan's contribution to the war effort.

"Wing Commander E. McNab dropped into the mess that evening from a nearby fighter wing, and we reminisced about the University of Saskatchewan," Spinks wrote. "Other memories are of strolling across Trafalgar Square and meeting Dr. Jim Campbell of Saskatoon, who was attached to one of the military hospitals. He said to me, 'Hello' as casually as if we had met on campus in Saskatoon, and took me off to a café for coffee and a bun."

The home front forces were active throughout the war. An article published by the *Regina Leader-Post* in June 1942 described a typical fundraising concert in the town of Shamrock, organized by the Victory Boosters Tobacco League: "Features of the evening were vocal numbers by Jean Lightbody, Mildred Miller,

Larry Collins and Mrs. Radcliffe," the story says, adding that some local pupils "presented a very cleverly conducted puppet show" and a quiz contest and that a total of $15.50 was collected "to provide cigarettes" for Canadian soldiers.

"I treasure that faded news clipping," Shamrock-born journalist and author Robert Collins recalled in his 1980 memoir *Butter Down the Well*, also excerpted in *The Middle of Nowhere*. "Not merely because I wrote it, as a *Leader* rural correspondent for ten cents an inch, but because it demonstrates how one small corner of Canada did its part in World War II. All over the land unimportant people like us were rallying to the war effort with knitting needles, bake sales, bingo games, variety shows and unflagging patriotism."

While many Saskatchewanians toiled behind the scenes in the push for victory, the province's soldiers were always front and centre — at Dieppe, Normandy and on countless other battlefields — in the fight for freedom.

Few, though, distinguished themselves the way Major David Currie did as he helped liberate France in the bloody aftermath of D-Day.

In the weeks following the historic June 6, 1944, landings along the coast of Normandy, Allied troops were engaged in a death struggle with entrenched German forces throughout the French countryside. During a critical offensive in August 1944, a contingent of Canadians was assigned to cut off a key corridor being used by enemy soldiers to escape the Allied advance in Normandy. Currie was put in charge of the small, mixed force of Canadian tanks, anti-tank guns and infantry that moved to close the escape route.

Born in Sutherland — an outskirts community just beyond Saskatoon's 1941 blackout — Currie was trained as an automobile mechanic at a Moose Jaw college. He enlisted with an Alberta regiment and by the summer of 1944, the thirty-two-year-old had distinguished himself repeatedly in the field, rising from lieutenant to captain to major.

In the official account of Currie's actions beginning on August 18, 1944 — actions that would earn him a Victoria Cross — he is described as having sworn off fear, failure and even sleep in what amounted to a marathon, virtuoso performance of soldiering:

"This force was held up by strong enemy resistance in the village of St. Lambert-sur-Dives and two tanks were knocked out by 88-mm guns. Major Currie immediately entered the village alone on foot at last light through the enemy outposts to reconnoiter the German defences and extricate the crews of the disabled tanks, which he succeeded in doing in spite of heavy mortar fire.

"Early the following morning, without any previous artillery bombardment, Major Currie personally led an attack on the village in the face of fierce opposition from enemy tanks, guns and infantry, and by noon had succeeded in seizing and consolidating a position halfway inside of the village.

"During the next thirty-six hours, the Germans hurled one counter-attack after another against the Canadian force, but so skillfully had Major Currie organized his defensive position that these attacks were repulsed with severe casualties to the enemy after heavy fighting.

"At dusk on the 20th August, the Germans attempted to mount a final assault on the Canadian positions, but the attacking force was routed before it could

Sutherland's Major David Currie, second from left with pistol in hand, accepts the surrender of several German soldiers, St-Lambert-sur-Dives, France, August 9, 1944

even be deployed. Seven enemy tanks, twelve 88-mm guns and forty vehicles were destroyed, 300 Germans were killed, 500 wounded and 2,100 captured. Major Currie then promptly ordered an attack and completed the capture of the village, thus denying the Chambois-Trun escape route to the remnants of two German armies cut off in the Falaise pocket.

"Throughout three days and nights of fierce fighting, Major Currie's gallant conduct and contempt for danger set a magnificent example to all ranks of the force under his command ...

"Since all the officers under his command were either killed or wounded during the action, Major Currie virtually had no respite from his duties and, in fact, obtained only one hour's sleep during the entire period. Nevertheless he did not permit his fatigue to become apparent to his troops and throughout the action took every opportunity to visit weapon pits and other defensive posts to talk to his men, to advise them as to the best use of their weapons and to cheer them with words of encouragement. When his force was finally relieved and he was satisfied that the turnover was complete, he fell asleep on his feet and collapsed.

"There can be no doubt that the success of the attack on and stand against the enemy at St. Lambert-sur-Dives can largely be attributed to this officer's coolness, inspired leadership and skillful use of the limited weapons at his disposal.

"The courage and devotion to duty shown by Major Currie during a prolonged period of heavy fighting were outstanding and had a far-reaching effect on the successful outcome of the battle."

There is a famous picture, taken by an official war photographer, that shows a gun-toting Currie giving instructions to a soldier while German prisoners are marched down a road at St. Lambert-sur-Dives. It's believed to be the only photograph showing a Victoria Cross recipient in the midst of his award-winning action.

Currie returned to Canada briefly in late 1944 and was given a hero's welcome. In a CBC Radio interview at the time, he said the men under his command were disappointed about facing at least another year of war in Europe but remained bound by duty and determined to get the job done: "They remind me a lot," Currie said, "of the Western farmer who has had a crop failure and says, 'Well, maybe next year.' "

There would be no next year, though, for many of the province's soldiers who fought in the Second World War. Among the dead in June 1944 was Gilbert

Tommy Douglas and supporters, shortly after the CCF won the election, Regina, 1944

Boxall, a twenty-four-year-old from northern Saskatchewan who was serving as a stretcher-bearer with the Regina Rifles during the D-Day invasion.

Years later, Sergeant Alf Allen described how one of his most vivid memories of the war was burying Boxall's body:

"He came from Canwood in northern Saskatchewan, grew up in the Depression and had very little of this world's goods. He'd never have had been the stick man in a British Guards parade but as a dedicated working man there was none better. He landed in the assault wave, gave first aid on the beach and in the battle inland. On D-plus-3, running to a chap he heard calling for help, he was cut down and killed. On his body we later found five dried shell dressings — he'd five wounds prior to being killed. He never said a word to anybody, just crawled away somewhere, put a dressing on and went back in."

For all of the self-sacrifice exhibited by Saskatchewan residents in the face of war, there remained among the province's farmers — and among a growing number of its urban citizens — a latent sense of injustice about the economic system underpinning Canadian society. The ongoing war failed to erase bitter memories of the desperate struggles experienced during the Depression and in some cases fuelled resentment over perceived unfairness in the distribution of work and wealth within the province and within Confederation.

At the outset of the war, the Co-operative Commonwealth Federation MP for Weyburn, Tommy Douglas, pledged his support for Canada's war effort but challenged the Liberal government of Mackenzie King to make the conscription of capital as much of a priority as the enlistment of soldiers.

"I make this plea," he had said in a June 1940 debate over granting special wartime powers to the federal government. "If men and women in Canada are prepared to serve the state, if they are prepared to offer their lives and to place their services at the disposal of the country, we should get some assurance from the government tonight that the material, financial and economic resources of the nation will be taken on the same basis as human service is taken, namely, without profit but for the service of the state and for the duration of the war."

In 1942, Douglas helped organize a farmers' protest in Ottawa that led to a slight increase in the per-bushel price of wartime grain. But Saskatchewan's citizenry was ripe for much bigger changes in the give-and-take of economic and social policy, and in 1944 — with Douglas at the helm of the provincial CCF — the party was elected in a landslide. It was the first socialist government ever put in power in North America and as the war wound down and the postwar era beckoned, Saskatchewan was in a position to export much more than wheat to the rest of Canada.

EXTRA **Saskatoon Star-Phœnix**

SASKATOON, SASK. SUNDAY, SEPTEMBER 3, 1939.

BRITAIN DECLARES WAR

FRENCH ENTRY BELIEVED IMMINENT

LONDON, Sept. 3.—Great Britain declared war on Germany today.

France had said she would follow automatically.

The announcement was made by Prime Minister Chamberlain in an address to the nation by radio.

It came at the expiration at 11 a.m. British Summer Time (3 a.m. M.S.T.) of a British ultimatum to Germany to call her armies out from Poland.

Mr. Chamberlain himself read the proclamation and ended with the prayer:

"May God bless you all and may He defend the right."

The Prime Minister assured his people that Great Britain had done her utmost to the end to arrange "a peaceful and honorable settlement" but "Herr Hitler would not have it."

"Consequently we are at war with Germany," he said.

"We have done all that any country could do to establish peace," he said, "but a situation in which no word given by Germany's ruler could be trusted and no people or country could endure has become intolerable, and now that we have resolved to finish it, I know that you will all play your part with calmness and courage.

"At such a moment as this, the assurances of support which we have received from the Empire are a source of profound encouragement to us.

"When I finish speaking, certain detailed announcements will be made on behalf of the Government.

"Please give your close attention.

"The Government have made plans under which it will be possible to carry on the work of the nation in the days of stress and strain that may be ahead.

"These plans need your help.

"You may be taking your part in the fighting services or as a volunteer in one of the branches of civil defence; if so, you will report for duty in accordance with the instructions you receive.

"You may be engaged in work essential to the prosecution of war, or the maintenance of the life of the people, in factories, in transport, in public utility concerns or in the supply of other necessities of life; if so, it is of vital importance that you should carry on with your jobs.

"Now may God bless you all and may we defend the right, for it is evil things that we shall be fighting against—force, bad faith, injustice, oppression and persecution.

"Against them, I am certain, the right will prevail."

The ultimatum was to fix a time limit on a "final warning" Britain and France gave Germany September 1.

It came on the third day after Germany's invasion of Poland.

Two columns of the German army were reported by German military authorities yesterday to have gone in from East Prussia and North Germany to pinch off the entire Polish Corridor (Pomorze).

There had been a one-day delay in the declaration of war in the hope peace might come out of a five-power conference which Premier Mussolini of Italy proposed.

Shortly before Mr. Chamberlain's proclamation 10 Downing Street had issued a communique setting the time limit and announcing that Sir Nevile Henderson, British ambassador in Berlin, had told the German Government that if assurances were not received by then a "state of war" would exist between Great Britain and Germany.

The announcement said Sir Nevile informed the German Government at 9 a.m. (1 a.m. M.S.T.)

Thirty minutes before the time limit expired the German embassy in Londoh disclosed it had "no news" and acknowledged it was "in constant communication" with Berlin.

The Prime Minister spoke to the House of Commons only five minutes. He started at 12.07 p.m. (4.07 a.m. M.S.T.) and sat down at 12.12 p.m. (4.12 a.m. M.S.T.)

In the meantime, the nation had felt the impact of war

An air raid alarm had cleared the streets of London in rehearsal of defence precautions and the "all clear" sirens were screaming even as Mr. Chamberlain arose behind the sandbagged walls of Parliament.

Sports events had been cancelled, theatres and movies shut and the populace had been exhorted not to collect in large crowds.

It was warned large crowds increased the menace of death from bombing.

"I trust I may see the day when Hitlerism has been destroyed," the Prime Minister told Parliament.

He explained the expiration of the ultimatum to Germany, telling the House it had expired without any reply from Berlin and that France—bound like Great Britain to help Poland defend her independence—was joining Britain in war "at this minute."

Mr. Chamberlain, his voice trembling with emotion, emphasized his words by banging the table with his hand as he exclaimed:

"There is only one thing left for me and that is to devote what strength and powers I have to forwarding the victory of the cause for which we have to sacrifice ourselves."

Arthur Greenwood, acting leader of the Opposition in the Commons, endorsed Mr. Chamberlain's statement.

"In this titanic struggle," he declared, "unparalleled, I believe, in the history of the world, Naziism must be overthrown.

"May the war be swift and short and the peace which follows stand proudly forever on the shattered ruins of an evil name.

"Poland we greet as a comrade. Our hearts are with you and all our power until the angel of peace returns to our midst."

Mr. Chamberlain himself read the radio proclamation from the Cabinet room at 10 Downing Street. He ended with the prayer.

Associated Press

PARIS, Sept. 3.—France gave Germany until 5 p.m. French summer time (8 a.m. M.S.T.) today to reply to her ultimatum demanding that German troops leave Poland or find herself at war with France.

French Ambassador Robert Coulondre delivered the note in Berlin at noon (4 a.m. M.S.T.), it was announced officially, declaring France would go to the aid of Poland if a satisfactory reply was not received by 5 p.m. French summer time (10 a.m. M.S.T.)

France's lag behind Great Britain in going to war was explained by the fact French forces were nearer Germany and could go into action more quickly while Britain needed a few more hours to mass her effectiveness.

At the moment that Coulondre entered the Wilhelmstrasse in Berlin Premier Daladier went to Elysee Palace to confer with President Albert Lebrun.

PARIS, Sept. 3.—The radio announced to the French nation today that Prime Minister Chamberlain had proclaimed Great Britain at war with Germany.

It was assumed France also would consider herself in a state of war with Germany unless Germany accepted immediately her demand for cessation of hostilities and retreat of the German armies from Poland.

Prime Minister Chamberlain's proclamation that Great Britain was at war with Germany left no doubt that France must follow suit.

The announcement that French Ambassador Robert Coulondre would call on the German foreign minister, Joachin von Ribbentrop, in Berlin at noon (4 a.m., M.S.T.) to demand a reply to France's ultimatum to Germany was considered merely a formality

Officials said Coulondre had asked for the appointment in advance and would "deliver a communication of the French Government to the German Government."

The rapidity with which the crisis came to a head caught the French public by surprise.

A drizzling rain rendered streets of the capital even more deserted than usual on Sunday.

Lobbies of the Chamber of Deputies had been alive with rumors of a possible German reply to the French-British demand that Germany cease her invasion of Poland and withdraw her troops or consider herself at war with the western powers.

Mr. Chamberlain's radio announcement which heralded war was heard by only a few here.

At the moment of the Prime Minister's historic announcement Premier Daladier was receiving Foreign Minister Georges Bonnet at the war ministry.

The Polish embassy issued a communique declaring German air raiders killed 1,500 persons in Polish towns Friday and Saturday despite the German agreement to confine bombings to military objectives.

"A barbarous bombing took place at the city of Czestochowa, the Polish Lourdes where homage is paid to the Miraculous Virgin," the communique said. "The city is in flames."

Premier Daladier conferred with President Albert Lebrun shortly after noon.

Robert Coulondre, French ambassador in Berlin, had called at the German foreign ministry at noon.

Coulondre had been instructed by his Government to demand a reply from the German Government to the French ultimatum requesting immediate cessation of hostilities with Poland and withdrawal of German troops.

WARSAW, Sept. 3.—A Polish general staff communique today said that in the first two days of the Nazi invasion the German forces lost 37 warplanes and Poland lost 12.

Air raids occurred throughout Poland, it said, without regardless of whether communities "represented military objectives or not."

(Shortly before the Reich's armed forces moved into Poland, Friday, Fuehrer Hitler said the air force had been instructed to aim their bombs at military objectives only.

(The Polish embassy at Paris announced German air-raiders had killed 1,500 persons in Polish towns Friday and Saturday.)

Precautions Continue

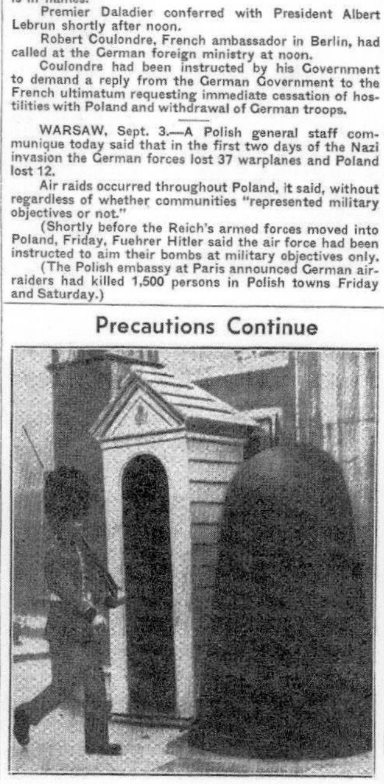

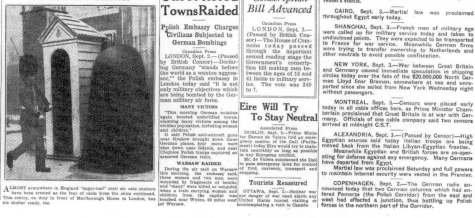

ALMOST everywhere in England "sugar-loaf" steel air raid shelters have been erected as the fear of raids from the skies continued. This sentry, on duty in front of Marlborough House in London, has his shelter ready, too.

Canadian Press

OTTAWA, Sept. 3.—Prime Minister Mackenzie King called the Dominion Cabinet to meet at 9 a.m. E.D.T. (6 a.m. M.S.T.) following receipt of news of Great Britain's declaration of war on Germany.

Word of Prime Minister Chamberlain's declaration reached Ottawa at dawn and found official Ottawa quiet but anticipating.

Mr. Mackenzie King was informed by The Canadian Press, through his secretary, and at once prepared to go to his office, from which the call for a Cabinet meeting went out shortly after.

The Canadian Press also informed Conservative Leader R. J. Manion who was at his home.

Parliament already has been called and will meet Thursday to hear the Government's proposal that Canada place itself squarely beside Great Britain in the struggle and provide the most effective assistance possible.

Canada, in fact, according to most authorities, is now at war. It remains for Parliament to decide to what extent the country will participate in the war and what forces if any shall be sent abroad.

The two major parties, as represented by their leaders, Mr. Mackenzie King of the Liberals and and Doctor Manion of the Conservatives, are agreed on that. A declaration to that effect was made by the Government in the House of Commons last session and received Doctor Manion's assent.

In a recent statement the Conservative leader quoted with approval the words of Sir Wilfrid Laurier, former Liberal Prime Minister, that "when Britain is at war Canada is at war."

On Friday the Cabinet proclaimed a state of apprehended war and brought into operation the War Measures Act of 1914. For the last week or more ministers and their officials worked quietly but speedily, preparing plans and orders as the crisis drew to its height.

Some of these war measures, such as the mobilization of troops and Government control of ship movements, already have gone into effect. Others are expected to come in today or tomorrow.

Still others will be proposed to Parliament. The War Measures Act is a legacy of the Great War. It was passed when Prime Minister Sir Robert Borden called a special session of Parliament in August, 1914, to obtain authority for Canada's efforts in that struggle.

Under it the Government has ample power to take whatever action may be necessary for the defence of Canada and the protection of the economic interests of Canadians pending the passage of such further legislation as may be necessary by Parliament.

The Prime Minister has not yet revealed the measures he will submit to Parliament and will not likely do so until the session opens. Whether a separate declaration of war shall be made by Canada has not been disclosed.

Records of the special session of 1914 do not disclose any special declaration of war on Canada's part, but Parliament of course voted to support the United Kingdom to the limit.

QUEBEC, Sept. 3.—The 8,000-ton Italian freighter San Guiseppe, held on an arrest warrant sworn charging breach of contract, was brought into dock here early today by Admiralty officials and Royal Canadian Mounted Police officers.

The warrant, sworn out by Joseph Pyke and Sons (Liverpool) Limited and claiming damages of $100,000, states the San Guiseppe was chartered to load a full cargo of grain at Three Rivers, Que. The freighter was boarded by R.C.M.P. officers and Arthur Lachance, Admiralty court registrar, when slowing down for a change of pilot in the port of Quebec.

Captain Paolo Sagiietti of the San Giuseppe told Lachance that he was en route to Sydney, N.S., for coal, and that his contract permitted him to "coal" before taking cargo. It is expected the freighter will lie here until Monday, when the case will proceed before the Admiralty registrar.

The freighter sailed from Montreal Saturday. Three Rivers is about half way between Montreal and Quebec.

Unfortified Towns Raided

Polish Embassy Charges Civilians Subjected to German Bombings

Canadian Press

LONDON, Sept. 2.—(Passed by British Censor)—Declaring Germany "stands before the world as a wanton aggressor,'" the Polish embassy in London today said "it is not only military objectives which are being bombed by the German military air force.

MANY VICTIMS

"This morning German aviation again bombed unfortified towns, claiming many victims among the civilian population, including women and children."

It said Polish anti-aircraft guns near Krakow brought down three German planes, four more were shot down near Gdynia, and near Chojnice Polish troops captured an armored German train.

WARSAW RAIDED

During the air raid on Warsaw this morning, the embassy said, three women and two men were wounded by fragments of bombs, and "many" were killed or wounded when a train carrying women and children from the capital was bombed near Wutno, 60 miles west of Warsaw.

Conscription Bill Advanced

Canadian Press

LONDON, Sept. 2.—(Passed by British Censor)—The House of Commons today passed through the important second reading stage the Government's conscription bill making men between the ages of 18 and 41 liable to military service. The vote was 340 to 7.

Eire Will Try To Stay Neutral

Associated Press

DUBLIN, Sept. 2.—Prime Minister Eamon de Valera told an emergency session of the Dail (Parliament) today Eire would try to maintain neutrality as long as possible in any European conflict.

Mr. de Valera summoned the Dail to pass emergency laws for control of food, currency, transport and shipping.

Tourists Reassured

OTTAWA, Sept. 2.—Neither war nor danger of war need alarm any United States tourist visiting or contemplating a visit to Canada

Canadian Press

LONDON, Sept. 3.—The King held a meeting of the Privy Council at 12.45 p.m. (4.45 a.m. M.S.T.) today.

LONDON, Sept. 3.—(Via Radio)—The British Broadcasting Corporation announced that the King will address his subjects in a world-wide broadcast at 6 p.m. (10 a.m. M.S.T.)

BERLIN, Sept. 3.—Adolf Hitler today received the new Soviet ambassador, Alexander Shkvartzeff, who arrived here yesterday by plane with a Russian military mission.

LONDON, Sept. 3.—(Delayed by Censor)—Air raid sirens sounded an alarm in London today at 11.32 a.m. (3.32 a.m. M.S.T.) The whole city was sent to shelters by the wail of the alarm but all-clear signals were sounded 17 minutes later.

Orders were issued forbidding the sounding of whistles or sirens except by police or air raid precautions wardens.

The system of air raid warnings was reviewed with unneeded urgings to "listen for them."

Churches and other places of worship will not be closed but the Government immediately broadcast orders shutting all movies and theatres until further notice.

It added they would be reopened in the future in less vulnerable sectors.

Sports gatherings outdoors and indoors were also prohibited as well as all other entertainments.

The Government "earnestly" requested the people not "to gather in large numbers."

Such meetings, it added, greatly increased the dangers of death from bombing.

Steel-helmeted A.R.P. squads went into immediate action as every London air raid siren screamed.

A few pedestrians on the streets ran for shelters.

The all clear signal, sounded first at 11.49 a.m. (3.49 M.S.T.) was reported intermittently until noon (4 a.m. M.S.T.)

RIO DE JANEIRO, Sept. 3.—The Brazilian Government Saturday declared its neutrality in any European conflict.

LONDON, Sept. 3.—The British Government will call conscripts by proclamation under the conscription bill given a second reading in the House of Commons Saturday.

The measure, permitting conscription of men between the ages of 18 and 41, requires employers to reinstate conscripts upon their return from service. An employer's non-observance of this rule would result in fines and payments to the employed.

LONDON, Sept. 3.—(Passed by British Censor)—The King and Queen heard Prime Minister Chamberlain's war declaration today over the radio in their private apartments at Buckingham Palace.

SAN FRANCISCO, Sept. 3.—The German merchant ship Portland, unheard from since it sailed from Everett, Wash., Wednesday, was reported early today being trailed by one Australian and two Canadian naval vessels somewhere off the Pacific Coast.

The marine exchange of the San Francisco Chamber of Commerce received the information, but attaches said they were not at liberty to disclose the source of it.

Credence to the report was lent by the fact that, although the Australian cruiser Perth and the Canadian destroyers Ottawa and Restigouche had been scheduled to arrive here Tuesday, it was later announced they would not come to San Francisco.

Inquiries as to the vessel's whereabouts at the British consulate here brought the reply: "No information."

On normal schedule the Portland would have arrived at Portland, Ore., three days ago. Mackay Radio said it had not been able to communicate with the ship.

The Portland's United States passengers left the ship at Everett after being held virtual prisoners several hours while the port authorities conferred concerning the vessel's status.

CAIRO, Sept. 3.—Martial law was proclaimed throughout Egypt early today.

SHANGHAI, Sept. 3.—French men of military age were called up for military service today and taken to undisclosed points. They were expected to be transported to France for war service. Meanwhile German firms were trying to transfer ownership to Netherlands and other neutrals to avoid possible confiscation.

NEW YORK, Sept. 3.—War between Great Britain and Germany caused immediate speculation in shipping circles today over the fate of the $20,000,000 North German Lloyd liner Bremen, somewhere at sea and unreported since she sailed from New York Wednesday night without passengers.

MONTREAL, Sept. 3.—Censors were placed early today in all cable offices here, as Prime Minister Chamberlain proclaimed that Great Britain is at war with Germany. Officials of one cable company said two censors arrived at midnight C.S.T.

ALEXANDRIA, Sept. 3.—(Passed by Censor)—High Egyptian sources said today Italian troops are being moved back from the Italian Libyan-Egyptian frontier.

Meanwhile Egyptian and British forces are co-operating for defense against any emergency. Many Germans have departed from Egypt.

Martial law was proclaimed Saturday and full powers to maintain internal security were vested in the Premier.

COPENHAGEN, Sept. 2.—The German radio announced today that two German columns which had entered Pomorze (the Polish Corridor) from the east and west had effected a junction, thus bottling up Polish forces in the northern part of the Corridor.

Despite the devastation of the Depression and the drought, Saskatchewanians moved with great speed and patriotism to support their young men — and women who could now enlist for the first time — on the home front. There was a steady stream of parades held to raise money for Victory Bonds, featuring floats that bore slogans such as "Stamp out U-Boats," "Finish Hitler," and "Men and Money are needed." Booths and posters urging the purchase of bonds and the virtues of sacrifice festooned cities and towns across the province: "I'm making bombs and buying bonds" emblazoned a poster of a woman working in the armaments factories; the *Star Phoenix* supported the Kinsmen Milk for Britain Fund and booths encouraging the purchase of War Savings Stamps, "Stop Hitler! Save Coupons from all Ogilvie products. Exchange them for FREE war savings stamps" and "Keep them Smiling! Lend some work for Victory" could be found on posters in restaurants, church basements and train stations. Women, in particular, organized themselves into support groups, working to distribute ration coupons, joining the Red Cross to send parcels overseas and organizing such groups as the War Mothers Association.

Victory Bonds parade, Regina, 1941

Training at Number 12 Vocational School, Saskatoon, circa 1942

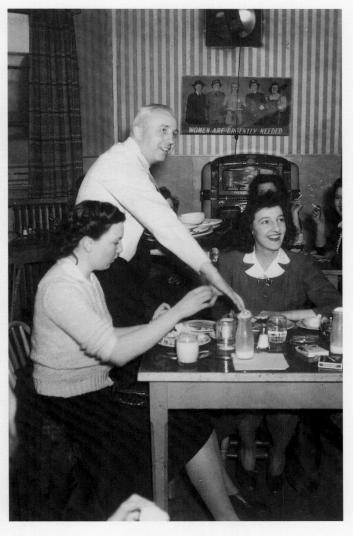

"Women urgently needed" recruitment poster at local restaurant, Saskatoon, circa 1941

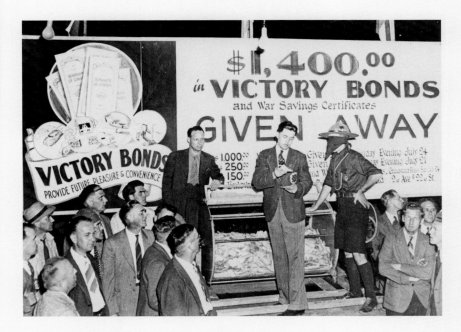

Victory Bonds rally, Saskatoon, 1942

Royal Canadian Air Force operators, Saskatoon, circa 1941

RCAF II Service Flying Training Class,
Yorkton, December, 1942

Triple Ferris Wheel, Regina Exhibition, 1942

King George VI inspects
the troops, Regina, 1939

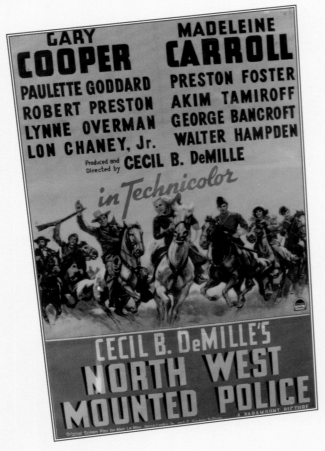

Sam Swimmer, chief of the Sweetgrass Reserve for almost forty-five years, with his grandson, Andrew, and his son, Bill, circa 1941

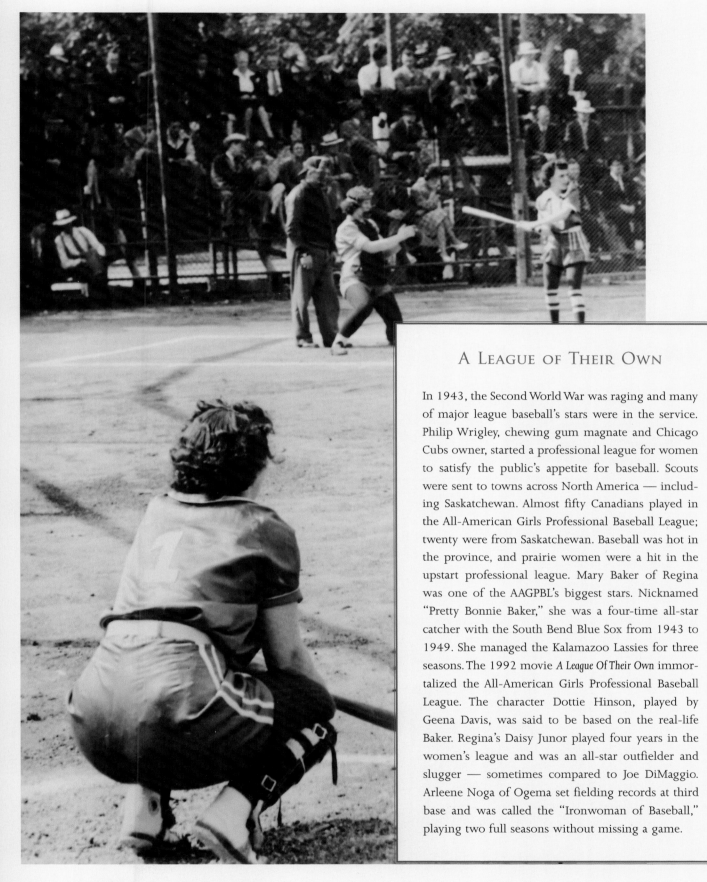

Women's baseball game, near Regina, circa 1943

A League of Their Own

In 1943, the Second World War was raging and many of major league baseball's stars were in the service. Philip Wrigley, chewing gum magnate and Chicago Cubs owner, started a professional league for women to satisfy the public's appetite for baseball. Scouts were sent to towns across North America — including Saskatchewan. Almost fifty Canadians played in the All-American Girls Professional Baseball League; twenty were from Saskatchewan. Baseball was hot in the province, and prairie women were a hit in the upstart professional league. Mary Baker of Regina was one of the AAGPBL's biggest stars. Nicknamed "Pretty Bonnie Baker," she was a four-time all-star catcher with the South Bend Blue Sox from 1943 to 1949. She managed the Kalamazoo Lassies for three seasons. The 1992 movie *A League Of Their Own* immortalized the All-American Girls Professional Baseball League. The character Dottie Hinson, played by Geena Davis, was said to be based on the real-life Baker. Regina's Daisy Junor played four years in the women's league and was an all-star outfielder and slugger — sometimes compared to Joe DiMaggio. Arleene Noga of Ogema set fielding records at third base and was called the "Ironwoman of Baseball," playing two full seasons without missing a game.

CHAPTER SEVEN

On the morning of November 24, 1945, a troop train carrying soldiers of the South Saskatchewan Regiment sped westward, toward home and a lavish welcome draped in bunting and washed by tears — of joy for the men who were returning from war, of grief for those who were not.

"The train was due to arrive at Weyburn at 10:30 hours and by that time a last polish had been given to all brass and leather, ready for the last parade," Lieutenant Colonel G.B. Buchanan recounted in a regimental history. "The train pulled into the station where thousands of cheering people voiced their welcome. After arrival, one half-hour was allowed for hellos to wives, sweethearts and families, before the regiment fell in for the big parade … through 15,000 wildly shouting, cheering crowds, through streets hung with banners, decorated store windows and lamp-posts with placards of the regiment's battles."

The unbridled excitement and relief of 1945 had already been captured in triumphant headlines and scenes of elation throughout Saskatchewan — a particularly memorable image, published in the *Leader-Post* that May and reproduced in a 1979 pictorial history of the province, showed a smiling youngster from Regina holding an "extra" edition of the newspaper with its blaring banner: "VICTORY! Surrender is unconditional."

The world to which the thousands of discharged soldiers were returning was much changed from 1939. Saskatchewan's population had, in fact, decreased by more than 50,000 during the Second World War because of an eastward outflow

LEFT PAGE: V-J Day celebration, Regina, August 15, 1945

ABOVE: *Leader-Post* V-E Day special edition, May 6, 1945

Teen Fashion Show, Saskatoon, September 10, 1951

of soldiers and factory workers who had helped drive the Canadian military machine. But the province was, like other parts of the post-war world, poised for a grand welcome home and to fully embrace the new era of peace — along with the impressive technological advances and relative material abundance it promised.

"The returning veterans carried home a broader view of the world," noted John Archer in *Saskatchewan: A History*. "Comradeship welded in war laid the basis for the concept of a cultural mosaic, for the battle rolls recorded that Ukrainian, German, French, Scandinavian, Hungarian, Indian, Métis, as well as Anglo-Saxon, had worn the uniform and won the day."

The coming age of growth would be a particularly interesting phase in the life of Saskatchewan, which had also elected North America's first socialist government a year before the war's end. All eyes were on the province and its unprecedented political experiment, which was to unfold not only during a decade of feverish economic activity but also at a time when allegations of — and paranoia about — Communist infiltration of Canada were at their height.

"As the war neared its end, people looked forward to the brave new world that was being promised," A.W. Johnson has written in *Dream No Little Dreams: A Biography of the Douglas Government of Saskatchewan, 1944-1961*. "People were ready for change, and the election of the CCF in Saskatchewan became the portent of that change.... The hope inspired by the CCF in Saskatchewan and its willingness to reach out to new frontiers of public policy were unmistakable. And that was what the majority of Saskatchewanians were looking for."

But the new premier, Tommy Douglas, was keenly aware of the pitfalls of pushing that frontier too far and too fast. During the election campaign, he had endured — and overcome — the dire warnings of such critics as the *Leader-Post*, which editorialized against the CCF and the "stultifying dictatorial system" it represented. So he was eager to disarm the alarmists as his government swung into action, soft-pedaling many of his reforms even as they shook the province's political foundations and made lasting impressions on the entire country's social fabric.

"We know that a co-operative commonwealth cannot be established at one jump," Douglas acknowledged soon after his election. "We know that it means moving forward step by step, along many roads simultaneously — health, education, social services, development of co-operatives and the establishment of socially-owned industries. These are the roads along which we propose to advance just as quickly as we feel that you will go with us."

Changes that were largely beyond the power of government were already reshaping Saskatchewan society. Advances in farm machinery were continuing to revolutionize agricultural production and recalibrate optimum farm size in the province, and consequently tens of thousands of people left the fields and farming villages for Saskatoon, Regina and other urban centres. Between 1941 and 1951, according to Archer, the rural population plunged from 514,677 to 398,279 — a 22.6-per-cent drop that, for the first time, made rural residents a slight minority among the province's 832,000 people.

"Farm mechanization had accelerated after the war," he wrote, "for the farm machinery industry was able to turn its full production for peaceful pursuits. There was a great increase in the production of tractors, gasoline engines, trucks and combines, though the sale of farm implements depended to a large degree on the farm income per year.... However, the most marked effect was on the size of farm holdings."

The changes were wrenching for many; thousands of small farmers — struggling to compete in grain and livestock markets — campaigned for a government-guaranteed "parity" price system for all agricultural products that they believed would correct unfair advantages enjoyed by large-scale farming operations. The parity movement peaked in September 1946 — and faded soon after — when members of the United Farmers of Canada picketed the Saskatoon stockyards.

"The marginal producers petered out along with their strike," writes John Herd Thompson in *Forging the Prairie West*. "The censuses of 1951, 1956 and 1961 provide a grim record of their decline and the ascendancy of the mechanized commercial farmer-businessman."

Beaux Arts Ball, Saskatoon, February 25, 1952

Modernization also brought electricity to remote corners of the province that were still operating with 19th-century household technology midway through the 20th.

A November 1953 story published in the *Western Producer* featured the reaction of rural residents to the switch-flicking "thrill" of instant power: "The biggest thrill of electricity coming to the farm is pressing a button and seeing a light go on," the article noted. "One farm woman said, "I tried all the switches and then I carried the coal oil lamps down to the basement, singing a triumphant little chant about 'No more lamp glasses to clean, no more lamps to fill....' Even a bare light bulb hung from the ceiling and operated by a pull chain seems wonderful ...""

At the same time, Saskatchewan began enjoying a boom in its relatively untapped mineral resource sector. Oil, uranium, sodium sulphate, natural gas and potash discoveries in the immediate postwar years combined to make the long held dream of diversification of the provincial economy a graspable reality.

"Alkali, the stuff which prairie pioneers cursed for years, today is proving to be the salvation of the Chaplin community, 104 miles west of Regina," notes one *Leader-Post* story from March 1951, when the chemical used by pulp and paper companies was in high demand.

"The eighteen-mile-long Lake Chaplin is the source of one of the richest and purest sodium sulphate deposits in the world and the product is providing a livelihood for many residents of the community who formerly were totally dependent on their grain crops or cattle sales," the article states. "The soil in the

Unidentified chief, just before the formation of the Federation of Indians, circa 1946

Chaplin area is poor and seldom do farmers get bumper crops, but crop or no crop, many of these farmers don't need to worry any longer. Since the Saskatchewan government's sodium sulphate plant opened in 1948, there has been a steady improvement in the financial position of many of Chaplin's residents."

The Douglas government would undertake massive hydro-electric developments, inaugurate an interprovincial oil pipeline in October 1950 and steer plans for extracting potash from the vast underground beds stretching across eastern and central Saskatchewan. It would take years for potash production to begin, but worldwide demand for the substance — a chief ingredient in fertilizer and other products — would eventually become a key part of the sustained effort to broaden the province's economic base.

"Lloydminster, initially an agricultural distributing centre straddling the Saskatchewan-Alberta boundary ... became Saskatchewan's 'first oil town,'" Jim Wright noted in a Golden Jubilee history of the province, published in 1955, that clearly demonstrated how an oil boom was also reshaping Saskatchewan.

"Saskatchewan's crude oil production in 1940 was 331 barrels; in 1945, more than 16,000 barrels, in 1947, 150,000 barrels; in 1954, some 5,000,000 barrrels as exploration involving millions of dollars resulted in new oilfields near Coleville, Fosterton, Smiley, Kindersley and elsewhere."

The fledgling CCF government's handling of such opportunities was a subject of controversy at the time and has been debated by politicians and historians ever since. Some analysts argue that concerns about Saskatchewan's socialist policies deterred investment in the province at a critical stage in its development, ensuring it would remain in the economic shadow of Alberta. Defenders of the Douglas government argue the creation of eleven Crown corporations early in its tenure — despite the failure of some public-ownership initiatives — helped stabilize and diversify the economy, and that the province ultimately struck a pragmatic, productive balance between co-operative principles and the power of private enterprise.

What isn't debated is the fact that the province was profoundly affected by events in the first decade after the Second World War, an era that cemented the image of Saskatchewan as having a distinct and dynamic political culture.

"As premier, Douglas was the unquestioned leader in cabinet, in caucus, and party of matters of policy," wrote Thomas and Ian McLeod in *Tommy Douglas: The Road to Jerusalem*. "He was the government's practical dreamer. The essence of his leadership, the source of his power over others, was his ability to dream and to cast his dreams in practical forms, to reduce his ideas to precise language and to articulate them in such a way as to inspire those around him."

Other historians have argued that Douglas and his political peers identified and skillfully tapped into a new kind of collective personality for the province that had been forged in the searing heat and hardship of the Depression.

"Saskatchewan appeared to have thrown off some of the pall of the 1930s as the mid-1950s approached," wrote Archer. "But physical scars remained — derelict houses, roadside fences that drifted over with blown dirt, weather-beaten buildings in small towns. These were the overt signs. There were deeper marks unseen, evident in a compulsion to build a protection against ill health, against foreclosure on farmland and to provide price support and protection against the elements and the machinations of men. The shadow of the 1930s lay across much of the legislation that was passed and affected the fortunes of those who strove for a seat in that body."

One legacy regularly trumpeted by chroniclers of the era was the creation of the Saskatchewan Arts Board in 1948.

Hailed as the first agency of its kind in North America, the SAB is credited with fostering a flowering of culture in the post-war

Saskatchewan, directed by Raoul Walsh, 1954

years that helped artists such as the Regina Five — Ron Bloore, Ken Lochheed, Art MacKay, Ted Godwin and Doug Morton — gain national reputations. Celebrated Prince Albert tenor Jon Vickers and Weyburn soprano Irene Salemka, who would go on to international acclaim, were also supported with funds from the board. Grants and workshops for painters, musicians, writers, handicraft artisans and a host of other artists contributed to a burst of creative energy among Saskatchewan's cultural communities.

"I've always maintained that the people of the Prairies ... are hungry ... for things of the mind and the spirit: good music, literature, paintings and folk songs," Douglas once said about the creation of the arts board.

"The board played a strong supportive role in all the arts — thanks in no small measure to its spirited executive director, Norah McCullough," Johnson, a leading bureaucrat in the Douglas era, observed in *Dream No Little Dreams*.

This blossoming of the province's arts scene followed the appearance of *Who Has Seen the Wind*, W.O. Mitchell's classic novel about drought-era Saskatchewan. A highlight of the early 1950s was the landmark publication of *So Little For the Mind*,

Gordie Howe, Detroit Red Wings' camp, circa 1954

a critical book on modern education by Saskatchewan historian Hilda Neatby.

Meanwhile, a future artistic talent from Saskatchewan was finding her voice at a Saskatoon hospital in the midst, oddly, of a polio epidemic that swept the province in 1952.

Nine-year-old Roberta Joan Anderson — who would become famous as the pop singer Joni Mitchell — was one of many Canadian youngsters struck by the potentially crippling illness. As she recovered at St. Paul's Hospital, Roberta faced the grim prospect of spending Christmas in the children's ward.

"Her singing was at first, literally, a form of self-healing," her biographer, Brian Hinton, has written. "As a nine-year-old stranded in a polio ward over Christmas, she had certainly needed something."

Mitchell has recalled how someone had sent her a colouring book with pictures of old-fashioned carolers and the lyrics to their songs:

"So, I started to sing Christmas carols, and I used to sing them real loud. When the nurse came into the room I would sing louder. The boy in the bed next to me used to complain. And I discovered I was a ham. That was the first time I started to sing for people."

Joni Mitchell's fame was yet to come. But by the early 1950s, another talented Saskatchewanian — who had also developed his special gift in the Saskatoon area in the 1930s and 1940s — was already the toast of the hockey world. Floral native Gordie Howe, every inch of him the strong, silent, strapping lad of prairie lore, was the NHL's perennial high scorer and most valuable player, leading his Detroit Red Wings to four Stanley Cups between 1950 and 1955.

Howe had also overcome serious adversity — a near-fatal head injury after crashing into the boards in 1949 — to achieve unparalleled greatness in his game. It made him the perfect poster boy for a province that, by the 1950s, had weathered the hardships of the Depression and the horrors of the Second World War to become a place of growing prosperity and even greater promise.

Weather Forecast
FAIR AND COLD

Saskatoon Star-Phœnix

VOLUME LXXII.—No. 206. 32 PAGES SASKATOON, SASK., MONDAY, MAY 7, 1945. * * * PRICE 5 CENTS

GERMANY SURRENDERS

—Photo by Karsh, Ottawa.
HIS MAJESTY KING GEORGE VI
monarch of Great Britain, India and the British Dominions beyond the seas, whose steadfast courage and resolute strength throughout the darkest days of the war was a symbol of hope to the peoples of the British Empire.

LONDON, May 7 (CP).—The greatest war in history ended today with the unconditional surrender of Germany.

The surrender of the Third Reich to the Western Allies and Russia was made at General Eisenhower's headquarters at Reims, France, by Colonel-General Jodl, chief of staff for the German Army.

This was announced officially after German broadcasts told the German people that Grand Admiral Karl Doenitz had ordered the capitulation of all fighting forces, and called off the U-boat war.

JAPANESE YET TO CONQUER

Joy at the news was tempered only by the realization that the war against Japan remains to be resolved, with many casualties still ahead.

The end of the European warfare, greatest, bloodiest and costliest war in human history—it has claimed at least 40,000,000 casualties on both sides in killed, wounded and captured—came after five years, eight months and six days of strife that overspread the globe.

Arrogant German armies invaded Poland September 1, 1939, beginning the agony that convulsed the world for 2,076 days.

Unconditional surrender of the beaten remnants of Hitler's legions first was announced by the Germans.

The historic news began breaking with a Danish broadcast that Norway had been surrendered unconditionally by its conquerors.

SUCCUMB AFTER SIX YEARS

Then the new German foreign minister, Ludwig Schwerin von Krosigk, announced to the German people, shortly after 2 p.m. (6 a.m. M.D.T.) that "after almost six years struggle we have succumbed."

Von Krosigk announced Grand Admiral Karl Doenitz had "ordered the unconditional surrender of all fighting German troops."

The world waited tensely. Then at 7.35 a.m., M.D.T., came the Associated Press flash from Reims, France, telling of the signing at General Eisenhower's headquarters of the unconditional surrender at 2.41 French time Germany had given up to the Western Allies and to Russia.

ALLIED CAPITALS EXCITED

London went wild at the news. Crowds jammed Piccadilly Circus. Smiling throngs poured out of subways and lined the streets.

(Cheers went up in New York, Toronto and Montreal, too, and papers showered down from sky-scrapers).

A discordant note came from the German-controlled radio at Prague. A broadcast monitored by the Czechoslovak Government offices in London said the German commander in Czechoslovakia did not recognize the surrender of Admiral Doenitz and would fight on until his forces "have secured free passage for German troops out of the country."

But the Prague radio earlier announced the capitulation of Breslau, long besieged by Russian forces

The B.B.C. said telephone conversations were going on between London, Washington and Moscow in order to fix the exact hour of the V-E Day announcement by Prime Minister Churchill, President Truman and Premier Stalin.

Grand Admiral Karl Doenitz, in an order broadcast today, ordered all his Nazi U-boats to cease hostilities and reports from Stockholm said V-E Day might be proclaimed without a battle for Norway.

The Flensburg radio broadcast a three-day-old order of the day by Doenitz to his submarine crews telling them:

"Crushing superiority has compressed us into a very narrow area. Continuation of the struggle is impossible from bases that remain."

Unconfirmed advices from Stockholm—repeated later by the Allied-controlled Luxembourg radio—said the Germans already had affixed their signature to Allied surrender terms for Norway.

EXPECTANT

Great Britain was clearly expecting a V-E Day announcement at any time. London began to dress up for the big occasion by draping flags on some downtown buildings. Prime Minister Churchill was declared to be busy at his desk, but close-mouthed as to his plans. The British Cabinet stood by for any possible emergency session.

The political correspondent for the London Evening News said: "Mr. Churchill is today expected to broadcast from the Cabinet room at 10 Downing Street that the war in Europe is over."

A headline in the London Star declared "today may be V-E night. Peace in Europe will be announced at any hour now."

Veteran parliamentary correspondents for two British press agencies—Press Association and Exchange Telegraph—said the general expectation was that Churchill will make an announcement "in a matter of hours."

Any V-E Day announcement by Mr. Churchill will be broadcast from his cabinet room at 10 Downing Street. Afterwards he is expected to address the crowds from a balcony overlooking Whitehall, where a special microphone apparatus is set up.

SIMULTANEOUS

Ed. Stackpole, Press Association's parliamentary correspondent, said perhaps the actual hour of the peace announcement was not definitely set, but that the three Allied leaders—Messrs. Churchill, Stalin and Truman—were undoubtedly trying to synchronize simultaneous release of the news.

Prime Minister Churchill remained in London during the week-end, and the King and Queen returned Sunday. There were reports that the Cabinet was called into an unusual Sunday session, but subsequently the Ministry of Information said no cabinet meetings had been called.

The excitement over Denmark's liberation had not entirely subsided. A small detachment of Americans entering Copenhagen Sunday was fired upon by roof-top snipers, presumed to be Danish Nazis.

Thousands of Danes thronged the square earlier to jeer and spit at more than 400 Danish Nazi sympathizers, loaded into trucks and paraded before them.

Occupation of Holland by the 1st Canadian Army was scheduled today. The formal surrender of all German troops in Holland took place Sunday at Wagningen, where Field Marshal Johannes Blaskowitz and his staff officers signed the necessary documents at the direction of Lt.-Gen. Charles Foulkes of London, Ont., 1st Canadian Corps commander.

V-E Day Tuesday

LONDON, May 7 (CP)—The Ministry of Information announced that Tuesday will be treated as V-E Day.

Prime Minister Churchill will broadcast at 3 p.m. Tuesday (7 a.m., M.D.T.), the King at 9 p.m. (1 p.m., M.D.T.)

The ministry statement said that in accordance with arrangements between the three great powers an official announcement will be broadcast by Mr. Churchill at 3 p.m., Tuesday.

OTTAWA, May 7 (CP)—Speaking over a national network of the Canadian Broadcasting Corporation at 2 p.m., M.D.T., Hon. J. L. Ilsley, acting Prime Minister, announced the issuance of proclamations making Tuesday, May 9, a public holiday in Canada and authorizing the observance of next Sunday, May 13 as a "day of prayer and solemn thanksgiving."

Nazis Had Purpose In News Break

By The Canadian Press

Germany, apparently purposefully, beat the Allies today in announcing her unconditional surrender to Britain, the United States and Russia. In so doing, the enemy was quick to get in an appeal for Allied mercy after Germany's "heroic fight of almost six years of incomparable hardness."

Knowing that the Allies, weeks ago, had arranged for simultaneous release in London, Washington and Moscow of the news for which the world had waited for more than 5½ years, the Germans, it was apparent, were determined to upset these carefully-laid plans.

The announcement today of the Flensburg radio that Grand Admiral Doenitz had ordered surrender of all German fighting troops was received in New York at 4.36 a.m., M.D.T. It was not until 7.35 a.m. that Edward Kennedy's flash from Reims, France, first story from the Allied side to announce cessation of hostilities, arrived in New York.

Goebbels Dead

MOSCOW, May 7 (Reuters).—Unconfirmed reports reaching here today said that the bodies of Joseph Goebbels and his family had been found in an air raid shelter near the Reichstag in Berlin.

VICTORY Editorial

A wrecked and desolated Germany has capitulated unconditionally—the day, which for five years, eight months and six days civilization has striven, has finally arrived. If this day means anything surely it must be that never again shall the peoples of the world be forced to undergo the privations, suffering and terrors of the past six years. There will be rejoicing everywhere, possibly even in the conquered country, but that cannot but be tempered by the realization of the loss of gallant lives, given in a glorious cause.

Nor must it be forgotten that this is not the end of the struggle. There is still a long road ahead before Japan gives in. There is the more tremendous task of rebuilding the world. Let us not relax for a moment in either objective. There is a pause today—but tomorrow backs must be bent afresh to the great tasks ahead. Tasks which today's events outline in all their stark reality.

Jubilant Canadians Celebrate Victory

Canadian Press

The 11,000,000 Canadians who went solemnly to war against Germany in September, 1939, had their victory today and they greeted it with an explosive enthusiasm that filled streets with paper and sound, hearts with thanksgiving and eyes with tears.

Reports that started flooding in from one end of the country to the other all bore the stamp of feelings unloosed in an unbridled celebration without parallel since the armistice of the First Great War.

Even the successive surrenders of great hordes of German troops on scattered fronts in past days, even the obvious fact that German defeat had been inevitable for weeks failed to sap the thrill from the anti-climax that was the official announcement of German surrender.

Giddily, loudly, vehemently the nation celebrated in its streets. But in countless homes there was a silent prayer of thankfulness for the massive blessing implied in the brief words of the announcement.

AT GREAT PRICE

And thousands of miles to the east, Canadian tanks and British Tommies rolled into the streets of Utrecht as the 1st Canadian Army began the formal completion of its last great task in the Second Great War—the liberation of a starving Holland. And behind them stretched the graves in the soil of Italy, Belgium, France, Holland and Germany to mark the price of the nation's five years and more of war.

From villages and towns and cities came the same reports. In North Bay, Ont., crowds poured into the streets, bells rang, whistles blew, fire trucks rumbled through the streets with sirens screaming. In Galt, Ont., factory workers surged into the streets and streamed up and down, shouting and singing.

PAPER SHOWERS

In Toronto, a warplane stunted amid the skyscrapers in the business district while in the streets below paper descended in endless showers upon the celebrants. In Halifax, ships of a dozen nations sounded their whistles and sirens in accompaniment to the joy running rampant in the streets.

In Montreal, crying, shouting people jammed famed St. James Street beneath clouds of ticker tape. In Winnipeg, stranger hit stranger on the back.

In nearly every city and nearly every town, it was the same. And as the first flush of enthusiasm began to wear off, the programs that had been prepared for weeks were

JUBILANT
Continued on Page 2, Column 3

Truman Holds Off

WASHINGTON, May 7 (AP).—President Truman said today he had agreed with the London and Moscow governments that he would make no announcement on the surrender of enemy forces "until a simultaneous announcement can be made by the three governments.

Premature Announcement Upset Plans

OTTAWA, May 7 (CP).—A premature German announcement of unconditional surrender over the Flensburg radio today disrupted Allied plans for simultaneous announcement on V-E Day in London, Washington and Moscow—an announcement believed to have been scheduled for Tuesday, The Canadian Press learned today.

Cut Sugar Ration

OTTAWA, May 7 (CP).—A cut in the individual sugar ration from 14 to nine pounds for the period June 1 to December 31, was announced today by the Prices Board.

The reduction will be made by allowing consumers one pound a month instead of the present two pounds for June, July, August, October and December. The September and November rations will remain at two pounds to allow as much home canning as possible.

The home canning allotment of 20 preserves coupons will be left intact and the two regular preserves coupons will continue to become valid each month.

In addition to affecting householders, the reduction will apply to the armed forces, jam and wine manufacturers, bakers, biscuit and breakfast cereal plants, soft drink manufacturers and quota users, such as restaurants and hotels.

Decision to make the cut followed a recent conference in Washington at which it was reported that United Nations requirements are 1,254,000 tons more than available supplies.

Another Secret Weapon Located

WITH THE U.S. 9TH ARMY IN GERMANY, May 7 (AP).—One of Hitler's last secret weapons—a piloted flying bomb—has been uncovered by the 9th Army advance.

The new V-weapon was just like the V-1 except that, 12 feet from the tip of the warhead, there was a small cockpit enclosed in glass. It was cramped and had a simple flying instrument panel, elevator controls and a light parachute.

The pilot could drop out in a hurry. The theory was expressed that the pilot would aim the bomb and then parachute. On the other hand there were reports the Germans planned to use suicide pilots.

Japs Want War To Be Pepped Up

SAN FRANCISCO, May 7 (AP).—Tokyo radio Saturday reported directors of the totalitarian political association of greater Japan were demanding a special session of the Japanese Diet.

This new evidence of dissatisfaction with the war situation followed Tokyo newspaper criticism of the policies of Baron Kanto Suzuki, third wartime premier, who only recently took office.

The broadcast, recorded by the Federal Communications Commission, said the party directors had also decided to establish special committees to deal with various production, defence and air raid matters.

Must Beat Japs Before Cheering

SAN FRANCISCO, May 7 (CP).—The Canadian people will receive news of the end of the European war with feelings which cannot be put easily into words "but this is no hour for exultation," Prime Minister Mackenzie King said today in a statement.

It is time for rededication and resolution, he said. The Japanese aggressor must be defeated and his ambitions crushed.

"The hard struggle for peace must go on long after the guns cease firing," he continued. "Until we win that struggle we cannot say we have won the war. This we should remember today."

"The people of Canada—like the people of the United States—will receive the news of the end of the European war with feelings not easily put into words," said Mr. King. "We think first of those who died to make this day possible; of those who lie wounded; of those who still fight on in other areas where the war continues.

"We rejoice that the righteous cause for which we fought in Europe has triumphed. But this is no hour for exultation. Rather, it is time for rededication and resolution. More objectives remain to be won. The Japanese aggressor must be defeated and his ambitions forever crushed.

"We must relieve the suffering and restore the devastated areas in the lands of our liberated Allies. Above all we must fight to a victorious end of the war against war itself; we must lay at San Francisco a solid foundation on which can be built an enduring structure of international co-operation and world peace.

"The hard struggle for peace must go on long after the guns cease firing. Until we win that struggle we cannot say we have won the war. This we should remember today."

"EVIL TRINITY"

SAN FRANCISCO, May 7 (AP).—Although the end of physical warfare is in sight "the world must cope with the evil trinity that accomplishes war—the scourges of devastation, pestilence and famine," M. J. Coldwell, C.C.F. leader, said today in a statement.

"Twice in a generation," said Mr. Coldwell, "the lights of peace in Europe have gone out. We rejoice today that after nearly six long and dreadful years they shine again. Here in San Francisco we hope and pray that they may be made to shine more brightly for evermore. As we do so we remember gratefully those who have suffered the horrors of battle, murder and sudden death for our sakes.

"Our task, of course, is not over yet—Japan may still resist the forces of liberation for some time and long suffering China may suffer still. The end of physical warfare, however, is in sight. Meanwhile the world must cope with the evil trinity that accompanies war—the scourges of devastation, pestilence and famine.

"We are face to face with a great challenge. Morally and economical-

MUST BEAT
Continued on Page 2, Column 5

Oswiecim Surpassed All Horror Camps

LONDON, May 7 (AP).—The Moscow radio said today more than 4,000,000 persons of various European nationalities were killed by the Germans in the Oswiecim concentration camp in Poland.

The broadcast quoted the Soviet Extraordinary State Commission describing the camp as "far surpassing all hitherto-known German death-camps in its elaborate equipment, technical organization and mass-scale extermination of people."

"German professors and doctors conducted here mass experiments on perfectly healthy men, women and children," the report said. "They conducted experiments in sterilization of women, castration of men, experiments on children, experiments on artificial infection of masses of people with cancer, typhus and malaria and they tested poisons on live people."

VICTORY LOAN

OTTAWA, May 7 (CP).—Canada's Eighth Victory Loan campaign, its minimum objective $1,350,000,000, today swung into its third and last week with loan workers heartened by the heavy purchases by individual buyers.

Sales to individuals for the first 12 days of the three-week drive amounted to a cumulative total of $455,389,950. At the end of the comparable period in last autumn's seventh loan campaign individuals had purchased $407,318,400.

Objective for individual purchasers in the eighth loan is $675,000,000, half of the over-all national objective. Cumulative figures for the first 12 days of the current campaign stand at $911,517,350, against $901,895,000 at the same stage in the seventh loan.

Wide gains in individual purchases in comparison with their subscriptions in the last loan were reported from various provincial headquarters. The largest gain was registered in Quebec which had a margin of $9,000,000 over comparable individual purchases in the seventh loan campaign.

Among the largest subscriptions in the "special names" group was $12,000,000 from the Great West Life Assurance Company of Winnipeg.

Urged to Stay at Work

OTTAWA, May 7 (CP).—Munitions Minister Howe, in a statement released by his office, today appealed to all Canadian workers to remain at their jobs for the balance of today.

Author Farley Mowat lived his early years as a writer in Saskatoon, date unknown

Abstract artist William Perehudoff, studio, Saskatoon, date unknown

Dorothy Knowles, landscape artist, Saskatoon, date unknown

THE ARTS

The establishment of the Saskatchewan Arts Board, the first of its kind in North America, allowed the many arts — painting, writing and music — to flourish in the postwar years. Among those who benefited from the arts-friendly environment were artists such as Dorothy Pawson and writers such as W.O. Mitchell. The post-1950s saw the emergence of many important artists, including landscape artist Dorothy Knowles and abstract painter William Perehudoff. Many artists found great support and encouragement in the art colony established by Gus Kenderdine at Emma Lake in the late Thirties that flourished during the 1940s.

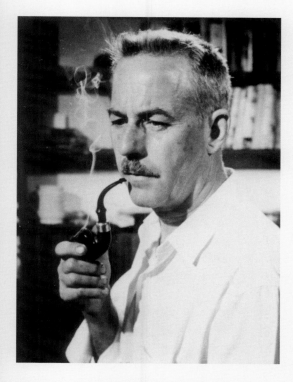

W.O. Mitchell, Saskatchewan literary icon, date unknown

Untitled, Prairie Road, by Ruth Pawson, 1950

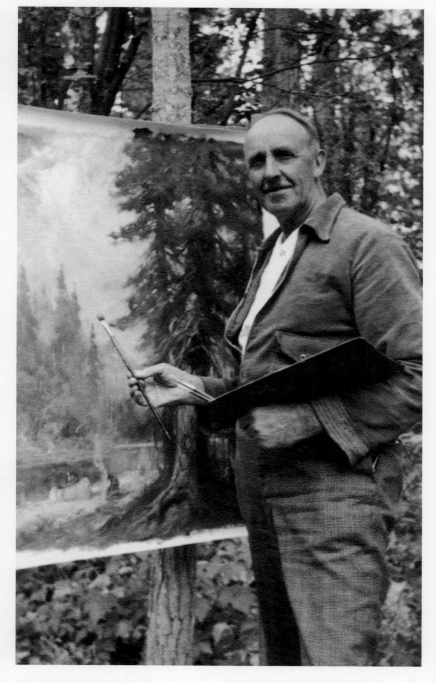

Gus Kenderdine, artist and founder of the Emma Lake arts school, Emma Lake, circa 1940s

Tommy Douglas campaigning with his mother, Anne, circa 1944

Tommy Douglas, far right, swearing in as premier, Saskatchewan Legislature, Regina, June 1944

Thomas (Tommy) Clement Douglas was born on October 20, 1904, in Falkirk, Scotland. The eldest of three children, he showed an early appreciation for the arts, performing monologues at family functions and eventually playing small roles in a Winnipeg vaudeville theatre after the family relocated to the Canadian Prairies in 1910. At the age of six, Douglas suffered a bone infection and was hospitalized four years later. He received several knee operations, but — since the family didn't have money for a specialist — was told that his leg would have to be amputated to stop the spread of infection. Douglas' parents were grateful when a visiting surgeon offered to perform another operation for free on the condition that his students could attend the surgery. Douglas' leg was saved and a flame was sparked that would later ignite his passion for universally accessible medical care.

With a fiery spirit and competitive nature, Douglas experimented with many careers in his youth — among which he worked as an amateur actor and apprentice printer. He began training to box at fifteen — but at 135 pounds, he quickly became more of a sparring partner than a prizefighter. Douglas' calling, of course, was to a fight in a different ring.

It was while Douglas was enrolled in classes at the Baptist Church's Brandon college from 1924 to 1929 that he refined his concept of the "social gospel," his vision of religion-in-action. In the winter of his graduating year, at the age of twenty-six, Douglas was asked to minister on a trial basis at the Calvary Baptist Church in Weyburn, Saskatchewan. After a number of years helping the people of Weyburn keep their faith through drought and the Depression, Douglas decided to try his hand at politics where he thought, possibly, he could make more of a difference. In 1935, he was elected an MP in the Co-operative Commonwealth Federation (CCF) and led his party to power in 1944 as the leader of the provincial CCF in Saskatchewan — North America's first-ever socialist government. As a passionate and aggressive public speaker, Douglas was often considered larger than life, though small in stature. After passing 100 bills during his first term, introducing Saskatchewanians to car insurance, labour reforms and his beloved universal medicare, Douglas said in 1961, then as national leader of the NDP: "My friends, watch out for the little fellow with an idea."

Tommy Douglas, 1944

Weather Forecast
CLOUDY, SHOWERS

Saskatoon Star-Phœnix

Rye Close
Winnipeg:
July 111¼ Oct 111¼ Dec 110⅝

VOLUME LXXI.—No. 244. 16 PAGES SASKATOON, SASK., FRIDAY, JUNE 16, 1944. PUBLISHED AT 6.15 A.M. ✣ PRICE 5 CENTS

C.C.F. LANDSLIDE IN SASKATCHEWAN

Huge U.S. Planes Bomb Japan's Industrial Areas

WASHINGTON, June 16 (AP).—American super Fortresses bombed Japan's homeland Thursday and the Tokyo radio, acknowledging attacks, said industrial areas of Moji and Shimonoseki were hit.

In Congress, Representative Joe Starnes (Dem., Ala.) told his colleagues he had information there was "great destruction" in Tokyo. There was no confirmation of Starnes' report from the War Department, which did not disclose targets.

Moji is a city on Kyushu, southernmost of the main Japanese islands. Shimonoseki is on Honshu Island just across a strait from Kyushu. They are about 586 miles, airline, from Tokyo.

FROM CHINA, BURMA

An Imperial Japanese communique estimated the number of raiding planes at 20 and made the usual claims that they were intercepted and "repulsed." It said several were shot down and Domei, Japanese news agency, said six were shot down.

Here, the only official information available late at night was that attacks were carried out by B-29's flying from bases in the China-India-Burma theatre.

The War Department disclosed that the long-secret flying giants had gone into action. The announcement said:

"B-29 super fortresses of the United States Army Air Forces 20th Bomber Command bombed Japan today."

To this was added some time

HUGE PLANES
Continued on Page 2, Column 2

5,000th Wren

OTTAWA, June 16 (CP). — When Lillian Edith Messenger of Calgary enlisted in the Women's Royal Canadian Navy Service she made history, though she didn't know it.

With her enlistment, Probationary Wren Messenger becomes the 5,000th Canadian girl to be attested in the naval service.

Big Battles Are Coming

By ROSS MUNRO
Canadian Press War Correspondent

WITH BRITISH AND CANADIAN FORCES IN FRANCE, June 16.—This campaign is sweeping to its first great climax and big battles, which would bring large armored formations into combat over the Norman farmlands, may be approaching rapidly.

A deep wedge was driven into German-held territory south of Bayeux by the thrilling dash of an Allied armored formation past Tilly-sur-Seulles and on toward Villers-Bocage, about six miles

BIG BATTLES
Continued on Page 2, Column 3

Is Rebuked In Commons

LONDON, June 16 (CP).Information Minister Bracken sharply criticized Capt. A. S. Cunningham-Reid, Independent, in the House of Commons Thursday for suggesting the Supreme Allied Commander, General Eisenhower, would have been blamed if anything had happened to Prime Minister Churchill on his visit to the Normandy beachhead Monday.

Cunningham-Reid had said:

"In the circumstances it would be he who would be to blame for allowing the Prime Minister to have gone out to France. The Supreme Commander is an American. If such a thing had occurred of it; if unfortunately, such a thing should occur, would it be to the advantage of friendly relations between the two nations."

The information minister reported that Cunningham-Reid had "come forward in a greasy way to show us the best method of establishing better relationships with the United States. He has no qualifications for smoothing relationships between England and the United States—much otherwise."

Cunningham-Reid appealed for a promise that the Prime Minister would not return to danger zones.

Bracken replied: "I think it a good thing that every Prime Minister should go into the frontline. . .

"Nothing said here today will make me take the unnecessary risk of trying to persuade the Prime Minister not to take risks."

He Has Left His Orders

LONDON, June 16 (AP).—Gen. De Gaulle announced Thursday that he had left instructions for administration of French civilian affairs during his visit to the Normandy beachhead, and this suggested an effort to eliminate the chief difficulty in British-American-French relations.

A communique issued through the French Press Service, emphasizing the "atmosphere of immense fervor" with which it reported De Gaulle was received in Allied-liberated towns Wednesday, said he gave directions "regarding resumption of civil administration, organization of supplies and public relief."

The instructions apparently were a step toward eliminating rough spots in the bid of De Gaulle's French Committee of National Liberation for full recognition as the voice of France.

De Gaulle returned to England Wednesday.

The communique referred to him as "President of the Provisional Government of the French Republic," a term which still lacks acknowledment by Britain and the United States.'

U.S. Forces Gain On Saipan Island

By LEIF ERICKSON
Associated Press Staff Writer

PEARL HARBOR, June 16.—American troops which landed 1,500 miles southeast of Tokyo Wednesday on Saipan in the Marianas have secured beachheads, captured a headland, fought their way into a sugar mill town and beaten off Japanese tank-paced counter-attacks, Admiral Nimitz announced Thursday night.

In a communique covering action through today, he reported that Agingan Point, a headland on the southwest corner of the 13-mile-long island, has been seized.

EXTEND MOVEMENT

The invaders, supported by a huge carrier-plane force and guns of battleships which knocked out enemy coastal guns and anti-aircraft batteries, have fought their way two miles north into the sugar mill town of Charan Kanoa.

The reports also indicate that the troops, transports and supporting warships have sprung their operation in behind the 500-mile-long chain of Marianas.

Garapan, Saipan's major town of about 10,000, lies about five miles north of the United States troops fighting in smaller Charan Kanoa.

Fleet headquarters reported the first landings on Saipan were made Wednesday under cover of a bombardment by warships and the bombing and strafing of carrier planes.

Additional assault forces were storming ashore despite enemy resistance.

This bold move to advance American bases 1,100 miles west of the Marshall Islands climaxed four days of pre-invasion assault by Powerful naval and air forces, starting last Saturday. The first day of the attack wiped out almost all of the enemy's air force based in the southern Marianas.

In invading Saipan, Vice-Admiral Richard Kelly Turner's forces vaulted far beyond Truk, major enemy base in the central Caroline Islands. When a firm hold is established on Saipan, it will place American forces 675 miles to the rear of Truk. Guam, southernmost of the Marianas, also would be outflanked.

The operation was believed to be the most spectacular of the Pacific war, due to the major use of rocket-firing planes and ships.

Saipan is the second largest island in the 500-mile long Marianas chain. Westward lies a clear ocean sweep to the Philippines, Formosa and the China coast.

Casualties

The latest casualty list will be found on Page 11.

Communique No. 20

SUPREME HEADQUARTERS, Allied Expeditionary Force, June 16 (AP).—Communique No. 20:

Further steady progress has been made west of Carentan and between the Rivers Vire and Elle.

Allied troops have repulsed several violent armored attacks in the Caumont-Tilly sector with considerable loss to the enemy.

In the Cherbourg peninsula ground gained in the area of Quineville has made available a valuable new outlet from the beaches.

During Thursday mobile batteries on the flanks were engaged as necessary by Allied warships. On the eastern flank H.M.S. Belfast (Capt. P. R. Parham, D.S.O., R.N.), wearing the flag of Vice-Admiral F. H. G. Dalrymple-Hamilton C.B., gave valuable support against enemy concentrations.

* * *

H.M.S. Nelson (Capt. A. H. Maxwell-Hyslop A.M., R.N.) engaged the batteries of Le Havre.

During an unsuccessful enemy air attack in the western assault area an enemy aircraft was shot down by the U.S.S. Augusta (Capt. E. H. Jones U.S.N.) wearing the flag of Rear Admiral Alan Goodrich Kirk, U.S.N.

Convoys of Allied merchant ships are arriving satisfactorily and the armies continue to be built up with men, stores and equipment.

Allied aircraft in great strength ranged from the Cherbourg peninsula southward to Loire and eastward to Chartres and Paris, continuing their attacks on communications, airfields and tactical targets.

Coastal aircraft kept up their attacks on enemy shipping in the Channel early today.

* * *

Heavy bombers in great strength attacked many targets in France this morning, including rail yards at Angouleme, airfields near Bordeaux and Paris and railway bridges near Tours.

They were escorted by strong forces of fighters which also strafed ground targets.

In these operations 12 enemy planes were destroyed. Three of our bombers and three of our fighters are missing.

Medium and light bombers attacked bridges at Conde-Su-Noireau, St. Lo, Lessay, Chartres and Coltainville and a road junction at Argentan.

None of these bombers was lost.

Fighter-bombers and fighters provided close support for the ground forces and swept over Normandy attacking supply dumps, troop concentrations, tanks, convoys and railway bridges.

Other fighters attacked a ferry at Quillebeuf near the mouth of the Seine.

In the course of a patrol this morning five enemy fighters were destroyed near Evreux.

Photographic reconnaissance shows German naval forces in the port of Le Havre suffered very severely from an attack by heavy night bombers on the evening of June 14.

Repulse German Counter-Attack In East Normandy

By JAMES M. LONG
Associated Press War Correspondent

SUPREME HEADQUARTERS, Allied Expeditionary Force, June 16 (AP).—A great armored battle of attrition ground ahead Thursday on the eastern wing of the Allies' beachhead in Normany, held by British and Canadian forces, and strong German counter-attacks were repulsed with what Thursday night's communique from supreme headquarters called "considerable loss to the enemy."

WELL SET IN WEST

On the western end of the 100-mile front American troops slashing westward from Carentan on a 10-mile front have reached firm ground within six miles of La Haye Du Puits, junction of the last German-held rail-highway lifeline to the port of Cherbourg, and within 4½ miles of the secondary junction point of St. Saveur-Lecomte. The communique said "steady progress" was made.

In the developing drive to cut off and capture the Cherbourg peninsula, similar steady advances were reported for a less clearly-defined thrust through the lowlands between the Vire and Elle Rivers southeast of Carentan.

This advance appeared to be aimed toward St. Jean de Daye, on the highway linking St. Lo and Carentan. Extent of the gain was not disclosed officially but it appeared probable that the road had been cut about five miles west of Lison.

On the extreme right flank of the Allies' beachhead, American capture of the coastal village of Quineville and surrounding territory was said to have provided "a valuable new outlet from the beaches."

These were the principal gains in the 10th day of the Allied invasion of France, which saw the offensive all along the 100-mile line gather force and either gain ground or repel repeated enemy counter-attacks.

Right around the irregular front, starting on the northwest, this was

REPULSE GERMAN
Continued on Page 2, Column 6

How Cabinet May Line Up

REGINA, June 16.—Veterans of C.C.F. campaigning in the Western Provinces probably will be included in the Provincial Cabinet to be formed by T. C. Douglas, Provincial leader, following C.C.F. victory in the election Thursday.

Mayor J. W. Corman of Moose Jaw, a lawyer, was said to be a likely appointment as attorney-general. Mayor C. C. Williams of Regina also is likely to obtain a Cabinet post, possibly that of minister of public works.

Maj. George Williams, former C.C.F. Provincial leader, now on active service with the Canadian Army, may be appointed minister without portfolio. Some other Cabinet office probably would be available for Major Williams, but his health has been indifferent since his return from overseas and he is expected to rest for a considerable period.

Mr. Douglas himself may assume the portfolio of minister of health. J. H. Brockelbank, a Tisdale constituency farmer and C.C.F. leader in the last Legislature, may become minister of resources.

Ald. C. M. Fines, long active in the C.C.F. movement in Regina and president of the C.C.F. Provincial section, may receive the municipal affairs portfolio.

Premier W. J. Patterson, head of the Liberal administration since 1935, had eight Cabinet ministers in his administration. He himself held the portfolios of Provincial treasurer and minister of telephones and telegraphs in addition to being president of the council.

Tabulated result of Saskatoon City vote on Page 3.

Standing

Latest party standing in Saskatchewan:

Elected

Liberal	4
C.C.F.	43

Leading

Lib. 2 (Meadow Lake, Athabaska).
C.C.F. 2 (Gravelbourg, Turtleford).
Deferred .... 1 (Cumberland).
Total 52

Gain Analysis

C.C.F. from Liberals	28
C.C.F. from Unity	2
C.C.F. from S.C.	2
Doubtful	5
Unchanged	15
Total	52

Douglas

(By a Canadian Press Staff Writer)

REGINA, June 16.—A short, slight man, the light step of a boxer and the quick retort of a skilled debater is the new Government leader in Saskatchewan.

T. C. Douglas—he is entitled to "Reverend" but seldom uses it—

has been a bright star in the C.C.F. firmament ever since he entered the political field in 1934, when he was a Baptist minister. He became a member of Parliament nine years ago.

On the wide Prairies, where men and wheat grow tall, political leadership in Saskatchewan in re-

DOUGLAS
Continued on Page 2, Column 6

Mere Corporal's Guard Remains Of Liberal Party

By Canadian Press Staff Writer

REGINA, June 16.—The first C.C.F. Government in history sailed into power on a blizzard of votes in Saskatchewan Thursday.

The vote left no more than a corporal's guard of the Liberal administration headed by Premier W. J. Patterson, provincial Premier since 1935. T. C. Douglas of Weyburn, a former member of Parliament, will head the new C.C.F. Government.

The election was one-sided from the start. Early returns showed C.C.F. candidates piling up large majorities, and then the series of individual C.C.F. successes turned into a landslide.

PATTERSON UNCERTAIN

Mr. Patterson had a small majority in his home constituency of Cannington, but could not be sure of a seat in the new Legislature until the votes cast by service men and women in Saskatchewan are counted on June 19.

Seven of his Cabinet ministers sought re-election. Five were defeated. One, Hon. T. E. Procter, Minister of Highways, was re-elected. Maj. the Hon. E. M. Culliton, minister without portfolio, ran second to a C.C.F. candidate in Gravelbourg but there was the possibility his position would be improved when the soldier vote was counted.

357,091 VOTES CAST

When the Legislature was dissolved on May 18, the Liberals had 33 seats, C.C.F. 10, Social Credit two, Unity (National Reform) two and five were vacant.

With 438 polls still to be heard from, a compilation showed 357,091 votes had been cast Thursday, with the C.C.F. obtaining 187,437; Liberals 126,878; Progressive Conservatives 41,133 and all others 1,543.

In the last Provincial election in 1938, the total vote was 440,273, with the Liberals securing 200,370, Conservatives 52,366 and C.C.F. 82,568.

The victory was paralleled only by that of the Liberals in 1934, when they elected 50 members to the Legislature which then had 55 seats compared with the present 52.

Hon. Charles Agar, speaker in the last Legislature, was defeated.

NO PROG. CONS.

Rupert D. Ramsay, Progressive Conservative provincial leader, suffered personal defeat in Saskatoon and not one of the 40 members of his party seeking election was successful.

Voting will be held on June 24 for the remote constituency of Cumberland, where a member will be chosen from Liberal, C.C.F. and Progressive Conservative candidates to complete the Legislature roster of 52.

Mr. Douglas said he would be prepared to take over the administration as soon as Mr. Patterson leaves his office.

It was estimated that more than 49 candidates lost their deposits, the majority of them Progressive Conservatives.

SOLDIER MEMBERS

The Saskatchewan men and women with the forces outside provincial boundaries will choose three additional members when voting arrangements are completed. One member will be elected by those serving in Canada, outside Saskatchewan, and in Newfoundland; one by those in the United Kingdom and with the invasion forces in France and one by those in the Mediterranean zone.

The three "soldier members" will sit for one term, following a pre-

C.C.F. LANDSLIDE
Continued on Page 2, Column 4

Election Comment

REV. T. C. DOUGLAS

REGINA, June 16 (CP)—T. C. Douglas, leader of the first C.C.F. Government ever elected, said in a statement following the Saskatchewan election Thursday that the victory was "a victory for the people of Saskatchewan as a whole."

His statement follows:

I am delighted at the outcome of the election. We do not take this as a personal triumph for the leadership or the C.C.F. membership. It is a victory for the people of Saskatchewan as a whole.

There is, of course, a certain element of personal elation but it is tempered by the great sense of responsibility at the undertaking which awaits us.

The election victory was the result of team work and co-operation on the part of thousands of workers and I want to thank them for their hard work. The same co-operation will be necessary to attack the economic and social problems that we will have as a Government.

The election also is an indication of the feeling of Western people with respect to Federal Government policies and is condemnation of the agriculture policies of Hon. J. G. Gardiner (Federal Minister of Agriculture), the man power policies of the Dominion and the failure to make provision for post-war reconstruction.

M. J. COLDWELL

REGINA, June 16 (CP).—M. J. Coldwell, C.C.F. national leader, said Thursday night that the C.C.F. victory in the Provincial election had exceeded all his expectations.

His statement follows:

The result of the Saskatchewan election exceeded all my expectations. It is a people's victory in the truest sense.

Our workers throughout the constituencies were volunteers. This made up for any lack of money we may have felt. We believe that this is a prelude to a victory in the Federal field, where alone the great national problems must be dealt with. Our success today rests on a firm basis of political and economic education.

We look forward to the future with confidence.

E. B. JOLLIFFE

REGINA, June 16 (CP).—E. B. Jolliffe, Ontario C.C.F. leader, said that the C.C.F. victory in the Saskatchewan provincial election was "a triumph for a people's movement

COMMENT
Continued on Page 2, Column 4

Thanks Opponent For Fair Dealing

BIGGAR, June 16.—Woodrow Lloyd, C.C.F., elected for the Biggar constituency, said the results of the election in the constituency and the Province are highly gratifying.

"I must express my appreciation to all my supporters and workers in the Biggar constituency. Likewise, I express my appreciation to Frank Freeman, Liberal candidate, for the type of campaign which he personally conducted. We look now to the forward march of our Province under a people's government.

HOW THE PROVINCE VOTED (Unofficial)

Names in black type denote elected. Premier W. J. Patterson has a slim lead in Cannington, with the soldier vote still to be heard from. Donald MacDonald is leading in Meadow Lake but a large number of polls are yet to be heard from. Only a few polls in Athabaska have been heard from.

Constituency	Liberal	Prog. Con.	C.C.F.	Lab.-Prog.	Social Credit	Others
Arm River	**G. H. Danielson***	T. A. Homersham	W. R. Fansher			
Athabaska	L. M. Marion	Fred Delaronde	Dr. D. Ayotte			E. G. Erickson (Ind.) F. X. Poitras (Ind. L.)
Battlefords	Paul Prince*	Wg. Com. McNair	**Alex Connan**			
Bengough	Thomas Waddell		**Allan Brown**			
Biggar	Frank Freeman		**Woodrow Lloyd**			
Cannington	**W. J. Patterson***	William A. Brigden	Mrs. Gladys Strum			
Canora	Steve Shabbits		**M. H. Feeley***			
Cumberland	D. A. Hall	R. O. St. Denis	L. W. Lee			
Cutknife	John A. Gordon		**J. C. Nollet**			
Elrose	Hubert Staines *‡	E. J. Ewing	**Morris Willis**			
Gravelbourg	E. M. Culliton*		**Dr. H. E. House**			
Gull Lake	H. H. McMahon*	Charles Howlett	**A. C. Murray**			
Hanley	Charles Agar*	J. H. Cannon	**J. S. Aitken**			
Humboldt	Arnold W. Loehr	F. D. Weese	**Ben. Putman**			
Kelvington	G. M. Ferrie	Samuel Hall	**Peter Howe***			
Kerr.-Kin.	Donald Laing*	W. S. Myers	**J. Wellbelove**			
Kinistino	R. M. Paul	A. Fraser	**W. J. Boyle**			
Last Mountain	Henry Mang	J. L. Blair	**Jacob Benson***			
Lumsden	J. G. Knox	A. M. Pearson	**W. S. Thair**			
Maple Creek	J. J. Mildenberger*	George Stewart	**Mrs. B. Trew**			
Meadow Lake	**Donald MacDonald***	Rev. W. Titley	Herschell Howell			A. Doucet (U.-Prog.)
Melfort	J. D. MacFarlane	S. B. Caskey	**O. W. Valleau***			
Melville	Lionel Stilborn	S. T. Regan	**A. N. Arthurs**			
Milestone	William Pedersen*		**F. R. Malcolm**			
Moose Jaw	George Baker*	A. H. Tiers	**J. W. Corman**		Frank F. Talbot	
	Harold Pope	R. Brownridge	**H. R. Heming**			
Moosomin	**A. T. Procter***		Alex Cunningham			
Morse	B. T. Hyde*	Clifford Martin	**S. M. Spidell**			
Notukeu-Will'bch	C. W. Johnson*		**Niles Buchanan**			
Pelly	R. J. M. Parker*		**Dan Z. Daniels**	William Derezowski		
Prince Albert	H. J. Fraser*	E. P. Woodman	**L. E. McIntosh**			
Qu'A.-Wolseley	Fred Dundas*	W. H. Acres	**Warden Burgess**			
Redberry	W. J. Langley	Ernest Wilson	**D. M. Lagarko**			Peter Semko (Ind.)
Regina	C. R. Davidson	H. McGillivray	**C. C. Williams**			
	B. J. McDaniel*	C. H. L. Burrows	**C. M. Fines**			
Rosetown	William Leith	John Stewart	**J. T. Douglas**			
Rosthern	**P. J. Hooge**	G. E. Goble	Henry Begand			
Saltcoats	D. A. MacKenzie	R. M. Salkeld	**J. L. Phelps***			
Saskatoon	J. W. Estey*	Rupert Ramsay	**John Sturdy**	Nelson Clarke		John Hilton (Ind.)
	R. M. Pinder*	H. O. Wright	**Arthur Stone**			R. Hartney (Ind.)
Shellbrook	Omer Demers*		**A. B. Stirling**			
Souris-Estevan	N. L. McLeod*	H. S. Penny	**Charles Cuming**			
Swift Current	J. G. Taggart*	B. M. Hill	**Harry Gibbs**			
Tisdale	Lt. Pat O'Connor	I. F. Stothers	**J. H. Brockelbank***			
Torch River	D. L. Menzies	Keith A. Baldwin	**Bruce Harris**			
Touchwood	Dr. J. J. Collins	Wm. Seneshen	**Tom Johnston***			
Turtleford	W. F. Kerr*	Chester Hicks	**Robert Wolffe**			
Wadena		Capt. G. R. Cook	**Maj. Geo. Williams***			W. E. Rogers (Ind.)
Watrous	Frank Krenn	Hugh Smith	**James Darling**			
Weyburn	J. W. Adolphe		**Rev. T. C. Douglas**			
Wilkie	Maj. J. C. Knowles*		**O. Hansen**			
Yorkton	A. A. Brown	Norman Roebuck	**Arthur Swallow**			

* Member at dissolution. *‡ Member, but for another constituency. Cumberland votes June 24.

Vote by Constituencies

Arm River, 44 of 45 polls: Danielson (L) 2,305; Homesham (PC) 1,081; Fansher (CCF) 2,180.

Athabaska, 3 of 18 polls: Marion (L) 250; Delaronde (PC) 6; Ayotte (CCF) 26; Erickson (Ind) 68; Poitras (Ind) 1.

The Battlefords 51 of 54 polls Prince (L) 2,370; McNair (PC) 408, Connon (CCF) 2,581.

Bengough 74 of 79 polls Waddell (L) 2,318; Brown (CCF) 3,460.

Biggar 73 of 77 polls Freeman (L) 2,022; Lloyd (CCF) 3,397.

Cannington, complete Patterson, (L) 3,186; Brigden PC) 684; Strum (CCF) 3,156.

Canora 30 of 39 polls Shabbitts (L) 2,178; Feeley (CCF) 2,936.

Cutknife, 42 of 60 polls: Gordon (L) 1,390; Nollett (CCF) 1,943.

Elrose, 64 of 73 polls: Staines (L) 1,604; Ewing (PC) 893; Willis (CCF) 3,026.

Gravelbourg, 69 of 70 polls: Culliton (L) 2,525; House (CCF) 2,602.

Gull Lake, 91 of 107 polls: McMahon (L) 2,208; Howlett (PC) 1,384; Murray (CCF) 3,524.

Hanley, 52 of 57 polls: Agar (L) 1,670; Cannon (PC) 832; Aitken (CCF) 2,050.

Humboldt, complete 47 polls: Loehr (L) 2,851; Weese (PC) 361; Putman (CCF) 3,519.

Kelvington: Ferrie (L) 1,535; Hall (PC) 573; Howe (CCF) 2,541.

Kerrobert-Kindersley, 82 of 108 polls: Laing (L) 1,844; Myers (PC); Wellbelove (CCF) 2,438.

Kinistino, 46 of 48 polls: Paul (L) 1,481; Fraser (PC) 655; Boyle (CCF) 2,885.

Last Mountain, 57 of 60 polls: Mang (L) 1,918; Blair (PC) 1,185; Benson (CCF) 3,454.

Lumsden, complete 66 polls: Knox (L) 1,873; Pearson (PC) 1,203; Thair (CCF) 2,817.

Maple Creek, 96 of 119 polls: Mildenberger (L) 2,605; Stewart (PC) 664; Trew (CCF) 3,156.

Meadow Lake, 26 of 60 polls: MacDonald (L) 1,250; Titley (PC) 261; Howell (CCF) 1,192; Doucet (UP) 414.

Melfort constituency complete, 53 polls: MacFarlane (L) 1,714; Caskey (PC) 1,347; Valleau (CCF) 3,296.

Melville, 46 of 48 polls: Stillborn (L) 3,088; Regan (PC) 792; Arthurs (CCF) 4,539.

Milestone, 58 of 61 polls: Pederson (L) 2,063; Malcolm (CCF) 3,042.

Moose Jaw, complete, 45 polls: Baker (L) 2,839; Pope (L) 2,824; Brownridge (PC) 1,265; Tiers (PC), 1,019; Corman (CCF) 6,087; Heming (CCF) 5,712; Talbot (SC) 237.

Moosomin, complete, 68 polls: Procter (L) 3,850; Cunningham (CCF) 3,234.

Morse, 65 of 76 polls: Hyde (L) 1,982; Martin (PC) 652; Spiddel (CCF) 2,526.

Nottukeu-Willowbunch, 79 of 8? polls: Johnson (L) 2,477; Buchanan (CCF) 3,509.

Pelly, 42 of 43 polls: Daniels (CCF) 3,173; Parker (L) 2,494; Berezowski (Lab) 494.

Prince Albert, 59 of 73 polls·

CONSTITUENCIES
Continued on Page 2, Column 2

The Weather

	Min.	Max.
SASKATOON	49	66
Jasper	40	49
Calgary	43	50
Edmonton	50	53
Lethbridge	48	57
Medicine Hat	48	63
Swift Current	43	67
Moose Jaw	—	72
Battleford	—	57
Prince Albert	54	64
Regina	49	70
Brandon	—	70
Winnipeg	54	74
Kenora	56	76

FORECAST

Cloudy with scattered showers, somewhat cooler in south portion.

Economy After the War

RCMP officers shooting cattle during a foot-and-mouth disease outbreak, near Regina, 1952

With the end of the Second World War in 1945, the First Batallion of the Saskatoon Light Infantry returned home to a more urban-based and affluent Saskatchewan than ever before. Transit systems were being built, museums erected and Saskatchewanians were succumbing to the euphoric optimism of postwar times. The discovery of oil reserves in the North West of Saskatchewan helped to broaden the province's resource base while a surge of European immigrants and returning soldiers helped replenish the province's depleted workforce. In 1948, the first electric trolley bus was put into service in Saskatoon, causing the Saskatoon Municipal Railway to be renamed the Saskatoon Transit System and marking a significant province-wide shift toward more urban-oriented services and amenities. Regina began to prosper again by 1951 — two years before its Golden Jubilee — after the construction of a new oil pipeline linked the growing city with the oil fields in Alberta and refineries in the eastern provinces. A federal census in 1951 calculated Saskatchewan's population at 831,728 — 71,319 in Regina and 53,268 in Saskatoon. And in May 1953, the Saskatoon *Star-Phoenix* predicted the city of Saskatoon would see "one of the biggest home-building booms in its history unless all the present signs are wrong."

Oilman covered in oil from a strike, Smiley, 1953

LIVING THE MODERN LIFE

Saskatchewan's prosperity continued into the 1950s as residents of the postwar Prairies leapt enthusiastically into the future. The broadening of Saskatchewan resources led to new office buildings, improved transportation systems and an increasingly urban focus. Architecture in Regina and Saskatoon began to favour the homogenous over the unique as the two cities embraced a new continental trend toward "sameness." And while the first television station — CKCK — opened in western Canada in 1954, film, music and radio continued to spread an emerging popular culture across the continent — enticing farmers, returning soldiers and war brides to celebrate North America's economic dominance with a love for "modern times."

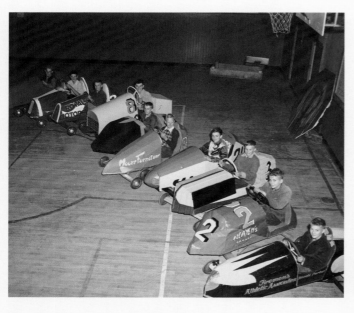

Speedbox derby, Optimist Club, Saskatoon, July 21, 1951

British war brides tea, Saskatoon, circa 1946

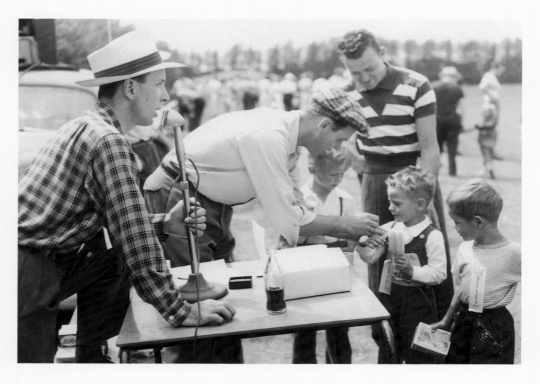

T. Eaton Company picnic, Forestry Farm, near Saskatoon, July 18, 1951

Digging out trapped train after blizzard, February 1947

Skaters, Regina, circa 1947

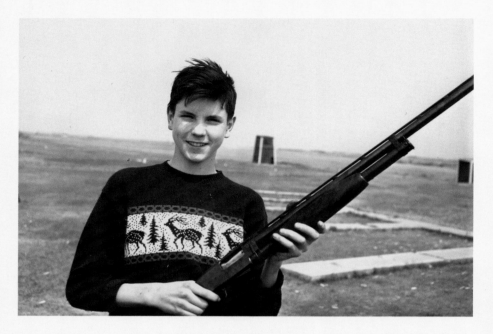

George Genereux, gold medalist in trapshooting at 1952 Olympics, date unknown

Saskatoon Quakers win championship cup, Saskatoon, April 4, 1951

PLAYING GAMES

Athol Murray, known as "Père" Murray, was born in Toronto in 1892 and sent to Regina on loan from the Diocese of Toronto after he was ordained in 1918. After a group of Protestant boys was caught stealing candy from a church basement in 1922, Père Murray decided to redirect young boys' energy by forming a sports club, later known as the Regina Argos Club. When he was appointed to St. Augustine's parish in Wilcox in 1927, fifteen young Argos followed. Educating his students in makeshift buildings acquired during the Depression, Père Murray finally founded Notre Dame Liberal Arts College in 1933 — a school of academics, athletics, leadership and spirituality. Students were allowed to pay their $10 monthly tuition in flour, meat or coal and were encouraged to participate in the school's vigorous sports program. The Notre Dame Hounds, as the college team was known, won several provincial titles in hockey, football and baseball, which gained them recognition across the country. A number of Hounds were drafted to the NHL and the school has since continued its sporting tradition. Père Murray was presented the Order of Canada in 1968, elected to the Canada Sports Hall of Fame in 1972 and inducted into the Hockey Hall of fame in 1998. In 1981, Notre Dame College was renamed the Athol Murray College of Notre Dame.

As two tornadoes ripped through Saskatchewan in 1944, one of Saskatoon's youngest whirlwind athletes was preparing to take the world by storm. Already six feet tall at fourteen, George Genereaux earned a surprise win at the midwestern invitational clay pigeon trapshooting handicap in Winnipeg in 1949. That year and the next, he won the Manitoba-Saskatchwan junior championship and, in 1951, took home the North American title. But it wasn't until he won the gold medal at the 1952 Olympic Games in Helsiki that Genereaux really blew Saskatchewan residents away. Canada's first gold medal since 1936, Genereaux's skillful performance gave Saskatchewanians some of the hope they were looking for: the winds of change.

Père Athol Murray, Wilcox, date unknown

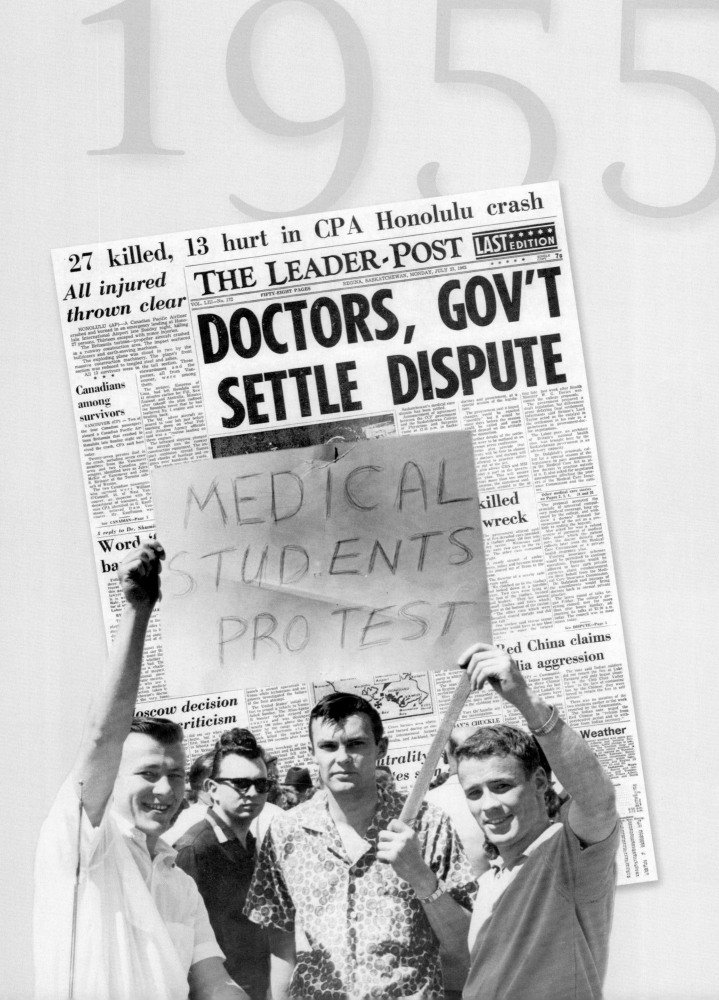

Chapter Eight

As turning points go, July 23, 1962, didn't have the drama of a battlefield conquest or the thrill of an explorer's discovery. But the day that ended the Saskatchewan doctors' strike — and cleared the way for the creation of North America's first medicare program — was a true watershed moment in the history of Canada and the development of a new national identity.

Though debates about the merits of public and private medicine continue to rage in Canada, few would dispute the notion that our system of universal health care — pioneered in Saskatchewan during the Sixties and eventually adopted coast to coast — is among the most cherished and distinctive of all Canadian institutions, the centrepiece of a vaunted social safety net that sets this country apart from the superpower society to the south.

But state-funded health care was born in the midst of a controversy that bitterly divided Saskatchewanians and dominated the province's political discourse for much of the 1950s and Sixties. The struggle over medicare would spark soul-searching deliberations — provincially, nationally and even internationally — about the ideal scope of the modern state, the balance between public and private enterprise and the very meaning of democracy.

Remarkably, it also prompted talk of possible violence in the streets of Regina and Saskatoon as a revered segment of Saskatchewan society rebelled against a government it deemed deluded and dictatorial.

Ross Thatcher, Saskatchewan Liberal party leader, James Gardiner, former Liberal premier and federal cabinet minister and Right Honourable Lester B. Pearson, Liberal prime minister, before Gardiner's death in 1962

The medicare clash, wrenching though it was, came during a time of continued economic growth for Saskatchewan and in the midst of various pride-boosting events that shone a spotlight on the province. The second decade of the postwar era also brought sweeping changes in the political leadership of the province and the country, including the elevation of two Saskatchewan politicians — John Diefenbaker and Tommy Douglas — to the leadership of national parties.

Saskatchewan also celebrated a royal tour in July 1959 as Queen Elizabeth and Prince Philip visited Saskatoon, Hanley, Chamberlain, Moose Jaw, Regina, Indian Head, Broadview and Moosomin during a memorable cross-Canada tour.

A Regina campus of the University of Saskatchewan was announced in 1961 and new buildings were soon erected at a site that would eventually be home to a separate and autonomous University of Regina.

Achievement in winter sports gave Saskatchewanians another reason to cheer. Native son Gordie Howe heaped goal upon goal, record upon record, trophy upon trophy en route to establishing the greatest career in hockey history. And the Richardson brothers — led by skip Ernie — dominated the curling world, winning a string of national and world championships between 1959 and 1964.

The tapping of Saskatchewan's mineral riches spurred development in the sparsely populated North and continued the critical process of diversifying the provincial economy beyond grain-growing and other agricultural industries.

"Potash was projected to place Saskatoon in the industrial limelight as oil had benefited Edmonton," writes historian John Archer. "Oil discoveries in the southeast and southwest areas seemed to herald a new era of expansion. Symbolic of a changing economy was the fact that in 1957 Saskatchewan had more oil and gas wells capable of production than there were grain elevators."

Diefenbaker, a brilliant Prince Albert lawyer and MP who had been chosen to lead the federal Progressive Conservatives in 1956, won a narrow, surprise victory in the 1957 general election to become the first prime minister ever from Saskatchewan. A year later, Diefenbaker's campaigning genius would transform his minority government into a stunning majority in the biggest election landslide in Canadian history. The Tory tide swept away all but one of the province's Co-operative Commonwealth Federation MPs — Hazen Argue — and gave hope to provincial Conservatives and Liberals that Saskatchewan's ardent commitment to social democracy and the CCF might finally be waning.

The 1960 provincial election did show cracks in the CCF regime but returned premier Tommy Douglas to power for the fifth time. Liberal leader Ross Thatcher, a former CCF MP from Moose Jaw and disenchanted socialist, made inroads with voters by attacking failed Crown corporations and the government's proposed health reforms. Still, the CCF held a majority and a mandate, it believed, to implement medicare.

Gordie Howe, circa 1956

Then, in 1961, Douglas stepped down as premier to become leader of the federal New Democratic Party. "Despite sincere differences over some of his government's policies, the people of Saskatchewan generally have respected Douglas while from his followers he has received their utmost admiration and adoration," a magnanimous *Leader-Post*, chief critic of the CCF for decades, opined upon Douglas's resignation. "He has stood forth during his seventeen years, which have seen premiers come and go in other provinces, as one of the most dynamic to hold this office in the nation. He has been an indefatigable worker, a zealous crusader, and an inspired and inspiring leader."

The creation of the public health insurance program was intended as a crowning achievement for the CCF government, which had wavered on some of its left wing policy plans during nearly two decades in office but was determined to construct the state-funded medical system. Douglas had directed the development of the ground-breaking policy and had rolled out a series of contentious, preliminary initiatives in the 1950s that presaged the adoption of medicare.

But it was his successor as premier, former education minister and treasurer Woodrow Lloyd, who faced the challenge of launching the provincial health plan over the loud objections of doctors who feared government meddling with the medical profession and socialist strictures on their incomes. The Saskatchewan College of Physicians and Surgeons had declared itself "unalterably opposed to a compulsory program of state-controlled medical care" and mounted a massive lobbying and publicity campaign aimed at igniting grassroots resistance to the provincial plan.

"The story of the government during the CCF's fifth term of office in Saskatchewan — 1960 to 1964 — was the story of medicare. All the rest of policy and of administration seemed frozen in time," writes A. W. Johnson in *Dream No Little Dreams*, a chronicle of the party's twenty-year reign during the province's postwar era. "The drama is to be found in the fundamentals of the dispute: in the clash between two fundamentally differing value systems …"

Former Saskatchewan MP Dennis Gruending, a leading writer and anthologist of provincial history, has described how "the tension had reached an almost fevered pitch" by May 1962, when Lloyd, "a rational and methodical man, walked into a hostile room" at a doctors' convention in Regina and made his case for medicare.

"Medical services are essential to health and to life itself. Good medical services are part of the basis for a healthy, productive economy," Lloyd declared in the address, which was recently included in Gruending's collection of the greatest speeches in Canadian history.

"Medical care is not an optional commodity, it is a necessity. When medical services are needed they should not in the interests of each of us or all of us be denied to any of us. When a commodity or service is essential, our society has long since accepted that consumers have a legitimate right to a voice in making the essential governing decisions in such matters. That voice has been for medical care …"

But the doctors were steadfast in their opposition. In a bid to shake the government's resolve, doctors announced a strike — they would close their offices on July 1, providing only emergency service until the premier agreed not to move forward with his medicare plan.

The Saskatchewan press was largely supportive of the doctors, but the province was the focus of unflattering media attention across Canada and around the world. Newspapers in Britain and the United States kept watch on the showdown between doctors and the government, with the British medical

TV March of Dimes Caravan
Dance, Davidson, circa 1962

journal *Lancet* calling the strike "wrong" and "out of keeping with the character of any profession, and especially that of medicine."

The *British Observer* dismissed the strike a "mutiny" and the *Daily Mail* argued, "when doctors strike and neglect patients, the voice of humanity protests."

A *Washington Post* editorial, as Johnson recounts in *Dream No Little Dreams*, skewered the doctors for their withdrawal of services: "Whatever the merits of Saskatchewan's new medical care act, the strike staged by doctors throughout the province is indefensible," the paper stated. "A strike by the doctors is a betrayal of their profession. It reduces medicine to the level of a business."

Father Athol Murray, a well-known priest from Wilcox who supported the doctors, told the *Prince Albert Herald*, "We must get off the fence and make our views known. This thing may break out into violence and bloodshed any day now, and God help us if it doesn't ..."

A coalition of citizens, businesspeople and anti-CCF political activists, operating under the banner Keep Our Doctors Committee, planned a mass rally in Regina for July 11. Up to 5,000 protestors were expected to crowd the grounds of the provincial legislature in a show of force that could well have thwarted the government's plans.

Full-page advertisements laid out the KODC's position: "No ruler in a free society may in conscience coerce a minority group of citizens in their way of life or in the conduct of their affairs, nor may a ruler under law discriminate against them in their profession, work or calling, however humane or beneficent the motives of the state may be thought to be"

Robin Badgely and Samuel Wolfe, in their 1967 history of the strike, give a clear sense of what was at stake in the outcome of the KODC rally. "The

Caswell's Limited,
130 21st Street,
Saskatoon,
September 1956

government, of course, awaited July 11 with apprehension. If 30,000 or 40,000 marchers converged on Regina, the anti-medicare campaign would succeed," they wrote. "Two girls carried effigies of Premier Lloyd and T.C. Douglas with the caption: 'Down with dictators.'

"Police intervened to protect a handful of government supporters who were cursed off the grounds with 'they are Communists. They are going back to the Kremlin.' " (But) the march was a failure. According to the Canadian Press, only 4,000 people attended. The momentum of the doctors and the KODC was never regained."

New rounds of negotiations were held. Lord Taylor, a British medical doctor who had played a key role in developing the United Kingdom's National Health Service, was brought in as a mediator for a series of talks in Saskatoon that, after several days, yielded an agreement and ended the strike.

"Saskatchewan's medical care dispute has been settled," the *Leader-Post* reported in its afternoon edition of July 23. "Announcement of agreement between the CCF government and the Saskatchewan College of Physicians and Surgeons came at 12:45 p.m. in Saskatoon.... The proposal accepted the principle of universal compulsory medical coverage, long opposed by the college, and withdrew a doctors' demand for suspension of the act as a prelude to ending the boycott ..."

The rancour sown by the medicare controversy further weakened the CCF in Saskatchewan. But Lloyd's supporters were hopeful that the province's increasing prosperity — evident in numerous mining projects and major public works, such as the mammoth South Saskatchewan River dam — would ensure the party's return to power in the coming election of April 22, 1964.

Leader-Post carriers, Swift Current, September 11, 1961

That year had already seen the province celebrate an important milestone in the construction of the great dam, which would eventually be named after former premier James Gardiner, who had championed it for years. The 200-kilometre-long lake created by the dam would be named Diefenbaker after the prime minister whose signature had finally put the project in motion.

"February 14 was a red-letter day in the history of Saskatchewan," the *Saskatoon Star-Phoenix* reported in 1964. "It marked the taming of the mighty river from which the province takes its name. The last seventy-foot gap through which water was flowing in the uncompleted part of the South Saskatchewan dam was closed off in fifty-three minutes. The water will henceforth flow, not in this part of the bed where nature has placed it since the final melting of the ice sheet of the Glacial Age, but through diversion tunnels which man will control, and where it will be forced to pay its tribute of power. Last Friday will be a focal point in history. The river, of course, is not yet paying tribute, but it is harnessed. It is now man's slave, not a rampaging monster carving its channel deeper and deeper and wearing away embankments of the good earth …"

Poster for movie filmed in Saskatchewan, 1961

Despite such impressive shows of progress, Saskatchewan was poised for seismic political upheaval. Thatcher and his Liberal party had successfully built a grassroots network of supporters modeled on the CCF's own system. And because of the medicare uproar, the Liberals had been able to pull together fragments of disaffected voters from across the province under a single banner.

"Thatcher's energy, confidence, and potential were depicted as appropriate to the new era of prosperity already unfolding, which contrasted with the known and worn leadership of the CCF after the tumult of medicare," wrote David E. Smith in *Prairie Liberalism: The Liberal Party in Saskatchewan 1905-71*. "Thatcher and the Liberals presented themselves as the independent spokesmen for Saskatchewan in national politics and exhorted voters to 'Pull Together With Pride.'"

The ensuing Liberal victory — thirty-one seats to the CCF's twenty-six — brought an end (at least temporarily) to Saskatchewan's experiment with democratic socialism. But a coming economic downturn and a period of flower-powered social change would make the next phase of the province's history another turbulent one.

Medicare

The Canadian Labour Congress called the 1962 strike of Saskatchewan doctors an "open and brazen defiance of constituted authority." A statement, signed by Congress Executive Vice President William Dodge, read: "In deserting their patients, the doctors of Saskatchewan have shown a callous disregard not only for the law but for the health and safety of the province." But at the same time as doctors across the province were preparing to strike, groups of citizens – calling themselves Community Health Services – had begun to sponsor small clinics of their own to ensure patients' needs were still being met. On July 3, two days after the strike began, Dr. Joan Witney and Dr. Margaret Mahood, wife of Ed Mahood, an unsuccessful NDP candidate for Saskatoon in the June 18 federal election, rented space in a downtown Saskatoon office building where they established their own makeshift clinic. Similar clinics were established in Prince Albert, North Battleford, Regina, Weyburn and Moose Jaw.

Erecting sign on Save our Saskatchewan headquarters, Regina, July 1962

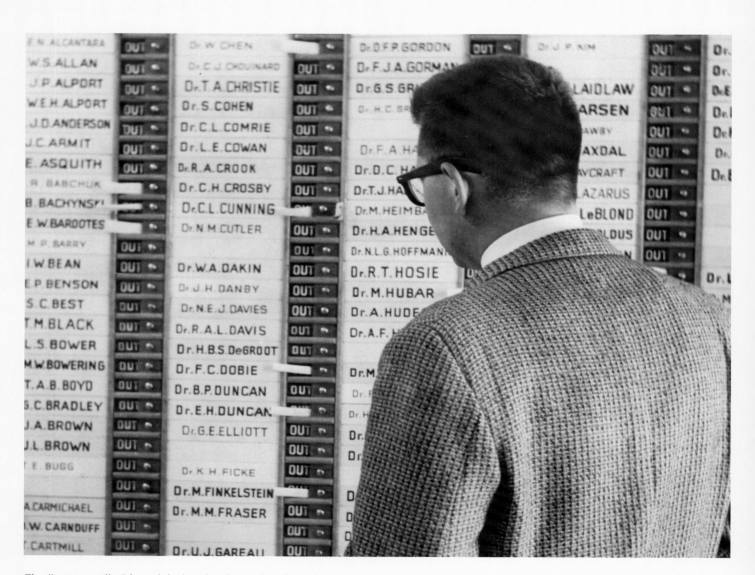

The "out on strike" board during the doctors' strike, July 1962

Saskatoon And District Welcomes Royal Visitors

Saskatoon Star-Phoenix

★ ★ ★ FINAL

57TH YEAR—No. 233. SASKATOON, SASK., WEDNESDAY, JULY 22, 1959 SINGLE COPY 7¢ ✦TWENTY EIGHT PAGES

Royal Blue Skies For Royalty

At the Museum and Pion-Era

GEORGE SHEPHERD, curator of the Western Development Museum, shows to the Queen and Prince Philip a sleigh made by the grandfather of Prime Minister John G. Diefenbaker.

QUEEN ELIZABETH and Prince Philip chat with Mrs. Bernice Norman, executive director of Pion-Era. The royal visitors were so interested in the show that Mrs. Norman had to leave her seat to answer their numerous questions.

Pion-Era Fascinates Royal Couple

Canada's pioneer west throbbed to life for Queen Elizabeth and Prince Philip on their arrival in Saskatoon Wednesday morning. A tour, which has already had spectacular moments, moved into the realm of the unusual as the Royal couple watched with fascination and wonder as giant steamers puffed and rumbled past them on their reviewing stand and old time threshing outfits spewed grain and chaff in a threshing circle behind them.

"This is the way it was done in the early days", Mrs. Bernice Norman, executive director of Pion-Era told the Queen and Prince Philip. And from that moment the royal pair plied Mrs. Norman with questions. The Queen told Mrs. Norman she found the show wonderful, it made the west real for her. The Prince was even more enthusiastic. He told Mrs. Norman the country should send out an SOS so that none of these old machines would be lost. She had explained to him that many of the relics of the Western Development Museum had been dug out of blown dirt in fence corners and brought together to tell the story and preserve the history of the agricultural west. At one point the Prince told Mrs. Norman, "But this is wonderful. We have never seen anything like it."

Within five minutes of the Queen's arrival she and the Prince entered the east door of the northern entrance of the Western Development Museum. Crowds had lined up outside, an hour before the royal arrival. For a sovereign who had expressed the wish that arrangements be kept simple, her entrance to the museum must have been much to her liking. Joe Phelps, the man most responsible for the creation of Saskatoon famous museum was there to greet the queen before she entered the door. Mr. Phelps, Saskatchewan farmer and director of the museum, appeared in his formal attire for the occasion. He had hidden away his greasy work-a-day overalls behind one of the exhibits, to be

PION-ERA
Continued on Page 6, Column 6

50 Years of City's History Spanned For Queen, Philip; Grain Threshing Show, University Visit Highlights

Queen Elizabeth and Prince Philip spanned 50 years of history during their visit to Saskatoon, the City of Bridges, today.

Within minutes of their arrival, the royal couple were treated to a demonstration of grain threshing as it was done in Saskatchewan in the early days of the province. Before their departure they saw the magnificent University of Saskatchewan buildings where nothing existed just 50 years ago.

The threshing demonstration was provided in a miniature version of Saskatoon's unique Pion-Era show presented at the Western Development Museum. The royal visitors showed animated interest in the display, which featured threshing in all its forms from the almost pre-historic flail to the steam engine and separator.

Whistles of the steam engines provided a noisy royal salute as the visitors left the museum grounds.

A link with an earlier period of Saskatchewan's history was provided at the Pion-Era grandstand with the presentation to the royal couple of Jean Dumont, 100-year-old nephew of Gabriel Dumont, trusted lieutenant of Louis Riel.

WANTED TO STAY

The Queen so enjoyed the show at the museum that she was reluctant to tear herself away. When the royal limousine drove up to take her to city hall she remained sitting on a small stage, firing questions almost a mile a minute.

The Queen first toured the Museum and then went to the grandstand where old but still functioning wood-and-straw - burning steam tractors, reapers, binders and threshers passed in review, wheezing, hissing, clanking and spitting cinders, one of which went into the Queen's right eye. She blinked it out unaided.

The Queen and Prince Philip obviously enjoyed the show and the Queen looked like a tennis fan at Wimbledon. She craned around to watch activities in the infield.

In one of the oddest but most enjoyable parades of the royal tour—and one of the best events staged anywhere — covered wagons, surreys, buggies and machinery went by, the drivers doffing their caps.

Treadmills and threshers were going like mad in the infield and the scene was one long burst of noise and activity.

The Queen laughed as she hasn't laughed for days.

She looked completely rested.

In the museum itself, the Queen saw a portrayal of early Prairie homesteading life with women making butter, spinning and the like. Philip went off on his own to inspect the old steamers which helped turn Saskatchewan into Canada's great wheat province.

There was so much to see that the Queen kept turning around to catch something she had missed.

GREETED BY WARM SUN

The threatening clouds of Tuesday night had turned to fleecy white and a warm sun beamed down as the Queen and her Prince stepped from the Royal Train at Avenue Y and Eleventh Street promptly at 10 a.m. The temperature was 64 degrees.

The Queen, looking fresh in the flag-snapping breeze, was wearing a two-piece flowered outfit in thunder blue, a small, soft turquoise hat and white accessories. Philip was wearing a subdued grey checked suit.

The city's population of about 85,000—already swollen by crowds attending the annual exhibition —was increased to 125,000 for the royal day. An estimated 1,000 of that number were on hand to greet the royal visitors as they were piped from the train by the Saskatoon Pipe Band, augmented for the occasion by a number of additional pipers and drummers.

The drive to the museum and, later, to the City Hall and the University, was made through flag-bedecked streets lined with cheering crowds. Members of the armed forces were in evidence everywhere, as were RCMP, city police and Civil Defence emergency police, who kept crowds in check.

The SASKATOON BERRY

At City Hall, the Saskatoon berry for which the city was named, came into its own. In an informal ceremony, not previously announced, Mayor Buckwold presented a jar of the berries to the Queen and told her 25 pies made from the fruit had been sent to the Royal Train.

Prince Philip was highly amused by the presentation and it was evident he was looking forward to enjoying the treat at future meals aboard the train, as suggested by the mayor.

Mayor Buckwold left no doubt in the minds of the royal visitors and the 6,000 others within the sound of his voice as to the proper spelling of the berry's name.

"We spell it with a capital "S", he said, pointing out that envious communities elsewhere in the province were inclined to belittle it with a small "S".

Flowers also had a part in the ceremonies at the City Hall, which was decked out in blue and gold bunting for the occasion. As the Queen approached the building she paused briefly to admire a floral arrangement in the form of a royal crown. A bouquet of flowers was also presented to the Queen by Linda Buckwold, the young daughter of the Mayor.

Ceremonies were opened by the Lions Club Band playing the National Anthem.

The Queen signed the city's official guest book, adding her signature to that she had put there in 1951 when she visited the city as Princess Elizabeth. The book also contained the signatures of the Queen's parents, King George VI and Queen Elizabeth put there in 1939 on the only other occasion on which the city had played host to a reigning monarch.

Members of City Council, school board chairman, Saskatoon MP Harry Jones and officials of the Saskatchewan Power Corporation were introduced to the Royal Couple at this point.

Official presentation from the city was in the form of two $500 bursaries, which the Queen, in turn, presented to two Grade 12 students who will be entering university this fall.

The Queen also received a Robert Hurley painting of the Queen Elizabeth power station of the SPC, believed to be the largest of its kind in Western Canada.

The Queen graciously consented to the use of her name in connection with the newly-completed power station and officially opened it. A meter above the platform sprang to life and showed the power surging through the generators at the station on the city's outskirts.

The royal party then moved on to the University, where the pre-

50 YEARS
Continued on Page 6, Column 8

Peaceful Clouds

There were more clouds over Saskatoon today than on June 3, 1939, when Saskatoon greeted the first Sovereign to set foot in the city. But the clouds today probably were not as ominous as the hardly visible clouds on that memorable day when King George VI and Queen Elizabeth visited here. Exactly three months after the visit, the British Commonwealth and Nazi Germany were at war. The clouds today, it was hoped, were more fleeting.

VISIT SIDELIGHTS

When King George VI visited here, the main function took place near the Massey-Harris building and thousands of youngsters in red, white and blue formed a monster Union Jack as a background for the ceremonies. Mayor of the city at that time was Carl Niderost.

In 1939, in violent contrast to this decade, Saskatoon was still in the throes of the depression. Thousands were jobless and money was a scarce commodity. Despite that, farmers and rural folk contrived to get to the city somehow. It was estimated that more than 100,000 persons converged on Saskatoon. Hundreds spent the night on the river bank and in City Park and the Royal Visit gave the entire area a real "shot in the arm."

There was no TV; radio had not been so well perfected. To get a feeling of intimacy with the event, it was necessary to visit the city. That's just what thousands did.

Groups of vets and small detachments of soldiers marched along the streets to checking points throughout this morning. This phase of activities was in charge of R. J. Sanderson, president of the Canadian Legion.

On University Drive, spectators began taking up positions by 9 o'clock. Many of them had light lawn chairs and sat on the boulevard, enjoying the sun while assured of a good spot to see the Queen.

Stanley Burke, columnist for the Star-Phoenix at United Nations and who is travelling wih the Royal Tour, told the Star-Phoenix editor today that Esmond Butler, secretary to the Queen, that Her Majesty had said today she was "deeply touched with the reception at all the western cities and small towns."

A little lad in a Cub uniform, who was selling programs long before the Royal Party arrived, was bragging that he had sold $6 worth but he wasn't sure just how much he would collect out of the deal.

Crowds were lined three and four deep along most of Second Avenue, as shops and offices emptied of staff in time to see the royal procession. Some enterprising spectators took up favored positions as long as an hour before time and provided themselves with comfortable chairs for the long wait. Every office window had its cluster of faces and many peered from the rooftops of buildings.

JOE PHELPS and Mrs. Phelps, both wearing old-time dress, explain to Her Majesty some details of some old furniture at the Museum.

Children's Greeting "Like a Wave"

Like a huge wave rushing out ahead of the tide to meet the shore, 5,000 resounding voices chorused their same greeting as the royal couple moved slowly into Griffiths Stadium from Cumberland Avenue at 11.50 o'clock this morning.

This was the city's gathering point for the children and the stadium bleachers were packed with anxious boys and girls humming excitedly in anticipation of the Queen's arrival and beside her, her husband Prince Philip.

For many of the youngsters this was their first glimpse of Queen Elizabeth II.

Their delight was spontaneous. As the royal limousine nosed carefully onto the quarter-mile cinder track, the screaming children sent up a welcome they had been holding back most of the morning.

And the royal couple returned the greeting with smiles as warm and friendly as the morning sun.

Only five minutes earlier the Queen and her husband had met and talked with officials of the University of Saskatchewan. Now they were in a different kind of atmosphere, one that shed completely any traces of the formality that had marked the royal visit to that point, a light-hearted atmosphere that only small and eager children could create.

The children had been waiting for hours, engaged in community singing, race events and listening to the fast-stepping Nokomis Chiefs band.

Hundreds of boy scouts, girl guides, brownies and cubs ringed the reviewing platform in a giant horseshoe, a regular scouting formation.

Then, escorted by the mayor,

CHILDREN
Continued on Page 6, Column 3

Best Yet!

Trouble about living in a place is that often you do not realize what you have!

Remarked a veteran visiting newsman after seeing the Western Development Museum and the Pion-Era show: "That's the best thing we've seen on this tour. I'd seen a film about the Museum but I never realized its scope. That visit was the best yet. It was obvious that Prince Philip was delighted."

The Weather

SASSY SAYS:

FIT FOR A QUEEN

Copyright —By Vavra

EDMONTON (CP) — Fine summer weather with maximum temperatures of 80 will persist today and Thursday. A few thunderstorms are expected in northern Saskatchewan this afternoon and in central and northern parts of Alberta late tomorrow.

Forecast valid until midnight Thursday:

SASKATOON—PRINCE ALBERT

Cloudy with scattered thundershowers this afternoon clearing this evening. Sunny and warm tomorrow. Light winds. Low-high Prince Albert 50-75; Saskatoon, North Battleford and Kindersley 55-80.

REGINA—YORKTON

Cloudy with sunny intervals; clearing tonight, mostly sunny Thursday; light winds; Regina 55 and 85, Yorkton 55 and 80.

Temperature at 7 this morning	64
A year ago	79
Lowest temperature in night	58
Maximum	69
Wind average velocity	6.8
Wind, maximum velocity	17
Precipitation	17
Sunshine	3.4
Sunset today	9.12
Sunrise tomorrow	5.14

Kamloops	97	62	
Prince George	79	44	
Prince Rupert	65	54	
Vancouver	77	63	
Victoria	71	57	
Calgary	76	56	
Coronation	78	53	tr.
Edmonton	78	56	
Fairview	77	56	
Jasper	81	45	
Lethbridge	79	56	
Medicine Hat	78	56	
Estevan	89	53	tr.
Moose Jaw	73	59	.28
Gretna	83	64	.25
Kenora	80	65	.14
Montreal	87	69	
North Battleford	68	55	.44
Prince Albert	73	48	tr.
Regina	71	54	.16
Swift Current	71	56	.90
Yorkton	71	58	.18
Brandon	80	59	1.23
Dauphin	79	55	.12
The Pas	77	62	.44
Fort William	77	56	.25
Ottawa	84	63	
White River	77	57	tr.
Quebec City	83	60	
Winnipeg	82	63	.79
Halifax	62	56	1.23
Toronto	86	63	
Saint John	77	54	.02

JOHN GEORGE DIEFENBAKER

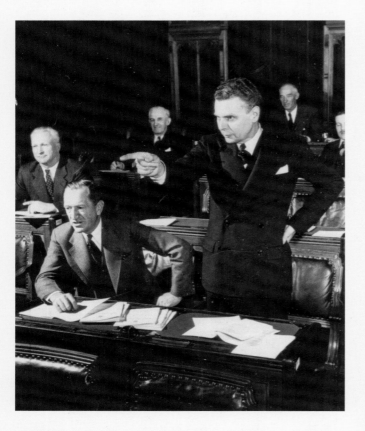

Diefenbaker in the House of Commons, Ottawa, 1948

John George Diefenbaker was born in Neustadt, Ontario, in 1895, but made his home in Saskatchewan after his parents moved the family to Fort Carlton, north of Saskatoon, in 1903. An avid reader and aspiring politician, Diefenbaker graduated from the University of Saskatchewan in 1916 with an M.A. in political science and economics. He served briefly as a lieutenant in the 105th Saskatoon Fusiliers from 1916 to1917, but soon found success as a criminal lawyer after passing the Saskatchewan Bar in 1919 and establishing a practice near Prince Albert shortly after. In Diefenbaker's early years, his attempts to enter politics were discouraging. He was defeated in general elections in 1925 and 1926, provincial elections in 1929 and 1938 and in the race for mayor of Prince Albert in 1933. From 1936 to 1938, however, he became leader of the Saskatchewan Conservative Party and was elected leader of the federal party from 1956 to 1967 as the Conservatives finally put an end to the Liberal's twenty-two years of rule. During his leadership, Diefenbaker became a strong, and for some overwhelming, advocate of social reform, bringing forward the Canadian Bill of Rights in 1958. In a speech delivered that same year, he declared himself the first prime minister of Canada of neither English or French descent, and told how he aspired to bring the nation's diverse cultural backgrounds under the umbrella of one national identity: Canadian.

On the hustings, Lake Centre riding, circa mid-1940s

Mary Diefenbaker (née Bannerman), date unknown

KENNEDY IS SLAIN

Connally, Johnson wounded

WASHINGTON (AP) – Government sources said Friday that President Kennedy is dead. He died at 1 p.m. CST.

Earlier two priests stepped out of Parkland Hospital's emergency ward and said President Kennedy died of his bullet wounds.

He had been given blood transfusions in an effort to save his life after he and Governor John Connally of Texas were shot in an assassination attempt.

The president was given the last rites of the Roman Catholic Church.

Vice-President Lyndon Johnson, travelling in a car behind the president's, was slightly wounded in the arm. After a visit to the hospital, Johnson's wife said he was not in danger.

Kennedy was reported taken to Parkland Hospital, near the Dallas trade mart, where he was to have made a speech.

Bell said Kennedy was transferred to an ambulance. He lay on a seat of the car.

Bell reported the shots were fired as the motorcade entered the triple underpass which leads to the Stemmons Freeway route to Parkland Hospital.

Pandemonium broke loose around the scene.

The secret service waved the motorcade on at top speed to the hospital.

Even at high speed it took nearly five minutes to get the car to the ambulance entrance of the hospital.

Reporters saw Kennedy lying flat on his face on the seat of his car.

Bell said a man and a woman were scrambling on the upper level of the walkway overlooking the underpass.

Mrs. Kennedy was weeping and trying to hold up her husband's head when reporters reached the car.

The secret service said the president remained in the emergency room and the governor was moved to the general operating room of Parkland Hospital.

THE LEADER-POST

VOL. LIV—No. 272 **92 PAGES** REGINA, SASKATCHEWAN, FRIDAY, NOVEMBER 22, 1963 **LAST EDITION** SINGLE COPY **7c**

BOB SHAW'S MOTHER DIES

Word was received late Thursday of the death of Bob Shaw's mother in Westerville, Ohio.

The Saskachewan Roughrider coach said Thursday night he will remain in Vancouver until after Saskatchewan's final playoff game with British Columbia Lions. The best-of-three series is tied 1-1 and the third game will be played Saturday afternoon.

Coach Shaw said his mother, 62, had been sick for a week of a malfunction of the liver. Shaw's father died some years ago.

The funeral will not be held until Shaw gets to Ohio.

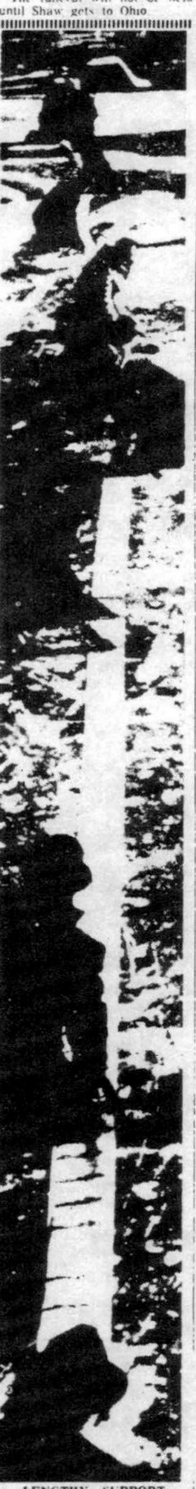

LENGTHY SUPPORT: A telegram nearly 100 feet long carrying the names of some 12,000 Saskatchewan Roughrider fans is being prepared for delivery in front of the telegraph office. By Saturday it is expected the cable will be 150 feet long. Target is 20,000 names.

REGINAN FACES MURDER CHARGE

By JIM PETRO
Police Reporter

A 27-year-old Regina pipefitter is in custody to face capital murder and attempted capital murder charges after a shotgun-wielding man entered a house at 2035 Francis about 1.10 a.m. Friday.

Dead is Ovide Berriault, 26, of 2052 Francis, who suffered a chest wound and had the lower portion of his jaw blown off.

Treated at General hospital for neck and back wounds was Mrs. Lorraine Florence Tuey, 25, of 2035 Francis.

Charged is Robert Charles Nesbitt, a resident at 2035 Francis until a short time ago.

He was arrested nearly four hours after the shooting as police surrounded a house in the 1800 block Ottawa.

Immediately after the shooting police and RCMP roadblocks encircled the city in search of a 1960-model Buick the suspect was believed to be driving.

Police went to the Ottawa address shortly before 5 a.m. after receiving information the subject could be there.

Insp. J. A. Juno, head of the criminal investigation division, said the suspect offered no resistance to arrest.

Police seized a 12-gauge shotgun.

Police were at the murder scene within minutes of the shootings.

Insp. Juno said Mrs. Tuey answered her back door shortly after 1 a.m., where some discussion took place with a man at the door.

Mrs. Tuey then fled out the front door and across the street, he said.

At this stage she was hit with a shot in the back, but continued on to the home of Mr. Irwin Leonard, 2079 Francis, from where police were contacted.

Police took Mrs. Tuey to hospital, but she was not detained.

Early in the investigation they were confused because they could not find traces of pellets at the scene.

Three expended cartridges were found at the scene, Insp. Juno said. Two were in the house, and one was outside.

He said police did not know how many shots were fired at the woman and how many at the man.

The house is a five-room bungalow.

Mr. Berriault lived with his brother, E. Berriault, and his wife at 2052 Francis.

He is survived by a wife and mother in Winnipeg, and at least one more brother and two sisters.

Mrs. Leonard Irwin, whose house Mrs. Tuey staggered into, said she knew neither the dead man or the woman.

She said Mrs. Tuey ran into the house about 1.15 a.m. while she was entertaining company from Manitoba.

"She could hardly talk and she told us to call the cops," Mrs. Leonard recalled.

"She (Mrs. Tuey) said he had a gun and was after her to shoot her," Mrs. Leonard added.

"I was so scared for fear the man would come into the house," she added.

She explained the occupants of the house locked the door and waited for police, who arrived within a matter of minutes.

It is believed Mr. Berriault was employed in work relating to the manufacture of chemicals.

PRESIDENT SHOT: President John F. Kennedy was shot Friday afternoon just as his motorcade left downtown Dallas, Tex. He was taken to Parkland hospital where he was given transfusions. Governor John Connally of Texas who was with the president was also wounde d.

Head-on collision in snow kills four

BROADVIEW (Special) — Three men and a women died instantly Thursday when a heavy car and light delivery truck collided head-on on the snow-swept Trans-Canada highway near this farming town, 95 miles east of Regina.

Police identified the dead as 56-year-old Frank Zimmer, Cudworth garage owner, and his wife Sylvia, 52, Richard George Bethell, 29, of 2801 Fourteenth, Regina and Hilden Crofford, 58, of the Regina district.

Police said falling and blowing snow shrouded the highway when the two vehicles rammed each other as the delivery truck tried to pass a small farm truck.

RCMP said they believed a swirl of snow from the farm truck obliterated the road as Bethell, driver of the delivery vehicle, pulled out to pass it.

Both vehicles were demolished, and the bodies of Zimmer and Bethell had to be cut from the wreckage.

The accident occurred on a straight stretch of road eight miles west of here at about 11.45 a.m.

Mr. and Mrs. Zimmer were returning to Cudworth from Windsor, Ont., where they had flown recently to take delivery of a new car. A luxury model, the car had been driven only 1,500 miles when the crash demolished it.

Mr. Bethell, an engineer

See FOUR KILLED—Page 12

Curtailed railway services suggested

Curtailment rather than abandonment of branch railway line services in Saskatchewan was proposed Friday morning to Canada's two railway systems.

The suggestion was made at the one-day conference in Regina of local railway retention committees. The conference had been arranged by the transportation branch of the provincial department of industry and information to enable the local committees to present their views to the railway companies.

There are 49 such committees organized with respect to 30 branch lines in Saskatchewan for which applications to abandon have been made by the railways. At noon there were 42 of the committee represented by official delegates.

The suggestion that railways might curtail rather than abandon branch line services was made early in a discussion period by A. L. Robin of Waldheim.

"We realize railways are losing money on branch line operations, but they might consider running freight trains only when there is a need to run them instead of running empty trains on regular schedules," he said.

Alfred Skinner of Winnipeg, general manager of the prairie region of the CNR commented that some branch lines in his company's system now are operating solely on a basis of need and others are being considered for that kind of service.

UNECONOMIC

He agreed it was uneconomic to send a train and crew on a scheduled run if there was no freight to be moved inward or outward.

"But, in some cases we have a crew, or crews available and they make the scheduled runs," he said.

Ha old Beamiss of Beechy questioned the difference in ton-mile standards that are considered by the two railways, noting one set the figure at 66,000 while the other noted 25,000.

A. M. Gossage of Winnipeg, vice-president and general manager of the CPR's prairie region said the 25,000 ton-mile figure was a net figure and could at least be doubled to reach a ross ton-mile figure for comparison with the 66,000 ton-miles noted by the CNR.

"A branch line dependent on grain shipments for revenue cannot be operated economically at present rates on a 25,000-

See CURTAILING—Page 12

Canada buys six DC-9s

OTTAWA (CP)—Prime Minister Pearson announced in the Commons today Trans-Canada Air Lines will buy six Douglas DC-9 jet aircraft, and touched off a stormy shouting match with Opposition Leader Diefenbaker.

Mr. Pearson read a lengthy statement to the House about TCA's choice of the Douglas aircraft, the prospective work load for the Canadair Limited plant in Montreal, and the retention of TCA turboprop overhaul facilities in Winnipeg. Parts of the DC-9 are to be made by de Havilland Aircraft Company in Toronto.

The DC-9 has two rear-mounted jet engines and will carry 70 passengers at speeds of better than 500 miles an hour.

When Mr. Diefenbaker rose to comment on the announcement, an unidentified backbench Liberal shouted a remark about the former government's cancelation of the Avro Arrow supersonic jet fighter program.

Mr. Diefenbaker said that his government had been condemned for the decision, but it was only recently revealed that the previous Liberal government under Prime Minister St. Laurent had decided the Arrow program must be discontinued—and was afraid to make the an-

See CANADA—Page 12

Keeping POSTed

Railways state abandonment case	—Page 3
Campus parties gear for election	—Page 9
Natural resources legislation for review	—Page 10
More activity in Sask. oil	—Page 24
Arctic oil dream of geologist	—Page 25
New, colder trade look aken	—Page 27
West, Atchison join Riders	—Page 30
Senator raps tax critics	—Page 41

Garage holdup nets pair $59

City police are searching for two men who robbed a service station attendant of $59 in cash early Friday morning.

Two masked men, who may have been armed, forced Andrew Kallichuk of 1443 Kent, into a back room while they rifled a till in Daval Petroleums, a British American station, at Albert and Twenty-fifth at 2.16 a.m.

The attendant said he saw no weapon, but one man had his hand thrust in his coat pocket as though he was carrying a gun.

The two bandits escaped in a car with two women.

The holdup men struck just as Kallichuk was depositing money from a gasoline sale in the till.

"The first man entered and told me to get away from the till," he said.

The attendant was pushed away from the till as the second bandit entered and said: "Get back if you know what's good for you."

He said both men were masked with what appeared to be cheesecloth and the second man to enter appeared to be carrying a gun.

Kallichuk said while he was being pushed into a back room he heard someone say, "hurry up."

He described one of the men as being around six feet tall with blond hair. He was wearing dark clothing. The other man, according to the attendant, was short, heavy set and dressed in a suit jacket.

Kallichuk attempted to chase the getaway car, which he said was a black 1952 or '53 Ford, in his own car, but got hung up on a concrete curb in the Golden Mile Plaza.

The attendant said he had to call police from another service station because the thieves had apparently destroyed the telephone connection in Daval Petroleums and a telephone booth on the parking lot was also not working.

He said there were two women in the car, but he did not get a look at them.

"This is the first time anythink like this has ever happened to me," Kallichuk said.

Weather

Milder weather will return to southern Alberta by Saturday morning but for the rest of the prairies the outlook still is continuing cold. Highs on Saturday will range from 15 to 30 above in southern Albertta and between zero and 10 below in Saskatchewan and northern Alberta. A Pacific system will bring increasing cloud and some snow to central and northern Alberta late today and tonight and to Saskatchewan on Saturday.

Regina - Yorkton - Weyburn - Estevan: Mainly sunny with not much temperature change. Winds light. Low-high 15 below and five.

Prince Albert - Saskatoon: Sunny today. Cloudy Saturday with light snow in the afternoon. Continuing cold. Light winds today, SE20 Saturday. Low-high 15 below and 10 below.

Maple Creek - Moose Jaw: Variable cloudiness occasional snow Saturday and not quite so cold. Winds NW15 becoming light tonight and SE15 Saturday. Low-high Swift Current 15 below and zero.

Regina Details

Forecast high today	15
Temperature at 8 a.m.	-7
One year ago	18
Relative humidity	81%
Record high 1939	58
Record low 1946	-27
Average high	27.2
Average low	9.7
Average	18.5
Sunset today	5.07 p.m.
Sunrise tomorrow	8.22 a.m.

Yesterday's Temperatures

	Max.	Min.	Precip.
Regina	9	-8	.06
Moose Jaw	9	-8	.08
Saskatoon	5	0	.03
Kindersley	12	-17	
Yorkton	6	4	.10
Battleford	4	-5	.05
Prince Albert	1	-1	.08
Broadview	5	1	.12
Dafoe	5	1	.12
Estevan	7	0	.14
Swift Current	6	-3	.04
Vancouver	42	33	.29
Victoria	42	39	.12
Calgary	4	-14	Tr.
Edmonton	-4	-23	Tr.
Jasper	3	-19	.02
Lethbridge	28	-7	
Medicine Hat	16	-7	Tr.
Brandon	8	4	.26
Dauphin	10	6	.28
The Pas	3	-1	.04
Winnipeg	17	15	.16

Japanese election to Ikeda

By JOHN RODERICK

TOKYO (AP) — Despite inroads by moderate leftists and independents, Premier Hayato Ikeda's conservatives maintained overwhelming control of the Japanese Parliament in final unofficial election returns today.

Though Ikeda appeared to have won a mandate to continue at the helm of the pro-Western government, the winning margin of his Liberal-Democratic party in Thursday's election of a new lower house fell below his expectations.

The final unofficial returns gave the Liberal-Democrats 283 seats in the 467-seat ruling lower house. This was 13 less than the 296 won in 1960 and three short of the 286 the conservatives held at dissolution three weeks ago.

Ikeda had asked for 300 seats and confidently expected at least 290.

Ikeda's main opposition, the Socialists, who lean towards Red China, won 144 seats, one less than the 145 chalked up in 1960 and seven more than they held at dissolution. Political experts had predicted they would score sizable gains.

Youth dies of injuries

Harvey Kuzuska, 17, of Sturgis, died early Friday in a Regina hospital of injuries received Sunday in a traffic accident near Stenen, 145 miles northeast of Regina.

Kuzuska was a passenger in a car operated by 14-year-old Lyda Bobowski when it went out of control and rolled over in a roadside ditch about 2¾ miles north of Stenen.

Miss Babowski was iiled in the accident.

TCA BASE WILL STAY

OTTAWA (CP) — Winnipeg's big Trans-Canada Air Lines maintenance base will not be removed by 1966 as previously planned but will remain in operation for at least 10 years, Prime Minister Pearson told the Commons today.

The original plan was to move the base to Montreal over the next three years as the Crown-owned air line moved into a pure-jet operation from turboprops.

Mr. Pearson reported the new decision at the end of a lengthy statement in which he announced TCA's plan to purchase the Douglas DC-9 jet airliner.

He said TCA's program for the next 10 years indicates the turboprop Viscount airliner will continue to be needed.

"I am therefore now able to announce a change from the previous expectation, which was made known a year ago, that the overhaul and maintenance base in Winnipeg might begin to be phased out early in 1966," he said.

"For at least as far ahead as planning now extends—that is, for 10 years—the Winnipeg facilities will continue to be used."

This decision was of great importance to Greater Winnipeg, he noted.

Winnipeg area MPs, along with various civic and provincial groups, have been campaigning for a year to keep the TCA base there.

16,871 ATTENDING COURSES

Registration for 1963-64 totals 16,871 for all courses offered by the University of Saskatchewan and its junior colleges, beginning with intersession last May. This is 1,961 higher than in 1962-63.

The figures were presented Friday to a meeting of the University senate by Registrar N. K. Cram.

The calculation is based on enrolment in daytime and evening classes at Saskatoon and Regina, Campion, Luther and St. Peter's colleges; on enrolment in the school of nursing and the school of agriculture; and on registration for summer school, intersession and correspondence courses. Certain non-degree credit courses and short courses are not included.

Mr. Cram reported that daytime, degree course students at Saskatoon number 6,902, an increase of 682 over the figure one year ago.

At Regina Campus, daytime enrolment (including matriculation students) is 1,003, an increase of 148.

The report for Saskatoon notes a decline in enrolment in the colleges of engineering and pharmacy of 32 and 1 respectively. All other colleges showed increases.

Enrolment of daytime, degree-course students, with 1962-63 figures in brackets, is as follows: agriculture 361 (323); arts and science 2,352 (2113); commerce 542 (467); education 1,252 (1,062); engineering 901 (933); graduate studies 336 (294); home economics 133 (105); law 115 (109); medicine 152 (137); nursing 350 (318); pharmacy 256 (257); physical education 121 (102).

Mr. Cram said that there are 2,145 first year students compared with 1,933 last year. 294 students from 46 countries who completed their secondary school work or additional work outside Canada are registered at the university this year.

Chief Abel Watetech and grandson, November 1958

Teepees at the Provincial Exhibition, Regina, July 1959

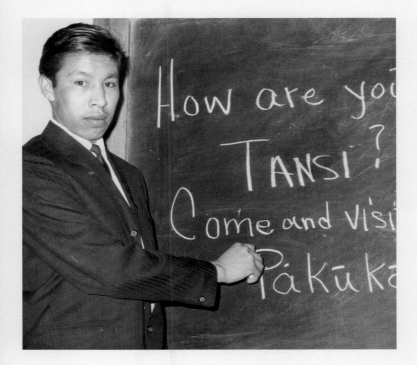

Hector Knife teaching Cree at the Indian and Métis Friendship Centre, Regina, January 1965

In 1958, a conference of First Nations from across Saskatchewan was convened at Fort Qu'Appelle to discuss the proposed extension of the provincial franchise to native people. The question of voting rights was not resolved at the time, but the gathering served as a watershed moment in the political cohesion of Saskatchewan's First Nations.

Under the leadership of John Tootoosis of the Poundmaker First Nation — a revered figure who had been battling for aboriginal rights since the 1920s — a loose coalition of native groups from across the province reconstituted itself as the Federation of Saskatchewan Indians, an entity destined to become a powerful force in provincial and national affairs. As its precursors had for decades, the new organization worked for the protection of treaty rights and the promotion of cultural, economic and educational development among First Nations. In 1960, under the Conservative government of John Diefenbaker, native people across Canada were granted the right to vote in federal elections. The proposal had been met with suspicion by many aboriginal leaders in Saskatchewan: "What I fear," said one elder, "is that by becoming voters in Dominion elections, we risk being treated as a mere interest group by the Canadian politicians rather than as independent peoples with special protections for our lands." Federal officials offered reassurances that participating in elections would not diminish other native rights, and the right to vote came to be seen as a milestone in an era when Saskatchewan's First Nations were asserting their identity with increasing determination and success. "One of the heartening developments of the period," wrote Saskatchewan historian John Archer, "was a reawakening of pride and energy among the Indian people."

Jubilee hoedown, Saskatoon, 1955

Big Muddy party, circa 1962

Broncos en route to the Calgary Stampede, June 1960

Regina, November 1963

Regina Riding Club, Light Horse Show, Regina, March 23, 1963

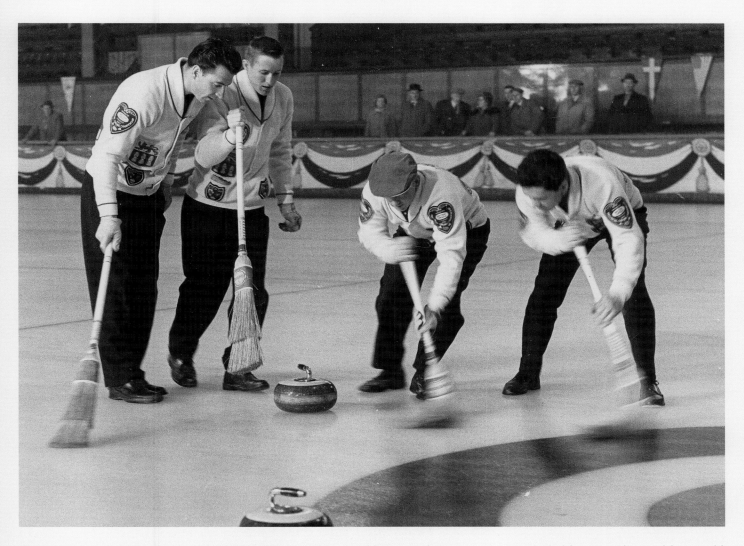

The Richardson rink, four brothers from Stoughton — Ernie, Arnold, Sam and Wes — won an unrivaled four Canadian and four world championship titles beginning in 1959

Chapter Nine

LEFT PAGE: Joni Mitchell appears on CFQC's Top of the Clock, Saskatoon, circa March 1969

ABOVE: Back to Batoche Days, Batoche, July 20, 1972

It was, on one hand, just a football game: a few fierce rushes by running back George Reed, a series of well-aimed passes from quarterback Ron Lancaster, a clutch grab in the end zone by receiver Hugh Campbell.

But the Saskatchewan Roughriders' upset win over the Ottawa Rough Riders in the 1966 Grey Cup was also, for many in the province, a truly transcendent triumph of West over East — a gridiron struggle that illuminated the growing animosity between the prairie provinces and Central Canada on a range economic, political and social issues.

By November 1966, when the western 'Riders defeated their eastern namesakes 29-14 to take the CFL championship, signs of the brewing bitterness were everywhere: freight rates, education, equalization payments, tax policies, wheat stockpiles and control over natural resources were all bones of contention between the provincial and federal governments.

But for a brief moment, the contest between Regina and Ottawa that mattered most was the one played on grass, Green against Black, Ron Lancaster vs. Russ Jackson.

"Reed bludgeoned his way for one first down in three cracks and it was now time to institute a pass pattern Hugh Campbell had told Lancaster and coach Eagle Keys he believed he could beat defender Joe Poirier with," the *Leader-Post* recounted. "Campbell ran a hook and it was good to the five. On the first play

Right Honourable John Diefenbaker, unidentified ambassador and Tommy Douglas, MP, Government House, Ottawa 1966

of the fourth quarter, he ran a shallow hook again and clawed the ball away from Poirier's desperate dive.

"The go-ahead score broke the back of the team a lot of people insisted was the finest team to come out of the East in fifteen years. The peppery Jackson was no longer clapping his hands attempting to jazz-up mates. They were dead and the dirge sounded moments later ..."

The Roughriders' victory uncorked decades of pent-up revelry.

"The Grey Cup champions returned to Regina Sunday night to be greeted by boisterous pandemonium unequaled, some said, by even the great celebrations here on V-E Day," an effusive *Leader-Post* scribe reported. "Regina celebrations began seconds after the final gun at Empire Stadium in Vancouver Saturday when shouts and cheers could be heard outside in any city neighbourhood and car horns sounded a din throughout the city. The feeling built to a great crescendo until it finally erupted from the throats of from 6,000 to 8,000 persons Sunday night when the Grey Cup was carried into the Regina Armory. The cup belonged to Saskatchewan for the first time in history."

Fans were "packed in back-to-stomach and shoulder-to-shoulder," the paper noted. "Mighty cheers shook the Armory roof when the Grey Cup was carried in, when coach Eagle Keys was the first to step up to the mike and then again when quarterback Ron Lancaster and other favourite players stepped up."

And among the celebrants at the Armory, the paper noted, was someone waving a placard that read: "The East plays lousy football." Saskatchewan premier

Ross Thatcher, who spoke to the crowd that day, must have nodded approvingly. Playing games with Ottawa was a major part of the premier's portfolio, and he was engaged at that time in a host of East-West battles of his own.

Thatcher presided over a province that was achieving unprecedented levels of prosperity. By the mid-Sixties, a string of bumper harvests and surging activity in the mining and forest industries had Saskatchewan booming.

"Wheat crops were good," wrote historian John Archer. "Capital investment in potash was high, with three companies mining and six others developing mines. Saskatoon christened itself the potash capital of the world."

The 1966 wheat yield was a record 537 million bushels, and farmers enjoyed a relatively healthy price of $1.69 per bushel. The provincial government had successfully courted an American pulp and paper giant — Parsons and Whittemore — to invest in a $65-million mill at Prince Albert that was hailed as the province's single largest industrial employer.

But prosperous times meant Saskatchewan would no longer be classified as a "have-not" province by the federal government. Reaching that milestone was a mixed blessing given the resulting loss of equalization payments — a much-debated development that led to fractious negotiations between Regina and Ottawa over how to phase out the grants.

Diefenbaker homestead, vandalized, Regina, circa 1967

There was further friction over what to do about stockpiles of surplus wheat. By 1970, more than 400 million bushels were being stored in temporary granaries awaiting the end of a glut in world markets. A federal program called LIFT (Lower Inventories For Tomorrow) paid farmers to convert wheat acreage to summerfallow, but the conception and administration of the plan sowed even more conflict between the provincial and federal governments.

"It was obvious to many farmers that they had done their part," noted Archer, "and that something was wrong with a system that left stored grain at one end of the food chain and hungry people unfed at the other end."

Even potash, the fertilizer resource that was helping to enrich Saskatchewan's economy, presented problems resulting from overproduction. Thatcher — "irritated by Ottawa's lack of action in defence of Saskatchewan's interests," David E. Smith observed in *Prairie Liberalism* — flew south to meet with the governor of New Mexico, the continent's other major potash producer and reached an agreement to curb total output and keep prices propped up.

In October 1968, a statue of Louis Riel was unveiled on the grounds of the provincial legislature, commemorating the Métis leader who had led a rebellion in territorial Saskatchewan and was hanged for treason at Regina in 1885. Thatcher and the country's new prime minister, Pierre Trudeau, stood side-by-side for the unveiling, but the event served mainly to highlight the widening divide between the two leaders and the turbulent social climate of the era.

Père Athol Murray and
Gordie Howe, Gordie Howe
Day, July 22, 1966

Thatcher was heckled and Trudeau was mobbed by hundreds of angry university students who were protesting tuition increases and what they considered regressive education policies being pursued by both the provincial and federal governments.

Against a backdrop of increased militancy among aboriginals across North America, Thatcher warned during the Riel dedication that "we are sitting on a time bomb in this matter of equal opportunity for our native people."

He also used the unveiling, noted historian John Herd Thompson, "to bash federal government policies with respect to the Prairies" and draw parallels to historic western grievances.

"Whether we realize it or not, we of 1968 face a situation which is similar in some respects," Thatcher argued. "If Riel could walk the soil of Canada today, I am sure his sense of justice would be outraged as it was in 1885."

Trudeau, widely viewed as an arrogant, ultra-urban easterner with little interest in the West, would go on to raise the ire of all Saskatchewan grain growers with his infamously flippant remark about the federal role in export marketing: "Why should I sell the Canadian farmers' wheat?"

It was an attitude that earned him enduring hostility across the Prairies. In July 1969, during an appearance in Saskatoon, Trudeau was bombarded with insults by protesters and shot back: "If you want to meet me in the future, don't bring signs saying that Trudeau is a pig and don't bring signs saying that I hustle women."

Amid the unrest and uncertainty of the Sixties in Saskatchewan, there was one instance of unmitigated horror. In August 1967, a deranged young gunman named Victor Hoffman murdered nine members of a family at their farmhouse near Shell Lake, a remote community about 80 kilometres from Prince Albert. Seven children and their parents, James and Evelyn Peterson, were shot to death in what was, to that time, the worst mass murder in Canadian history.

"Fourteen shots from a .22-calibre weapon snuffed out the lives of nine of ten members of a family here sometime Monday night," the *Star-Phoenix* recounted from the scene. "The children were aged one to seveteen years. Bodies were found on the front porch, the back yard and in the home.... The lone survivor of the massacre was four-year-old Phyllis, (who), according to one report, was lying in a bed between her brothers and sisters and may have slept through the entire blood bath."

For all of the tumult of the times, there were poignant moments, too.

Detroit Red Wings hockey star Gordie Howe, probably the most famous of all Saskatchewan-born citizens, returned to Saskatoon in July 1966 for a day of tributes.

"Thousands of people lined the streets of Saskatoon this morning to pay homage to the 'monarch' of hockey," the *Star-Phoenix* reported. "Young, old, brush cut to Beatle cut, stood knee-to-knee and hooted, hollered and waved signs as 'their' hockey player was honored by his native city. Gordie Howe Day was officially kicked off by a parade complete with bands, floats and visiting sports personalities....

"Homemade signs were jauntily waved in the air as the Howe family was escorted by in an open convertible.... Tribute to the hockey great was not restricted to signs and cheering. One mother decked her daughters out with special, full skirts. As Howe's car came by, the girls, who were standing in front of the crowd, spread their skirts out to show the word 'Gordie' emblazoned across the bottom...."

Two other celebrated Saskatchewanians were making their mark in the music world. Buffy Sainte-Marie, a native songstress from a Cree reserve in the Qu'Appelle Valley, and the young Saskatoon folk singer she'd mentored in the business, Joni Mitchell, mingled easily among the world's biggest musical talents in the 1960s and Seventies.

Buffy Sainte-Marie was born on the Piapot Cree reserve in the Qu'Appelle Valley and later raised in Maine and Massachusetts

The two women, Mitchell biographer Brian Hinton has written, shared "a sense of the Canadian landscape which is nostalgic and angry, proprietorial and dispossessed...."

Saskatchewan's landscape, in fact, got something of a makeover around that time. As part of its successful bid to host the 1971 Canada Winter Games, Saskatoon built a ski hill — Mount Blackstrap — out of excavated dirt. A similarly innovative, can-do attitude led the University of Saskatchewan to begin accepting surplus grain from hundreds of farm students in lieu of tuition — a move that deflected some of the criticism surrounding fee hikes and also eased (at least symbolically) the wheat-stockpiling problem.

September 22, 1969, marked another landmark moment in the province's history: "Saskatchewan ran its first official flag up the flagpole Monday," the *Leader-Post* noted in a story that described the unfurling of the banner — "the Saskatchewan coat of arms and a prairie lily on a green and gold field" — at a ceremony in Regina.

"The flag, although flying in the face of tradition to the extent that it did not gain approval from Britain's College of Arms, was chosen by a free vote in the legislature from 4,025 designs submitted in a contest by Saskatchewan and former Saskatchewan residents," it was reported. "It was designed by Anthony

Flood, Regina, 1971

Drake, a British school teacher who taught at Pontiex and Hodgeville for three years, prior to returning to England this summer to continue his studies ...

"Premier Thatcher, whose government set up an all-party legislative committee to choose 'a distinctive flag' for the province, said it should fly 'as a symbol of our determination to build an even better Saskatchewan for future generations.'"

Thatcher, though, who had won a second majority in the 1967 provincial election, faced declining fortunes. By 1970, there was growing unease about the economic health of the province and the level of foreign investment in Saskatchewan's resource sector.

That same year, the NDP chose a successor to Woodrow Lloyd. In an exciting leadership contest that featured a tight race between two future premiers, the party selected Allan Blakeney by a slim margin over Roy Romanow.

The revitalized party started tapping into a vague but widespread sense of dissatisfaction with the Thatcher government. It made the most of rising concern about rural depopulation and the future of the family farm and harnessed strident opposition among unions, students, native people and environmentalists to major Liberal policy initiatives.

In the June 1971 election, Blakeney and the NDP surged to a surprisingly solid majority victory.

"It must be something I did," a shocked and dejected Thatcher stated after his defeat. "It wasn't our supporters' fault." The ousted premier died just a month after the election. "His death stunned the Liberal party as much as its recent defeat," Smith noted in *Prairie Liberalism*, "its policies repudiated and its leader gone."

The early years of the Blakeney era would witness another burst of economic growth in the province, but ongoing — in fact, deepening — discord with the federal government. Saskoil, a Crown corporation set up in 1973 to increase state influence in the petroleum industry, typified the NDP's belief in the need for a major public-sector presence in the provincial economy. The philosophy, however, would bring Blakeney's government into repeated conflict with business and federal authorities.

But the new premier made one decision that was universally popular. October 7, 1973, was officially designated "October 34" and declared George Reed Day as Saskatchewan celebrated the illustrious career of Canadian football's all-time greatest running back. The Roughriders' unstoppable Number 34 — "honoured at half-time by almost 22,000 cheering and devoted fans at Taylor Field," the *Leader-Post* reported — was still smashing CFL records seven seasons after the team's Grey Cup win back in '66, and more than a decade after he'd arrived in Canada from his native Mississippi.

Ron Lancaster, Roughrider quarterback from 1963-1978

Blakeney presided over a ceremony that saw Snowbirds from Canadian Forces Base Moose Jaw create a smoke-trail heart above the stadium and during which Reed — surrounded by his family — was given mounted footballs commemorating two of his league records: most rushing yards and touchdowns. Reed's equally prodigious contributions to charity were also recognized.

Then the game resumed and, as if to script, he scored three fourth-quarter touchdowns in a 24-9 Saskatchewan win over the B.C. Lions.

"It is doubtful that any other Roughrider player has ever earned the respect of people in the province or the country that Reed has," wrote Bob Calder and Garry Andrews in *Rider Pride*. Upon retiring a few years later, they noted, Reed paid his own tribute at a retirement gathering to the country and province he's made his home: "I came, I played, I stayed."

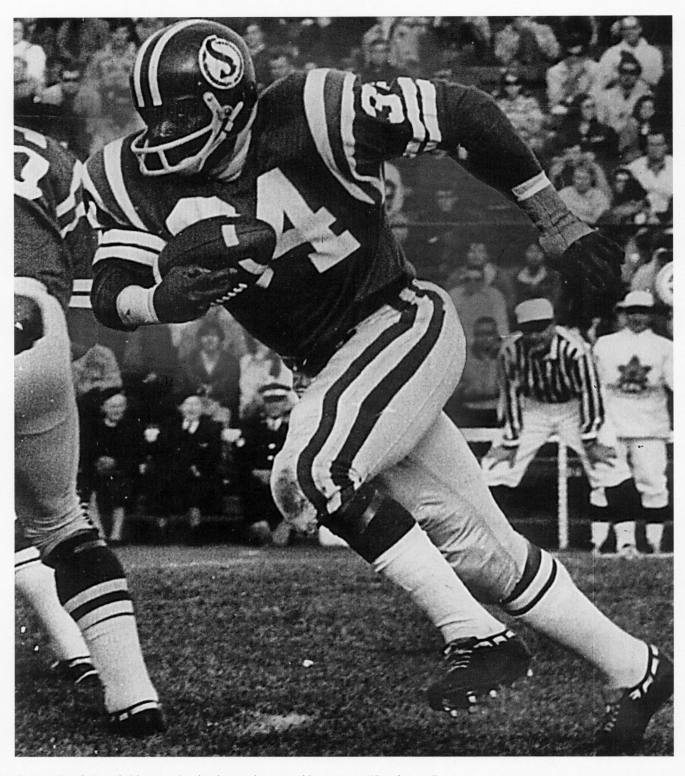

George Reed, Roughrider running back, was honoured in 1973 on "October 34"

[cooler
Low-high 50, 75
Details on Page 2]

the Star Phoenix

[Final EDITION]

35TH YEAR—No. 254   SASKATOON, SASK., WEDNESDAY, AUGUST 16, 1967   10 CENTS   ◆FORTY-EIGHT PAGES

Nine in farm family slain

Farm-to-farm check on weapons pressed in search around Shell Lake

By DERIK HODGSON
Staff Reporter

SHELL LAKE — A house-to-house, bush-to-bush search for clues continues today with, so far, no result as police attempt to find any information which may lead to the person or persons who killed nine members of the Peterson family here sometime Tuesday morning.

Inspector B. D. Sawyer, of the North Battleford detachment, RCMP, described the search as 'expanding.'

Fourteen shots from a .22-calibre weapon snuffed out the lives of nine of 10 members of the family.

The mystery killer gunned down James Peterson, 47 years, his wife Evelyn, 42, and seven of the eight children who were at home. The children were aged one to 17 years.

Some of the bodies of the slain family were found in the front porch, others in their bed. The mother and baby had been shot down in the back yard . . .

apparently fleeing the killer or killers. Their bodies were found under an open window.

Mr. Peterson was found clad only in his undershorts, lying near the front door of the house on his farm four miles west of the town of Shell Lake.

The dead children are: Larry, 1½ years; Colin, 3; William, 6; Pearl, 9; Dorothy, 11; Mary, 13; Jean, 17.

All the children except Larry were in two double beds in one room.

Four-year-old Phyllis—the only survivor of the massacre — is being kept away from the prying eyes of the public.

An eye-witness account from a police officer on the scene said Phyllis told of 'loud bangs' and that she then "snuggled down next to her sister, Jean."

One of the girls was found shot to death with both hands under her head, apparently without ever hearing a thing.

Mrs. Peterson's sister, Eva, married to Shell Lake district farmer, Helmer Helgeton, is caring for Phyllis.

Insp. Sawyer said the tiny survivor had 'helped in some way . . . but she is understandably confused . . . she is so young.'

"There is no indication at this time as to who might have done the shooting," the inspector said.

A total of 30 officers, armed with sidearms and rifles and using two dogs and a mine detector, are taking part in the search which, Insp. Sawyer said, "is not a manhunt yet."

"The shocking thing about this is that we haven't been able to determine a motive," he said.

The inspector said this was the most gruesome killing he has seen in his police career.

As the search widened, all roadblocks have been lifted.

"We are using the house as a focal point," Insp. Sawyer said, "and working out from there."

Inspector Sawyer said the roadblocks were lifted so all manpower available could be used in the search for clues.

He said a farm-to-farm search was now being conducted, checking any weapons on the properties.

The only confirmed clue turned up so far are five spent cartridge casings. An unconfirmed report told of a .22-calibre weapon being found by youngsters but this has so far been denied by police.

A neighbor, W. J. Lange, discovered the lonely farm house killings when he called on Mr. Peterson to begin haying operations at about 9 a.m. Tuesday.

Mr. Lange opened the door to the Peterson home to kid Mr. Peterson that he had slept in when he saw Mr. Peterson's body by the kitchen door. The house was not ransacked.

Mr. Lange found the keys in the Peterson family's 1957 station wagon and drove the car to the nearest telephone at Shell Lake, four miles away.

Coroner Dr. Calvin S. Lambert of Leoville estimated the time of death at "possibly 2:00 a.m." A coroner's jury, called to the scene to view the bodies, estimated 14 shots had been fired.

Dr. Lambert said Mr. Peterson may have struggled with the killer or killers. He had been shot in the abdomen.

The coroner speculated that Mrs. Peterson and son Larry, might have come to see what was happening, tried to escape through the window and were shot just outside the four-room house. They also were shot in the head.

(More stories, pictures on Pages 2, 3)

Ed Simonar, who operates a garage at Shell Lake, said powder burns indicated the victims were shot at close range.

RCMP said there was no apparent motive for the slayings, and the coroner said that, because no weapon was found, "I don't think there was a suicide."

Another daughter, Mrs. Kathy Hill, 20, has returned here from her home in British Columbia.

At the scene Tuesday night, RCMP officers were on their hands and knees going through long grass of the farm yard looking for anything.

More officers were inside the tiny, white, five-room homestead. Chickens pecked in the front yard and pigs rooted in a pen behind the house.

The family dog, a black mongrel with white markings covered under the back porch while police searched for clues as to who killed his masters. The dog never wagged his tail.

A neighbor had taken the rest of the stock—otherwise the tiny home looked like it always has on a hot summer afternoon. A boy's bicycle was in the dirt yard, a wash rag was hanging on the clothes line, and an old washing machine held blooming pink flowers.

Through the garden, under the clothesline and through the pines another officer with a tracking dog searched.

★ NINE SLAIN
Continued on Page 2, column 4

—CP Wirephoto

Shooting victims

Nine members of the James Peterson family of Shell Lake were found shot to death in their home Tuesday. This is the most recent picture of the entire family taken this spring at the christening of the youngest member of the family. Left to right are Mary, 13; Dorothy, 11; Jean, 17; Pearl, 9; Phyllis, 4; a married daughter, Mrs. Lee (Kathleen) Hill of Chetwynd, B.C.; Colin, 2; Mrs. Evelyn Peterson, 42; William, 6; Mr. Peterson's mother, Mrs. Martha Peterson, and Mr. Peterson who is shown holding son Larry, one and a half. Phyllis was the only member of the family in the house at the time of the shootings who survived. Mrs. Hill was at her British Columbia home and Mrs. Peterson Sr. was in hospital.

THE PETERSON FARM HOME NEAR SHELL LAKE   —Star-Phoenix Photo by Jack Statham

—CP Wirephoto

Two survivors

The two survivors of the 11-member Peterson family which was gunned down during the early morning hours of Tuesday at the family home just west of Shell Lake. The little girl is Phyllis, a four-year-old who was lying in bed between two sisters when the murder took place. With her is sister Kathy Hill, 20, who was recently married and is living in British Columbia. She flew home today after receiving word of the tragedy. Both are staying with an aunt, Mrs. Eva Helgeton, who also farms in the area.

'Something terrible happened'

WINNIPEG (CP) — The four-year-old survivor of a mass killing at Shell Lake, told her uncle she saw a strange man in the house the night nine members of her family were slain.

The uncle, Helmer Helgeton, now is caring for the child in his home, 3½ miles from the house where his sister and brother-in-law and seven of their children were killed.

Mr. Helgeton said in a telephone interview with the Free Press that Phyllis Peterson "knows something terrible happened" but that she hasn't been told the fate of her family.

Mr. Helgeton said Phyllis told him there was a strange man in the home, but she couldn't tell what time.

"She said the man looked in the dresser drawer," Mr. Helgeton said. "When I asked her what she was doing at the time, she said she was sleeping. She definitely knew something was going on and she heard the shots all right, but she didn't know exactly what."

He said he believes Phyllis must have hidden under the covers where she was found unharmed beside her dead brothers and sisters.

"When I first got to the house, I asked where her daddy was and she said 'on the floor', but she didn't say why," Mr. Helgeton said.

"She told me she saw her mother run out to the car with the baby in her arms."

Both the mother and the one-year-old child were found dead outside the home.

Skrien fired

VANCOUVER (CP) — Head coach Dave Skrien today was fired by B.C. Lions of the Canadian Football League. Jim Champion of St. Louis, a former assistant coach with the Lions, will replace him.

MAP PINPOINTS LOCATION OF SLAYING

STAR GAZING

Almanac	12
Classified	41 to 45
Comics	36
Editorial	29
Local	3, 12
Markets	46
Movies	39
Sports	30, 31, 32, 33, 34
TV-Radio	39
Women's	18, 19, 20, 21, 22

When Saskatoon made its bid to host the 1971 Winter Games, the city was forced to deal with quite an obvious issue: with an abundance of rolling plains and open sky, one thing Saskatoon was short on was varied altitude. Winter Games meant winter sports, including alpine skiing; if the city's bid were to succeed, its residents would have to move mountains — or at least build one. The bid was won and the seeds of Saskatoon's man-made mountain were planted. Originally scheduled for construction near Devil's Dip, an unexpectedly weak shoreline prompted organizers to make a last-minute move to the shores of Blackstrap Lake. The great pile of earth, known as Mount Blackstrap, was still settling when it opened in December of 1970, but the *Star-Phoenix* reported that "there is no cause for any fear that the mountain one day will give an agonizing sigh and deflate into the valley over which it stands." The elevation of the ski hill, the story read, was 2,045 feet above sea level, but would reach 2,080 feet following the completion of a ski jump structure.

Mount Blackstrap, built for the 1971 Canada Winter Games, near Saskatoon, 1973

Saskatchewan native Frances Hyland as Doll Tearsheet, scene from the Stratford Festival production of Henry IV, Stratford, Ontario, 1965

Celebration of Saskatchewan's 60th anniversary as a province, Regina, 1965

showers
Low-high 50-80
Details on Page 2

the Star-Phoenix

Final EDITION

65TH YEAR—No. 234 | SASKATOON, SASK., SATURDAY, JULY 22, 1967 | 10 CENTS | SEVENTY-SIX PAGES

A dream comes true—South Sask. dam opens

By FOSTER BARNSLEY
Staff Reporter

CUTBANK—Saskatchewan's mighty Gardiner Dam was dedicated Friday afternoon by four politicians but not before the weather got in a taunting lick.

Federal Agriculture Minister J. J. Greene had just introduced the platform guests and had asked the estimated 12,000 people to give them an old-fashioned Saskatchewan welcome.

Before anyone could lift a hand in applause, an ear-ringing clap of thunder split the air.

Amid laughter from the crowd and dignitaries alike, Mr. Greene said he and Prime Minister Pearson had ordered the thunder for the end of the ceremonies.

Later, he said: "Never before in history has there been such a variety of politicians on one stage and never again will there be."

Mr. Pearson, Opposition Leader Diefenbaker, Premier Thatcher and national NDP leader Douglas all took part in unveiling four plaques to dedicate the three-mile-long dam, realization of a dream.

The plaques were to honor the dam, Diefenbaker Lake, the Saskatchewan Rivers Development Association and the Prairie Farm Rehabilitation Administration.

Mr. Pearson said the dam is an illustration of the need for vision in natural development.

"This achievement magnificently underlines the importance of the individual with a dream.

"Although the idea of damming the South Saskatchewan River was first mentioned 100 years ago, without the vision of two men whose names we are formally enshrining in our history today, this accomplishment would still be no more than hope and aspiration," he said.

"I pay tribute to the vision of the late Jimmy Gardiner, who fought for so many years to have this project started, and to the vision of John Diefenbaker who took the bold decision as leader of the government (in 1958) to begin construction."

NDP Leader T. C. Douglas wasn't left out. Premier Ross Thatcher said a park, near the dam, would be named after him. Mr. Douglas, Saskatchewan's premier for 18 years before moving into federal politics and was premier when the agreement between the federal and provincial governments were signed.

The late Mr. Gardiner, after whom the dam was named, had been a strong promoter of the dam. He was a premier of Saskatchewan 30 years ago and federal agriculture minister for 22 years until 1957.

Mr. Diefenbaker, now Progressive Conservative opposition leader, was prime minister in 1958 when the agreement between the federal and Saskatchewan government for construction of the dam was signed.

Mr. Pearson said the project will have many economic benefits.

"But among the most exciting is the creation of Diefenbaker Lake, 140 miles long and with nearly 500 miles of shoreline.

"This will provide a vast new recreational resource within easy reach of half the population of the province. It will do much for the life of this province.

★ GARDINER DAM
Continued on Page 2, column 2

—CP Wirephoto

ARC DE TRIOMPHE REPLICA ERECTED FOR DE GAULLE

UN session ends; Reds, Arabs split

UNITED NATIONS (Reuters) Soviet - Arab differences and bitter recriminatory speeches marked the end of the United Nations General Assembly's attempts to solve the Middle East crisis Friday night as it threw the problem back to the Security Council.

The assembly voted 63 to 26, with 27 abstentions, to adjourn its five - week Soviet - inspired emergency session on the Middle East so the council might resume "as a matter of urgency" its consideration of the crisis. Canada voted for the resolution.

The resolution included a clause leaving the way open for recall of the assembly, but no further debate on the Middle East is expected before its next regular session scheduled for Sept. 19.

Informed sources said the council is expected to meet next week, although the possibility of a longer delay to permit the delegates to take a hard look at the situation was not excluded.

All 13 Arab states voted against the resolution to adjourn, which had been approved in private by the Soviet Union and the U.S.

The Arab states described the proposal as an attempt to mask the assembly's failure to come to grips with the basic issues.

Soviet Foreign Minister Andrei A. Gromyko sat passively through a host of pre-vote speeches critical either directly or by inference of Soviet policy.

Iraqi delegate Adnana Pachachi led the list of critics, which also included Algerian Foreign Minister Abdelaziz Bouteflika, one of the most militant of the Arab spokesmen.

But the real bitterness came out after the vote on the proposal, when Pachachi, pounding the rostrum angrily, denounced the Latin American countries for blocking assembly action on proposals for the immediate unconditional withdrawal of Israeli troops from Arab territory.

Gromyko also criticized the Latin American nations, who held the balance of power throughout the emergency session.

U.S. Ambassador Arthur J. Goldberg rejected Gromyko's charge about American pressure as "ludicrous." He said the American position throughout the session was dedicated by the principle of live and let live.

The only two major substantive resolutions adopted during the session were aimed at ending Israel's takeover of the former Jordanian - held Old City of Jerusalem. Israel has refused to give up control of the section.

Israeli Foreign Minister Abba Eban praised the assembly for refusing "to violate justice or betray peace" and repeated Israel's offer of direct negotiations with Arab states—an offer which the Arabs rejected.

Fedorenko may be dropped

UNITED NATIONS (Reuters) Nikolai T. Fedorenko, Russia's resident United Nations representative, is expected to return to Moscow shortly on leave. But there was some doubt being voiced as to whether he will be back at the UN.

A number of Western delegates to the UN said Friday night they would be surprised if he returns to his post. They pegged Deputy Foreign Minister A. A. Soldatov as his possible successor.

Meanwhile, Soviet Foreign Minister Andrei Gromyko prepared to leave for home today—empty handed after a series of defeats for Russian resolutions introduced during the General Assembly's emergency session on the Middle East.

Fedorenko's predecessor, Valerian Zorin, was sacrificed after Soviet diplomacy suffered a sharp defeat in the 1962 Cuban missile crisis.

Western diplomats assume Fedorenko's advice contributed at least in part to Rusian mishandling of the Middle East situation and that his continued usefulness in the UN must be questioned.

One of the worst errors, in terms of UN tactics, was to permit a vote to be taken on the resolution personally introduced by Kosygin.

It is normally the resident delegate's duty to "count heads" and make a judgment of the likely response that a given resolution will receive. The Russians grossly over-estimated the support they could obtain for Kosygin's resolution.

Instead of withdrawing it, they allowed it to go to a vote, paragraph by paragraph, and each one was rejected.

Race rioting spreads in U.S.

By THE ASSOCIATED PRESS

Racial violence in New Jersey cities spread to Englewood Friday night. Eight policemen were injured in a brief rock-throwing, window-smashing outbreak by Negro youths. Calm was restored early today.

In Minneapolis national guardsmen kept a tense peace, but firemen were busy putting out two fires touched off by arsonists.

A Black Power conference in Newark shouted support for a statement backing the "right of black people to revolt when they deem it necessary," calling for a United Nations observation team to come to the city, and demanding the replacement of its white mayor with a Negro.

In Englewood, 16 miles north of riot-ravaged Newark, more than 200 city and county policemen were summoned to deal with the disturbance. None of the eight injured officers was seriously hurt.

After bands of Negro youths hurled bottles and bricks and smashed store windows, Negro ministers and a Negro councilman walked the streets urging teen-agers to "cool it." Three hours after trouble erupted, Mayor Austin Volk said the disturbance was under control.

In Plainfield, N.J., also hit by rioting last week, Mayor George F. Hetfield charged that he had sufficient proof that his city's troubles were caused by non-residents and said the proof would be divulged "in due course." National guard troops were removed from the city Friday.

The Congress of Racial Equality announced to delegates at the Black Power conference that it would seek a recall election to replace Mayor Hugh Addonizio "with a black mayor." The city's 400,000 population is more than half Negro.

In Minneapolis, a two-alarm fire at a church and school three blocks from the site of three fires Thursday night led to the movement of national guardsmen.

Faced with a Sunday deadline to meet Negro demands, Cairo, Ill., officials clamped on an 8 p.m. curfew and closed bars and liquor stores. Mayor Lee Stenzel and city officials conferred with federal and state representatives on possible action to satisfy the Negro community.

Negro spokesmen warned the officials to meet demands for new job opportunities, organized recreation programs and an end to alleged police brutality by Sunday afternoon.

Elsewhere, Adam Clayton Powell sent word from Bimini in the Bahamas that he had decided against attending the Newark Black Power conference. His decision left a sheriff standing by to arrest him at a New York airport.

Ottawa-Quebec division on de Gaulle visit widens

QUEBEC (CP)— The Quebec government's office of information and publicity packed its province - boosting literature Friday night and moved its press room for state visits out of the Canadian government's military drill hall here.

The move appeared to be yet another escalation in a wide-open battle between federal and provincial officials over details of the visit by President Charles de Gaulle of France, who arrives in Quebec City Sunday morning.

Official reason given for the information office's move was that the federal quarters were not sufficiently large for the crowd of international journalists swarming into town to report the coming of de Gaulle.

However, informants indicated that the office's midnight move to a big bar in the cosy confines of the Chateau Frontenac hotel was linked to the federal-provincial shenanigans of the past several days.

They said they understand that the information office has no intention of returning to the drill hall despite the dozen state visits to the capital scheduled to follow this French foray.

Premier Daniel Johnson of Quebec acknowledged Friday that protocol people at Ottawa and Quebec City were roughing it up. But this is only normal because it "reflects the political situation" in Canada, Mr. Johnson said.

Among the incidents has been a fight over the first stop in the tour, the sort of vehicle president de Gaulle will ride, and who will sit at what table at the Quebec government's state dinner for de Gaulle Sunday night.

The French president is making waves of his own en route up the St. Lawrence River to Quebec aboard the French cruiser Colbert. The general will be making a five-day state visit to Canada.

His visit arises from Canada's Centennial Year and France Day at Expo 67 in Montreal Tuesday.

Quebec City has taken on a festive air, with flags of France and Quebec decorating the streets, along with red, white and blue bunting.

Almost every single telephone and electricity pole along the 180 miles of Highway 2 to Montreal, which de Gaulle will travel Monday, has been decorated with cardboard cutouts representing flags of France and Quebec. Fleur - de - lys' have been painted on the road.

Veto may block Tshombe's death

ALGIERS (Reuters) — Only Algerian Premier Houari Boumedienne stands between former Congolese premier Moise Tshombe and a death sentence in his homeland across the Sahara.

Boumedienne has the right to veto a Supreme Court ruling Friday in favor of a Congolese request that Tshombe be extradited to Kinshasa where he faces the death sentence for treason.

The Supreme Court verdict was handed down three weeks after the exiled former premier's hijacked charter plane was forced to land in Algeria.

Kinshasa Radio, announcing the court's verdict Friday night, told its listeners "the traitor Tshombe will be here in a few hours."

The radio said the Congolese cabinet will meet today to study the situation "after the favorable reply of Algeria on the extradition of Africa's greatest traitor."

But there was no indication that the Algerian government is in a hurry to send Tshombe to Kinshasa.

The former Congolese premier heard the verdict without emotion.

600 Viet Cong killed in clash

SAIGON (AP) — Nearly 600 Viet Cong and North Vietnamese soldiers were killed Friday in a series of fierce battles with U.S., South Korean and South Vietnamese troops, military sources reported today.

Large - scale ground action developed after an 11-day lull. The U.S. command said an outnumbered U.S. cavalry troop fought off a Viet Cong ambush and killed 90 guerrillas. U.S. losses were reported as 13 dead and 59 wounded.

Premier Nguyen Cao Ky announced that the 620,000-member South Vietnamese armed forces would be increased by 55,000 men and that the Vietnamese military organization would be overhauled from top to bottom.

In the air war, U.S. B-52 bombers conducted two raids Friday night and today against troop-staging areas in the A Shau valley in northwest South Vietnam. The sector has been hit by B-52s at least 25 times since late June.

U.S. Gen. Maxwell D. Taylor, former ambassador to South Vietnam, was expected in Saigon Monday. He is expected to press the Vietnam allies to increase their commitments to the war.

U.S. defence department sources in Washington have said between 80,000 and 100,000 men will probably be added to U.S. forces in South Vietnam within the next year, bringing them to a total of more than 540,000.

In the ground war, U.S. marines clashed twice with Communist units near Quant Tri City in the northern part of South Vietnam. Seven marines were reported killed and 52 wounded.

Federal govt. agrees to share drought aid

Premier Ross Thatcher told a news conference near here Friday that the federal government has agreed "in essence" to pay 50 per cent of government support costs for emergency hay shipments in this drought-stricken province.

Mr. Thatcher said the province is importing hay from Manitoba and Alberta and moving it from northern Saskatchewan to the south in order to maintain cattle herds during the current dry weather.

He said the provincial and federal governments each will pay a maximum of about $4 a ton for hay shipments depending on mileage.

Prime Minister Pearson, who attended the news conference with Mr. Thatcher after the Gardiner Dam dedication ceremony, said the Saskatchewan government had made representation to Ottawa for federal drought aid.

"We are aware of the situation. We accept the responsibility that is ours," Mr. Pearson said.

The prime minister said the long-range answer to prairie droughts must be more comprehensive crop insurance. But until insurance coverage was broadened, emergencies required fast action.

Agricultural officials in Ottawa said Thursday that a crop failure on the prairies this year would effect the entire Canadian economy.

Mr. Thatcher told the press conference that "this is the most critical year agriculturally in this province since the '30s."

The premier said that in order to be prepared for similar emergencies about 10,000 acres of crown land will, over the next few years, be irrigated from the Gardiner Dam reservoir here in west-central Saskatchewan.

The government plans to grow three hay crops a year on the irrigated land and stock pile millions of bales to meet possible future needs.

—CP Wirephoto

Ministerial ride

Kalapik, 11, perches on the shoulders of Northern Development Minister Laing during an outing for Eskimo children in Ottawa Friday. One hundred Eskimo children are visiting the nation's capital, and are sponsored by the Hillcrest Community Council as a centennial project. Mr. Laing praised it as one of the most generous projects Canadians have undertaken.

Police fall guys in bare-bottom pinch

TORONTO (CP) — The policeman who made the pinch in the bare - bottom caper wishes he hadn't.

"The policeman is the fall guy no matter what happens," sighed Constable George Kipling, the officer who laid information against two small children for parading on a Toronto Island beach without clothing.

"We had to do something," he said Friday. "The people who complained would ask what action we took. It's not my job to say what is a bad law.

"And now I'm the villain. I can see why there are so many resignations from the department."

Constable Kipling this week had to turn in a report on the activities of Marc, 1½, and Lisa, 2½, children of Dutch-born Mr. and Mrs. Martin ter Woort.

Mayor William Dennison thought it was all a publicity stunt by the parents. Controller Allan Lamport said the children should go to a nudist camp "for this kind of thing," and Controller Fred Beavis believes people coming to Canada from "places where nudity is perfectly legitimate must be made to understand it isn't permitted on beaches here."

Susan Staveland, an island resident, says it is not safe for children to be running around naked "with the kind of men you get around here today looking at them."

Not that there is that much to see—the policeman who made out the information that is going to take the parents into court for breaking a bylaw admitted he thought the babies were both boys.

The parents, Martin ter Woort, an economist at the University of Toronto, and his pretty wife Johanna, thought it was all a joke.

"It's just plain ridiculous," says the 27-year-old Mrs. ter Woort.

"They say we have to have a community standard and I say blah."

Her children take off their bathing suits because the wet suits make the sand stick between their legs, she said.

The summonses, which the ter Woorts were told are in the mail, charge that the children violated a parks bylaw by "walking in public disorder." The usual fine for parks bylaw offences is $25, but it can be $100 on each offence.

Controller Paul Hunt thinks the bylaw is silly, and Controller Margaret Campbell says it is stupid.

Linda Clark, a summer resident on the island in Toronto Harbor, says it is hard to imagine who could be corrupted by nude children at that age, but Nanci Lye, supervisor of a day camp, says "this sort of thing is just not done."

Marc and Lisa, meanwhile, are back on the beach, their bare bottoms tanning under the summer sun.

STAR GAZING

NATIVE LIFE

Near the end of the 1960s, disagreements between the federal government and the country's native peoples were heating up — from land claim disputes to issues of self-government. In 1969, the federal government published what it called the *White Paper*, rejecting special First Nations' rights in favour of a more assimilationist approach to native issues. Angry Aboriginal leaders quickly presented their own counter argument, titled *Citizen Plus*, which, along with criticism from the Canadian public, eventually caused the government to withdraw its controversial publication.

On March 26, 1970, the *Saskatoon Star-Phoenix* reported that the provincial government intended to make the hiring of a percentage of First Nations workers mandatory for contractors working on government jobs. In 1972, the newspaper reported that the Saskatoon police force was working hard to recruit Aboriginal men into service. "We have sent out letters to the chiefs of the thirteen Indian reservations in Saskatchewan asking them to recommend any young men they feel are suitable for the job," said Lieutenant T.H. Guest, personnel director of the Saskatoon police department. If thirteen positions were open and thirteen qualified Aboriginals applied, the *Star-Phoenix* quoted him as saying, all would be hired.

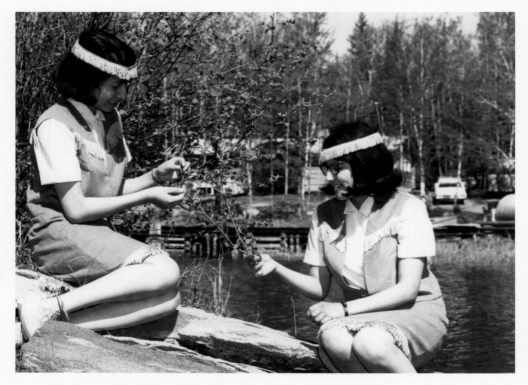

Rosalie Sewap and Bernadette
Merasty, waitresses at Pelican
Narrows fishing camp, June 1969

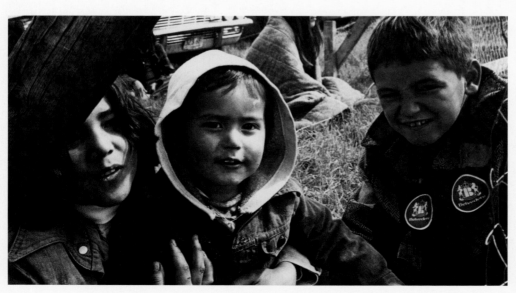

Métis children at Batoche,
circa 1965

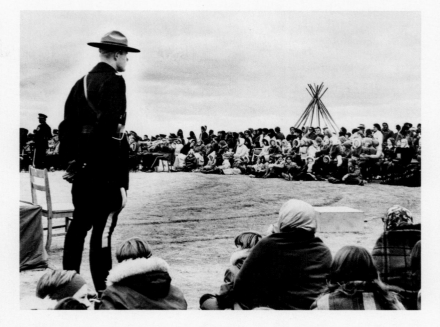

Unveiling ceremony honouring Chief Poundmaker as an eminent Canadian, Poundmaker Reserve, October 17, 1972

Gordon Tootoosis of the Poundmaker Reserve and three-year-old Alanna Glynis, powwow at Saskatoon, December 20, 1971

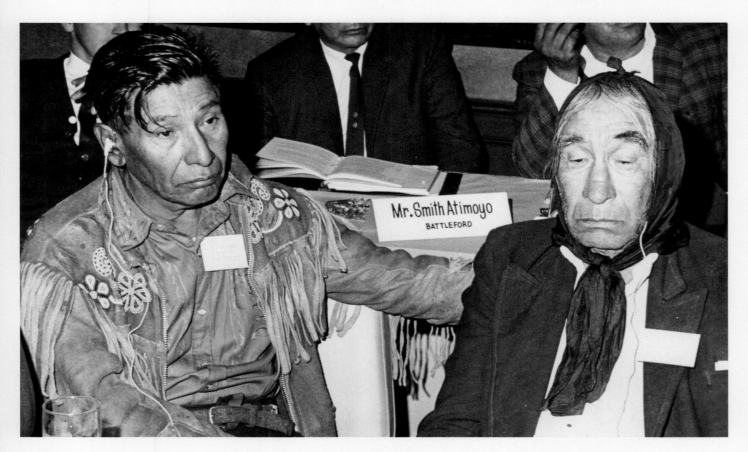

George Whitefish and Harry Harris, of Pelican Narrows, Indian Act hearings, Regina, September 1968

CHURCHES

The continued growth of the country's immigrant populations into the 1960s excited a religious revival throughout the Prairies and inspired the architecture of some of Saskatchewan's most cherished churches. The Silton Chapel, at Qu'Appelle Lakes, was designed by Clifford Weins, one of Canada's better-known architects, in 1967. Nestled in a ravine, the open-air Christian chapel featured a cross-style, timber-supported ceiling and a baptismal font that filled with rainwater from the roof. Ukrainian places of worship had also begun to appear across the plains by the end of the war, featuring onion-domed chapels and bell-towers — religious monuments to the growing diversity of Canada's cultural landscape. These photos are from collections of works by Joanne M. Abrahamson, Keith Ewart and Hans Dommasch held by the University of Saskatchewan Archives.

Near Robinhood

TOP LEFT: Near Pense
TOP RIGHT: Near West Bend
CENTRE: Near Gravelbourg
BOTTOM: Near Krydor

1975

THE COLIN THATCHER STORY

The murder of JoAnn Wilson, the
ex-wife of Progressive Conservative
MLA and former cabinet minister
Colin Thatcher, touched off what
many have described as the most
spectacular police investigation
and trial in the province's history.

to end,
province and
press
contains all the
murder novel
money,
divided
courtroom drama
in the

Chapter Ten

In the late summer of 1979, the people of Saskatchewan gathered in golden fields and at dusty rail crossings, on overpasses and at small town stations, to watch the train that carried John Diefenbaker home for the last time. In Prince Albert, where he had built his career as a lawyer and politician, thousands thronged the tracks as the funeral car arrived on August 21 under sunny skies and a billowing, half-staff maple leaf. It was the flag Dief had so vehemently, so characteristically rejected in favour of the old red ensign that would, in posthumous protest, drape his coffin the following day in Saskatoon.

So much of the history of the province and the country was recaptured in that poignant westward trek. It was the path Diefenbaker's family — like so many families — had taken from Ontario to Saskatchewan in the first decade of the 1900s, when the boy was barely ten and the province barely born. The same stretches of steel would later carry him to local fame as the pioneering prairie lawyer from Wakaw (via Borden and Saskatoon) who pumped his way by hand car from client to client. The rails would carry him again, during the 1950s, from whistle-stop to whistle-stop as the Conservative dynamo who swept the country in a series of historic election campaigns.

The railroad — a mythic presence in so much Saskatchewan history — is there, as well, in the tale about Diefenbaker's awakening to politics:

Weyburn Co-op seed clean-
ing plant, March 11, 1982

"John's first claim to fame was his now legendary encounter with the Canadian prime minister, Sir Wilfrid Laurier, in 1910," Verne Clemence has written in *Saskatchewan's Own: People Who Made a Difference.*

"Diefenbaker was a paperboy for the Saskatoon daily and he approached Laurier to sell him a paper after the prime minister stepped off the train."

So it was a moment rich with layers of memory and meaning when another train, a lifetime later, reached Saskatoon with the remains of Saskatchewan's most accomplished citizen.

The burial took place on the campus of the University of Saskatchewan, where Diefenbaker had earned his B.A. and a law degree by 1919. The gravesite, a leafy retreat along the banks of the South Saskatchewan River, was just downstream from the long, winding lake named for the province's first prime minister and — who would deny it? — the country's most colourful personality of the 20th century.

"John Diefenbaker did not tiptoe through the public life of Canada, he strode through, and as he offered passion to his fellow Canadians, he drew passion in return," observed eulogist Joe Clark, prime minister at the time and heir to the leadership of Diefenbaker's beloved Progressive Conservative party. "John Diefenbaker attracted every reaction from the people of this country except indifference."

Clark, knowing full well that the range of responses to Diefenbaker's politics included fierce antagonism even within his home province, simply urged Canadians "to celebrate the frontier strength and spirit of an indomitable man, born to a minority group, raised in a minority region, leader of a minority party, who went on to change the very nature of this country — and to change it permanently."

"One Canada" — Diefenbaker's passionate plea for tolerant but un-hyphenated nationalism — and a Bill of Rights that presaged the Charter of Rights and Freedoms were among his chief legacies. So, too, as the crowds of '79 made clear, was a confirmed belief within his province and country that anyone from anywhere — with enough pride of place, gritty determination and willingness to serve — could achieve success and even greatness. "Arguably," concluded Clemence, "he became Saskatchewan's most celebrated son as he stubbornly rose from humble beginnings to the pinnacle of political power in Canada."

Yet the province Diefenbaker's train traveled through that summer was in the midst of serious social and political change. Even the rails that took him west — and which played such a central role in Saskatchewan's history and development — faced an uncertain future. One expression of the changes underway in the province was the creation in April 1982 — one day before Canada's newly

Trent Catley, 7, from Craven, at 4-H competition, June 29, 1977

repatriated constitution was officially signed into existence — of the country's first native legislative assembly.

The Federation of Saskatchewan Indian Nations had evolved over the decades from an ad hoc assembly of chiefs into the most powerful aboriginal organization in Western Canada. And its final metamorphosis into "a true federation of nations" would serve as a model for aboriginal governance and a sign that the country's First Nations were organizing like never before to secure their place — and assert their influence — in Canadian society.

With an avowed aim of "breathing life into the solemn treaty promises" given to their 19th-century forebears, the leaders of the FSIN not only lobbied federal and provincial governments on behalf of Saskatchewan's native people, they also pioneered key cultural and educational institutions throughout the 1970s and Eighties, including the Regina-based First Nations University of Canada.

The gradual trend toward urbanization in the decades following the Second World War had quickened by the end of the 1970s. Defined for so long by its agricultural identity and settlement patterns — and more recently by its quest for a diversified industrial economy — Saskatchewan was now struggling to slow rural depopulation, to prevent the abandonment of grain elevators that had been landmarks for generations and to stop the planned closure of key branches of the railway lifeline.

"Demographically, prairie people became less distinguishable from the rest of Canada with each passing year as the cities grew and the countryside emptied out," John Herd Thompson writes in *Forging the Prairie West*. "Despite generally good grain prices during the 1970s, operating costs increased faster; 2,500 farms a year disappeared, and those that remained became larger and more mechanized.... The rural associational life that had been the cultural base of the agrarian movement decayed as depopulation and distance made it unsustainable. As huge 'inland terminals' replaced local grain elevators, and semi-trailers hauled the crops instead of branch-line railways, rural service centres died."

The threatened scrapping of the Crow Rate — the federal railway subsidy that for generations had helped defray the cost of shipping grain out of Saskatchewan — loomed like a dark cloud throughout the era. Farmers and towns across the Prairies saw their futures as inextricably connected to the "sacred" freight deal, and many predicted doom for grain growers if transportation costs were left to the vagaries of the market and the whims of ruthless rail conglomerates.

Otto Lang, Saskatchewan's key figure in the federal Liberal government of Pierre Trudeau, had already faced outrage from Wheat Pool farmers over proposed changes to international grain marketing. During that uproar, Thompson notes, many farmers had placed periods between the letters on their POOL baseball caps to make it an abbreviation of "Piss On Otto Lang." Lang, now assigned to spearhead possible railway closings and changes to the Crow Rate, appointed the distinguished Saskatchewan judge Emmett Hall to examine the issue in a federal commission.

"The Hall commission became to the people of the rural West what the Berger commission, occurring simultaneously, was to the native people of the

75th anniversary
celebrations, Regina, 1980

North — an opportunity in the face of change to make their case to someone they trusted," Dennis Gruending wrote in his 1985 biography *Emmett Hall: Establishment Radical*. "In Wishart, Saskatchewan, a hamlet southeast of Regina, a crowd of 200 packed the hall. Every local person presenting a brief, from an eleven-year-old school child to senior citizens, called for retention of the community's rail line. An old woman said, 'The CPR brought me here and now they are going to abandon me.'"

Though Hall's report called for the maintenance of the Crow Rate, the shutdown of some branch lines — and, in effect, communities — was deemed inevitable. But were closed rail lines and abandoned elevators dire wounds for a way of life or mere growing pains for a maturing province, one ready to experience an economic metamorphosis? Such were the terms of a debate that began to shape Saskatchewan politics as the 1970s gave way to the Eighties.

The provincial NDP government under premier Allan Blakeney had, by the late-Seventies, distinguished itself as a fierce defender of Saskatchewan's interests in the face of unpopular federal policies — wildly unpopular in the West — over the control of natural resources. The province's renewed push into the oil and potash industries was resisted by the Trudeau government and "federal-provincial relations sank to a new low," recalled John Archer in *Saskatchewan: A History*. In 1977, Blakeney slammed the "aggressive attempt of the federal government to limit and abridge the clear constitutional rights of the provinces in dealing with resources."

But the NDP's championing of uranium development in northern Saskatchewan generated considerable opposition even among many of the party's traditional supporters. "It has been argued that the popular support for the Blakeney government began to fade after they won the October 1978 election," writes University of Regina political economist John Warnock in *Saskatchewan: The Roots of Discontent and Protest*. "But the dissatisfaction began in 1976 with the growing public division over uranium mining ... There was strong opposition to this policy from many within the NDP, the peace movement, environmentalists, major elements of the Christian churches and even the Saskatchewan Federation of Labour."

The alienation of several key NDP constituencies coincided with a rise in the fortunes of the long-moribund provincial Conservative party. The resurgence had come about thanks to the selection of an impressive new leader, Grant Devine, and a swelling of Tory ranks caused by the collapse of the provincial Liberals — seen by many voters to be too closely aligned with a federal Trudeau regime widely condemned as anti-West.

An election was set for April 1982. It would come just a week after the official adoption of the Charter of Rights and Freedoms and the repatriation of the Constitution — a watershed moment in modern Canadian history that Blakeney and his attorney general, Roy Romanow, were instrumental in achieving. It was Romanow, along with his Ontario counterpart, Roy McMurtry, and then-federal justice minister Jean Chrétien, who had struck the famous "kitchen accord" that broke a logjam in negotiations and made repatriation possible.

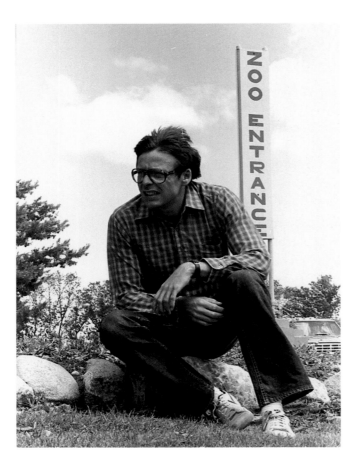

Guy Vanderhaege, author,
Saskatoon, 1983

But even the Blakeney government's notable foray into constitutional matters backfired back home, where it reinforced a growing sense that the party had lost touch with its grassroots and was more open to playing political games with Ottawa. On the eve of his election call, the NDP premier had also approved a back-to-work order that forced 5,000 non-medical hospital workers to end a strike — a move that angered unions across the province and weakened labour support for Blakeney on the campaign trail and at the ballot box.

Devine promised tax cuts, a cap on mortgage rates and less government involvement in the economy. The result, unimaginable just weeks earlier, was a massive Conservative majority.

"Premier-elect Grant Devine is set to take the reins of Saskatchewan's first Progressive Conservative government in forty-eight years following the greatest election upset in the province's history," the *Saskatoon Star-Phoenix* reported the day after a vote that gave the Tories fifty-seven of sixty-four seats. "As the polls showed the eleven-year-old NDP government of Allan Blakeney collapse around him in every direction, Devine admitted he hadn't counted on such a landslide. 'This is fantastic,' he told a crowd of about 300 frenzied supporters at the Derrick Hotel … Throughout the campaign, he has compared the wealth of Alberta to what he saw as economic standstill in Saskatchewan, promising an administration that would fight Ottawa over resources and see that benefits are passed on to Saskatchewan residents. He said his promises brought hope to the 'competitive edge' in people which has been lying dormant under the reign of the NDP."

Blakeney, in conceding defeat, acknowledged to the *Regina Leader-Post*: "It is very clear from the results that we were not responding to the aspirations and expectations of the people of Saskatchewan."

Blakeney's fall from power, as it happens, coincided with the 1982 publication of *Man Descending* — Saskatchewan writer Guy Vanderhaeghe's award-winning collection of short stories about male identity in the modern age. When it was announced he'd been named winner of the Governor General's Award for fiction — a surprise pick in a field of competitors that included Alice Munro and other writers Vanderhaeghe had idolized — the humbled and giddy Esterhazy native told the *Saskatoon Star-Phoenix*: "I feel like a rookie coming into the league and playing with Gordie Howe.… It was something I hoped might happen twenty years from now. This is almost for me like one of those Thirties musicals."

No man in Saskatchewan descended farther or faster in the 1980s than Colin Thatcher. Among the few well-known figures in Devine's fledgling administration, Thatcher was the son of the late Liberal premier from the

First class of women RCMP officers, 1975

1960s. A charismatic crusader for free enterprise, the younger Thatcher was given the energy portfolio and pursued the privatization of Saskoil — his mandate was to "whip it into shape and sell it," he once explained. But he was soon making headlines for other reasons.

His ex-wife, JoAnn Wilson, was bludgeoned to death in 1983 and Thatcher became a suspect in the killing. In May 1984, police recorded a damning conversation between Thatcher and an accomplice who had helped the politician hire a hit man and dispose of a bloody car. A few days later, on May 7, 1984, the powerful cabinet minister was reduced to a criminal quarry in downtown Moose Jaw, where he was the centre of a dramatic police takedown.

"As he neared the major intersection, he saw a Royal Canadian Mounted Police cruiser, lights flashing, waving him down," author Maggie Siggins noted in her recounting of the arrest through the eyes of Inspector Ed Swayze.

"Thatcher glanced around in a manner that seemed to Swayze like 'an animal trapped in a cage,'" Siggins wrote in *A Canadian Tragedy: JoAnn and Colin Thatcher, A Story of Love and Hate.* "Out of nowhere police cars had materialized to block the three other streets at the intersection. Other police in the vicinity had cordoned off the area to keep motorists away. There were even some Moose Jaw cops who had nothing whatsoever to do with the operation; they had come to watch history being made ... Swayze noticed that Thatcher's tongue had turned white and he kept swallowing as though the saliva had dried in his mouth. 'He's in a state of shock,' thought the policeman."

The shock was felt province-wide. And the court drama that followed, described frequently as the most sensational trial in Canadian history since Louis Riel was convicted of treason in 1885, captivated the country. Thatcher was found guilty, and on November 6, 1984, the forty-six year-old rancher-politician stood clutching a Bible in a Saskatoon courtroom as he was sentenced to life in prison for first-degree murder.

DIEFENBAKER GRAVESITE

Construction for the Right Honourable John G. Diefenbaker Centre began six years after Diefenbaker pledged his memorabilia, personal papers and library to the University of Saskatchewan in 1969, when he was elected chancellor of the school. A decade later, on July 9, 1979, the *Saskatoon Star-Phoenix* reported that Diefenbaker had also asked to be buried on the grounds of the centre, along with his late wife Olive. Diefenbaker died a mere month after his request, at the age of eighty-three, and was buried on August 23 on a grassy area of the university grounds, overlooking the South Saskatchewan River. Honorary pallbearers, family, fellow politicians, members of the military and friends attended the massive funeral as native drummers and members from five reserves performed a mourning song for the man they credited with giving Aboriginal Peoples the right to vote.

John Diefenbaker leaves Prince Albert for the last time, August 21, 1979

John George Diefenbaker 1895-1979

JOHN GEORGE DIEFENBAKER: P.C., Q.C., M.A., L.L.B., D.C.L., F.R.S.C., D.S.L., L.L.D., D.H., Litt. D., MP and PM (June 21, 1957 - April 21, 1963).

"I am one of those who believe that this party has a sacred trust, a trust in accordance with the traditions of MacDonald. It has an appointment today with destiny, to plan and to build for a greater Canada . . . one Canada, with equality of opportunity for every citizen and equality for every province from the Atlantic to the Pacific."

John Diefenbaker to the January, 1956, Conservative convention which chose him as party leader.

Within six months of speaking these words, John Diefenbaker, having inherited a party which had not been in power for 22 years, kept his appointment with destiny.

On June 10, 1957, in the greatest-upsurge of Conservative strength since R.B. Bennett led 137 PCs to victory in 1930, Diefenbaker's Conservatives made electoral gains in every province to swell their members to 110 – more than double the 50 seats held prior to the election.

Personifying a vision of an expanding, dynamic Canada, he had led the party to an astonishing, but minority, victory.

Perhaps angry and disillusioned with the government of Louis St. Laurent for having rammed through Parliament the trans-Canada pipeline legislation in the summer of 1956, and attracted to what one commentator described as Diefenbaker's "contradictory miracles of sky-

'I thought how wonderful it would have been if my father had lived to see his dreams come true.'

high spending with lower taxes," the voters had surprised political observers by electing the kinky-haired rhetorician from Prince Albert.

Perhaps no one was more surprised than Blair Fraser, then Ottawa editor of MacLean's. For he knew the June 22 dated issue – to be on the streets the morning after election day – contained his editorial, written well before the election, beginning: "For better or for worse, we Canadians have once more elected one of the most powerful governments ever created by the free will of a free electorate . . ."

Fraser also predicted, in the Dec. 1, 1953, MacLean's that Diefenbaker lacked the stamina to become party leader.

On election night, Diefenbaker, then 62, sat at home in Prince Albert, clutching a biography of Abraham Lincoln, as the stunning results began coming in.

Later that night, after a brief television address to the nation from Regina, ("My fellow Canadians, this is a moment of deep dedication rather than elation for me . . .") he flew to Saskatoon to visit his mother in hospital.

"My abiding memory of my mother is on election night in 1957," he said. On that night she advised him, as prime minister, not to forget "the poor and afflicted" and "to do the best you can as long as you can."

Paying their own fare on a commercial flight, John and his wife Olive arrived in Ottawa June 14. One week later he and his cabinet were sworn in.

Thus began his prime ministership, the culmination, as he said in his memoirs, of "a long, long trail to the mountainpeaks" from his arrival with his parents and brother, Elmer at Fort Carlton, 54 years earlier. And he regretted his father had not lived to see his dreams come true.

"I thought how wonderful it would have been if my father had lived to see his dreams come true. It had been a long, long journey from our arrival at Fort Carlton fifty-four years earlier," he reflected in his memoirs.

Two days after the first session with his new cabinet, the Diefenbakers spent 10 happy, heady days in London. The occasion was the Commonwealth Prime Minister's Conference.

Passionately advocating increased Commonwealth trade at a time when the United Kingdom was toying with the idea of entering a European free-trade pact, Diefenbaker was hailed as the "new strong man of the Commonwealth."

After his pro-Commonwealth declarations, one BBC interviewer asked: "Where did you find him? He can have the Crown jewels after this."

Diefenbaker had an audience with the Queen, lunched with Nehru, and – with Olive – attended a formal state dinner with Winston Churchill and Harold MacMillan.

Mrs. Diefenbaker commented on the apparent widespread interest in the Canadian election. Churchill said: "Interest? Why shouldn't there be? It's the most important event since the end of the war."

Back in Ottawa, Diefenbaker moved quickly on a series of his election promises: tax cuts, pension increases, a new scheme of agricultural price supports, cash advances for farm-stored Prairie grain, more money for housing, some tax concessions to provincial governments and special financial aid to the economically-depressed Atlantic region.

The legislative drive of the freshly elected Conservatives through September, October, November and into December fairly bowled over the surviving Liberals.

St. Laurent, who resigned Sept. 5 but agreed to act as Liberal party leader until the leadership convention in January, led dispirited opposition against the enthusiastic PCs who seemed to able to do no wrong.

If these were the brightest hours of Diefenbaker's political career to date, they were to be matched or even surpassed in March, 1958.

On Jan. 20, new Liberal leader Lester Pearson, on the advice of one of his ministers, rose in the Commons and flabergasted the government by proposing power be transferred back to the Liberals.

Seizing advantage of the blunder, Diefenbaker delivered a devastating two-hour harangue against Liberal arrogance, and capped his performance by flourishing a secret Liberal document which had warned the party, when in power, of a decline in the national economy.

Sensing he could sweep the country, Diefenbaker dissolved Parliament 10 days later, and immediately launched his famous 1958 campaign.

With an active run of parliamentary legislation just behind him, Diefenbaker needed only to promise an exciting future.

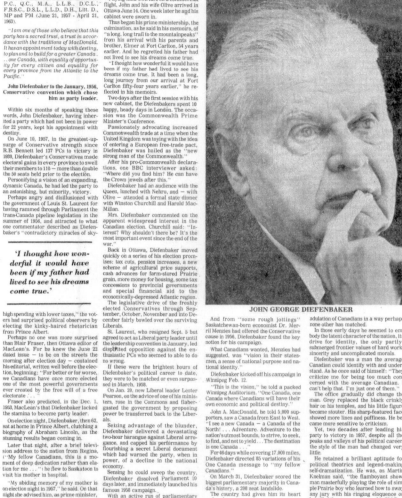

JOHN GEORGE DIEFENBAKER

And from "some rough jottings" Saskatchewan-born economist Dr. Merril Menzies had offered the Conservative cause in 1956, Diefenbaker found the key notion for his campaign.

What Canadians wanted, Menzies had suggested, was "vision in their statesmen, a sense of national purpose and national identity."

Diefenbaker kicked off his campaign in Winnipeg Feb. 12.

"This is the vision," he told a packed Winnipeg Auditorium. "One Canada, one Canada where Canadians will have their own economic and political destiny."

John A. MacDonald, he told 5,000 supporters, saw a Canada from East to West. "I see a new Canada – a Canada of the North! . . . Adventure. Adventure to the nation's utmost bounds, to strive, to seek, to find, and not to yield . . . The destination is one Canada . . ."

For 46 days while covering 17,000 miles, Diefenbaker directed 85 variations of his One Canada message to "my fellow Canadians."

On March 31, Diefenbaker scored the biggest parliamentary majority in Canada's history, a 208 seat landslide.

The country had given him its heart and soul.

In the early part of his prime ministership, John Diefenbaker commanded the adulation of Canadians in a way perhaps none other has matched.

In those early days he seemed to embody the latent character of the nation, its drive for identity, the only partly-submerged frontier values of hard work, sincerity and uncomplicated morals.

Diefenbaker was a man the average Canadian could identify with and understand. As he once said of himself: "They criticize me for being too much concerned with the average Canadian. I can't help that. I'm just one of them."

The office gradually did change the man. Grey replaced the black crinkly hair on his temples, and his little figure became stouter. His sharp-featured face showed more lines and puffiness. He became more sensitive to criticism.

Yet, two decades after leading his party to victory in 1957, despite all the peaks and valleys of his political career, the style of the man had changed very little.

He retained a brilliant aptitude for political theatrics and legend-making self-dramatization. He was, as Martin Knelman said, "the flamboyant showman masterfully playing the role of simple Prairie boy who learned how to sway any jury with his ringing eloquence on behalf of the common man or his Old Testament furies directed at the bastions of special privilege."

PRIME MINISTER DIEFENBAKER WITH MEMBERS OF HIS CABINET IN 1963

Given Diefenbaker's undisputed oratorical capabilities, his commanding presence, his expressive face, theatrical metaphors are inevitable in any substantial discussion of him.

If his oratorical histrionics and unrelenting tirades against those who dared presume against him were the characteristics which earned him the affectionate title of the Chief, his critics saw them as a facade which, conscionably or not, he used to hide unpleasant political realities.

Journalist Bruce Hutchison, a strong critic of his prime ministership, said Diefenbaker "mistook acting for action and gradually came to believe in his own act . . . he made himself an orator before he ever made up his mind on policy and must drown in the flood of his own rhetoric because he had no policy to keep him afloat."

So it was with Diefenbaker: people rallying around or against this remarkably resilient compaigner as he set out to write a new page or footnote to history. During three mercurial decades in Parliament the intense Prairie orator stimulated an all-or-nothing reaction. He was revered and reviled, fought and fawned upon, loved and loathed as he roared through Canadian political history turning defeats into victories and victories into defeats.

For example, even with the enormous majority of 1958, Diefenbaker postponed central decisions and procrastinated overly long on controversies, taking only peripheral actions on issues which pressed him harder and harder as a consequence.

"When a matter was difficult," he stated in his memoirs, "when there was deep uncertainty, I took my time in deciding. Time is often the politician's best friend. The best example of this was John A. Macdonald who was called Old Man Tomorrow."

Diefenbaker said he agreed with Sir Ivor Jennings' view that Parliament's function "is not to govern but to criticize, to modify government policy, and to educate public opinion."

"Parliament's mission is freedom," Diefenbaker wrote, "and the assurance that all the people shall receive justice. It is not a slot machine into which a slug is dropped to produce ready-made legislation."

Elsewhere he stated: "Incredibly, I think our major difficulty after the 1958 election was that we had too large a majority."

Peter Newman, Diefenbaker's strongest critic, suggested the biggest difficulties were, rather, that once in office he tried to respond to every gust of public opinion, became "intoxicated" with the authority of his office, insisted on cabinet unanimity, and that such an approach led inevitably to administrative chaos.

Newman reported one minister saying: "Instead of discussing what we should do next, we spent most of our time arguing: How do we get out of this one?"

But in defeat or facing hard criticism, Diefenbaker could fire up his oratory, muster old loyalty, and fight the good fight.

"When anyone counts me out of the way, I count myself right back in again," he once proclaimed.

Blazing blue eyes, menacing forefinger stabbing the air, Diefenbaker was his combative best when under political attack or sensing what he regarded as an injustice.

No one who saw photographs of Diefenbaker aiming his finger at party president Dalton Camp at the November, 1966, Conservative convention will soon forget the Chief's fierce scowl as he launched his verbal tirade against Camp for his treachery.

Camp was mustering a core of party dissidents into a vote to "reassess" the party leadership. Following a 564-to-502 vote in Camp's favor, the Chief, to hearten his frayed loyalists, many in tears, recalled a British ballad:

"Ffight on my men," sayes Sir Andrew Barton,

"I am hurt, but I am not slaine;
I'le lay mee downe and bleed a-while
And then I'le rise and ffight againe."

On Jan. 18, the old warrior gamely called for a leadership convention himself "at the earliest possible date."

He added, "Let me say at once – this is no swan song. Those who interpret it in that way do not know me."

The convention date was set for Sept. 9.

As the voting began, Mr. and Mrs. Diefenbaker sat bravely facing the convention. The handwriting was on the wall, and virtually everyone could sense it.

The results of the first ballot were: **Robert Stanfield 519; former Manitoba premier Duff Roblin 349; former justice minister E. Davie Fulton 343; former trade minister George Hees 295; John Diefenbaker 271.**

Six other candidates trailed the Chief, but that was little consolation.

There was now absolutely no doubt Diefenbaker was about to lose the leadership. He could have withdrawn from further voting, but that would have been quitting. Through the heat of the afternoon voting he kept his head high as his supporters dwindled to 172 on the second ballot and then to 114 on the third.

As Mrs. Diefenbaker fought back tears, her husband scribbled out his withdrawal notice. It was all over.

The man who 10 years earlier had brought the Conservatives to power was toppled from the party leadership.

This was his darkest hour.

After the convention became bogged down in interpretations over "two nations," and Stanfield had been elected new leader, his predecessor mounted the podium to cheers and tears.

"Now that I am taking my retirement, I say this with the deepest of feeling . . . I have nothing to withdraw in my desire to see Canada one country, one nation . . ."

And, speaking from some experience, he said: "Don't, as the fires of controversy burn around your leader, add gasoline to that fire."

He had confided to an acquaintance that if he lost the leadership, he would no longer want to stay in the House of Commons.

"My course has come to an end."

But of course his parliamentary career had not ended. The man who had so often said "I love Parliament" could not stay away.

He rose to "ffight againe" those who sought to discredit or oppose him. He returned to the front row, although five seats removed from the chair of the leader of the Opposition.

The power of his debating skill didn't diminish. He gradually took on more wrinkles, his hearing became a bit worse and he began to stoop slightly – but he remained a verbal heavyweight, incisive, determined and a voice commanding Commons attention.

'Parliament's mission is freedom and the assurance that all people shall receive justice.'

It was four years after Diefenbaker said his course was at an end that the Speaker of the Commons welcomed him back from a bout of illness by saying he looked "dangerously well."

At 76, he was readying himself for the next general election – the 11th since the Prince Albert lawyer first won a Commons seat at the age of 44.

Exchanging the entire constituency of Canada for only the single riding of Prince Albert, he campaigned through the 1968 election with youthful abandon. He was back among "the average Canadians – the little fellows."

And there were no more personal attacks. Diefenbaker no longer held something others wanted.

He didn't forget easily, however, if at all. And he remained a lone wolf, unafraid to throw a shaft at his own party if its official views differed fromhis.

Despite years of unrelenting attack and the humiliation of having been stripped of leadership, Diefenbaker was able, astonishingly, to carry the aura of a man of unswerving dignity with thunder in his voice and majesty in his brow.

These were the characteristics Bob Bossin, of Stringband, had in mind when, in 1974, he wrote the song Dief Will Be the Chief Again.

Bossin said he was thinking of Diefenbaker not as a politician so much as a symbol of a sense of peace.

"Sure there's folly about the man, but there's also great nobility," he said.

Knowing himself to have achieved goals which were beyond all likelihood of his humble beginnings, Diefenbaker began his memoirs with the questions: "What determines the character of a man? Whence does he get his strength to endure, to abide by his principles, and to reject the concept of the impossible in human affairs?"

And he answered: "It is my conviction that a man is the end product of his ancestors, proximate and remote, that he is endowed at birth with a heritage of character, but that this character may be influenced by fortuitous circumstances."

His memoirs make clear the "fortuitous circumstances" refer mainly to the influence of his parents.

His father, William Thomas Diefenbaker, was "an unusually good student with a high regard for education . . . his greatest affection was for Shakespeare . . . he had deep respect for the law . . . the House of Commons lived for him . . . he was an unusual person . . . not a driver in any sense of the word, but a dreamer who loved books . . . had an affection for all who were in difficulty . . . His philosophy of life: do unto others as you would they do unto you."

His mother, Mary Florence Bannerman: "an unusual woman, deeply proud of her Highland ancestry, canny and 'a wee bit "careful, and determined never to spend a dollar that could be saved . . . she never knew the meaning of defeat."

He described both as "devout Christians," adding "When I look back, mother gave me drive, father gave me the vision to see what could be done."

Diefenbaker's paternal forbears came to Upper Canada from south Germany in 1816. His great-grandfather on his mother's side emigrated from the Scottish Highlands with Lord Selkirk in 1812.

The family name was originally Diefenbacker but grandfather George Diefenbacker, a noted carriage-maker in western Ontario, dropped the "c" during the 1890s.

His father met and married Mary Bannerman in 1894 at Chelsey, Ont., where he taught school.

Their first son, a future prime minister, was born Sept. 18, 1895, at Neustadt, a village south of Owen Sound. Three years later, after the birth of Elmer Clive, the Diefenbakers moved to Todmorden on the outskirts of Toronto.

In 1903, at the urging of Mrs. Diefenbaker, the family decided to seek greater opportunities in the newly-opening Canadian West.

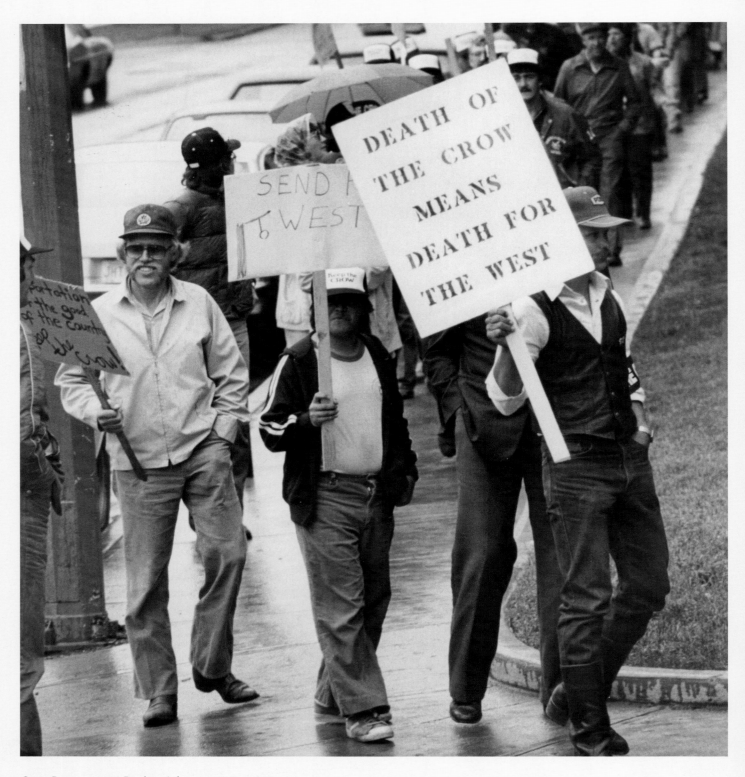

Crow Rate protest, Regina, July 15, 1982

A Vanishing Horizon

Since first erected at the turn of the century, Saskatchewan's grain elevators had become more than just keepers of grain. As large, rectangular signposts on a flat prairie landscape — symbols scattered across the province's skyline — they had become emblems of an enduring prairie spirit, of community pride and perseverance. But by the mid-1970s, due to the abandonment of railway lines and a redesign of grain-handling systems, these agricultural icons began to fall from the horizon, giving way to an era of rationalization. Once numbering 6,000 as they stood every few kilometres along the railway lines of Alberta, Saskatchewan and Manitoba in the mid-1930s, the Prairies' grain elevators were estimated at fewer than 900 at the beginning of the 21st century. Many were soon replaced with larger, inland grain terminals — destroying important cultural centres for towns, shifting business to larger centres and eventually pushing many smaller ones to extinction. The ghost towns left in the wake of this agricultural shift continue to be haunted by the enduring prairie spirit for which the province's grain elevators once so proudly stood.

Tearing down the water tower, Melville, October 26, 1982

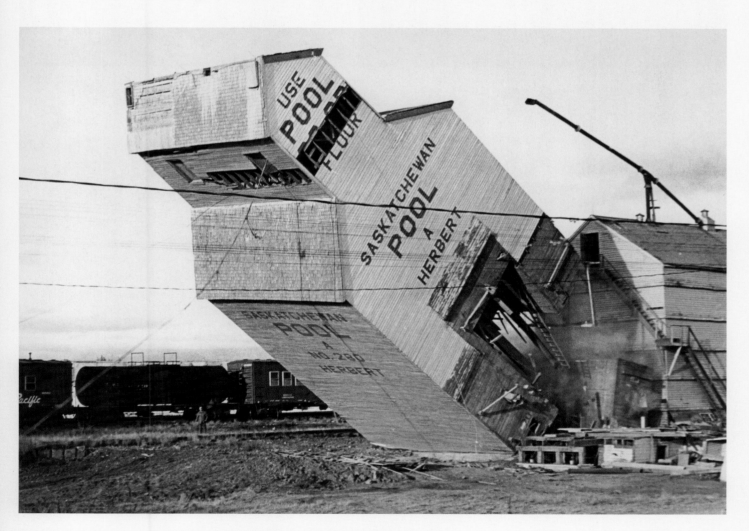

Tearing down a Saskatchewan Wheat Pool elevator, Herbert, October 7, 1977

Farm equipment auction, Regina, June 1982

Doukhobor women, 1983

Hutterites head to the corn fields, Vanguard Colony, September 6, 1980

Vanguard Hutterite Colony, September 6, 1980

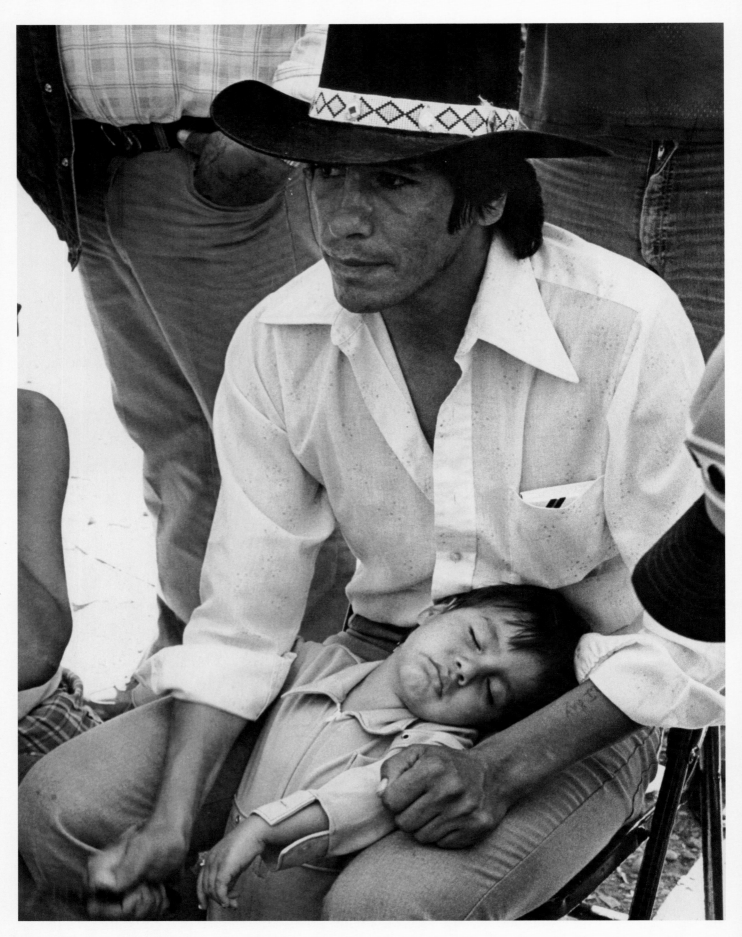

Mike Kay with his son Sheldon, powwow, Regina, 1975

Rodeo

The Canadian Cowboys Association (CCA), the country's largest semi-pro rodeo association, was founded in 1963 and quickly made its home in Saskatoon. It wasn't until 1977, however, that the Saskatchewan Indian Cowboy Association was formed, following the establishment of the National Indian Rodeo finals in the United States. Just as the Saskatchewan Indian Cultural College opened in April 1976 to educate First Nations students in reclaiming their cultural heritage, the province's aboriginal rodeo riders were preparing to show off the cultural legacy of skill they had developed over generations.

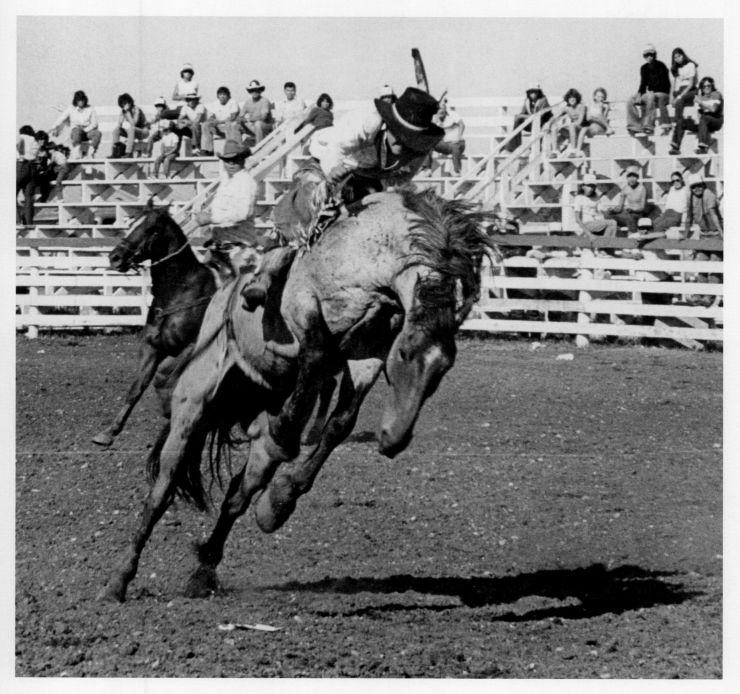

Donnie Hall, Rodeo at Indian Cultural and Agricultural Fair, Regina, August 1981

Candy Cane Disco, circa late Sixties

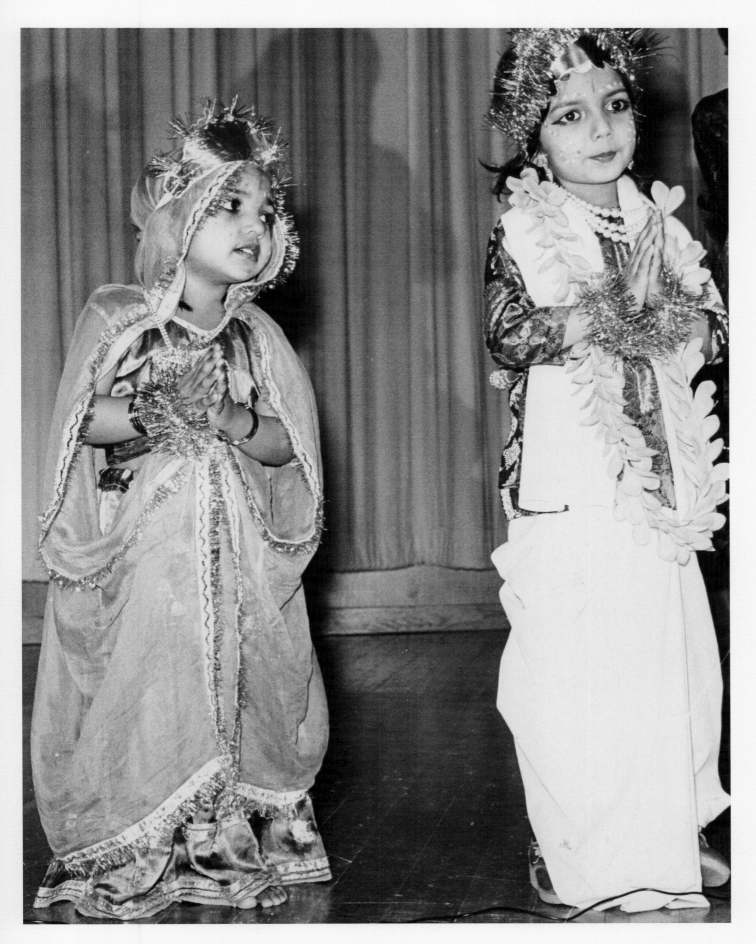

Urvashi and Sashi Sharman Sain, Holi Spring festival, Regina, March, 1977

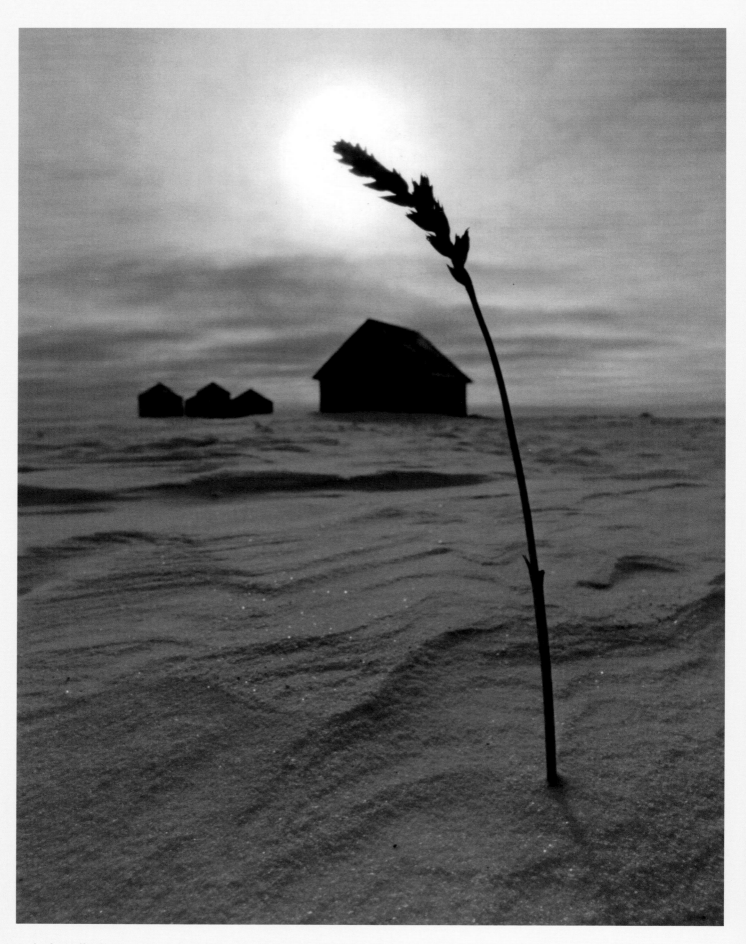

A single stalk of wheat rises above the snow after a record snowfall, Regina, February 1, 1994

Sunola field near Pilot Butte, July 28, 1998

Tractor in a field near Regina, September 16, 1993

Canary seed crop, southwest of Regina, October 4, 2002

Crop along Rochdale Boulevard, Regina, August 6, 1991

Kalina farm, southeast of Regina, August 1993

Foxleigh Anglican Church, Saskatchewan, October 2002

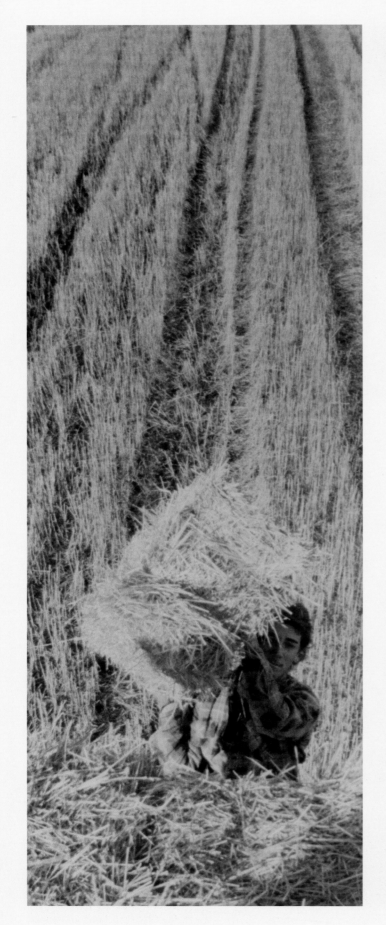

Black Angus cow, Mel McCrea's farm near Baldwinton,
May 22, 2003

Keith Izsak throws a bail of hay onto the back of a truck,
southeast of Regina, October 21, 1985

circa 1970s

Flax field near Regina, October 1993

Old farm machinery, east of Regina, February 1998

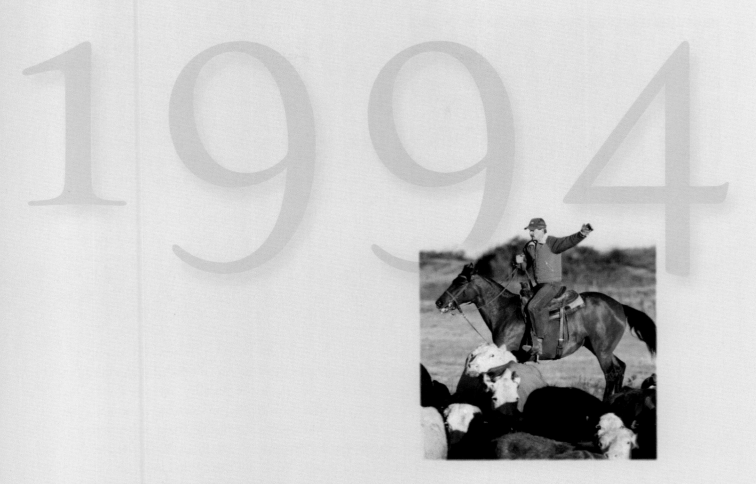

1994

Chapter Eleven

LEFT PAGE: **Leaving the farm,**
Saskatchewan, January 1990

ABOVE: **Cattleman cuts out
the herd for branding,
June 1988**

There was Grey Cup jubilation and there were grasshopper horrors. There was an inspiring little girl who survived a freezing night in the cold, and a daughter who died — was it murder or mercy? — at the hands of her father. The population surged above the million mark and then — chagrin — it slipped below again as thousands left the province looking for better prospects. Political history was made with Saskatchewan's first female lieutenant governor, its first female party leader and its first all-woman native council; it was made again with a corruption scandal that disgraced the legislature and shocked the country.

There was a best-of-times-worst-of-times aspect to the late 1980s and early 1990s in Saskatchewan. Signs of progress and achievement — a popular new science centre, an historic First Nations land claim agreement, the luring of Crown Life's national headquarters and 1,100 jobs to Regina — were countered by devastating hailstorms, failed privatization schemes, rising unemployment, depressed grain prices and general economic stagnation.

The Conservative government of Grant Devine, rocked by the murder conviction of a key minister, Colin Thatcher, and then confronted with a farm crisis, limped to re-election in 1986. But it was trounced in 1991 as Roy Romanow — backed by rural residents who had largely given up on social democracy in the 1980s — led the NDP out of the wilderness and back into power.

Tommy Douglas's gravesite, Beechwood Cemetery, Ottawa. Douglas died at eighty-one on February 24, 1986

Deepening worry about the state of agriculture underlay the anxiety of the era. Farm families facing ruin or the absorption of their lands into industrial-scale grain or livestock operations appealed to the government for help. Though bailouts came, threats loomed and a way of life remained in doubt. But, in the great Saskatchewan tradition of making the best of things in hard times, the crisis helped inspire a literary hit: Eastend writer Sharon Butala's non-fiction masterpiece *The Perfection of the Morning*.

"I don't think the repopulation of the Great Plains will be easy, nor do I claim to have a clear notion of how to do it," she observed in the book that earned widespread acclaim for its eloquent probing of the lost connections between people and the land. "But any such repopulation has to be based on a belief in what I have been saying, that in a renewed relationship with Nature, as a people and in a flourishing rural life, lies the salvation and the foundation of our nation."

Grappling with rural depopulation and falling farm incomes were key priorities of the Conservative government, a fact Devine drove home by handling the agriculture portfolio in addition to his duties as premier. But even with his outspoken advocacy of farmers at the federal level and at international conferences, and despite the Tories' introduction of various farm-support programs, the Devine government faced possible defeat in the October 1986 election. The NDP under Allan Blakeney had rebuilt itself following its 1982 defeat and appeared ready to seize upon the province's economic troubles to topple the Devine government.

That set the stage for what historians have dubbed the "Devine intervention" of Brian Mulroney's federal Conservative government. "The election was a close, hard-fought campaign with the Tories' hopes for victory hinging on their rural support," James Pitsula and Ken Rasmussen recount in their political history of the era, *Privatizing a Province*.

"The most dramatic moment came midway through the campaign," the authors argue, citing an announcement of $1 billion in federal aid for western farmers. "This was the first time the federal government had mentioned a specific amount of money. Then and there, the NDP lost the election. The point spread between the Tories and the NDP in the rural swing ridings immediately jumped to thirteen points."

Despite losing the popular vote by a fraction, the Conservatives captured thirty-eight out of sixty-four seats compared to the NDP's twenty-five. A lone Liberal seat was won by the party's leader, Ralph Goodale. He would go on, a decade later, to become Saskatchewan's most powerful federal politician and a key cabinet minister in the Jean Chrétien and Paul Martin governments.

"While people are hurting because of the economic conditions which are beyond our control, they hang in there with a provincial government that believes in the future," Devine told a cheering crowd on election night. "We will continue to listen and work hard for your respect."

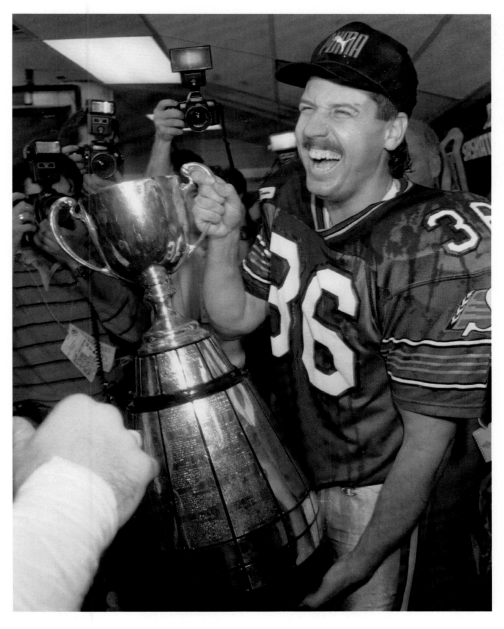

Dave Ridgway, hero of the 1989 Grey Cup

It was during Devine's second term as premier that Sylvia Fedoruk became Saskatchewan's lieutenant-governor, the first woman to hold the post. She was appointed after a distinguished career as a professor, nuclear physicist, researcher and pioneer in radiation therapy at the Saskatoon Cancer Clinic.

And there were other political milestones for women. Lynda Haverstock took the helm of the provincial Liberals in 1989 to become Saskatchewan's first female party leader, and Chief Big Eagle of the Ocean Man Band led the province's first all-woman native council.

But the biggest celebration of the era was sparked by a football that soared through the uprights in the final seconds of the 1989 Grey Cup game in Toronto. The Saskatchewan Roughriders captured the club's second ever Canadian Football League championship on November 26 with a spell-binding 43-40 win over the Hamilton Tiger-Cats — a match that is still often described as the most dramatic CFL final in history.

"Six seconds left in a game tied 40-40. Thirty-five yards from the spot where the tee lay to the goal posts, standing up there brilliant yellow, with thousands of green-painted crazies forming a blurry, moving mural behind them," sportswriter Cam Cole recounted in his description of the pressure-packed moment. "Time-out, Saskatchewan. Time-out, Hamilton. Tick, tick, tick. Not much on the line. Only twenty-three years of disappointment, and a chance to end all that for a whole province."

Dave Ridgway, the place-kicker who had spent his entire career in Regina, took his position on the field.

"What was I thinking?" he later recalled. "I was thinking: 'OK, they got you in makeable range, now just don't hit the uprights and get zero points.' All I had was time to think. You try to block everything out at a time like that, but it doesn't always work...."

It did this time. And as the ball sailed between the posts, a perfect strike, Ridgway said he "thought about the people of Saskatchewan. It's not the best province economically. When you make your living on the whims of the weather, a lot of times there's not much to cheer about. Your football team is one of the few things that you have to root for and those fans have stuck with us. I was thinking about all those little towns I've done speaking engagements in — I mean, those people bleed green. Well, I hope they're having a beer tonight."

Many, apparently, were. Thousands poured onto the streets of Regina to celebrate the victory, a sea of smiling faces, many painted green. Horn-honking cars were jammed in a line that went on for kilometres along Albert Street and the pedestrian mall on Scarth Street was packed with revelers on foot. A group of men danced down the street chanting: "Dave Ridgway for Mayor!"

"It's unbelievable," said an overjoyed Devine, who had watched the game with his family in Toronto. "It's like, well, it's like dying and going to heaven."

By 1989, the premier was, in fact, on borrowed time politically. Despite growth in Saskatchewan's mining sector, continued hardship among farmers and continuing job losses dogged the province. Federal and provincial payouts fuelled deficits but failed to halt the troubles facing rural parts of the province.

"Larger farmers gobbled up the subsidies, just as larger farms continued to gobble up the smaller ones," historian John Herd Thompson has written of the 1980s' agricultural compensation schemes.

Meanwhile, behind the scenes, an unseemly abuse of taxpayers' money was being perpetrated by high-level players in the Conservative government. It would take years and a full-blown RCMP investigation for the details to emerge, but between 1987 and 1991 a dozen Tory members of the legislative assembly and caucus workers — including several cabinet ministers — took part in defrauding taxpayers of more than $1 million. Using a system of false invoices and numbered companies, members of the Conservative caucus took public funds earmarked for legislative expenses and paid for private trips and other personal luxuries. A breakthrough came in the investigation when, at a Regina bank in 1992, police discovered a stash of $1,000 bills — about 150 of them — in a safety deposit box. Though the name attached to the box was bogus, it was accurately registered to Room 203 of the Saskatchewan legislature: the Tory caucus office.

Investigators had already begun probing the case by the time a tired, frustrated and unpopular Grant Devine called an election in the fall of 1991. His government had left the province creaking under billions of dollars of debt, and voters — even the farmers who were the Conservatives' power base — were ready for a change.

Blakeney had been replaced as NDP leader by his former lieutenant, Roy Romanow. The Saskatoon member of the legislative assembly, having distinguished himself provincially as attorney general and on the national scene during constitutional talks in the early 1980s, was poised to ride a wave of NDP popularity that had recently put the party in power in Ontario and British Columbia.

The campaign, in many ways, was a replay of 1986. The ongoing travails of farmers were a key focus of debate, and once again the federal Conservative government announced an $8-million relief package that provincial Tories hoped would propel them back into office.

But election day, October 21, 1991, saw the NDP take more than fifty per cent of the popular vote and all but eleven of the sixty-six seats in the legislature. The ousted Conservatives were reduced to ten seats and Haverstock was the only Liberal elected.

"I'm very, very happy," Romanow, the fifty-two-year-old premier-elect, declared at his Saskatoon victory party. "Let the word go forth from every corner of our province tonight that Saskatchewan is back. The people have entrusted us with a great responsibility of rebuilding this province. We are going to make the Nineties Saskatchewan's decade."

Devine, who was re-elected in his own riding, somberly accepted the voters' verdict: "The people are always right, and they were right tonight," he said.

A number of defeated Conservative members of the legislative assembly still faced the verdicts of Saskatchewan courts in connection with the expense

Drought ravaged
Saskatchewan,
circa 1987 and 1988

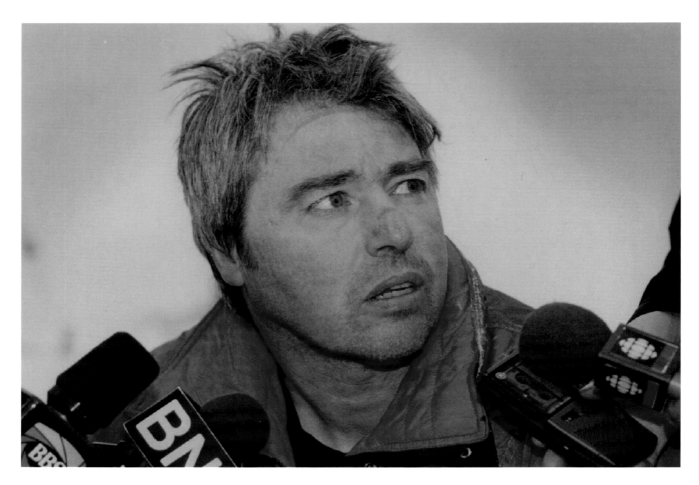

Robert Latimer, after hearing Supreme Court decision on a new trial, Wilkie, February 6, 1997

account scandal. But two other judicial dramas in Saskatchewan held the province — and the country — rapt during the early 1990s.

David Milgaard, who had been convicted of murder in the 1969 death of Saskatoon nursing assistant Gail Miller, was exonerated and released from jail in April 1992 after spending twenty-three years behind bars. The thirty-nine-year-old was given $270,000 in compensation and a trust fund that promised to disburse $1 million by the time he turned sixty-five. But at a press conference held a few days after his release from the Stony Mountain penitentiary, Milgaard said: "If you miss your sister getting married or your grandmother dies or something, there's no price tag for that kind of stuff. There really isn't any way you can compensate people for something that goes a little bit deeper than money."

He also urged police to pursue the real killer and urged the government to hold an inquiry to probe his wrongful conviction: "The same thing might happen to someone else ... I wouldn't consider it revenge. I'd consider it a proper way to clean house."

Meanwhile, another Saskatchewan man would soon be facing charges for killing his severely disabled daughter in circumstances that, in the minds of many people, didn't constitute a crime at all. Robert Latimer, a farmer from Wilkie, used a hose attached to an exhaust pipe to deliver a fatal dose of carbon monoxide to his twelve-year-old daughter, Tracy. Despite defence arguments that the girl was "in a vegetative state and was undergoing tremendous pain,"

Karlee Kosolofski, at home in Rouleau, April 1994

her death sparked a nation-wide debate about euthanasia and led to her father's conviction.

Then there was Karlee Kosolofski, the two-year-old from Rouleau who made a "miraculous" recovery — scientists and tabloids alike were using the word — after being found frozen outside of her family's house. The little girl had followed her father outside when he left for work in the wee hours of a bitterly cold February morning. Still dressed in pyjamas, with just a light coat and boots to protect her against minus 40° weather, she couldn't get back in through the locked door and spent six hours outside before being found stiff in the snow.

Rushed to hospital clinically dead, with a body temperature of fourteen and no apparent brain activity, Karlee was slowly thawed out and successfully revived by doctors in Regina. No human being had ever been so cold and survived.

She lost part of one leg but suffered no other significant damage. Saskatchewan, the notoriously unforgiving land, had spared a sweetheart. And hearts everywhere melted.

Signing of the Treaty Land Entitlement Framework Agreement, Wanuskewin Heritage Park, September 22, 1992

After an early frost and snow damaged Saskatoon's crops in 1992, Brian Mulroney set out to meet with prairie farmers to see what could be done. But while Saskatchewan's often unforgiving weather had drawn the prime minister to the Prairies, it is the province's land that drew the attention of the nation. On September 22, 1992, during that trip to Saskatoon, Mulroney, Premier Roy Romanow, the Chief of the Federation of Saskatchewan Indian Nations and twenty-two Entitlement Bands signed the Treaty Land Entitlement Framework Agreement — a $440-million plan to help aboriginals buy back land, mineral rights and improve buildings and structures over the following twelve years. "This is money that should have been paid 100 years ago, so I'm not concerned about the naysayers," Mulroney was quoted by the *Edmonton Journal*. By the end of the summer of 1993, settlements with nineteen First Nations had been reached.

Rally in support of aboriginal rights, Regina, March 1987

Soil-filled ditch on McFarlane's farm, Harris, May 1988

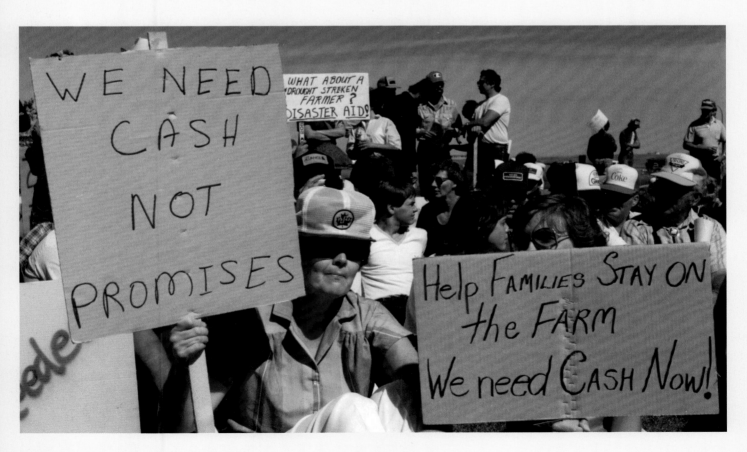

Farmers' protest, Swift Current, circa 1985

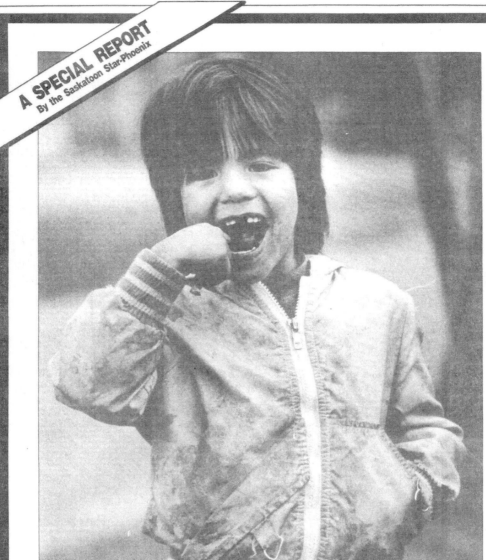

A SPECIAL REPORT
By the Saskatoon Star-Phoenix

—S-P Photo by Richard Marjan

A PEOPLE APART

NATIVES in SASKATOON

Strangers in Canada's cities. Refugees in their own land. A people apart.

Catchphrases like these describe the tens of thousands of natives who, during the last 20 years, moved to the blighted cores of our cities, areas abandoned by all but the poor.

This special report documents the shocking poverty of Saskatoon's native community, and the problems experienced in employment, education, housing and health care.

But it also has some hopeful stories about native languages and culture, native-run schools and community-initiated housing programs, and child welfare and self-help groups.

With the help of a scientifically valid survey conducted over the summer, it gauges the ambivalent, puzzled response of Saskatonians to the migration.

"The Indians arrive in the cities," journalist Larry Krotz wrote in a 1980 book about the native populations of Regina, Edmonton and Winnipeg, "and run up against closed doors or blank or hostile faces. We study one another from a distance. No one understands."

This supplement — prepared by a team of Star-Phoenix reporters led by native affairs reporter Earl Fowler — is an ambitious and no doubt flawed attempt to bridge that gap with a little understanding.

Fowler

Tuesday, October 7, 1986, Saskatoon, Saskatchewan Star-Phoenix **Natives in Saskatoon** 17

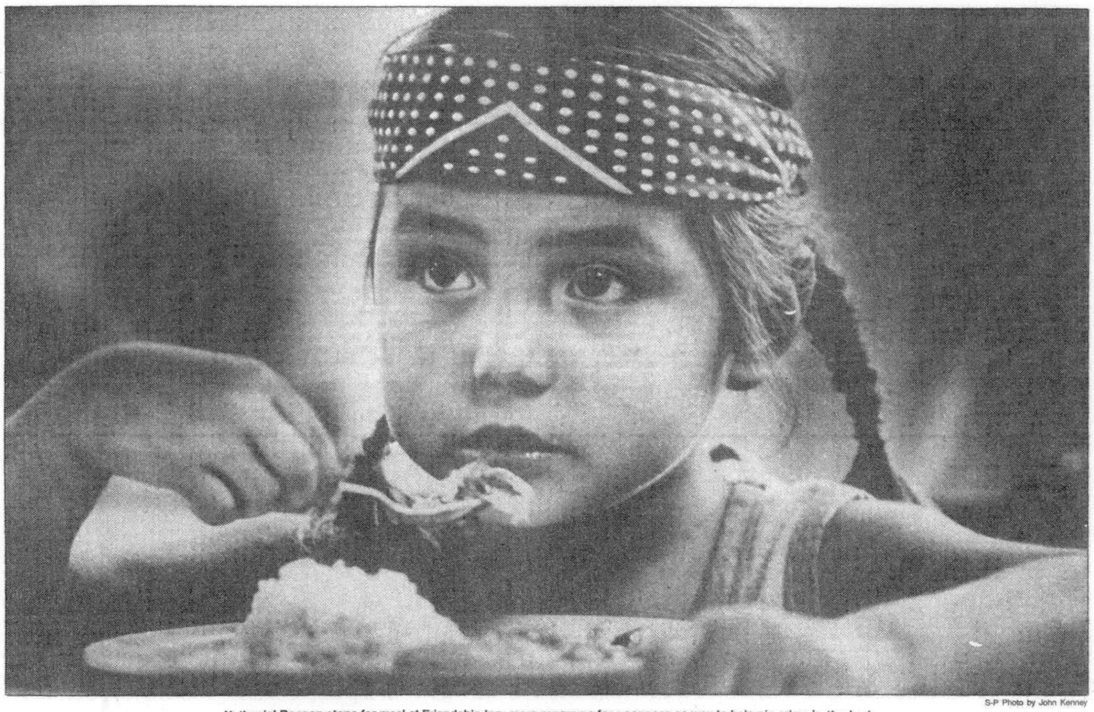

S-P Photo by John Kenney

Nathaniel Benson stops for meal at Friendship Inn; more programs for poor seen as way to help nip crime in the bud

Incarceration not long-term solution

In 1981, according to The Canadian Encyclopedia, there were more than 60,000 police and 21,000 correctional personnel in Canada. Expenditures for corrections alone were $845 million . . . a 24-per-cent increase over 1978-79.

"Official expenditures for social defence in Canada are now between $2 billion and $3 billion annually. The private security industry is larger in many places than the official police force. More attention is paid to housing design, street lighting and security installations, measures that unfortunately also encourage the creation of a fortress mentality."

Closer to home, it costs $100,000 to build an institutional bed in a holding facility like Kilburn Hall, and $105 a day to keep a teen there, said director Dennis Chubb.

Ottawa and Regina are spending $13.75 million to build new "living units" for 125 federal inmates at the provincial correctional facilities in Saskatoon, Regina and Prince Albert.

The operating budget for the Saskatoon police department this year exceeds $20 million.

The threat of punishment is supposed to deter the average person from committing crime, just as the imposition of punishment is supposed to deter offenders. That's the theory.

But the high recidivism rates mentioned earlier raise questions as to the effectiveness of incarcerating non-violent offenders.

Some people feel punishment isn't severe enough and sentences are too short. But if many of the crimes committed by natives are due to the whole web of destructive social conditions born of poverty and powerlessness, perhaps it would make more sense to concentrate on finding social and political solutions.

Sticking native mothers in prison for fraud or shoplifting or prostitution often has the effect of breaking up families and exacerbating an already bad situation, said Arla Gustafson of the Elizabeth Fry Society in Saskatoon.

Male and female inmates can take advantage of drug and alcohol rehabilitation programs, upgrading and trades training while serving their time. But in the absence of adequate community support mechanisms, people unable to find jobs tend to fall back into the same lifestyle that led to jail in the first place, agreed former native court worker Margaret Ruda and Irene Hanna of Saskatoon's John Howard Community Justice Services.

Wouldn't it make sense — in straight economic terms, if nothing else — for governments to spend more money on programs that might nip crime in the bud by helping poor families cope?

Wouldn't it make more sense — again, with an eye to saving money in the long run — to develop and improve alternatives to incarceration wherever possible?

Yes, said most of the people interviewed for this series. "There needs to be an understanding by all concerned that the best way to spend money is at the preventive end, where kids can be changed and families kept together," said Chubb.

"The system and our community contribute to making criminals by not developing the resources these kids need. The idea that kids can be punished and fixed up in a place like this is just not grounded in reality."

As the 1980s opened in Saskatchewan, status Indian children were represented in foster and group homes and other "substitute care" institutions at more than six times the rate f the general child population.

Many of these children suffer from behavioral problems, and have been bounced from home to home as they wear out their welcome. The relationship between childhoods spent in successive foster homes and later stays in jail has been noted by many observers, including Associate Chief Judge Edwin Kimelman, who said this in one of his recent reports on Indian and Metis adoptions and placements in Manitoba:

"For the majority of children who become permanent wards, infants and young children excepted, there is only the remote hope of an adoption placement. For most of these children, the reality is that they will be placed in a series of foster homes, group homes and institutions, with the very real possiblity of spending some of their adult years as residents of the province's correctional facilities."

The Riel Local of the Association of Metis and Non-Status Indians of Saskatchewan observed in a 1984 review of child welfare services in Regina that "the proportion of native children to total children in care of the Department (of Social Services) and the proportion of native people to (the) total population in correction centres in Saskatchewan are very similar."

That relationship may be spurious, but Hanna said "early intervention, early detection of children facing problems" could prevent much of the "acting out" typical of teens from unstable backgrounds. "Young children are much easier to work with than adults or juveniles."

Family and child welfare laws introduced in Ontario and Alberta in the mid-1980s — and the new Family Services Act in the works for Saskatchewan — all provide for the rechanneling of resources into keeping families together, as opposed to the more traditional practice of removing children from troubled homes.

Social Services Minister Gordon Dirks announced almost two years ago that under the new act, there will be a greater concentration on in-home support services, individual and family counselling, mediation and similar services.

It's worth noting that the existing act provides for delivery f extensive in-home services to troubled families by social workers. These services have been limited by tight budgets more than legislative constraints.

Hanna said that when MPs and MLAs react to uninformed public demands for more jails and more severe punishment of offenders, services designed to prevent future problems tend to get lost in the shuffle.

Adult mediation services co-sponsored by the John Howard Society may be shut down next June, and a plan to introduce a new "community dispute resolution" system next year may never get off the ground, because of lack of government funding.

"The (nation-wide) budget for alternatives to incarceration is extremely small compared to the budget for incarceration," said Hanna.

Statistics from 1980-81 indicate that 79 per cent of all correctional service expenditures in Canada were absorbed in the operation of correctional facilities. Of the remainder, approximately nine per cent went toward community supervision services, and 12 per cent toward administration.

Hanna said that if governments are serious about rehabilitating offenders without increasing spending on corrections, money has to be taken out of the correctional facilities budget and put into alternatives to incarceration.

"The real debate around (the new Family Services Act) should be whether or not the legislation should require resources be granted in certain circumstances as a right and not based on budgetary decisions mandated by Treasury Board officials," said Saskatoon lawyer Bill Wardell.

—Analysis
By Earl Fowler

Only one native on 330-member force

Providing more support services to children and families would help prevent crime in the long term, says Saskatoon lawyer Bill Wardell.

Steps to address the high unemployment, welfare and alcohol dependency, and training deficiencies of native people are also clearly part of the long-term solution.

But that doesn't mean there aren't simpler, more immediate changes that could be made to reduce native crime rates.

Arla Gustafson, executive director of the Elizabeth Fry Society in Saskatoon, said a feasibility study done by her society demonstrates a great need in Saskatoon for a "halfway house" exclusively for female offenders — a house-like setting, where supervisory staff would help the women get back into school, jobs and stable relations with their children.

Legal aid lawyer Kearney Healy said the appointment of native representatives to the police commission and to relevant city council advisory committees, coupled with the adoption by city police of an affirmative action hiring program, would help counter the widespread notion that the criminal justice system is stacked against the interests of poor native people.

Almost 60 per cent of the Saskatonians surveyed this summer for the *Star-Phoenix* indicated unqualified support for the idea of appointing a native person to the police commission, and another 30 per cent expressed qualified support.

About 55 per cent said they want to see more natives hired as city police officers, and another 38.6 per cent offered qualified support for this proposal.

But echoing Mayor Cliff Wright, Saskatoon Police Chief Joe Penkala said only members of city council should be appointed to the police commission, the body that oversees police affairs, because they alone are responsible for spending public money.

Penkala said an affirmative action program would not be appropriate for police work, if it forced the department to hire people who don't meet entry requirements, including a Grade 11 education. Under-qualified native officers would be unable to compete with whites for promotions, he said.

He said only one of the 330 officers now on staff is of Indian ancestry, and he would gladly hire more natives. But he said few who meet the eligibility criteria are interested in police work.

The department has no plans to develop a race relations unit to improve relations with native people, he said, nor does it make any special effort to recruit native officers. The lone native officer turned down a request for an interview.

Paul Wilkinson, director of a social work education program for Indians in Saskatoon, said he found the attitude of the Saskatoon police department discouraging while working for the provincial government on a program designed to get more natives into police work and other careers.

"In Regina, where problems between the city police and the native community have been more overt, the police realize there's a problem and have been making a serious effort to hire native constables," he said.

"In Saskatoon, they said they don't discriminate because native people have an equal chance of being hired. But that's simply not true in the absence of a special program to ensure that there are native constables."

Sgt. Brian Lynch, co-ordinator of the RCMP's special native constable program in Saskatchewan, said the 48 special constables now working for the force throughout the province have greatly improved relations between the RCMP and native communities.

Lynch said many of the special constables, who receive a 17-week training course instead of the 25-week course given to regular officers, have gone on in the last decade to become regular constables and into other government jobs.

In Saskatchewan, 17 former special constables are now working as regular officers, Lynch said, adding that he doesn't know of any who have gone on to join municipal police forces. In late August, he said there was a waiting list of about 80 men and women who had applied for training as special constables.

Wardell said the appointment of a respected native person to the police commission would help dispel the "commonly held view within the native community that there's no point in complaining about the police, because the policeman's word against the native person is going to stand up anyway."

He said the idea that police standards would have to be lowered as part of an affirmative action program is ridiculous.

Natives who go on to become lawyers frequently enter the University of Saskatchewan's Native Law Centre without the "academic underpinnings" of other students, Wardell said.

"What they find at the centre after time is that these folks have come up to the standard that's required. Surely to goodness if we can qualify them to be lawyers, they should be able to qualify as policemen."

If Penkala is correct in thinking that natives don't wish to work for his department, "then it's his job to earn their respect," Wardell added.

"There's lots of unemployed native people out there who, with a little bit of extra push from an affirmative action perspective, would be very happy to do the job."

Executive director Dennis Chubb of Kilburn Hall said there is an urgent need in Saskatoon for youth hostels, where troubled teens, "who are mostly just pushing away from their families, could have a place to hang their hats until they decide what to do."

Right now, kids wind up "crashing on a friend's rug when they leave home, and then get involved in spontaneous activities when hanging out with kids on the street."

Ron Camponi, manager of a company that provides low-rental houses to Indians and Metis on social assistance in Saskatoon, put it this way:

"If a 14-year-old girl came into my office right now and said: 'Look, I just got kicked out of my house and kicked out of school. What can you do to for me?'

"I'd say: 'I'm sorry. You haven't got in deep enough yet. Go and get yourself pregnant, get an alcohol problem, and we'll have scads of people to look after you.'

"Our whole social services system — who does it cater to? The adults, that's who. Nobody is doing anything about the children."

—By Earl Fowler

Clifton Innis, Folkfest, Saskatoon, August 1994

Saskatchewan Legislature, Regina, March 1994

THE MAKING OF A METROPOLIS

Saskatchewan's urban centres continued to prosper as the province's population reached 988,928 in 1991. As the Prairies embraced a diversification of industry and an increasingly urban lifestyle, new buildings appeared in both Regina and Saskatoon and populations of the two cities continued to swell. Although Saskatchewan's rich agricultural heritage still remained an essential aspect of prairie identity, manufacturing, telecommunications and other technological industries had begun to take hold. Near the end of the Eighties, the Saskatoon Blades had played in the first event held at the Saskatchewan Place Arena, STV Regina had begun its first television broadcast and the Saskatchewan Science Centre had opened. The Nineties brought a leisure centre and IMAX theatre to Regina and a new City Hospital to Saskatoon. As an urban focus brought increasing urban development, the province prepared itself to meet the 21st century.

Lan Huy Dhan and Phuoc Tran, Regina, June 1985

Pacers' practice, PeeWee B division, Regina, 1994

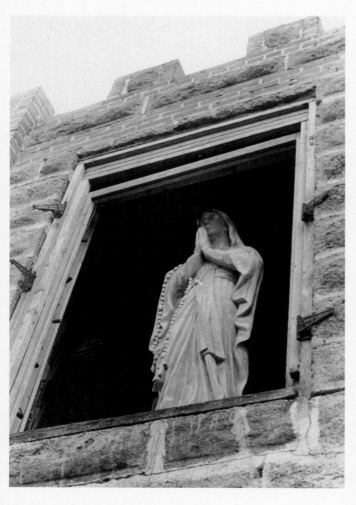

Virgin in the tower, Candiac, 1992

Summerfallow fields, Waldheim, 1988

Crowd leaves the Capitol theatre after the last picture show, Regina, May 12, 1992

Forget Village, 1990

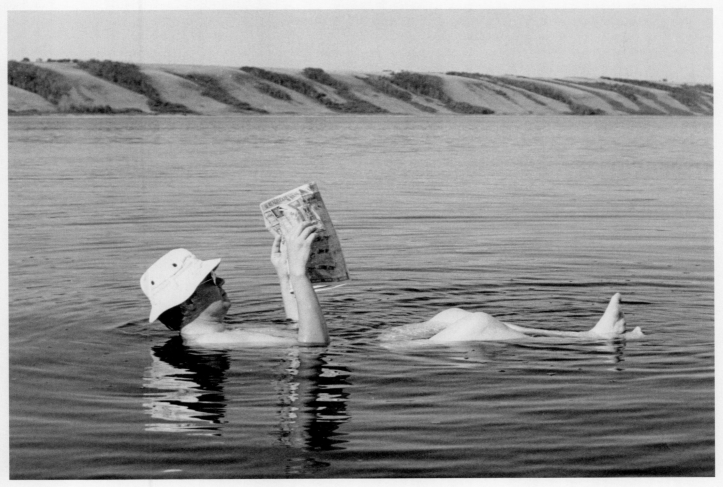

Mineral-rich waters of Little Manitou Lake, 1989

1995

Leader-Post

Regina, Saskatchewan ■ Friday, December 31, 2004 ■ www.leaderpost.com

Sports

Canada's hockey teams win at the World Juniors in the U.S. and at the Spengler Cup in Switzerland on Thursday.

C1, C2

CELEBRATING 100 YEARS

WEATHER

Today

High -18
Low -24

Tomorrow

High -13
Low -25

INDEX

Arts & Life   A8
Business   B4
City & Province   B1
Classified   D5
Comics   C10, G5, G8
Crossword   D7, G9
Dating Girl   A8
Death Notices   D5
Horoscopes   D8
Letters   B10
Petrie   B1
Sports   C1
Travel   C11
TV Listings   G5
Churches   G6
Viewpoints   B9
Weather   D10
Weekly   G1

About   TODAY

tribute
nnial

n's

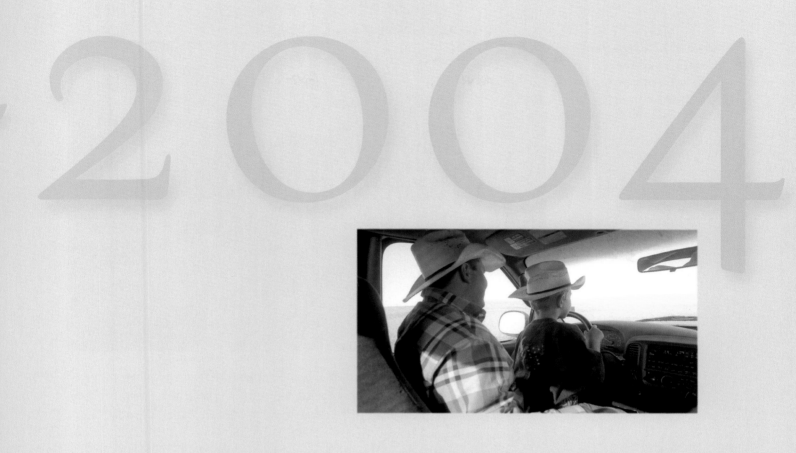

Chapter Twelve

A few months before New Year's 2005 marked the official start of Saskatchewan's centennial year, about 300 scientists, university officials, politicians and assorted dignitaries gathered in Saskatoon to celebrate another milestone in the province's history. In an impressive new building the size of a football field at the University of Saskatchewan, a rainbow array of laser beams danced to the sounds of a symphony in a spectacular show highlighting the inauguration of Canada's first — and the world's most advanced — synchrotron.

The hoopla surrounding the unveiling of the $174-million research tool, which is to be used for experiments that will shed super-powered light on everything from the structure of subatomic particles to the very origins of the universe, would surely have bewildered the hardy men and women who peopled the Prairies 100 or more years before. But as a sign of how Saskatchewan is set to embark on its second century —and to embrace a future more likely to be shaped by strivings of the mind than by labours on the land — the synchrotron may one day stand alongside the locomotive, grain elevator and oil rig as a symbol of the province's progress and prosperity.

"The construction of a transcontinental railway was a national dream of the 19th century," university president Peter MacKinnon announced at the October 2004 opening ceremony for the synchrotron. "It is now the 21st century and the demands of nation building in our era urge upon us a new national dream, one centred on knowledge, discovery and innovation."

LEFT PAGE: Saskatchewan's Gold medal curlers, Atina Ford, Marcia Gudereit, Joan McCusker, Jan Betker, Sandra Schmirler, Nagano, February 14, 1998

ABOVE: Jason Hicks lets his son, Tyler, take the wheel, Parkbeg, August 2002

Federal finance minister Ralph Goodale, the province's leading national politician, praised the "audacious" Saskatchewanians who had secured the synchrotron prize for the country: "Dreamers every one of them and Canada is now the better for them," he declared.

Premier Lorne Calvert also saw history in the making: "One hundred years ago, Saskatchewan pioneers were determined to build a future on this prairie. They were making decisions based on building a better life for themselves and their children. Today we are focused more than ever on an opportunity to build a future for our young people," he said. "The synchrotron will provide a wide range of opportunities for our youth and for our province. We can only dare to imagine what Saskatchewan's contributions to humankind will be as a result of this new synchrotron."

The baptism of the Canadian Light Source couldn't have come at a more fortuitous time — on the eve of the ultimate provincial birthday bash and with Saskatchewan in the midst of efforts to refurbish the image it projects within the country, and beyond to a global marketplace.

The province's "Wide Open Future" promotional campaign, a sometimes controversial but mostly applauded marketing initiative, has combined big-sky-and-breadbasket imagery with upbeat illustrations of Saskatchewan's modern, high-tech makeover. The 100th anniversary of the creation of the province — officially designated "100 Years of Heart" by centennial officials — was being hailed as a further opportunity to shine the spotlight on Saskatchewan's success stories, to celebrate its contributions to Canada and the world and to look forward to its next century of development. And the decade leading to Saskatchewan's centennial celebrations offered a host of examples of notable achievers from the province. Most notable among them was Biggar native Sandra Schmirler.

The ever-smiling, bespectacled skip and her Regina rink became curling legends in the 1990s, collecting a string of Tournament of Hearts national titles, three world championships and — in a dramatic final against Denmark — Olympic gold at the 1998 Nagano Games. It was the first time Olympic medals had ever been awarded in the sport, and all of Saskatchewan celebrated the achievement with Schmirler, third Jan Betker, second Joan McCusker and lead Marcia Gudereit. "To be able to curl in something like this is great," said a jubilant Schmirler, thirty-four at the time of her greatest victory. "To be able to do it with such close friends is the best feeling in the world ... We're just four brave little girls from Saskatchewan."

Schmirler's prowess on the ice was matched by an endearing humility and truly winning personality, making her one of the country's most popular sports figures. That's why her death from cancer in March 2000 created such an enormous sense of loss in Saskatchewan and triggered a nation-wide outpouring of sympathy and tributes.

"In the morning of the day Sandra Schmirler died, a nation wept, its tears washing from one end of the country to the other, its grief profound and from the soul. Just as she had made us laugh and cheer, just as she had made us feel proud and inspired, just as she had charmed and warmed us, Sandra was gone," the *Leader-Post* observed in an eloquent front-page story about her passing. "It felt as if we had all lost the battle, such was the strength of her pull on our hearts. If Sandra Schmirler was passionately devoted to curling and to her family and, really, to all that can be good about life, then this was a province that became equally devoted to her. She was not so much looked upon as a superstar in sports, an Olympian, a world champion, all of which she was. In Saskatchewan, we looked at her as a friend, a daughter, a mother, a sister, a wife, a neighbour. Sandra Schmirler was so down to earth, she had to be from small-town Saskatchewan...."

The triumph and tragedy of the Sandra Schmirler story highlighted an era of remarkable exploits among Saskatchewan female athletes. Saskatoon speed skater Catriona LeMay Doan had her own harvest of Olympic gold at Nagano in 1998, and then repeated as 500-metre champion at the 2002 Games in Salt Lake City. Images of her performing a victory lap with the yellow-and-green provincial flag billowing behind her are seared into the memories of many sports fans. And, like Schmirler, LeMay Doan has been admired just as much off the ice for

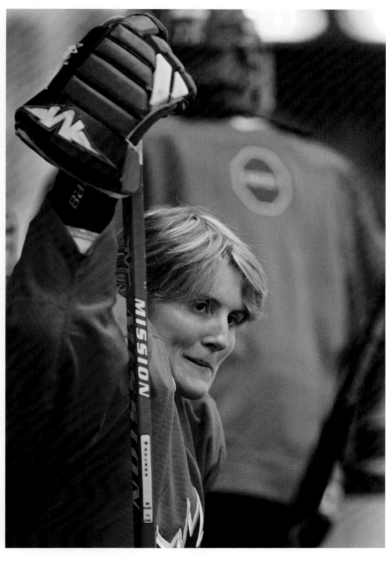

Hayley Wickenheiser of Shaunavon, assistant captain of Canada's women's hockey team in 2002 Olympics

Premier Lorne Calvert, waiting for a news conference to
begin, provincial legislature,
Regina, November 6, 2003

her sunny disposition and sense of sportsmanship. Saskatchewan natives also
played a key role as the Canadian women's hockey team took gold at Salt Lake
over the favoured host squad from the United States. Hayley Wickenheiser of
Shaunavon, possibly the best female hockey player ever, led Canada to victory
while fellow Saskatchewan natives Dana Antal (Esterhazy), Kelly Bechard
(Sedley) and Colleen Sostorics (Kennedy) shared in the limelight.

Meanwhile, another woman from Saskatchewan made national headlines in
2002. Wadena-born Pamela Wallin, who had already become one of the country's best-known and most-admired broadcasters, was named Canada's top
consular representative in New York that year.

The world of television produced another star from Saskatchewan in 2004.
Brent Butt, a funny guy from Tisdale, became an unlikely sensation on national
TV when his Saskatchewan-based sitcom, *Corner Gas*, shot to the top of the rat-
ings. Shot in Rouleau and co-starring Indian Head native Eric Peterson, *Corner
Gas* has emerged as a classic of Canadian comedy. "It was always my thought that
Canadians want to watch Canadian shows," Butt told the *Leader-Post* in March

2004. "They just don't want the shows to be crammed down their throats and be about moose every time and really 'look how Canadian we are!'" Gags such as the building of a giant hoe as a town tourist attraction have poked fun at his home province, but Butt's brand of humour is proving to be universal.

"If there is any justice in this TV world," one critic has argued, "several elements will enter Canadian TV lore, like the way in which the befuddled citizens of fictional Dog River, Saskatchewan, collectively spit — anywhere, anytime — when they hear the name of their town's rival."

Roy Romanow, too, did a turn on the national stage, though the subject matter was decidedly more serious. The dominant figure in provincial politics throughout the 1990s, he resigned as Saskatchewan's premier in 2001 then returned to prominence by leading a landmark royal commission on the future of health care in Canada. The appointment — followed soon after by Order of Canada honours — capped a distinguished career in public service that stretched back to the 1960s and included a pivotal role in fed-eral-provincial constitutional negotiations in the early 1980s.

Romanow's time as premier had been marked by turbulence and, in the end, eroding popularity. His deficit-fighting agenda, which included the closure of scores of rural hospitals, tax hikes and other controversial measures aimed at stabilizing the provincial economy, turned many rural residents against the NDP. The Romanow government was reduced to a minority in September 1999 in an election that rocked the province's political landscape. The Saskatchewan Party, a centre-right coalition that rose from the ashes of the scandal-plagued Conservatives, won the popular vote and came within three seats of forming a government under leader Elwin Hermanson.

"Voters in small towns and farms abandoned the NDP in droves, leaving the party with just two members in the province's thirty rural ridings," the *Star-Phoenix* reported at the time. "It was an expression of concern by rural Saskatchewan and a plea for federal assistance," Romanow explained, arguing that his party's poor showing resulted from a farm-income crisis rather than rural resi-dents' displeasure with NDP government policy. "I have heard you and all of Canada has heard you and we shall act in your interests to make sure the inequities you face in the world scene are rectified so there is justice brought to the farm families of this province," Romanow vowed. But just over a year later, he stepped down and was succeeded as premier and NDP leader by Lorne Calvert.

A veteran minister in Romanow's cabinets as well as a minister of the United Church, Calvert was widely respected politician who, neverthe-less, was not expected to hold off Hermanson and the Saskatchewan Party in the next election. So it was a surprise to many in the November 2003 showdown

RCMP hot air balloon above Regina, June 1998

Ryan Preece, chuckwagon races, Buffalo Days, Meadow Lake, July 30, 2002

when the NDP not only held on to power but won the popular vote and restored its majority in the legislature. "Saskatchewan's New Democrats defied the political odds Wednesday, winning a fourth-consecutive mandate in a nail-biter of an election that seemed out of reach to them just a few months ago," the *Leader-Post* reported. "The party took thirty of fifty-eight seats in the provincial legislature, as a majority of voters put aside concerns about the government's performance during the last four years and maintained the status quo. The Saskatchewan Party, which boldly predicted a majority victory in the final days of the campaign, finished second with twenty-eight seats."

The electoral triumph would extend the NDP's hold on power in the provincial legislature to at least the fifteen-year mark. "They said it couldn't be done. We did it!" Calvert exclaimed in his victory speech.

"The momentum changed. The momentum came to the New Democrats. The momentum is now with Saskatchewan."

Remarkably, as the province prepared to celebrate its centennial with Calvert at the helm, headlines were dominated by a struggle between the province and the federal government over resource revenues. The details might have been different, but the story would have struck a chord with every provincial premier since 1905. Some things never change.

But 2005 did promise unique and memorable celebrations of Saskatchewan's heritage, its citizens, and its future. A planned royal visit by Queen Elizabeth was expected to be the highlight of anniversary events. Special

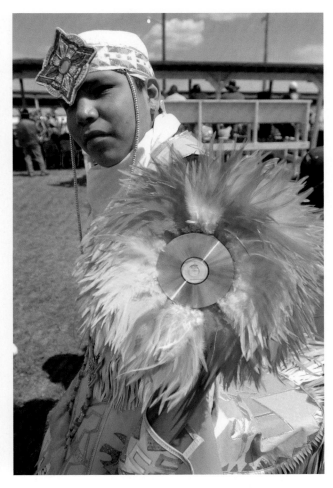

days were declared to commemorate the births of Tommy Douglas and John Diefenbaker, the two most renowned political figures in the province's history. And a special medallion was minted to honour thousands of living heroes — teachers, veterans, entrepreneurs, volunteers and other achievers at the dawn of Saskatchewan's second century. "Saskatchewan is an extraordinary place to live, work and celebrate — and it's a place that's best characterized by our people," Calvert said in announcing plans for the 100th birthday party. "The centennial anniversary allows us to take note of how far we've come as a province and how much we've contributed to Canada and the rest of the world."

ABOVE LEFT: 18-year-old Garrett Lavallee dances with two-year-old Sincere Toto, Native dance fair, August 3, 2002

ABOVE RIGHT: Teddy Cutine Bison of Ocean Man First Nation shows part of his traditional costume mixed with modern-decorations, Sakimacy First Nation, north of Grenfell, June 21, 2004

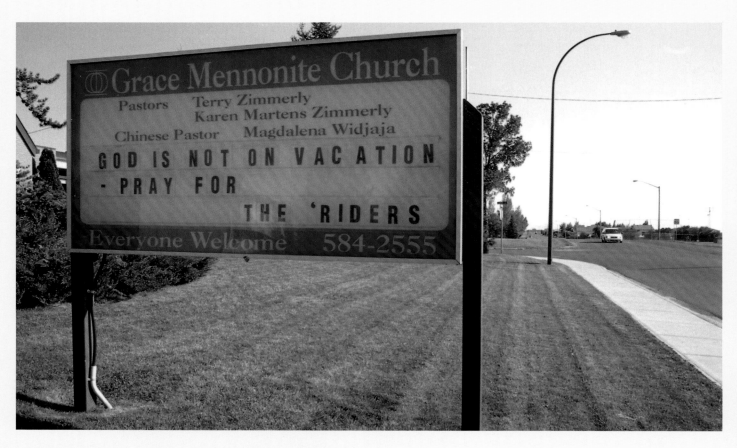

Grace Mennonite Church sign, cheering on the 'Riders, Regina

Campbell Collegiate students cheer the Tartans, Regina, September 1996

QUEENS OF ICE

Over the decades, Regina's historic union station had seen the arrival of a variety of travelers: immigrants and workers, war veterans and passers-through. But by the end of the 20th century, the majestic building underwent multi-million-dollar renovations in order to greet another kind of guest: gamblers. In 1996, Union Station was reopened as Casino Regina, which quickly rolled into place as the province's leading tourist attraction.

But while the casino continued to bring visitors to the Prairies, many Saskatchewan residents were getting excited about another kind of arrival — one that didn't seem such a gamble. For many Saskatchewanians at that time, the success of the province's women athletes was becoming a sure bet. Biggar's Sandra Schmirler was skip for a Saskatchewan rink that won the first gold medal awarded for women's curling at the 1998 Nagano Olympics, raising the profile of women's curling to an international level. Saskatoon's Catriona LeMay Doan earned a gold medal in the 500-metre speed skating competition in the 2002 Winter Olympic Games, setting a world record as the fastest woman on ice. And also at the 2002 Olympics, Hayley Wickenheiser, of Shaunavon, Saskatchewan, skated to a gold medal win as assistant captain of Canada's women's hockey team.

Putting the finishing touches on some slot machines before the official opening of Casino Regina, Regina, January 24, 1996

Hayley Wickenheiser, Colleen Sostorics and Dana Antal, members of Canada's National Women's hockey team, Calgary, 2004

Catriona LeMay Doan, after earning a new world record in the 500-metre speed skating competition, Essent ISU World Cup, Olympic Oval in Calgary, December 9, 2001

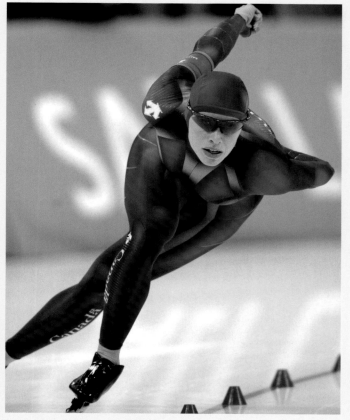

Catriona LeMay Doan finished ninth in the women's 1000-metre speed skating competition at the 2002 Winter Olympics, Salt Lake city, February 12, 2002

TODAY HO L-6 TOMORROW HO L-11

The StarPhoenix

Monday Feb. 16, 1998

Saskatoon, Saskatchewan   Suggested Price: 70¢ Mon.-Thurs.; $1.17 Fri.-Sat. Tax not included

SASKATCHEWAN GOLD

NAGANO 1998

Heavy medal weekend

By Scott Larson
of The StarPhoenix

The excitement was almost too much for Shona and Iain LeMay as their daughter, Catriona LeMay Doan, stepped to the starting line for what would be an historic women's 500-metre speed skating race in Nagano.

"We were all so excited," said Shona in a telephone interview from Nagano.

Shona usually finds watching her daughter race too nerve wracking, but she stayed in the M-Wave skating oval for this one early Saturday morning local time.

After a couple of chattering steps LeMay Doan and teammate Susan Auch stretched into full stride. Auch hit the 100-metre mark first in 10.27 seconds with LeMay Doan a blink of the eye behind.

At the crossover LeMay Doan took the inside lane and started to chase down Auch, pushing past her as they headed home.

LeMay Doan flashed across the finish line in 38.21 seconds, breaking the Olympic mark she had set the day before, for an aggregate time of one minute, 16.60 seconds. Auch was next, 33 one-hundredths of a second behind for the two races.

It was the first time Canadians had finished one-two in the Winter Olympics.

"I don't enjoy watching her, maybe if it was someone else's child," said Shona. "Now, I can sit back and enjoy the rest of the Games."

LeMay Doan was 13th in the 1,500 metres this morning and competes in the 1,000 on Wednesday at midnight.

Shona was armed with a Canadian and Saskatchewan flag at the oval for Saturday's race.

"When Catriona came by she said, 'Throw me the Saskatchewan flag,' " said Shona.

Shona tossed it out, but her aim was off. Someone grabbed it and gave it to Catriona, who was waving it when she stood on the podium to receive her gold medal.

In Saskatoon, about 30 people from the speed-skating community watched the race with Henrietta Goplen, LeMay Doan's former coach in the Lions Speedskating Club.

They partied until 5 a.m.

"It was such a roller-coaster (of emotions)," said Goplen, of watching LeMay Doan capture gold.

"It was thrilling to see her set a goal, succeed and know you had a little bit of help in it," she said.

"Catriona is just the perfect recipe, she has all of the ingredients," added Goplen.

Goplen said Catriona's parents should be given a lot of the credit for putting her in a number of sports when she was young.

"She was in dance, soccer and skating and that helped a lot. She is a natural athlete, but she has trained hard.

"I guess I'd like to say, thank you very much Catriona, you were great."

Meanwhile, there was a family get-together cheering on Saskatchewan's other gold medallist late Saturday night.

Sandra Schmirler's family watched Schmirler and her rink of third Jan Betker, second Joan McCusker and lead Marcia Gudereit, as well as spare Atina Ford, capture the women's curling gold medal with a 7-5 win over Denmark.

Sandra's parents, Art and Shirley, drove to Acme, Alta. along with Sandra's baby, Sarah, to watch the semis and final with their other two daughters, Carol and Beverley.

"You knew it was there and you knew they could do it, but gosh, you still gotta do it," said Shirley, while changing Sarah's diaper after arriving home in Biggar.

Schmirler scored three in the first and never relinquished the lead. After taking a point in the eighth end, after a measurement in the four-foot showed Canada's rock was a hair closer than Norway's stone. McCusker iced the game with a remarkable triple peel in the 10th.

"Getting the three on the first end was the big one," said Shirley, who talked a couple of times on the phone to Sandra during the week and communicated via e-mail every day.

"Most of the conversation was about our baby," said Shirley.

She said it was great to watch the finals with her daughters.

"What a hoot, they are more fun to watch — they scream, they holler, they hide their face. It was fun."

Sandra's sister, Carol, had a good feeling about the final before they even hit the ice.

"We felt they were going to win right from the start," she said. "Sandra looked very confident."

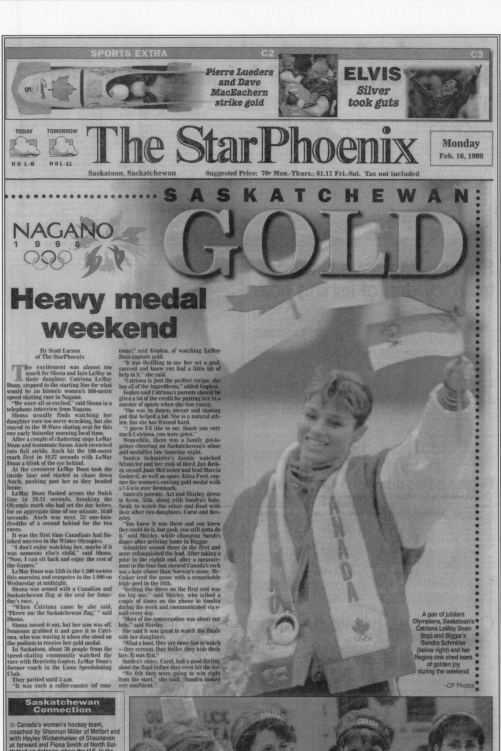

A pair of jubilant Olympians, Saskatoon's Catriona LeMay Doan (top) and Biggar's Sandra Schmirler (below right) and her Regina rink shed tears of golden joy during the weekend

—CP Photos

Saskatchewan Connection

■ Canada's women's hockey team, coached by Shannon Miller of Melfort and with Hayley Wickenheiser of Shaunavon at forward and Fiona Smith of North Battleford on defence, plays the U.S. in the gold medal game at 3 a.m. Tuesday

A.M. UPDATE

Monday-Thursday

STARLINE

NBA
Heat 116, Raptors 95
Rockets 90, Lakers 88
T'Wolves 115, Mavs 89
Bulls 99, Pistons 90

Publications Mail Contract No. 460885

The StarPhoenix On-line:
http://www.saskstar.sk.ca

In Tuesday's StarPhoenix: Dance final

Saskatchewan Indian Federated College powwow, held at the Agridome in Regina, April 19, 1992

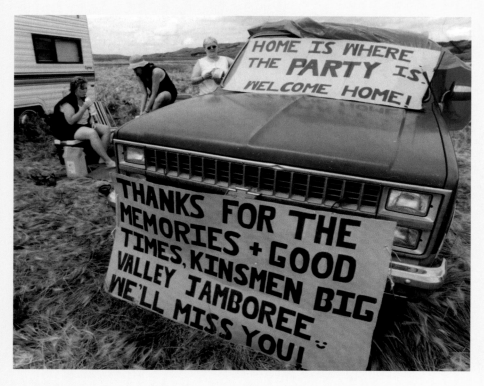

HOME IS WHERE THE PARTY IS! WELCOME HOME!

THANKS FOR THE MEMORIES + GOOD TIMES, KINSMEN BIG VALLEY JAMBOREE WE'LL MISS YOU!

Goodbye to the Jamboree, July 1999

Tisdale-born Brent Butt, star of TV's *Corner Gas*, June 27, 2004

Students from St. Dominic Savio School, Saskatchewan Science Centre, Regina, May 2002

Joyce Walters and
Leah Husley, Big Valley
Jamboree, July 1999

TOP STORIES:
Sask. standouts

Douglas prominent/A3

HIJACK: Hostages
freed from plane

Canadian Macklin OK/E7

RUSSIA: Yeltsin
steps down

World surprised/C8

Saturday, January 1, 2000

Section A

Today

High: -8

The LeaderPost

Regina, Saskatchewan

Informing Regina and Southern Saskatchewan since 1883

Mon.-Thurs. 70¢/Fri.-Sat. $1.17

Looking
Forward,
Looking **Back**

Inside Today:

Look inside today's Leader-Post for a special 40-page section marking the start of 2000. Here's a quick look at some of what you'll find:

■ **G2:** *A Love Affair a Century in the Making* — The start of 2000 is, for many, a time of reflection. What makes Regina the great place it is to live? Leader-Post Editor Bob Hughes shares his opinion.

■ **G9:** *Canada Y1K* — The state of our country at the start of the last millennium, when the sophisticated societies of Canada's First Nations dotted the land from sea to sea.

■ **H1:** *Regina: From Pile o' Bones to Prairie Powerhouse* — The Leader-Post's Will Chabun examines the history of our city, with a look at where we've come from, and where we might be going.

■ **H4:** *Shaping our World* — A timeline of the last 1,000 years, highlighting the political, social and scientific milestones that shape our lives today.

■ **I1:** *The Battle over Medicare* — Many consider it to be one of our province's defining moments of the last 100 years. Reporter Anne Kyle revisits the divisive debate over the introduction of medicare, one of Saskatchewan's lasting legacies to the rest of our country.

■ **I3:** *Farmers at a Crossroads* — After enduring the 1900s, a new millennium begins with farmers facing a crisis that could forever change the face of our province.

■ **J1:** *Canada: Diary of a Century* — A year-by-year look at the forces that have shaped our country during the last 100 years.

On The Web

www.leader-post.sk.ca

Friday-Saturday

Please Recycle in your Big Blue Bin

7 71960 00021 1

Canada Post Canadian Publications Mail Sales Product
Agreement No. 454435

Regina Welcomes 2000

TERRY CHEVALIER / The Leader-Post
Celebrants at Saskatchewan's Millennium Party in Regina welcome the new year

Reginans join in peaceful wave of celebrations that swept globe

By LISA SCHMIDT
of The Leader-Post

As the last party of the 1900s raced around the globe, and calendars in country after country ticked over to 2000, southern Saskatchewan eagerly awaited its turn to celebrate Y2K.

"I've been waiting. We've watched New York, Ottawa and Toronto happen — now it's our turn," said Preston LeCaine, who had lined up in front of the stage with his friends since the first band started four hours earlier.

But midnight would just be the start, he said.

"We're going until the sun comes up, which will be about eight o'clock."

While many resident greeted 1999 with families at home or with friends at a house party, the largest crowd of the evening was the Saskatchewan Millennium Party at Regina Exhibition Park.

Last count of ticket sales put attendance over 3,000, but Don Chatwin of Regina Exhibition Park reported many last-minute buyers.

The show, which featured ten bands on three stages, drew a mixed crowd.

"We haven't gone out for a couple years, so we thought why not now," said Scott Buchan of Regina before being led onto the dance floor by his girlfriend to dance to a Jack Semple tune.

Randy Loustel and Michelle Shawaga of Emerald Park enjoyed the band at the country music stage.

Welcome to 2000

More Inside:

■ **E8:** As fireworks lit the skies above Canada, melting away many Y2K fears, people celebrated the year 2000 in typical Canuck fashion: singing and dancing, shivering and stamping their feet to stay warm.

■ **E8:** Millions joyously packed streets around the world to join in a worldwide welcome for the new year

■ **More Coverage:**
Pages A3, A5, A9, and D9

"We thought it was a good place to be," said Loustel, adding he had few fears about Y2K bug problems.

"I don't think anything will happen."

In fact, few people seemed to be worried about being away from home when the clock struck 12. Ian Wiley came in from Yorkton with about 30 people to celebrate the evening.

"This is great because there's people from all over that we've seen here," he said.

"I just wish a lot more women here were single," his friend Dallas Hydamaka added.

"Especially this one walking around with black pants and a silver tank top."

Several party-goers were also hoping to find someone special for 2000, though some of their methods seemed less than successful.

"We're having a great night," shouted Ian Punab, between catcalls and whooping. He eventually doffed his shirt to flex a bicep.

The crowd was wearing everything from blue jeans to tuxedos.

One woman wore an angel costume, complete with wings.

Some had donned their best duds.

"We're single," admitted Lisa Holly, who was wearing a full-length black evening gown.

Please see *Revelers* / A2

After all the hype, Y2K bug a Y2K bust

By ANNE KYLE
of The Leader-Post

The hype and predictions of Y2K glitches associated with the dawning of 2000 fizzled Friday night like the spent bottles of champagne.

"Nothing dire happened. The situation is normal across the province," said Tim Whelan, co-ordinator of the province's Y2K preparations. "I've got a headline for you: Y2K Sk. OK . . . I've been working on that for months," said Whelan, who was sharing a bottle of non-alcoholic champagne with co-workers who spent the night working the phones.

The evening was a relatively routine New Year's Eve with the only big bang being the sound of fireworks at the White Night celebrations at the Saskatchewan Centre of the Arts, which drew a capacity crowd.

"We were pretty slow here tonight and that's the way we like it," said Dave Quick, head of emergency planning for the City of Regina, as he and other emergency personnel staffing the city's Y2K Emergency Operations Centre monitored events in the city and across the country.

"Things unfolded exactly as I expected," he said.

Nothing out of the ordinary occurred to mar the celebrations as revelers in Saskatchewan ushered in the new year in high spirits, emergency personnel said.

However, earlier in the evening a few Regina residents may have experienced momentary panic when they couldn't get cash out of the Royal Bank automated banking machines before heading out to celebrate New Year's Eve. But a spokesperson for the bank said the problem wasn't Y2K related.

"Our machines were temporarily down in the Regina area, but it wasn't Y2K related. The problem was with the telephone service provided by SaskTel. There was a problem with their switching system and our machines were down for a three to five minute interval. But they are all up and running now," said Donna Fairbrother after checking out the situation.

Some automated bank machines went off-line and phone lines were down in the city for a few minutes around 6 p.m. after a minor equipment breakdown at SaskTel.

See *No Major Problems* / A2

QUOTABLE

"

I've got a headline for you: Y2K Sk. OK

"

Tim Whelan

Inside Today

canada.com

Call 565-8212 or 1-800-667-8751 for Daily Home Delivery

$2.90 Per Week in Regina, $3.00 Per Week Outside Regina

Jesse Oliver, Windhorst, June 2002

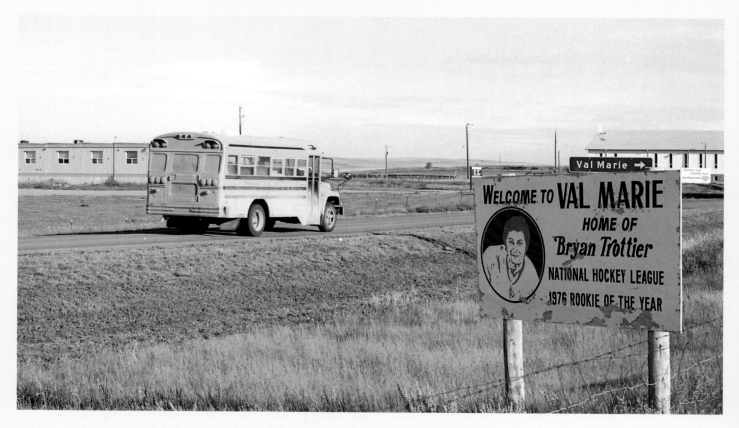

Val Marie, September 2002

At a Crossroads

In the fall of 2002, the *Regina Leader-Post* ran a 10-part Crossroads series that examined the future of rural Saskatchewan — what will live and what will die. The stories and photographs in this series contrasted dying communities with those that are thriving thanks to the decisions they made to reinvent themselves. These photos are drawn from the Crossroads project.

Manitou Springs Resort and Mineral Spa, Watrous, September 2002

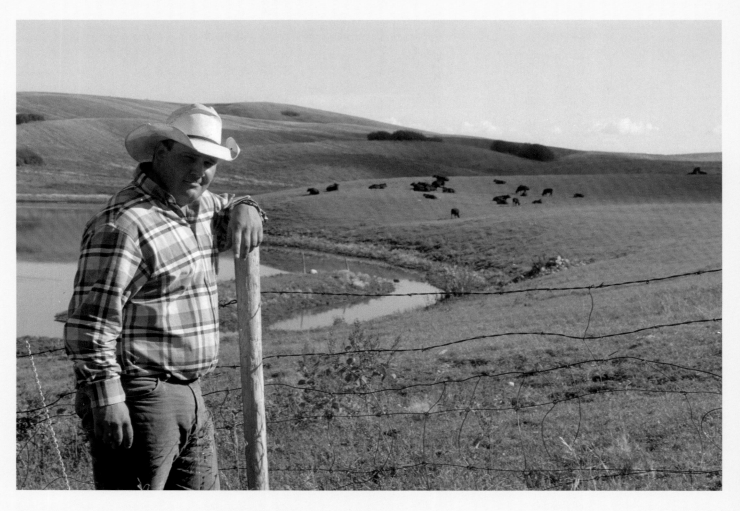

Jason Hicks, Bluestone Stock Farms, Parkbeg, August 2002

Drought-ridden flax, near Tisdale, July 2002

The StarPhoenix

Saskatoon, Saskatchewan — Wednesday, May 18, 2005 — www.TheStarPhoenix.com

Belinda bombshell

❑ Stunning defection of Stronach rocks Parliament; anticipated defeat of minority gov't in question/**A8**

Diary of the deal
❑ Former Ontario premier David Peterson responsible for getting the deal done.
/A8

Romance over?
❑ The fairy-tale romance with Tory bigwig Peter MacKay appears to be over.
/A10

Inside:
- Stronach in her own words/**A8**
- Don Martin column/**A9**
- Stronach a sellout: Vellacott/**A12**
- Calvert defends decision/**A12**
- StarPhoenix editorial/**A14**
- Loonie rises on news/**C12**

—CanWest News Photo

Queen Elizabeth II arrives in Regina Tuesday for her nine-day visit to Saskatchewan and Alberta

Queen arrives in Regina

❑ First Nations University first stop on Sask. tour

Saskatchewan News Network

REGINA — Queen Elizabeth II kicked off a nine-day tour of Western Canada Tuesday with a trip to the First Nations University of Canada in Regina and a word about the "special relationship" between the sovereign and First Nations people.

The monarch addressed an assembled crowd of First Nations veterans and dignitaries inside the university, presenting a stone tablet carved with the initials of both her and Queen Victoria.

"This stone was taken from the grounds of Balmoral Castle in the Highlands of Scotland, a place dear to my great-great-grandmother Queen Victoria," said the Queen.

"It symbolizes the foundation of the rights of First Nations people reflected in treaties signed with the Crown during her reign."

More than 300 people crowded barriers along the walkway to the university to watch the Queen and Prince Philip, who arrived at the university in a 13-vehicle motorcade just before 5 p.m.

"I'm just here to see the family that signed treaties with my people here in Treaty 4," said Rick Favel from Kawacatoose First Nation, as he waited outside the university for a glimpse of the couple.

"Even though we didn't get very much out of the treaties we still think they are very sacred because they were done in a spiritual way between two nations."

Inside, the Queen, wearing a peach, brown fur-trimmed suit and matching hat, and Prince Philip, the Duke of Edinburgh, were flanked on stage by university president Eber Hampton, Chief Alphonse Bird of the Federation of Saskatchewan Indian Nations and Grand Chief Philip Favel of the Saskatchewan First Nations Veterans Association.

The monarch admired a traditional star quilt presented to her, while Prince Philip accepted a pair of moccasins.

Hampton said the Queen's visit holds a lot of significance for First Nations people.

■ CONT'D: Please see Queen/**A10**

■ Royal itinerary in Saskatchewan/**A10**
■ A home away from home/**A10**
■ Best locations to see the Queen/**A10**

93¢ Monday - Thursday (taxes not included)
Publications Mail Contract No. 40006989
Return undeliverable
Canadian addresses to:
The StarPhoenix
204 5th Avenue North
Saskatoon, SK S7K 2P1

WEATHER
High 15
Low 10
Details Page B8
canada.com
★ ★

Women of distinction
Thirty-four women and one group will be recognized in 10 categories at the 24th annual YWCA Women of Distinction Awards being held June 2. Please see story on **Page C1.**

PlayStation 3 unveiled
The new Sony PlayStation 3 was touted as the most important entertainment and digital media platform of the decade during its launch this week. Please see story on **Page C15.**

Holocaust lesson
A group of Canadian students left the U.S. Holocaust Memorial Museum shaken, but aware of the need to prevent a similar tragedy from happening again. Please see story on **Page C11.**

Officers don't want strike
City police officers didn't call for a strike vote at a Monday meeting. Instead they endorsed a review of issues affecting the police service. Please see story on **Page A3.**

Her Majesty, the Queen, Depot Division, Regina, May 19, 2005

The Queen, Saskatoon, May 19, 2005

The Queen visiting near Regina to mark the province's centennial, May 18, 2005

LEADER-POST

Regina, Saskatchewan ■ Saturday, May 21, 2005 ■ www.leaderpost.com

Summer travel season has started! We have some tips / A10

ONLINE EXTRAS

For unique online-only content for *Leader-Post* subscribers, point your Web browser to www.leaderpost.com and look for the Online Extras link at the bottom of the page.

Here's some of what you'll find today:

■ A Yorkton-area farmer was trapped under a piece of farm machinery for three days before being rescued by a neighbour, as **Heather Polischuk** reports on Page B3. Go online to read Saskatchewan Labour's Farm Safety Guide.

■ Inflation jumped by 3.2 per cent in Saskatchewan in April over the same month one year earlier, as **Colleen Silverthorn** reports on Page B4. Online, view the consumer price index report from Statistics Canada.

■ Turn to Page G3 for Games, Gadgets, and Gizmos and then get more G3 by going online.

■ Some of our best writers are our readers. We have an online-only selection of some of your letters.

$1.40
Friday and Saturday

Canada Post
Canadian Publications
Mail Sales
Product Agreement No. 454435

A Royal Farewell

'The spirit of nation building in Saskatchewan and Canada truly falls on fertile soil. With this spirit the promise of the future is boundless.'

— Queen Elizabeth II

Her Majesty accepts flowers during an impromptu walkabout at Government House.
BRYAN SCHLOSSER/Leader-Post

By JANA G. PRUDEN
Leader-Post

In her last public appearance in Saskatchewan, Queen Elizabeth II spoke fondly of her time in the "vast, colourful tapestry" of Western Canada, and shared kind words about past premier Tommy Douglas.

"In a lifetime of most remarkable service — first to province and later to country — premier Douglas brought social consciousness to life in the policies that directly affected the lives of Canadians," Her Majesty said, speaking at a luncheon at the Centre of the Arts Friday afternoon.

The Queen, dressed in a lively aqua suit and hat ensemble, recalled being greeted by Douglas during her first visit to the city in 1951, and said she's seen a similar spirit of service during her travels throughout the week.

"During the past four days, Prince Philip and I have caught glimpses of your ancestors' dreams that have been brought to life, not by accident but through determination, perseverance and hard work," she said, speaking in French.

The Queen began her day at Government House, where sunny skies brought out hundreds of spectators eager to catch a glimpse of the monarch on her last day in the province.

The enthusiastic crowd broke into applause when the Queen's motorcade arrived shortly after 11 a.m. and pulled into the portico area of the building, where the Queen was met by Lt.-Gov. Lynda Haverstock.

Walking slowly toward the new entrance, the Queen stopped to wave at onlookers and looked pleased when she unveiled a plaque officially opening the newly completed wing in her name.

The new building bears the cypher of Queen Elizabeth, just as the original structure bears Queen Victoria's.

Sisters Kayla and Tannis Coliboba presented flowers to the Queen as she walked into the building, and shared their thoughts about the experience afterward.

"I thought she'd be taller," noted 11-year-old Kayla.

The Queen was "pretty" and "really nice," added six-year-old Tannis.

Inside, the Queen toured the new addition and the second-floor interpretive centre, which focuses on the history of the Crown and First Nations people.

She then attended a reception and signed the guest book before heading outside for a brief, unscheduled walkabout, and proceeding by motorcade to the Centre of the Arts.

See Queen on Page A2

MORE INSIDE

■ Complete coverage of the final day of the Royal visit to Saskatchewan.

Page A4

Her Majesty Queen Elizabeth II and Lt.-Gov. Lynda Haverstock chat while on a walkabout at Government House Friday morning.
BRYAN SCHLOSSER/Leader-Post

ALBERTA

Police examine the wreckage of the collision between a bus and a transport truck on Friday.
CanWest

Four killed, dozens hurt as transport strikes bus

By JIM FARRELL
and RYAN CORMIER
CanWest News Service

EDMONTON— Four people were killed and 25 others injured after a transport truck slammed into a commercial bus that was stuck after trying to turn around on a highway north of Edmonton early Friday morning.

Police said the accident happened shortly before 1 a.m. when a bus carrying 43 oilfield workers got stuck while attempting to turn around on Highway 28 north of Gibbons, Alta.

The four dead men have been identified as Stephen Joseph Batherson, 56, of North Sydney, N.S.; William Carl Ingram, 53, John Daniel Hernon, 54, and Steve Raymond Wallis, 42, all of Edmonton.

The southbound bus had been the last in a long line of vehicles waiting for police to reopen the highway following an earlier, unrelated accident. Police said the driver attempted to turn it around in order to find an alternate route. When the back wheels of the bus dropped off the edge of the pavement onto the grassy shoulder it became stuck, leaving its front wheels parked almost exactly on the centre line of the highway.

"Because Highway 28 is a two-lane with a small shoulder, the bus's back wheels dropped into the ditch and became stuck, blocking traffic in both lanes," said RCMP Const. Laurel Kading. "Because it was obvious to passengers it was going to take a while for the bus to get out, many exited onto the road facing the accident."

Many of them were standing on the passenger side of the bus when a semi-trailer full of peat moss slammed into the driver's side, and sent the bus skidding into the workers.

Hillery Scheidl got back onto the bus only seconds before the impact. "I wasn't on the bus more than 10 seconds. I went to my seat and was bending down to get a pop. Then I heard someone say: 'He's not slowing down,' " Scheidl said.

"Everything went flying. I went flying backwards and there was glass everywhere. Parts of the seats came off, everything from the overhead racks. It was a huge mess."

After the bus and truck stopped moving, Scheidl crawled out the window to see bodies on the highway, in the ditches and under the bus.

Eleven of the 25 injured were released from hospital by Friday afternoon. Eight remained in critical condition, one in serious condition and five in stable condition. The driver and passenger of the tractor trailer were also sent to hospital and released.

Paramedics and emergency personnel from the first accident nearly a kilometre away were the first on the scene.

"We were just packing up our equipment and the ambulance was still on the scene when we got another call," said Gibbons' fire captain Ken Munro. "It was mass chaos. There were walking wounded on the road and in the ditch. The more-seriously wounded were laying on the road. There were also victims trapped under the bus."

The female driver of the bus was unconscious in her vehicle, having sustained serious head and internal injuries.

See Crash on Page A2

QUOTABLE

"
It was mass chaos.
"

Fire Captain Ken Munroe

No paper on Monday

Because of the Victoria Day holiday, the *Leader-Post* will not be published on Monday, May 23.

Image Sources

Title Page and Introductions
Title page: Saskatchewan Archives Board R-A 15,198 (Saville); p.VIII Pamela Wallin courtesy of the *Ottawa Citizen*, Bruno Schlumberger, Tony Cote, courtesy of the *Regina Leader-Post*; p.IX Dale Eisler, courtesy of Brigitte Bouvier, Prime Minister's Office, Government of Canada, Shirley Douglas courtesy of V. Tony Hauser.

Chapter One: Pre-1905
p.8 *StarPhoenix* files, October 17, 1902 (newspaper), Saskatchewan Archive Board R-B 3382 (buffalo jump); p.9 SP files (settlers); p.10 RLP files (Chief Piapot); p.11 RLP files (Riel); p.13 SP files (pile of bones); p.14 RLP files (RCMP Noncoms); p.15 Glenbow Archives NA-4035-185 (Business district); p.16 RLP files (Chief Big Bear), RLP files (Riel trial); p.17 RLP files (Chief Poundmaker), Glenbow Archives PA-3629-3 (Cree woman), Saskatchewan Archive Board R-A 6605-1 (Cree family); p.18 RLP Files November 19th, 1885 (newspaper); p.19 Glenbow Archives NA-3811-99 (haying crew), RLP files (Barr tents); p.20 RLP files (Barr homestead), RLP files (pool table); p.21 Saskatchewan Archive Board R-B 3376 (Doukhobor woman); p.22 City of Regina Archives CORA-A-1549 (Davin), Glenbow Archives NA-387-30 (*Leader* building); p.23 SP files (businessmen), SP files (stone school).

Chapter Two: 1905-1914
p.24 GBA NA-3818-17 (*Leader* front page), SAB R-A3739-2 (Legislative building); p.25 GBA NA-1687-38 (Immigrant family); p.26 E.B. Curlette, RLP files, (Laurier); p.28 SAB R-A 350 (Saunders); p.29 GBA NA-2642-6 (Ladies' group); p.30 RLP files (Weyburn store); p.31 CORA RPL-B-362 (Duke visits); p.32 RLP files, September 6, 1905 (newspaper); p.33 CORA B-719 (inauguration), SAB R-B 9442 (Legislative building); p.34 GBA NA-1749-3 (letter), GBA NA-2878-63 (immigrant with child), RLP files (two coal miners); p.35 SAB R-B 1918 (Ukrainian children), GBA NA-359-5 (Russian family); p.36 RLP files (homesteaders), SAB R-A 5796 (threshing); p.37 CORA RPL-B-61 (Rose Theatre Orchestra), CORA RPL-B-395 (*Leader* building); p.38 CORA B-772 (Princess Theatre), RLP files (Regina cyclone); p.39 RLP files, July 2, 1912 (newspaper); p.40 Canada Science and Technology Museum CSTM/CN image no. CN000397 (trains); p.41 CSTM/CN image no. CN000937 (Saskatoon skyline), SP files (Victoria Bridge); p.42 SAB R-A 8490 (McNaughton and friends), GBA NA-3818-13 (women's suffrage cartoon); p.43 SAB R-A 23037 (Beaupré the Giant), GBA NA-3035-35 (Spindel); p.44 SAB R-B 628 (Gibson with aeroplane engine), RLP files (Bonspiel); p.45 GBA NA-3026-41 (baseball team), RLP files (Regina rugby team).

Chapter Three: 1915-1924
p.46 SP files, August 5, 1914 (newspaper), SAB R-D 444 (77th Regiment); p.47 PH 95-92.1 courtesy of Saskatoon Public Library — Local History Room (enlistment); p.48 2930_2 courtesy of Saskatoon Public Library — LHR (Clinkskill), SP files June 2, 1921 (cartoon); p.49 GBA NA-3229-27 (pupils); p.50 RLP files (flu masks); p.51 SAB R-A 7553 (Ramsland); p.52 RLP files (storefront); p.53 SAB R-A 15, 198 (Saville); p.54 GBA NA-2642-47 (95th Rifles), CORA RPL-A-340 (File Hills Regiment); p.55 courtesy of Diefenbaker Canada Centre Archives-JGD 64 (Diefenbaker), GBA NA-2642-52 (27th Light Horse); p.56 RLP files, November 11, 1918 (newspaper); p.57 GBA NA-2117-5 (Prince Edward and Knight); p.58 SAB R-A 28209 (Coombe's widow), SP files (McClelland Aviation); p.59 RLP files, July 26, 1917 (newspaper); p.60 CSTN/CN image no. CN003942 (farmer); p.61 CSTN/CN image no.

CN000059 (horse-drawn harrows); p.62 GBA NA-1574-4 (racing cars), GBA NA-1574-1 (CKCK radio station); p.63 GBA NA-3853-23 (bar), GBA NA-2878-76 (swimming).

Chapter Four: 1925-1928
p.64 SP files (Diamond Jubilee edition), University of Saskatchewan Archives (Saskatchewan Wheat Pool); p.65 SP files (paperboy); p.66 GBA NA_871_1 (Cree and Métis pilgrimage); p.67 LH 2630 courtesy of Saskatoon Public Library-LHR (Catherwood with Mayor); p.68 LH 4166 courtesy of Saskatoon Public Library-LHR (Chinese Nationalist League Headquarters); p.69 RLP files ("Firey Cross"); p.71 RLP files, February 18, 1932 (newspaper); p.72 RLP files (Meadow Lake elevators); p.73 GBA ND_13_10 (Sapiro), PH 89210 courtesy of Saskatoon Public Library — LHR (Meeting of Wheat Pool): p.74 SP files, August 6,1928 (newspaper); p.75 RLP files (ladies' golf), LH 3475 courtesy of Saskatoon Public Library — LHR (Olympic team); p.76 CORA RPL-B-93 (Regina Pats), CORA E-2.123 (girls' softball team); p.77 PH 95-177 courtesy of Saskatoon Public Library — LHR (ukulele players), RLP files (carriers).

Chapter Five: The Depression
p.78 RLP files, July 2, 1938 (newspaper), RLP files (Dundurn Camp); p.79 GBA NA-2256-1 (Bennett buggy); p.80 RLP files (TB van); p.81 GBA NA-2291-4 (tractor); p.82 RLP files (erosion); p.83 LHR A1614 courtesy of Saskatoon Public Library-LHR (storefront); p.84 RLP files (On-to-Ottawa poster); p.84 GBA NA-2629-10 (poster); p.85 RLP files (Cree reserve); p.86 GBA NA-3092-82 (corn crop); p.87 RLP files (fence), CSTM/CN image no. CN000948 (settler); p.88 CORA RPL-B-110 (trekkers); p.89 RLP files (Regina Riot), CORA RPL-B-393 (Riot/bottom image); p.90 RLP files, October 21, 1929 (newspaper); p.91 RLP files (Rex Theatre); p.92 SP files, October 30, 1937 (newspaper); p.93 SP files (Grey Owl with beaver), SP files (Grey Owl).

Chapter Six: World War II
p.94 RLP files, June 6, 1944 (newspaper), Canadian Press PLS5407823 (soldiers); p.95 CORA E-2.59 (boy with flag); p.98 A422 courtesy of Saskatoon Public Library — LHR (parade float); p.100 courtesy of National Defence, Government of Canada (Currie); p.101 SAB R-B-2895 (Douglas); p.103 SP files, September 3, 1939 (newspaper); p.104 CORA E-2.47 (parade float); p.105 RLP files (war training), B2125 courtesy of Saskatoon Public Library — LHR (women needed), SP files (victory bonds); p.106 SP files (RCAF operators), RLP files (training class); p.107 CORA E-2.191 (Ferris wheel), CSTM/CN image no. CN003787 (King George VI); p.108 Patrick Pettit, RLP files (North West Mounted poster), RLP files (Capitol brochure), LH78 courtesy of Saskatoon Public Library — LHR (Chief Sam Swimmer); p.109 CORA E-2.203 (women's baseball).

Chapter Seven: 1945-1954
p.110 RLP files, May 8, 1945 (newspaper), CORA B-719 (China joins); p.111 SAB S78-114 (victory); p.112 SAB SP Collection 870_1 (teen fashion); p.113 SAB SP Collection 1430_12 (Beaux Arts Ball); p.114 3555 courtesy of Saskatoon Public Library — LHR (chief); p.115 RLP files, Patrick Pettit (RCMP Rockies Poster); p.116 QC 3949-1 courtesy of Saskatoon Public Library — LHR (Howe); p.117 SP files, May 7, 1945 (newspaper); p.118 PH 92-23 courtesy of Saskatoon Public Library — LHR (Mowat), CP6940-3-1 courtesy of Saskatoon Public Library — LHR (Perehudoff), CP6940-4-1 courtesy of Saskatoon Public Library — LHR (Knowles); p.119 Courtesy of the OC (W.O. Mitchell), LH1225 courtesy

of Saskatoon Public Library — LHR (Kenderdine), University of Saskatchewan Archives Pawson MG 204, 4. Estate 187-1994 (Pawson painting); p.120 SP files (Douglas and mom), RLP files (swearing in) p.121 SP files (Douglas); p.122 SP files, June 16, 1944 (newspaper); p.123 RLP files (Foot Mouth disease), CSTM/CN image no. CN005025 (oil man); p.124 SAB SP Collection 832_1 (speedbox derby), B6131 courtesy of Saskatoon Public Library — LHR (war brides), B4323 courtesy of Saskatoon Public Library — LHR (Eaton picnic); p.125 Larry Shaw, RLP files (snow train), CORA E-2.301 (skating party); p.126 SAB SP Collection 32_1 (Genereux, boy with rifle), SAB SP Collection 1175_2 (Quakers win); p.127 RLP files (Murray)

Chapter Eight: 1955-1964

p.128 RLP files, July 23,1962 (newspaper), RLP files (medical students); p.129 RLP files (boy with lamb); p.130 SP files (Thatcher, Pearson, Gardiner); p.131 QC 205-1 courtesy of Saskatoon Public Library — LHR (Howe); p.132 QC 2085-1 courtesy of Saskatoon Public Library — LHR (dance); p.133 B13671 courtesy of Saskatoon Public Library — LHR (storefront); p.134 RLP files (carriers); p.135 SP files (The Canadians poster); p.136 RLP files (SOS), RLP files (strike board); p.137 SP files, July 22, 1959 (newspaper); p.138 SP files (Diefenbaker), SAB SP Collection 11_10 (Diefenbaker on Hustings), RLP files (Diefenbaker's mother); p.139 RLP files, November 23, 1963 (newspaper); p.140 RLP files (Chief Watetech); p.141 RLP files (teepees), RLP files (Hector Knife); p.142 SAB SP Collection 3548_1 (hoedown), RLP files (Big Muddy party), RLP files (horses); p.143 RLP files (Lions Band), RLP files (Regina Riding Club), RLP files (Richardsons)

Chapter Nine: 1965-1974

p.144 RLP files, November 28, 1966 (newspaper), QC4646 3 Saskatoon Public Library — LHR (Mitchell); p.145 SP files (boy with cotton candy); p.146 CP (Ted Grant) PLS 1272893 (Diefenbaker with Douglas); p.147 RLP files (Diefenbaker, broken window); p.148 CP5063-24 courtesy of Saskatoon Public Library — LHR (Murray and Howe); p.149 courtesy of the OC (Sainte-Marie); p.150 RLP files (flood); p.151 RLP files (Lancaster); p.152 Courtesy of the Montreal Gazette (Reed); p.153 SP files, August 16, 1967 (newspaper); p.154 SP files (Blackstrap), RLP files (60th anniversary), courtesy of Stratford Festival Archives, reproduced with permission of Canadian Actors' Equity Association and Evan McCowan (Hyland); p.155 SP files, July 22, 1967 (newspaper); p.156 RLP files (native girls), RLP files (Batoche children); p.157 SP files (powwow man and boy), SP files (Poundmaker tribute), RLP files (Whitefish); p.158 USASK Abrahamson MG 244, Robinhood, 1994 (church); p.159 USASK Ewart MG 259, Pense, 1978 (church, top left), USASK Ewart MG 259, West Bend 1993 (church, top right), USASK Ewart MG 259, Gravelborg, 1985 (church, centre right), Dommasch MG 172, Prairie Giants, Krydor, Slide 39 (church, bottom)

Chapter Ten: 1975-1984

p.160 RLP files, November 13, 1984 (newspaper), RLP files (75th anniversary, balloons); p.161 RLP files (modern dance); p.162 RLP files (Weyburn seed clean); p.163 RLP files (4-H Club); p.164 RLP files, Robert Watson (75th anniversary bus); p.166 91174 courtesy of Saskatoon Public Library — LHR (Vanderhaege); p.167 SP files (women RCMP); p.168 RLP files (Diefenbaker train); p.169 SP files, August 16, 1979 (newspaper); p.170 RLP files (farmers' union); p.171 RLP files (Melville water tower), RLP files (Herbert elevator); p.172 RLP files (auction), RLP files (Doukhobors); p.173 RLP files (Hutterites), RLP files (Hutterite girls); p.174 RLP files (native man with boy); p.175 RLP files (bronco); p.176 RLP files (disco, top), RLP files (disco, bottom); p.177 RLP files (Holi festival); p. 178 RLP files, Bryan Schlosser (winter drift); p.179 RLP files, Bryan Schlosser (sunflowers), RLP files, Patrick Pettit

(tractor in field); p.180 RLP files, Charles Melnick (canary seed crop), RLP files, Roy Antal (Rochdale Boulevard); p.181 RLP files (Kalina Farm), RLP files (Foxleigh Church); p.182 RLP files, Patrick Pettit (bails), courtesy of CP (Gord Waldner) PLS 4588094 (angus cow), RLP files (farmer swathing); p.183 RLP files (combine tractor), RLP files (old machinery)

Chapter Eleven: 1985-1994

p.184 SP files, November, 27, 1989 (newspaper), RLP files (leaving the farm); p.185 RL files, Bryan Schlosser (cowboy cuts); p.186 courtesy of the OC, Wayne Hiebert (Douglas' grave): p.187 RLP files (Ridgway); p.189 RLP files, Ian Caldwell (drought); p.190 SP files, Greg Pender (Latimer); p.191 RLP files (Karlee); p.192 SP files (treaty), RLP files, Patrick Pettit (aboriginal rights); p.193 RLP files (McFarlane's farm), RLP files (farmers protest); p.194 SP files, October 7, 1986 (newspaper); p.195 SP files, October 7, 1986 (newspaper); p.196 SP files (limbo dancer), RLP files, Charles Melnick (Legislature); p.197 RLP files (kids with drink), RLP files, Bryan Schlosser (baseball); p.198 RLP files (Candiac), SP files, Glen Berger (drifts), RLP files, Robert Watson (Capitol Crowd); p.199 RLP files (Forget Village), RLP files (Manitou Beach)

Chapter Twelve: 1995-2004

p.200 RLP files, December 31, 2004 (newspaper), courtesy of CP PLS 539639 (athletes); p.201 RLP files, Dan Healy (learning to drive); p.202 courtesy of the OC, Wayne Hiebert (Beaudry); p.203 RLP files (Wickenheiser); p.204 courtesy of CP, Adrian Wyld (Calvert); p.205 RLP files, Bryan Schlosser (RCMP balloon); p.206 RLP files, Joshua Sawka (Chuckwagon races); p.207 RLP files, Bryan Schlosser (Lavallee), RLP files (Teddy Bison); p.208 RLP files (Mennonite church), RLP files, Roy Antal (Campbell students); p.209 RLP files, Don Healy (slot machines); p.210 courtesy of the Calgary Herald, Leah Hennel (women's hockey team), courtesy of the Calgary Herald, Mikael Kjellstrom (LeMay Doan, right top), courtesy of Reuters, Jerry Lampen (LeMay Doan); p.211 SP files, February 16, 1998 (newspaper); p.212 RLP files (powwow), RLP files, Bryan Schlosser (jamboree); p.213 courtesy of CTV, (Butt, Corner Gas), RLP files, Patrick Pettit (mailboxes); p.214 RLP files, (students science centre), RLP files, Bryan Schlosser, (Big Valley); p.215 RLP files, January 1, 2000 (newspaper); p.216 RLP files (Oliver), RLP files (Val Marie); p.217 RLP files (spa); p.218 RLP files (Hicks), RLP files (flax); p.219 SP files May 18, 2005 (newspaper); p.220 RLP files (Queen and Mounties), SP files (Queen with flowers), RLP files (Queen with umbrella); p.221 RLP files May 21, 2005 (newspaper)

Every effort has been made to contact copyright holders. In the event of omission or error, please notify the editor at canwestbooks@canwest.com.

The following institution names have been abbreviated:

CORA: City of Regina Archives
CP: Canadian Press Images
CSTN: Canada Science and Technology Museum
GBA: Glenbow Archives
LHR: Saskatoon Public Library-Local History Room
OC: Ottawa Citizen
RLP: Regina Leader-Post
SAB: Saskatchewan Archive Board
SP: Saskatoon StarPhoenix
USASK: University of Saskatchewan Archives

It takes many people to pull together to make a book like this work and many of them toil in anonymity, giving generously of their time and goodwill. There too many to thank by name, but a few standout. Thanks go to the many archivists and librarians who showed great patience and enthusiasm as we plumbed their files for photographs, especially Sue Marshall, the librarian at the *Regina Leader-Post*, researcher Margaret Hryniuk, archivist Carey Isaak of the City of Regina Archives, Nadine Charabin of the Saskatchewan Archives Board in Saskatoon and the energetic staff of the Local History Room at the Saskatoon Public Library. Photo desks and technicians at the *Regina Leader-Post*, the *Saskatoon StarPhoenix* and the *Ottawa Citizen* met our many requests with great grace and efficiency. Tracy Nixon of CanWest Books undertook the mammoth task of organizing photo orders and keeping track of permissions. Thanks to Silas Polkinghorne of the *StarPhoenix* for contributing to writing sidebars, and also to Kerry Macgregor, of CanWest Books, who not only wrote and researched sidebars and cutlines but also is a terrific copy editor with a keen eye for detail. Thanks too, to Susan Johnson for her professional, quality proofreading — invaluable.

And finally, deepest gratitude to Tom Childs of Quadratone Graphics.

— Lynn McAuley, Editor-in-chief, CanWest Books

SOURCES

– www.usask.ca/agriculture/sahf/capsule.php

– http://scaa.usask.ca/gallery/ukrainian/introduction.php

– http://collections.ic.gc.ca/exploring/homestead/farming.htm

– www.regina.ca/content/info_services/archives/index.shtml

– Barnhart, Gordon L. *Building For the Future — a photo journal of Saskatchewan's Legislative Building*. Regina: Canadian Plains Research Centre, 2002

– www.reginalibrary.ca/history_highlights.html– www.mb.ec.gc.ca/air/summersevere/ae00s07.en.html

– www.fsin.com

– www.city.saskatoon.sk.ca/org/clerks_office/archives/ar-dates.asp

– http://scaa.usask.ca/gallery/art/– www.cbc.ca/greatest/top_ten/nominee/douglas-tommy.html

– www.saskndp.com/history/douglas.html

– www.city.saskatoon.sk.ca/org/clerks_office/archives/ar-dates.asp

– www.foundlocally.com/saskatoon/Local/Info-CityHistoryRecent.htm

– Maxwell, Grant. "One of the biggest home-building booms in the city's history expected this year; mortgage money to flow freer — heavy demand for it." *Saskatoon StarPhoenix*, May 6, 1953

– Ring, Dan. *The Urban Prairie*. Saskatoon: Mendel Art Gallery and Fifth House Limited 1993

– www.legendsofhockey.net:8080/LegendsOfHockey/jsp/LegendsMember.jsp?mem=b199801&page=bio

– www.globalseek.net/CoNTiNeNTs/NAMeRiCa/CaNaDa/ADDiTiONaL/LeGeNDs/murray.html

– www.thecanadianencyclopedia.com/index.cfm?PgNm=TCE&Params=A1ARTA0000377

– www.notredame.sk.ca/about/founder.html

– "Saskatoon Lad Olympic Winner." *Saskatoon StarPhoenix [Souvenir Edition]* , July 26, 1952

– "Two-doctor clinic set up by citizens in Saskatoon." The *Leader-Post*, Thursday, July 5, 1962

– "'Brazen defiance' of authority." The *Leader-Post*, Thursday, July 5, 1962

– www.collectionscanada.ca/primeministers/h4-3325-e.html

– www.usask.ca/diefenbaker/dates.html

– www.creative-native.com/biograp.htm

– Niedermyer, Don. "Mount Blackstrap settles into its new home." *Saskatoon StarPhoenix*, October 20, 1970

– http://cms.nortia.org/Org/Org38/Content/Games/1971%20Saskatoon.asp?mnu=3

– www.collectionscanada.ca/archivianet/02012001/20_e.html

– MacDonald, Bruce. "Police try to get Indians on force, prejudice possibly cited." *Saskatoon StarPhoenix*, May 8, 1972

– "Hiring of Indians, Métis to be mandatory in Sask." *Saskatoon StarPhoenix*, March 26, 1970

– www.heritagecanada.org/eng/news/article.html#faith

– www.rcmp.ca/women/women1_e.htm

– www.sfn.saskatoon.sk.ca/arts/scha/dief/dief.html

– http://parkscanada.pch.gc.ca/clmhc-hsmbc/pm/Diefenbaker_E.asp

– http://142.206.72.67/01/01b/01b_supp/01b_supp_004_e.htm

– www.cbc.ca/ideas/features/shows/horizon/horizon.htm

– www.foundlocally.com/Regina/Sports/Spo-Rodeo.htm

– www.canadiancowboys.sk.ca/history.html

– "INFR Main Attraction at FSIN 50th Anniversary." *Saskatchewan Indian*, December 1996

– "Students Becoming Aware of Culture." *Saskatchewan Indian*, March 31, 1975

– www.muskeglake.com/tleHISTORY.htm

– www.pdac.ca/pdac/advocacy/land-use/pa-saskatchewan.html

– www.sicc.sk.ca/saskindian/a93aug20.htm

– Beltrame, Julian. "PM hints at aid plan for farmers; assistance 'not political.'" *Edmonton Journal*, September 23, 1992

– www.sasksport.sk.ca/media/2004/jan28.html

– www.curling.ca/news/articles/92.asp

– www.sk.bluecross.ca/spokesperson/bio.html

– www.oval.ucalgary.ca/oval_olympics/oly_HayleyW.asp

– http://soudogcurling.tripod.com/schmirler_tribute.html

– www.virtualsk.com/current_issue/lucky_lady.html